THE TRIALS OF
EDWARD VAUGHAN

THE TRIALS OF EDWARD VAUGHAN

Law, Civil War and Gentry Faction in Seventeenth-Century Britain, c.1596–1661

LLOYD BOWEN

UNIVERSITY OF WALES PRESS
2024

www.uwp.co.uk
British Library Cataloguing-in-Publication Data

A catalogue record for this book is available from the British Library.

ISBN   978-1-83772-177-1
e-ISBN   978-1-83772-178-8

Typeset by Richard Huw Pritchard
Printed by CPI Antony Rowe, Melksham

Contents

Genealogical tables

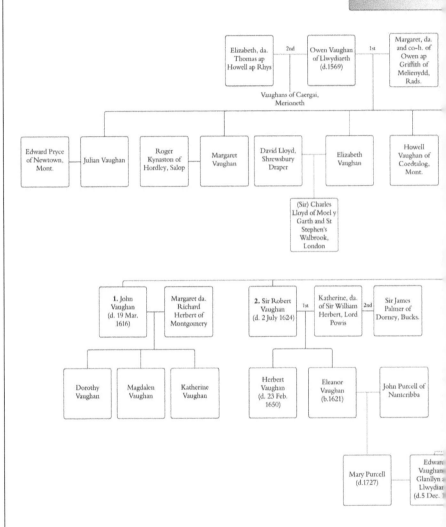

LLWYDIARTH

Howell Vaughan of Glanllyn, Merioneth

John Vaughan of Glanllyn

John (ap) Owen Vaughan, (d. 21 August 1599)

Dorothy Vaughan

John Vaughan of Glanllyn

Owen Vaughan (d. 5 Oct. 1617)

Catherine, da. and h. of Moris ap Robert of Llangedwyn, Denbs.

Howell Vaughan of Glanllyn

Charles Vaughan (1657)

Margaret, da. Edward Price of Eglwysegle, Denbs.

4. Roger Vaughan (d.bef.1620)

5. Edward Vaughan (d. 15 Sept. 1661)

2nd

Frances, da. Andrew Meredith of Glantanat (d. Jan. 1672)

1st

James Phillips of Llanddewi, Rads. (d. June 1633)

1 daughter

3 sons

6. Celynin Vaughan (d. Mar. 1619)

7. Rowland Vaughan (d. Apr. 1667)

1. Mary Vaughan

Arthur Price of Vaynor

2. Dorothy Vaughan

William Salesbury of Rug, Merioneth

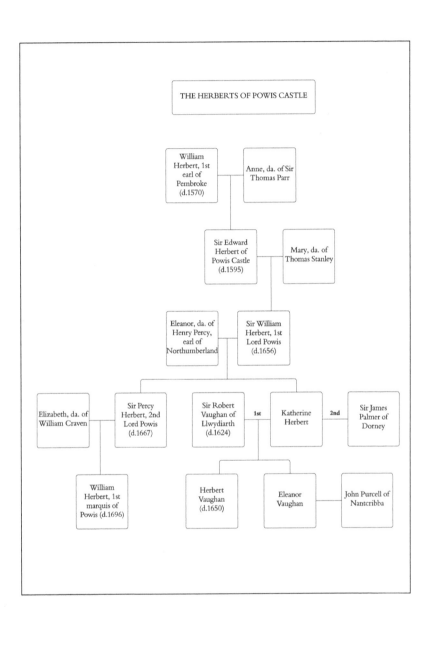

THE HERBERTS OF POWIS CASTLE

William Herbert, 1st earl of Pembroke (d.1570) — Anne, da. of Sir Thomas Parr

Sir Edward Herbert of Powis Castle (d.1595) — Mary, da. of Thomas Stanley

Eleanor, da. of Henry Percy, earl of Northumberland — Sir William Herbert, 1st Lord Powis (d.1656)

Elizabeth, da. of William Craven — Sir Percy Herbert, 2nd Lord Powis (d.1667)

Sir Robert Vaughan of Llwydiarth (d.1624) — 1st — Katherine Herbert — 2nd — Sir James Palmer of Dorney

William Herbert, 1st marquis of Powis (d.1696)

Herbert Vaughan (d.1650)

Eleanor Vaughan — John Purcell of Nantcribba

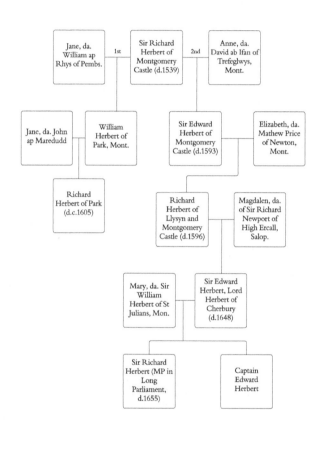

THE HERBERTS OF MONTGOMERY CASTLE

Jane, da. William ap Rhys of Pembs. — 1st — Sir Richard Herbert of Montgomery Castle (d.1539) — 2nd — Anne, da. David ab Ifan of Trefeglwys, Mont.

Jane, da. John ap Maredudd — William Herbert of Park, Mont.

Sir Edward Herbert of Montgomery Castle (d.1593) — Elizabeth, da. Mathew Price of Newton, Mont.

Richard Herbert of Park (d.c.1605)

Richard Herbert of Llysyn and Montgomery Castle (d.1596) — Magdalen, da. of Sir Richard Newport of High Ercall, Salop.

Mary, da. Sir William Herbert of St Julians, Mon. — Sir Edward Herbert, Lord Herbert of Cherbury (d.1648)

Sir Richard Herbert (MP in Long Parliament, d.1655)

Captain Edward Herbert

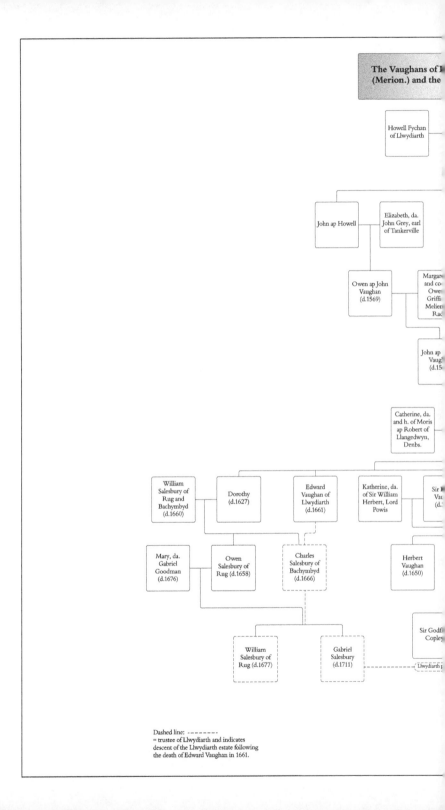

The Vaughans of
(Merion.) and the

Howell Fychan
of Llwydiarth

John ap Howell | Elizabeth, da.
John Grey, earl
of Tankerville

Owen ap John
Vaughan
(d.1569) | Margare
and co-
Owe
Griffi
Melier
Rad

John ap
Vaug
(d.15

Catherine, da.
and h. of Moris
ap Robert of
Llangedwyn,
Denbs.

William
Salesbury of
Rug and
Bachymbyd
(d.1660) | Dorothy
(d.1627) | Edward
Vaughan of
Llwydiarth
(d.1661) | Katherine, da.
of Sir William
Herbert, Lord
Powis | Sir
Vau
(d.

Mary, da.
Gabriel
Goodman
(d.1676) | Owen
Salesbury of
Rug (d.1658) | Charles
Salesbury of
Bachymbyd
(d.1666) | Herbert
Vaughan
(d.1650)

Sir Godf
Copley

William
Salesbury of
Rug (d.1677) | Gabriel
Salesbury
(d.1711) | Llwydiarth

Dashed line: --------
= trustee of Llwydiarth and indicates
descent of the Llwydiarth estate following
the death of Edward Vaughan in 1661.

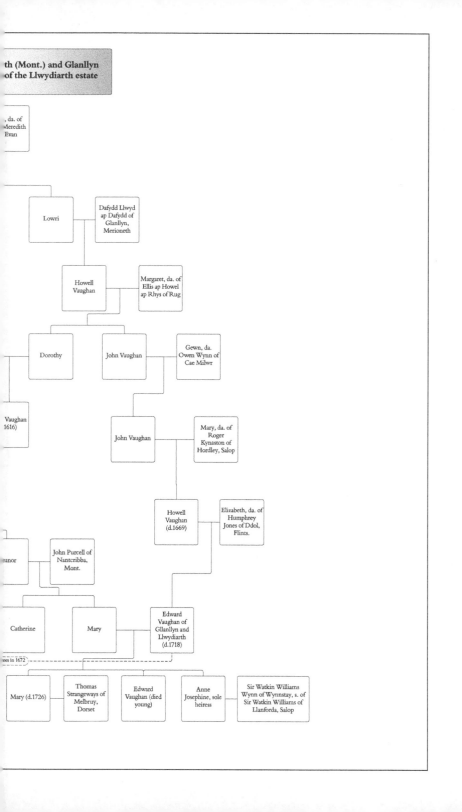

th (Mont.) and Glanllyn
of the Llwydiarth estate

, da. of
Meredith
Evan

Lowri

Dafydd Llwyd
ap Dafydd of
Glanllyn,
Merioneth

Howell
Vaughan

Margaret, da. of
Ellis ap Howel
ap Rhys of Rug

Dorothy

John Vaughan

Gewn, da.
Owen Wynn of
Cae Milwr

Vaughan
1616)

John Vaughan

Mary, da. of
Roger
Kynaston of
Hordley, Salop

Howell
Vaughan
(d.1669)

Elizabeth, da. of
Humphrey
Jones of Ddol,
Flints.

eanor

John Purcell of
Nantcribba,
Mont.

Catherine

Mary

Edward
Vaughan of
Gllanllyn and
Llwydiarth
(d.1718)

ees in 1672

Mary (d.1726)

Thomas
Strangeways of
Melbruy,
Dorset

Edward
Vaughan (died
young)

Anne
Josephine, sole
heiress

Sir Watkin Williams
Wynn of Wynnstay, s. of
Sir Watkin Williams of
Llanforda, Salop

Maps

Counties of North Wales and the Marches

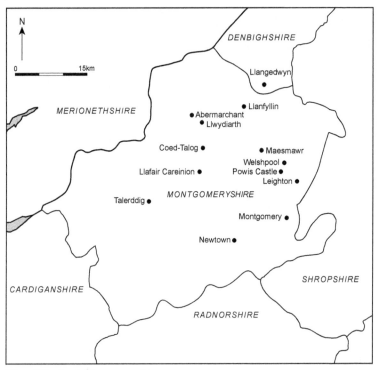

Edward Vaughan's Montgomeryshire

Abbreviations

A&O	C. H. Firth and R. S. Rait (eds), *Acts and Ordinances of the Interregnum, 1642–1660*, 3 vols (London, 1911)
APC	*Acts of the Privy Council of England*
BL	British Library
BLB	R. N. Dore (ed.), *The Letter Books of Sir William Brereton*, 2 vols, Record Society of Lancashire and Cheshire, 123 (1984); 128 (1990)
Bodl.	Bodleian Library
CJ	*Journals of the House of Commons*
CSPD	*Calendars of State Papers, Domestic*
dep(s).	deposition(s)
Dodd, *Studies*	A. H. Dodd, *Studies in Stuart Wales* (Cardiff, 1952)
Dwnn, *Visitations*	S. R. Meyrick (ed.), *Heraldic Visitations of Wales … by Lewys Dwnn*, 2 vols (Llandovery, 1846)
HL	Huntington Library
HMC	Historical Manuscripts Commission, reports
HoC, 1640–60	Stephen K. Roberts (ed.), *The House of Commons, 1640–1660*, 9 vols (Woodbridge, 2023)
HPO	History of Parliament Online (all biographies can be found at *https://www.historyofparliamentonline.org/*). Citations indicate relevant volume entries in brackets

LJ	*Journals of the House of Lords*
Lloyd, *Sheriffs*	W. V. Lloyd, *The Sheriffs of Montgomeryshire … from 1540 to 1639* (London, 1876)
Lloyd, 'Sheriffs'	W. V. Lloyd, 'Sheriffs of Montgomeryshire [1639–1658]', *MC*, 27 (1893)
MC	*Montgomeryshire Collections*
NEWA (D)	North East Wales Archives (Denbighshire)
NEWA (F)	North East Wales Archives (Flintshire)
NLW	National Library of Wales
Phillips, *Justices*	J. R. S. Phillips (ed.), *The Justices of the Peace in Wales and Monmouthshire, 1541–1689* (Cardiff, 1975)
TNA	The National Archives
WSTY	Wynnstay manuscript at NLW

Acknowledgements

I first encountered Edward Vaughan in the Wynnstay manuscripts more than twenty years ago. I recognised that there was *something* important in Wynnstay MS 90/16, but I was not sure quite what. I revisited the material a number of times over the years, and it was through the help of the recent re-cataloguing of the collection that the contours of its importance began to take shape. I would like to thank the enormously helpful staff at the National Library of Wales, who are always unfailingly attentive, courteous and accommodating on my many visits to their archival eyrie. I would also like to thank the staff at the National Archives at Kew, who have always been very accommodating and supportive as I order up yet another box of documents.

A chance encounter with Melvin Humphreys in the reading room of the NLW led to him generously sending me a copy of his book on Talerddig, and also providing a transcript of civil war sequestration materials which he and Murray Chapman had uncovered while cataloguing part of the vast Powis Castle collection. I am most grateful for his help and assistance. I am also very grateful to Stephen Roberts and Vivienne Larminie at the History of Parliament Trust for allowing me to see some draft biographies (including that of Edward Vaughan) prior to their publication in the monumental *House of Commons, 1640–1660* volumes. Stephen has been a longstanding friend and erstwhile colleague, who has always taken an interest in and supported my work, and for that I am very grateful indeed.

The History Department at Cardiff University is full of very talented, helpful and friendly colleagues, and it is my pleasure to thank them collectively for their assistance and support over the years. Special mention goes to David Doddington, Mark Williams, Keir Waddington and Stephanie Ward. I am very fortunate to have such splendid colleagues and friends who also take the time to introduce me to novel cuisine ('It's meant to look like that'), and who make me laugh every day. I am also grateful for the support and friendship of David Appleby, Andy Hopper and Ismini Pells. Mark Stoyle, in particular, has been a hugely important source of assistance and scholarly inspiration over the years, and I am very grateful for his support and friendship.

It is a pleasure to record my debt once again to Llion Wigley and the staff at the University of Wales Press for their help and assistance in seeing this volume across the finishing line. I would like to thank Adam Burns for his excellent work in designing the book's cover. I am also very grateful to HEFCW for supporting the publication of this work as an Open Access volume.

My friends have contributed nothing to this volume. This is not surprising, but it still cuts deep. Skies has been captured by #Project55; Dar has possibly been kidnapped by Des; while Dids remains resolute in his refusal to engage. It is also a pleasure to acknowledge the support of Heathcote Pursuit, Sharon Parawee, Iqbal Achieve, Jonah Fonts and Pandy.

It is great when your children are cleverer and funnier than you, and I am a lucky dad twice over. Thanks so much to my two extraordinary boys, Tal and Osian, for making me prouder than they will ever realise, for making me laugh so much, and for not becoming historians. Nicki keeps us (and me) together, and I am enormously grateful for her support, patience, sage advice, understanding, and for stopping me from murdering the dog.

Introduction

E dward Vaughan (*c*.1596–1661) of Llwydiarth in Montgomeryshire is not well known to historians, and there are good reasons why this is so. Although Vaughan was elected as an MP on four occasions, he was not a political figure of national importance and did not make a significant impression on those parliaments in which he sat. He did not write any important texts or leave to posterity a large volume of personal correspondence. Rather Vaughan was the fifth son of a provincial gentlemen in one of the lesser-known counties of a largely ignored corner of early modern England and Wales. So why write a biography of the man? I have done so, in part, to argue that Vaughan was, in fact, more important than most historians believe, particularly in the history of the civil wars in north Wales, and to suggest that his involvement in local and national politics deserves to be more widely known. This book also argues that charting Vaughan's life throws light onto several important areas of historical debate and research, which include: the nature and dynamics of seventeenth-century gentry faction; the culture and tactics of litigation among the Welsh gentry; the role of kinship and lineage in provincial politics; the significance of factional division in parliamentarian politics in north Wales during the 1640s; the structure of parliamentary administration and its attendant conflicts in that region during the civil wars and the republic; and the nature of moderate Presbyterian politics in a part of the kingdom whose civil war history has largely been constructed through the eyes of religious and political radicals.

In addition to these elements, Edward Vaughan is also a fascinating figure whose life story is full of arresting and revealing episodes. A younger son with no realistic prospect of succeeding to an estate, he was an indefatigable lawyer who clawed his way into possession of one of the key landed interests in north Wales and who faced down one of the great aristocratic figures in the region. Vaughan helped bring down a major regional court – the Council in the Marches of Wales – partly by joining forces with the controversial Archbishop of Canterbury, William Laud. He contracted a secret marriage in the 1630s and put his wife aside soon afterwards but had the validity of this union tried in court in the 1650s. He was accused of treason by both the king and parliament, although neither side managed to get the charges to stick. He established his own parliamentary garrison but also tried to bring down his commanding officer. He was imprisoned at least twice by his enemies in the 1640s, once after the New Model Army's purge of parliament in December 1648. He also participated in a multi-generational legal battle for his patrimony, using scandalous allegations against his opponents, while he himself was accused of conspiring to murder his nephew on at least two occasions. Remarkably, given his efforts to secure the estate, Vaughan failed to leave a clear line of inheritance after his death in 1661. Exploring Edward Vaughan's life, I argue, can reveal much about the cultural, social and political worlds he inhabited.

* * *

This introduction will briefly discuss some of these important themes, but, as Vaughan is not well known, it will be useful to provide a rudimentary sketch of his life before proceeding further. Edward Vaughan was born into a significant landed dynasty located at Llwydiarth in the northern part of Montgomeryshire, a county that lay on the Anglo-Welsh border. Through marriage, purchase and some illegal enclosures during the sixteenth century, the Llwydiarth estate became a sprawling interest in north Wales, reaching into the neighbouring counties of Merioneth and Denbighshire. From the mid-Elizabethan period onwards, Vaughan's family was involved in a bitter power struggle with the Herberts of Montgomery and subsequently the Herberts of Powis Castle. This feud was a critical, indeed a structuring, feature of Vaughan's life, but it was also at the heart of Montgomeryshire's political dynamics between *c*.1580 and *c*.1660.

As a fifth son, Edward Vaughan would never have expected to be on the frontline of the factional politics conducted between his family and the Herberts; instead, he received an education at the Inner Temple and was destined to become a lawyer. However, the vagaries of early modern mortality and of mental incapacity among his siblings meant that in the early 1620s Vaughan stood to inherit from his elder brother, Sir Robert, the enormous wealth and influence bestowed by the 120,000 acres of the Llwydiarth estate. Through a complex set of circumstances involving intermarriage and Sir Robert's premature death, however, Vaughan's ancestral lands came into the hands of his mortal enemies, the Herberts of Powis Castle, and more particularly into those of Sir William Herbert, who in 1629 became Baron Powis of Powis. The story of the remainder of Vaughan's life, in some respects, is his struggle to regain and then to retain his family's lands. This effort involved Vaughan mobilising all the resources he could muster in the 1620s and 1630s to defend his claim in a bewildering variety of legal arenas, the most important of which were Star Chamber and the Court of Wards. In this effort Vaughan was at something of a disadvantage as his Herbert adversaries were well connected at Court whereas Edward Vaughan relied mainly on his kinship associations in north Wales. However, the collapse of King Charles I's Personal Rule and the meeting of the Long Parliament in November 1640 provided new opportunities for Edward Vaughan to regain his ancestral estates, and he rushed to take advantage.

In the new political climate of 1640–1, Vaughan's Herbert antagonists had two major disadvantages: first, their legal claims to Llwydiarth had been upheld by courts which relied on the prerogative power of the king rather than of the common law, and such prerogative jurisdictions came under sustained attack by the Long Parliament. Secondly, the Herberts of Powis Castle were Catholics (or, at the very least in the case of Lord Powis, Catholic sympathisers) while the Vaughans were Protestants, and in the backlash against the religious policies of the 1630s, the potent instrument of anti-popery was readily weaponised by the adaptable Edward Vaughan against his longtime antagonists. The Long Parliament thus provided new opportunities for Vaughan, who gained a degree of parliamentary sanction for his claim to Llwydiarth, both because his opponents were tainted with popery, and because their title rested on decrees from legal jurisdictions which were now routinely figured as 'arbitrary'. At the moment when Vaughan's path to recovering his estate seemed on the point of becoming clear, however, the crisis of civil war ensured that it remained beyond his grasp; for the moment at least. Montgomeryshire's prevailing royalism meant that parliament's fiat had little traction in a region where the Herberts rallied to the king's standard and appeared in the vanguard of his cause. Edward Vaughan was forced out of north Wales and spent a period in exile in London.

Edward Vaughan's route back to his estates lay with the parliamentary party, and he appeared in their colours as mid Wales began to be reduced to parliament's control in 1645. He established his own garrison in northern Montgomeryshire and was in a good position to press his claims to Llwydiarth as a man supposedly put in possession by a ruling from the Long Parliament itself. However, although he did indeed gain possession of the lands, matters did not fall out as straightforwardly as he would have wished because of the complexities of local parliamentary politics. The civil wars were not simply a conflict between royalists and parliamentarians: this was a period in which the factional disputes *within* the parliamentary party were of critical importance. The downfall of the royalist Herbert interest meant that Edward Vaughan had a route to becoming one of the most powerful parliamentarian gentlemen in north Wales. However, there were interests within the local parliamentarian group for which this was an unappetising prospect. Vaughan was a moderate within the parliamentarian coalition, a Presbyterian, and he was also a man who resisted the interests of the army and who wished to return to a settled and traditional form of local and national government as quickly as possible after the royalists' defeat. Because of these positions, he quarrelled with two successive leaders of the parliamentary army in north Wales in the mid-1640s, Sir Thomas Myddelton and Thomas Mytton. Vaughan helped devise and promote proposals for reforming parliament's local bureaucracy and for reducing the army's authority in north Wales during this period. Although these initiatives were not successful, they nevertheless help to reveal his priorities, and those of his Presbyterian allies, and they thus provide a crucial insight into a thread of parliamentarian politics that has received little attention in its Welsh context.

The conflicts between the different wings of the parliamentarian party in north Wales generated a good deal of friction and instability in local administration. This antagonism was institutionalised with Edward Vaughan's appointment as the head of Montgomeryshire's sub-committee of accounts in December 1645. In this role, he clashed dramatically with one of Sir Thomas Myddelton's chief supporters and the leader of Montgomeryshire's executive sequestration committee, Lloyd Pierce of Maesmawr. The political narrative of 1646 and 1647 in north Wales can be read partly as a battle between Vaughan and Pierce and the constellation of interests and ideological positions within the parliamentarian phalanx that they represented. The accounts sub-committee was an instrument of the Presbyterian interest designed to clip the wings of the military and its Independent supporters. In Montgomeryshire, this army-Independent interest coalesced around Lloyd Pierce, the Montgomeryshire sequestration committee, and also the Committee for North Wales which, from late 1645, supported parliament's military forces in the region. These clashes also had a more material and less ideological dimension, however, for Lloyd Pierce was in the vanguard of attempts to secure Llwydiarth and its revenues for the state, arguing that the property had been sequestrated by parliament because of the royalist activism of Edward Vaughan's nephew and Lord Powis's grandson, Herbert Vaughan, who had resided at Llwydiarth during the First Civil War. Moreover, Pierce and his allies asserted that Edward Vaughan, although in possession of the property from 1645, had never sufficiently proven his title to the estate. Vaughan thus had much more at stake than his political priorities in facing down the challenges of Pierce and his army-supporting associates during the mid-1640s.

The complex political manoeuvring that accompanied the protracted reconquest of north Wales involved struggles over who should fill the parliamentary seats which had been vacated by members who had died or been disabled for their royalism. The year 1647 witnessed Edward

Vaughan securing the plum prize of the Montgomeryshire seat alongside his close associate for the borough constituency, George Devereux of Vaynor, although local factional disputes translated into Westminster as both men faced challenges from the army-Independent interest upon their arrival. Vaughan managed to survive these attacks (Devereux did not) and pursued a Presbyterian agenda in the Commons.

Edward Vaughan's political Presbyterianism placed him on the wrong side of history in the later 1640s. His moderation and opposition to the army and the Independents left him vulnerable following the defeat of the Presbyterian interest at Westminster in the summer of 1647. Following the Second Civil War in 1648, Vaughan's opposition to the Independents' plans for settling the kingdom meant that he became a victim of one of the most famous episodes in this period's turbulent history: Pride's Purge. Secluded from parliament and imprisoned, Vaughan's political stock plummeted and, as a result, he faced renewed attacks from his local enemies. Lloyd Pierce, and later a Merioneth lawyer, Rice Vaughan, pursued Vaughan for huge sums which they claimed he owed to the state, but they also headed up dogged efforts to sequester Llwydiarth, and thus to ruin Vaughan entirely. It says much about Edward Vaughan's lawyerly resilience and creativity that he withstood these attacks and managed to retain hold of his ancestral lands. His successful opposition to Rice Vaughan's candidacy at the Merionethshire election of 1654 shows that he was still a force to be reckoned with, and his political capital rose as the more moderate politics of the Protectorate from the mid-1650s allowed a return to the political stage for the Presbyterian interest.

Vaughan's return to influence is underlined by his election as Montgomeryshire's MP in 1659, and his successful negotiation of the Restoration was demonstrated by his election in the same capacity to the Cavalier Parliament in March 1661. The return of monarchy threatened the revival of old animosities with his Herbert antagonists, but despite some attempts to query his title to Llwydiarth, Vaughan's beloved ancestral estate remained in his hands. He did not enjoy his victory for long, however, as he died, childless, in his chambers in the Inner Temple in September 1661. His death touched off a new and protracted struggle for Llwydiarth, which was ultimately won by Edward

Vaughan's namesake, a distant relative who was subsequently elected to parliament for Montgomeryshire sixteen times. The Vaughan estate then became incorporated into the empire of Sir Watkin Williams-Wynn, a Tory magnate of extraordinary power and influence who dominated north Wales in the first half of the eighteenth century.

* * *

Such is Vaughan's story in outline. It is complex and convoluted, but it repays close attention. This is not a life that has been entirely neglected by scholars, although Vaughan has not been the subject of an extended treatment such as that found in this volume. Important early forays into his family's history were undertaken by William Valentine Lloyd, a cleric and co-secretary of the Powysland Club, who, in the late nineteenth century, produced a series of scholarly and well-researched essays on Montgomeryshire's sheriffs between 1541 and 1658.[1] Among these essays was a discussion of Edward Vaughan's grandfather, John Owen Vaughan (sheriff in 1583), and Lloyd also provided an extended treatment of the Vaughan family genealogy and heraldry in an 1881 article on their heraldic pew in Llanfihangel-yng-Ngwynfa church. Although these contributions provide extremely helpful information on Vaughan's family, neither discussed the seventeenth-century squire directly. Indeed, standard reference works such as W. R. Williams's *Parliamentary History of the Principality of Wales* (1895) confuse the identity of our Edward Vaughan and he is ignored entirely by the *Dictionary of Welsh Biography* (1959), which incorrectly states that the family's male line ended with the death of his elder brother, Sir Robert. There is no entry in the *Dictionary of National Biography* for our subject. Edward Vaughan was occasionally noticed in publications such as A. H. Dodd's *Studies in Stuart Wales* (1952), but these were passing references only and added little to our knowledge of the man or his milieu.

The most important treatments of Edward Vaughan emerged with his entries across three sets of volumes from The History of Parliament Trust which were published in 1983, 2010 and 2023.[2] Collectively these publications provide a critical overview of his life, establishing for the first time the basic facts of his career, as well as his effort to secure the family estates and his disputes with Sir William Herbert of Powis Castle. The most recent entry by Stephen Roberts provides the first real analysis of Vaughan's civil war activities and of his work on the parliamentarian sub-committee of accounts. Valuable as these biographies are, however, they vary in detail (the 1983 biography is particularly brief and uninformative) and they necessarily focus on Vaughan's (often unimpressive) activity in parliament. Moreover, none of them make full use of the materials relating to Vaughan available at The National Archives and in the National Library of Wales. These are extremely valuable contributions of the highest scholarship, but they are also partial snapshots of a life and do not fully excavate the wider dimensions of Vaughan's struggles over Llwydiarth or of his activities as part of the parliamentarian administrative machine in north Wales.

Beyond the History of Parliament volumes, the most significant treatment of Edward Vaughan was in a lecture delivered as far back as 1981, but which only appeared in print in 2019.[3] This was a discussion by the late E. Ronald Morris, an industrious local historian of wide-ranging interests, which did an excellent job of outlining Vaughan's background and his struggles with the Herberts. The Morris piece is particularly noteworthy as being the first to utilise (some of) the Vaughan papers among the Wynnstay muniments at the National Library of Wales. As will be seen from the chapters that follow, this archive provides invaluable evidence about Edward Vaughan, but also about the parliamentarian war effort in north Wales more generally. The Morris article thus constitutes a pioneering foray into this material and offers a cogent, albeit partial, narrative of Vaughan's political life. The piece has its problems, however, particularly as it frames its subject through the historiographical preoccupations of the mid-twentieth century. Vaughan is located within the framework of the now-antiquated 'Rise of the Gentry' debate, while his political motivations are presented as largely personal and economic in nature and as being subject to the vagaries of impersonal but only dimly perceived 'social forces'. Vaughan is also presented as a resolute localist who was largely uninterested in the wider ideological currents of the time, and the article suffers from an outdated approach both to the dynamics of central politics and also of provincial connections with the capital. It is also the case that Morris fails to understand the nature of the parliamentary administration in Montgomeryshire and in north Wales during the 1640s. He is unaware that there were two rival committees in Montgomeryshire and that Vaughan headed up the sub-committee of accounts. Morris does not draw on any of the voluminous material relating to Vaughan in the Commonwealth Exchequer papers or in the archive of the Committee for Compounding with Delinquents. The discussion which follows in this book makes full use of these and other materials to better explain how Vaughan found himself caught up in the web of national politics as well as in the struggles of local gentry interests.

* * *

This book uses the voluminous records that surround Edward Vaughan (but which, unfortunately, are rarely *by* him) to explore and examine the conjunction of family faction and ideological crisis in seventeenth-century Britain. It is the first work to exploit fully the relevant material in both the National Library of Wales and in The National Archives; it also draws on the Wynnstay deposit in the North East Wales Archives at Ruthin. Bringing this material together, I argue, provides us with a novel perspective on seventeenth-century gentry faction, legal manoeuvring, the parliamentary conquest of north Wales, civil war administration and much else besides. This study is important too in examining a provincial gentleman of a kind which has received little attention in the recent historiography. We are often drawn to focusing on aristocratic behemoths and political grandees of the seventeenth century, or, in more recent times, on previously neglected groups such as women and the marginal poor. There are many kinds of omission and absence in our historical studies, but I would argue that developed analyses of provincial gentlemen – particularly from early modern Wales – represents one such lacuna, and one which can offer valuable perspectives on the social and political dynamics of seventeenth-century life. And Vaughan, moreover, provides an unusual case study as a scrappy lawyer who, by accident of mortality, came into possession of one of the most important estates in north Wales. Indeed, one of the key themes that runs through the volume concerns the vagaries of inheritance in an era of high death rates, but also the unwillingness of gentlemen to make clear provision for their estates. Edward Vaughan occupied a world in which inheritance and the transmission of family title was of central, indeed consuming, importance. Yet his father, his brother and he himself made only partial and inadequate provision for their inheritances. Such neglect speaks to a reluctance to make a final determination of estate transmission, probably as this was a key bargaining chip in the era's familial and dynastic politics.

The voluminous legal papers arising from suits over inheritance provide one critical corpus of material upon which this book is based, and this volume represents something of a novel methodological enterprise: an attempt to write the biography of a seventeenth-century gentleman from legal and administrative sources. As noted earlier, Edward Vaughan bequeathed hardly any of the usual evidence that underpins a biography, such as personal correspondence or something akin to a diary.[4] Indeed, I have only come across a couple of examples of letters that he himself wrote. What Vaughan did leave, however, was a record of his life in litigation. He and his family were constantly involved in disputes within the varied legal ecosystem of early modern England and Wales. The records of courts, including those of Star Chamber, Chancery, Exchequer, Wards, the Council in the Marches of Wales, the great sessions, the High Court of Chivalry, parliament, and others, form the basis for much of the discussion that follows. This evidence is augmented in the 1640s and 1650s by material generated by disputes arising within the committee system established by parliament, including the Committee for Taking the Accounts of the Kingdom, the Committee for the Advance of Money, and the local and national committees for sequestrating delinquents. Utilising such material to write something approximating a biography presents serious challenges. The subject is constantly refracted through the binaries imposed by the structures of the legal system, as well as through its conventions of presentation as wronged litigant or oppressed defendant. This book cannot claim to present a complete or intimate picture of Edward Vaughan; rather it offers up for view the gentleman of the courts, a common figure of the early seventeenth century when rates of litigation were at unprecedented heights.[5] Edward Vaughan's career also provides an opportunity to trace his legal entanglements across the rupture of the civil wars and through parliament's novel local and central jurisdictions. In exploring Vaughan's multifaceted engagement with early modern litigation, we are presented with a series of narratives from which the 'litigious subject' of Edward Vaughan emerges. He was a trained lawyer, but also an unscrupulous and determined one, and in the bills, answers, depositions, and breviats which make up much of what follows, a clear picture emerges of a man determined to hold onto his family estate by any means necessary.

Rather than the historian's usual approach of tracing the course and fate of an individual lawsuit, then, this book tries to do something rather different: to track an individual's engagement with the law across several decades, often in jurisdictions where record survival has been poor but where the Wynnstay archive provides rare access. Such an approach affords an unusually full picture of one provincial gentleman's legal business, but it also constitutes important evidence about the nature, pervasiveness and reach of the burgeoning culture of gentry litigation in this period. The scholarship of the late Christopher Brooks and others has established the remarkable rise in rates of litigation in this period, but Vaughan's case offers up an illustration of the intensity of such litigation in a case of contested inheritance among the provincial gentry class.[6] The Llwydiarth inheritance dominated Vaughan's life from the early 1620s; it was the driving force in so many things he did, but it was also something of a curse that he bequeathed to subsequent generations and which blighted their lives and depleted their purses.

Tracing Edward Vaughan as a 'litigious subject' thus affords us with an opportunity to examine the intersection of legal, family and political history as these were refracted through, and partly constituted from, the effort to control Llwydiarth. In examining Vaughan's engagements with the law, we are reminded forcefully that inheritance disputes of this kind and on this scale involved economic considerations of land and money as one would expect, but that they were also about lineage, honour and power. It is also the case that following Vaughan's legal entanglements allows us to see how such disputes morphed and shifted as they were introduced into different jurisdictions, but also how they developed over time. As it moved through different courts, so the Llwydiarth case shifted from questions of violence and illegal entry to forgery and corruption; from non-payment of legacies to suborning witnesses and perjury; from libel and defamation to religious nonconformity and Catholicism. All of these various elements were bound up with the single 'cause' of confronting the Herbert family, but the various narratives told in these courts and the strategies adopted by both prosecution and defence highlight the litigants' need to adapt their tactics to the jurisdiction in question. Following this 'grand cause', as one contemporary called it, also highlights the intergenerational nature of the suit and the ways in which enmity could be handed down along with title across the generations. As Jason Peacey has argued in his recent study of law and conflict in this period, albeit in a very different context, a case such as this allows us to do something which most studies have eschewed: to analyse the nature of the disputes which lie behind the suits, and to creatively relate the two.[7]

While the analysis presented here remains cognisant that its evidential base tends to foreground conflict and disputation, it nevertheless argues that the feud between the Vaughans and the Herberts was a structuring element of public life in late sixteenth- and early seventeenth-century Montgomeryshire in ways that previous scholars have not fully appreciated. It is a central argument of this book that the region's civil war politics were also profoundly shaped by the legacies of this feud. There is a tendency in current scholarship to overlook older factional alignments when writing a region's civil war narrative, and to see family politics as a secondary consideration to new and ideologically freighted concerns during the 1640s. Of course, there is a great deal of truth in this, but we should be wary of writing out of the picture deep-seated and profound factional rifts of the kind seen in Montgomeryshire when examining the course of its civil war history.[8] As is discussed in chapters 3 and 4 below, it was not inevitable that Vaughan would become a parliamentarian, but the fact that the Herberts were staunch royalists and that the Long Parliament provided Vaughan with a route back to his inheritance meant that civil war alignments in the region were strongly inflected with long-established factional enmities and antagonisms. Although the confrontations between these power blocs in the pre-war period were not primarily ideological in nature, we should also recognise that the Vaughan-Herbert dispute did possess such a dimension: the Herberts' royalism stemmed in no small measure from their Catholic sympathies, while Edward Vaughan demonstrated a moderate but reformist Protestantism that was sympathetic to 1640s Presbyterianism.

In exploring Edward Vaughan's legal entanglements as well as his activities across the period of the civil wars and interregnum, this book also seeks to contribute to the historiography of local communities and their relationship with the political centre during the mid-seventeenth century. Although Edward Vaughan sits at the centre of the book, the volume is also a treatment of early modern Montgomeryshire's politics, a subject that has not received any sustained treatment to date beyond the constituency articles and biographies of the History of Parliament volumes. Analyses of county politics in the 1640s fell from favour in recent decades as historians moved away from models of the 'county community' which portrayed shires like Montgomery as self-contained and isolated social and political communities that resisted the national mobilisations of the political centre.[9] However, recent stimulating scholarship, particularly Richard Cust and Peter Lake's 2020 study of Cheshire on the eve of the civil wars, has suggested some of the ways in which the county study can be reshaped and reintegrated into our scholarly landscape by recognising the county as one dimension of an integrated ecosystem of political consciousness and activity.[10] The current book seeks to adapt and build on such insights by demonstrating the interconnections and interplay between various levels of political action that focus on Montgomeryshire, the England-Wales border, north Wales and also London. In many ways, the Llwydiarth estate itself facilitates such an approach and demonstrates how someone like Vaughan needed to operate across administrative boundaries. Llwydiarth reached into three shires and constituted a regional interest rather than something bounded by a 'county community'. When a kinsman from Merioneth addressed a Welsh poem to Edward Vaughan in 1652, for example, it lauded his 'throne of three counties'.[11] Although Edward Vaughan's principal sphere of interest was Montgomeryshire, he was first elected to parliament for Merioneth and he also served as Denbighshire's sheriff. Moreover, when examining his legal battles and political disputes, we encounter a network of family and kin upon whose resources he drew that reaches across north Wales.

The advent of the civil wars also underlines the need to adopt a regional rather than simply a local or county perspective to understand the dynamics of political life. The activities of the parliamentary committees which ran Montgomeryshire from the mid-1640s were intimately connected to wider political and administrative structures. One of Vaughan's closest allies on the accounts sub-committee, for example, was the Shropshire man Samuel More, and there were strong connections between the parliamentary administrations in Montgomeryshire and in Shropshire. The emergent machinery of the parliamentary state in this area was also regional in scope and Vaughan needed to engage with the bureaucracy of north Wales rather than just of his home county. It is also the case that parliament's army was a regional force and needed to be engaged with as such, and something that emerges from the analysis of this period is the relative ease and speed with which officers and army figures moved between the counties of north Wales and the Marcher shires.

It is also the case that both the Llwydiarth dispute and Vaughan's political troubles in the 1640s and 1650s demonstrate how his 'local' battles were not simply local but were intimately connected with London and the wider currents of national political life. Vaughan was a lawyer who lived for extended periods in his chambers at the Inner Temple. His protracted dispute with Sir William Herbert involved machinations and manoeuvrings in Wales, but his cases were heard largely before the courts at Westminster. Connections to parliament and the Court were important for the fate of the Llwydiarth suit. Vaughan's involvement with the sub-committee of accounts shows an intense and sustained interplay between developments in Montgomeryshire and the locus of parliamentary power in the capital. Similarly, when Vaughan was under attack by his local enemies between 1649 and 1655, it was executive committees in London that decided his fate and with which he needed to negotiate (and to obfuscate). The account given below, then, provides an important illustration of the overlapping and interconnected spatial dynamics of political life in this period. It argues that we need to appreciate the many ways in which local politics was bound up with wider regional and national structures. It remains cognisant, however, that there was a unique dimension to the dynamics of Montgomeryshire faction, and that we should be careful not to overwrite or ignore this when discussing the national mobilisations of the mid-seventeenth century.

At the heart of this book, and perhaps its main contribution to historical scholarship, is a new study of civil war administration and parliamentary politics in north Wales during the 1640s and 1650s. Edward Vaughan provides a route into this discussion as he became part of the bureaucracy that was established in Montgomeryshire when the county was reconquered by parliament in 1644–5. Our knowledge of this region during the civil wars has been partial and often military in character. Norman Tucker, Norman Dore and, more recently, Jonathan Worton, have provided excellent narratives of the civil wars in north Wales and, to a lesser degree, Montgomeryshire, but they tend to focus heavily on strategy, military narratives and major personalities within the respective armies.[12] A. H. Dodd in 1952 provided an invaluable discussion of civil war administration in Wales, but he worked only from published committee lists which, as is discussed further below, missed many of the appointments made by Sir Thomas Myddelton in places like Montgomeryshire.[13] Moreover, such official nominations 'bore little relationship' to the activism or otherwise of those nominated.[14] More recently, Sarah Ward Clavier has produced a valuable analysis of north-east Wales between 1640 and 1688, but her work is focused squarely on royalist cultures and is little concerned with the region's parliamentary politics.[15] The perennial concern of Welsh radical puritanism in this region has garnered much more attention, with numerous studies that focus on individuals such as Morgan Llwyd and Vavasor Powell, as well as on the activities of the Commission for the Propagation of the Gospel in Wales (1650–3).[16] Moderate parliamentarians such as Edward Vaughan have thus received scant notice as the 'Presbyterian impulse' with which they are associated lost out to the counsels and influence of the Independents. However, as Stephen Roberts has recently reminded us, this strand of parliamentarianism was significant in eastern Wales before the revolution of 1648–9, and Vaughan provides us with an entry point into important aspects of its political dimensions.[17]

Chapters 4 to 6 of this volume thus explore Vaughan's role within the fledgling parliamentary administrative structures of north Wales as they were instituted in the wake of Sir Thomas Myddelton's reconquest in 1644–5. It is the first study to examine fully the establishing of parliamentary committees in north Wales and the spectacular feud which erupted between Edward Vaughan as the head of the Montgomeryshire sub-committee of accounts, and Lloyd Pierce who ran the county's sequestration committee. This discussion contributes to our knowledge of the role such accounts sub-committees played in the provinces, but it also helps us understand the nature and development of political polarisation and parliamentarian factionalism in north Wales. The emergence of 'Presbyterian' and 'Independent' positions can be seen with Vaughan's campaign against Pierce and his allies, and our evidence also allows us to explore the processes by which each side appealed to authorities at the political centre for support and assistance. Deeply implicated in this confrontation, and to a degree helping to determine the rival positions that were adopted, were the respective sides' attitudes towards the army in north Wales. For his part, Vaughan wished to reduce the army's power and influence and that of its appointees on the sequestration committee which sat at Powis Castle. He helped draft position papers and presented petitions that called for the end of committee rule and the return of traditional forms of local government. He also wished to reduce the taxes that supported the army in north Wales and orchestrated a tax strike in the autumn of 1646 which caused the army leadership serious anxiety. His local opponents, of course, were closely connected to army circles and sought to undermine Vaughan's case and to have him imprisoned. Vaughan's actions brought him into direct confrontation with the two commanders of parliamentarian forces in north Wales during this period, Sir Thomas Myddelton and Thomas Mytton. In early 1646 the two men orchestrated a campaign against Vaughan, with the likely collusion of Lloyd Pierce, which attempted to have him removed from the accounts sub-committee on charges of royalist sympathies during the First

Civil War. The discussion below is the first to excavate the full story of this confrontation and explore its implications for the functioning of parliament's war effort in 1646.

Chapters 4–6 also establish for the first time the nature of the bureaucratic apparatus which supported the army establishment in north Wales, and identify and discuss the nature of the Committee for North Wales, a critical body but one which has been misunderstood or ignored in previous scholarship. Earlier scholars have confused this institution with a county committee in Denbighshire, but the analysis below establishes that it was a peripatetic executive body which was established in the wake of the Self-Denying Ordinance and Thomas Mytton's assuming of command in north Wales in late 1645. The analysis provided in these chapters establishes that a parliamentarian local bureaucracy was in place in this region much earlier than has previously been recognised, and that we need to understand this body as an ally of Pierce's sequestration committee if we are to make sense of the factional dynamics within the local parliamentary party from 1646 onwards. This discussion thus has important implications for our understanding of the origins and development of parliamentarianism in north Wales, and of the fractures and disagreements which lay at its heart from the very beginning.

The discussion of Vaughan's involvement with the army and parliament's local bureaucracy also brings home a point that is insufficiently appreciated in the scholarly literature: the protracted nature of the war in north Wales and the enormous burdens which it placed upon local communities. The reduction of Montgomeryshire in the autumn of 1644 was an initial inroad into hostile royalist territory, but it took another two and a half years to conquer north Wales. The war thus continued here long after most regions in England had been reduced. The reconquest of north Wales is often considered to be something of a 'mopping up' exercise, a sideshow to the main event in England where the respective parties become involved in negotiations for a peace settlement from mid-1646. Such a perspective, however, ignores the significant burdens of taxation and free quarter on local populations in north Wales, and it also overlooks the continued significance of Mytton's provincial army and its officers as critical players in the region's politics.

We should also remain cognisant of the fact that this was something of an 'alien' force, which had been raised largely in England and which was now fighting in a heartland of indigenous Welsh culture.[18] Part of the momentum behind Vaughan's opposition to the army, then, arose from a population which had to endure the burdens of civil war for longer than most. When in 1649 a petition was presented to parliament from Montgomeryshire which reflected on the 'many and (as wee thinke) unparaleld sufferings of this poore countie in … the hardest & saddest times', its rhetoric was only somewhat exaggerated.[19] Any analysis of religion and politics in north Wales during the later 1640s, then, needs to take account of the protracted and onerous nature of the war in the region and of the army's potent influence in local politics.

Although Vaughan's activities on the sub-committee of accounts reflected his political inclinations and ambitions, the analysis below also illustrates how he provides us with a fascinating example of the commixture of public and private interests. Although Vaughan was keen to clip the wings of the army and the radicals in this region, he was also desperate to establish and maintain his title to Llwydiarth. The Herberts' royalism had seen them (and their intimate ally Herbert Vaughan, Edward's nephew and until mid-1645 Llwydiarth's possessor) effectively barred from the property, and Vaughan was eager to move in and establish himself as the new parliamentary master of his ancestral house. His problem was that his local antagonists wanted the property for the state, claiming that he had never sufficiently demonstrated title and thus that Llwydiarth had been sequestered. The ongoing battle for Llwydiarth therefore ran through all of Vaughan's exchanges with Pierce, Myddelton and Mytton. It is impossible entirely to disentangle Vaughan's personal motives from his public politics, but the analysis below discusses how Vaughan sought to strike a delicate balance of articulating his position in terms of defending the public interest, while simultaneously ensuring that his private estate was secure.

Out of these tensions and confrontations came the so-called 'recruiter elections' in the spring of 1647. Edward Vaughan was returned as Montgomeryshire member, while his close political ally on the accounts sub-committee, George Devereux of Vaynor, was elected for Montgomery

Boroughs. Chapter 6 provides a full analysis of these elections and brings new evidence to bear on the ways in which they embodied a clash between the moderate 'Presbyterian' interest on the one hand, and the pro-army 'Independent' interest on the other. This bitter factionalism followed the newly elected members to Westminster, where Edward Vaughan faced renewed attacks from Myddelton (which he answered in kind) while Devereux was unseated. As chapter 7 demonstrates, in parliament Vaughan was allied to the Presbyterian party and attempted to press initiatives, such as the halting of sequestrations in Wales, which would undermine the army interest while simultaneously ensuring that Llwydiarth remained beyond his enemies' reach. Such activities ensured that he became a target for the resurgent Independents in 1647–8, which led to his exclusion in Pride's Purge in December 1648.

The historiography of the interregnum period in Wales is, for good reason, routinely told from the perspective of the 'Saints', the political and religious radicals who were able to seize the levers of power.[20] Edward Vaughan once again offers us a novel position from which to explore this period as a parliamentary moderate who found himself out 'in the cold'. Chapters 8 and 9 explore his journey from pariah back to parliament man and how he doggedly sought to frustrate his enemies' campaign to prise Llwydiarth from his hands. Drawing on an extensive but unused cache of papers from the archive of the Committee for Compounding with Delinquents, these sections offer up for scrutiny some novel forms of public politics in a series of manuscript exchanges between Vaughan and Lloyd Pierce in which both men claimed to speak on behalf of Montgomeryshire's political community. Edward Vaughan showed remarkable resilience and some inventive sleight of hand in managing to retain his estate as Pierce, and later Rice Vaughan, waged an extended campaign against him through the state's sequestration apparatus. Chapter 9 demonstrates how his stubborn resistance eventually ground his opponents down, but also how he returned to a degree of local authority with the coming of the Protectorate.

The volume's final chapter traces the fate of Llwydiarth after Edward Vaughan's death in September 1661, but also explores the voluminous depositional material among the Wynnstay manuscripts to reflect on two important dimensions of Vaughan's life. The first is his secret marriage to Frances Phillips (neé Meredith), which occurred in 1636. For reasons that are not entirely clear, Vaughan set his wife aside shortly thereafter, but she comes back into view in the mid-1650s (when Vaughan's title to Llwydiarth finally seemed secure) suing for alimony payments. Historians have not previously recognised that Vaughan was married, but material among the Hanmer of Pentrepant papers in the Shropshire Archives allows us to piece together the remarkable tale of his clandestine union and his subsequent callous and uncaring treatment of his wife. The depositions following Vaughan's death also illuminate his attitudes towards family and kin. This section argues that Vaughan held distinctly conservative opinions regarding his kin and lineage and suggests that an intimate connection between pedigree and place helps us better understand his fierce attachment to Llwydiarth as the repository of his 'name' as well as the source of his wealth and power.

* * *

This book argues, then, that attending to Edward Vaughan helps us illuminate and better comprehend some poorly understood and lesser-known aspects of seventeenth-century history. Although Vaughan himself remains a perplexing and elusive figure, by studying his life and career we can gain some novel and informative perspectives on the intersection of law, politics and conflict. His activities during the civil war years are particularly revealing and add a new dimension to our understanding of the conflict in north Wales. Vaughan's life was full of colour and incident, and this book argues that, although his experiences were atypical, they can nevertheless reveal much about the nature of litigation, faction, gentry culture and political Presbyterianism in an understudied part of the realm during the turbulent seventeenth century.

PART ONE:

FAMILY, FACTION AND THE LAW

CHAPTER 1

Families and Faction in Elizabethan and Early Stuart Montgomeryshire

The narrative of Montgomeryshire's politics in the late sixteenth and early seventeenth centuries is, in many respects, the story of two dynasties: the Herberts of Powis and Montgomery Castles, and the Vaughans of Llwydiarth. This book's focus is on the Vaughans, but during the later Elizabethan and early Stuart eras, the family existed in a kind of antipathetic symbiosis with the Herbert family. This chapter explores the origins and background of the Vaughans of Llwydiarth and the development and course of their feud with the Herbert clan. It considers the role of lineage, honour, kin networks, public office and electoral politics to understand the world into which Edward Vaughan was born and which shaped his life of struggle with his family's inveterate enemies. Family was a touchstone for Edward Vaughan, and he had a reverence for kin and blood that can only be understood by examining the deeper history of his lineage.

The Vaughans of Llwydiarth: origins

The Vaughans originated in south Wales, but their appearance in Montgomeryshire, perhaps appropriately given the disputatious history that will be detailed in the following pages, arose from an act of violence. In the early fourteenth century one Celynin ap Rhirid, an individual who claimed descent from the kings of Dyfed, killed the mayor of Carmarthen and fled into what was then Powys in eastern Wales.[1] He obtained an estate centred on Llwydiarth in what would later become northern Montgomeryshire through his marriage to the daughter of a prince of Powys. The name 'Vaughan' was introduced into the family around the turn of the sixteenth century when Howell ap Griffith's son was also named Howell, and so Vaughan or 'fychan', meaning 'small' or, more specifically in this case, 'younger', entered the naming convention. The family was, however, not especially prominent in local affairs before the sixteenth century. At the start of Mary I's reign, the grandson of the above named Howell Vaughan, Owen ap John ap Howell Vaughan (or 'Owen Vaughan', he was the first of the family to use the appellation as a true surname), appeared as a justice on the Montgomeryshire and Merioneth commissions of the peace, a sign of distinction and prestige.[2] That his appearance on these county benches came at the beginning of Mary's rule might indicate that he was a Catholic and that the authorities viewed him as a trustworthy local governor in an age of Counter-Reformation. If this was indeed the case, however, he was sufficiently adroit in his confessional allegiances to retain these positions under the Protestant Elizabeth. Indeed, he advanced in favour under the new queen, becoming for a brief period in 1561 the *custos rotulorum*, or chief magistrate, in Merioneth.

Owen was a hinge figure in the emergence of the Vaughan clan during the sixteenth century: his first wife, Margaret, was an heiress of Maelienydd in north Radnorshire, which brought a substantial estate to the family. By his second wife, Elizabeth, Owen established the Vaughan family at Caergai in Merioneth, creating a cadet branch that would produce the famous poet and antiquarian Rowland Vaughan in the seventeenth century; this individual would pen an ode to his kinsman Edward Vaughan in 1652.[3] Owen Vaughan was steeped in the vernacular culture of north Wales and in 1567 was named one of the commissioners for the Caerwys eisteddfod, a celebration of Welsh-language poetry which also acted as a meeting for regulating the bardic order.[4] Owen died in 1569 and described himself in his will as of Llanuwchllyn, the parish in which Caergai was situated; he had already given over the Llwydiarth estate to his eldest son by his first wife, John (ap) Owen Vaughan, who was then about twenty-three years old.[5]

John Owen Vaughan succeeded to a long-established estate in Montgomeryshire and a family whose influence reached into several north Wales counties and which possessed a dense network of kin relationships in the region. John Owen Vaughan married Dorothy, the daughter of a relation, Howell Vaughan of Glanllyn in Merioneth. This family would ultimately provide the heirs to the Llwydiarth estate in the later seventeenth century after the death of the childless Edward Vaughan, something which is discussed further in chapter 10. This John Owen Vaughan was probably the 'J. Vaughan' who appears on the Montgomeryshire commission of the peace in 1571, and was also the individual who served in 1565 as the leading town official, the bailiff, of the borough of Llanfyllin, which lay a short distance from Llwydiarth.[6] Vaughan was also Montgomeryshire's sheriff in 1583, but he never achieved the prominence in local office which might have been expected given his landed presence in the county and his prestigious lineage. The Vaughans, for example, never secured a seat in parliament during the sixteenth century. The reasons for their relatively modest public profile can be traced to the opposition of a newer but more powerful family in Montgomeryshire's politics: the Herberts.

The Herbert families of Montgomery and Powis Castles

While the Vaughans were established in the Montgomeryshire area from the early fourteenth century, the Herberts only arrived around 1507. The man who began their presence there was Sir Richard Herbert, who settled at Montgomery Castle and who was a prominent supporter of the Acts of Union in the 1530s, the statutes which created the county of Montgomeryshire itself.[7] Sir Richard was a cousin of Charles Somerset, first earl of Worcester, a dominant figure in south Wales and a prominent individual at Court. Sir Richard's connections to Worcester, who was steward of Montgomery lordship and constable of Montgomery Castle, was the source of his commanding presence in the area. Following Sir Richard's death in 1539, his son, Sir Edward Herbert, dominated the shire for the next four decades.[8] He was routinely returned as knight of the shire to parliament, the principal accolade available to the greater provincial gentry in this period, while those elected to parliament for Montgomery Boroughs were his nominees or individuals who had obtained his blessing.[9] The Herbert family's local power was a thorn in the side of John Owen Vaughan who bridled at their dominance.

The Vaughan family's problems were compounded when another branch of the Herbert family, this one descended from the line of the earls of Pembroke, established themselves at Powis Castle near Welshpool in 1587. This was an issue for the Llwydiarth clan as their presence directly challenged the Vaughan position in north Montgomeryshire. As one early historian of the family appositely put it:

> From the time when the Herbert family established themselves in the county, their interests seemed to have conflicted with those of the Vaughans. Suits at law, and fierce disputes between the retainers of these dominant but rival houses seem, with the ascendancy of the Herberts, to have culminated in an open rupture.[10]

Both lines of the Herbert family had strong connections at Court, and this was critical in securing their local power as well as easing a path to advancement in central office. The Vaughans, by contrast, were unable or did not wish to cultivate patrons and protectors in London, and so operated at something of a strategic disadvantage. They could, however, call on a strong network of allied local families to assist them in their multifarious disputes with the Herbert clan as they developed in the Elizabethan and early Stuart eras, and they frequently did so with what seems to be a violent relish.

John Owen Vaughan was a vigorous and confrontational individual and it was he who sparked the intergenerational feud which structures much of the discussion that follows in this book. Even before he directly confronted the Herberts, however, Vaughan was crossing swords with another local magnate, Edward Grey, Lord Powis.[11] In 1575 Grey was considering selling up his Welsh lands and appointed a commission to survey and assess his estates. The commissioners included Sir John Throckmorton, the local assize judge and member of the Council in the Marches, and Edward Herbert, but Grey also appointed John Owen

Vaughan and his brother Howell to assist. John Owen Vaughan had made unlawful enclosures within the barony of Powis, and, consequently, he attempted to hinder the survey which would have uncovered them.[12] Vaughan also displaced the duly elected bailiffs of Llanfyllin, appointing his own men and orchestrating a riot against a fellow surveyor who was Lord Grey's brother-in-law. In November 1580, William Herle, a pro-Herbert figure, noted that Vaughan had put himself forward for selection as county sheriff, but that this was because he had suits against Sir Edward Herbert and he 'desire[d] this office only to hinder justice in his own causes'. Moreover, Herle continued, Vaughan was a 'factyous fellow' and could be rejected for the office on those grounds.[13] The recipient of the letter was the powerful Court favourite Robert Dudley, earl of Leicester, who held large tracts of land in Montgomeryshire, and was someone who could readily cross Vaughan's efforts to secure the shrievalty.[14] The same day that he wrote to Leicester, Herle also penned a missive to Sir Edward Herbert, in which he referred to the recipient's desire that Vaughan be prevented from gaining the shrievalty as a 'person unffyt for many respectes'. Herle noted that he had pressed Herbert's suit with Leicester 'till I had talked hym aslepe', and found the earl amenable to 'have such a sheriffe as your self [i.e. Sir Edward Herbert] cowd lyke with'.[15] The man who was chosen in the role for the Herbert interest was Griffith Lloyd of Maesmawr; his grandson, Lloyd Pierce, would become Edward Vaughan of Llwydiarth's nemesis in the civil wars of the 1640s.

Feud, faction and Elizabethan conflict

The grumbling antipathy against Herbert power in Montgomeryshire exploded into violence in the 1580s. Factional networks of gentry followers and their plebeian entourages mobilised against one another in set-piece confrontations driven by kinship and blood, with the Herberts and their dependants on the one hand and the Vaughans and their allies on the other; there was little ideological difference discernible in these disputes.[16] In January 1588 the house of David ap Cadwaladr was deliberately burned down. Suspicion centred on a Vaughan associate, John Griffith John, who

was brought before the county justices. Rumours then circulated that
a powerful Herbert supporter, Edward Price (who married Sir Edward
Herbert's daughter, Catherine), had suborned witnesses against Vaughan's
man. Griffith John was ultimately executed, but he loudly proclaimed his
innocence on the scaffold, asserting that 'if he were pryvey or consenting
therunto [he] wyshed that he might never see God in the face and that his
soule and bodye never receave any rest'.[17] This episode was the prelude
to a more serious outbreak of violence a month later. The disputed town
of Llanfyllin was the site of the disturbance which involved Vaughan's
dependants facing down Edward Price's followers. In the melee William
Vaughan, John Owen Vaughan's kinsman, killed Edward Price's brother,
Thomas, by stabbing him through his leg with a rapier. As a result,
William Vaughan found himself before the county's great sessions courts
on a murder charge (he was ultimately convicted of manslaughter).[18] It
may have been these broils to which the Shrewsbury chronicler referred
in March 1588, when he described a meeting of the Shropshire assizes,
to which:

> cam sutche a boundans of people that the lycke hath not been seene; by
> the reasoon of the apparance owt of Wales [of] Sir Edw[ard] Harbert,
> beinge playntyfe, and John Owen Vaughan and Howell Vaghan (his
> brother) deffendants, whoe had matters then and there to be trieed.[19]

Legal evidence around these cases describes a situation in which violent
individuals refused to appear for good behaviour before 'Mr Herbert nor
his freinds, neyther will Mr [John Owen] Vaughan on the other syde, in
respecte they bee hys freinds, offer to theym anye molestacion'.[20] Justice
in Montgomeryshire had become so violently partisan that the Council in
the Marches of Wales became a necessary arbiter in county administration.

These lawsuits and violent confrontations foreshadowed a challenge
to Sir Edward Herbert's electoral dominance at the county hustings of
1588. He was opposed by Arthur Price of Vaynor, a family that would
maintain close ties to the Vaughans down to and beyond the civil wars.
Although John Owen Vaughan was not the orchestrator of Price's
candidacy, he weighed in on the anti-Herbert ticket, attempting to make

pro-Price voters by granting freehold leases in Llanfyllin hundred the day before the election.[21] At the election Richard Herbert, Sir Edward's son, publicly challenged several of John Owen Vaughan's voters and threatened to pursue them in the courts.[22] Herbert ultimately prevailed, but the main significance of this episode is in revealing that Sir Edward Herbert's dominance was no longer taken for granted in the shire. Part of this shift in the local balance of power was the appearance of the other branch of the Herbert family who bought the lordship of Powis in 1587, a purchase that included Powis Castle (also known as 'Red Castle'). The previous lords Powis had been absentees and had not involved themselves in local business.[23] The Herberts, by contrast, came to reside in the shire and were much more interventionist in county affairs. This caused problems for the Llwydiarth clan because the Powis Castle estates abutted and overlapped with their own sphere of interest in northern Montgomeryshire. This was a recipe for further strife and contention between the Vaughans and the Herbert dynasty.

Indeed, soon after the Herberts arrived at Powis Castle disputes with the Vaughans began. As noted above, the Vaughans had been making illegal entries onto land in Powis lordship and Sir Edward Herbert, leader of the Powis Castle family until his death in 1595, attempted to recover these concealed properties.[24] The dispute centred particularly on the manor of Talerddig which had once been part of the estates of the dissolved monastery of Strata Marcella.[25] This was a substantial recovery effort by Herbert, with one report mentioning that several thousand acres were at issue, and the Privy Council register recording it as 'the great Welsh land case'. In 1589 the business was to be tried in Shropshire where Herbert complained that Vaughan possessed 'many friends and kinsmen and there the complainant is likely to be defeated'.[26] Herbert prevailed in the matter, however, and John Owen Vaughan and his brother Howell received a Privy Council directive ordering them to stop destroying Herbert's enclosures in the lordship.[27]

In January 1589, as John Owen Vaughan was en route to London, a riot broke out in Shrewsbury between his followers and those of Francis Newport, brother-in-law of Richard Herbert of Llysyn, who was also steward of Powis lordship.[28] Vaughan claimed that Newport and his men had said that they would not be satisfied until Vaughan and his son, Owen, were 'slaine and murthered'. Later that autumn, it was Richard Herbert himself who faced the wrath of Vaughan (to paraphrase Star Trek) at Llanerfyl churchyard. Importantly, the occasion was the execution of the commission of enquiry into enclosures, and a large number of Vaughan followers came to the venue. Richard's son, Edward, Lord Herbert of Cherbury, recalled in his *Autobiography* how on this occasion John Owen Vaughan and his brother, Howell Vaughan of Coed-talog (which lay in Llanerfyl parish), ambushed his father. One of Vaughan's 'villains' wounded him with a forest bill:

> until he fell down; tho recovering himself again, notwithstanding his skull was cut through to the *pia mater* of the brain, he saw his adversaries fly away ... and after he was cured, he offered a single combat to the chief of the family by whose procurement it was thought the mischief was committed, but he disclaiming wholly the action as not done by his consent ... flying to Ireland, whence he never returned.[29]

In fact, there is no evidence that Vaughan went to Ireland, and Richard Herbert brought a suit against John Owen Vaughan and his brother in Star Chamber, a court that was kept busy with the bad blood running freely in Elizabethan Montgomeryshire.[30] In one bill Richard Herbert accused the Llwydiarth squire of seeking revenge because Richard, as a diligent JP, had been pursuing Vaughan's servants who were thieves and felons.[31] John Owen Vaughan, for his part, maintained that Richard and his allies had, for years, through 'sundry practizes, conspiracyes & unlawfull demises soughte the distruction of your subiecte & [the] perpetuall overthrowe of his howse'.[32] Herbert, meanwhile, asserted in a later bill against John's son, Owen Vaughan, that he possessed 'an ancient and inveterat hatred to him and the whole name and family of the Herberts'.[33] This invocation of a hatred of the 'name' of the Herberts suggests how familial faction animated and informed a good deal of the county's public politics in this period. Indeed, this was a violent feud which resists easy accounts of the supposed 'civilising' effects of the Acts of Union and gentry recourse to the law by Elizabeth's reign.

The Vaughan armorial pew

In the context of this discussion of John Owen Vaughan, his struggles with the Herberts and the clash between two lineages, we should consider a striking monument which Vaughan produced in Llwydiarth's parish church of St Michael's at Llanfihangel-yng-Ngwynfa in 1577. This monument can help give us some indication of the central role played by lineage and kin in the mental world of this squire, but also in that of his heirs. This monument was an imposing 8-foot-high family pew inside Llanfihangel's chancel screen which was composed 'of panelled and heraldically emblazoned oak, heavily canopied and corniced'; the heraldic panels which covered the pew were painted, and this structure must have dominated the small church.[34] W. V. Lloyd suggested in the 1880s that the famous herald Lewys Dwnn of Welshpool may have assisted with the construction of this 'heraldic pew' which displayed the blood of three main familial lines converging in the person of John Owen Vaughan.[35] These lines were those of his grandmother, the Greys, earls of Tankerville and lords of Powis; the line from Celynin ap Rhirid, founder of the Llwydiarth dynasty; and finally that of his mother Margaret, an heiress whose forebears included a hero of Agincourt. This illustrious heritage was delineated in thirty heraldic panels showing the impaled familial shields of husband and wife with their names carved in Gothic script below. The red lion of Powys Wenwynwyn, the medieval kingdom encompassing northern Montgomeryshire, featured prominently on these panels, anchoring Vaughan's heritage in the native royal blood which ruled the area before the Edwardian Conquest. Through the Grey line, the panels also connected him to the barons of Powis from the fourteenth and fifteenth centuries. Also prominent, of course, was the insignia of Celynin of Llwydiarth: a silver he-goat with golden horns and hooves on a black background.

Like many other gentlemen of this period, John Owen Vaughan was clearly a man who was deeply concerned with lineage and the legitimacy and authority it bestowed.[36] The Elizabethan and Jacobean periods witnessed a spectacular growth of interest in, and display of, pedigrees and heraldic imagery such as that seen in the Vaughan pew. This was not simply a form of empty ornamentation, however. Contemporary ideas about gentility and honour connected the qualities of leadership, integrity and virtue with elevated bloodlines and a prestigious ancestry.[37] In the context of the power struggles involving the Vaughans and the Herberts, then, the decision to commission and build what must have been an expensive piece of architecture at the heart of the parish community is revealed as an intervention in contemporary power politics rather than an indulgent fancy. With this pew Vaughan was making a clear statement about his family's illustrious pedigree and thus also about the qualities of gentility and the capacity for exercising authority that such an ancestry bestowed. The pew demonstrated that the Vaughans descended from the native rulers of the area and so were endowed with the innate qualities required to wield power in the region. This display of the many esteemed families to which Vaughan was connected by marriage also acted as a declaration of the complex kin network within which his family sat and from which they could draw support and succour. As we have seen, John Owen Vaughan mobilised such associations, sometimes violently, against his antagonists, and the Llanfihangel pew thus emerges from the local context not only as a statement about the family's readiness to rule, but also as a form of cultural ammunition to be used against the Herbert clan.

'Imboldned to live in all licentiousnes and disorder': Owen Vaughan and the Herbert feud

John Owen Vaughan wrote his will on 8 August 1599, 'beinge weake and sicke in bodie' and died thirteen days later.[38] This brief document designated his son, Owen Vaughan, as his heir and executor. Owen was the father of this book's subject, Edward. In 1588 Owen had married Catherine the daughter and heiress of Moris ap Robert of Llangedwyn which, although lying in Denbighshire, was only a short distance from Llwydiarth.[39] The marriage settlement brought around 4,000 acres of land to the couple so it is likely that Owen already had some experience of running a modest estate by the time that he entered his patrimony in 1599.[40] The main Llwydiarth estate was of a different order to his marriage lands, however. Its holdings amounted to some 120,000 acres, principally of upland pasture, in northern Montgomeryshire.[41] It seems likely that a good deal of its revenues were generated by rents and the husbanding of cattle for export to England, and also of sheep to supply the still-lucrative cloth trade which ran through the nearby towns of Oswestry and Shrewsbury.[42] There is little reason to believe that the mixed farming of the Llwydiarth estate as described by a surveyor in 1763 had departed radically from that which obtained at the turn of the seventeenth century: he recorded the 'ordinary methods of making rents' as being 'by sheep, milking cows, rearing small black cattle and horses, and also the manufacturing of flannels and a strong woollen cloth called webs'.[43] From the proceeds of this wealth, and to proclaim his arrival in the county, in the early seventeenth century, Owen Vaughan rebuilt Llwydiarth Hall as a grand Renaissance house which impressed poets such as Owain Gwynedd.[44] In addition to succeeding to the substantial Llwydiarth estate, however, Owen also inherited his father's feuds.

In September 1598, probably as his father's health was failing, Owen Vaughan appeared on the Montgomeryshire commission of the peace, taking John Owen's place.[45] And it was as a JP that Owen, along with his brother Cadwalader, faced a Star Chamber suit from his fellow justice and deputy lieutenant, Richard Herbert of Park (a different individual to the man injured in the Llanerfyl encounter) in 1603.[46] Owen Vaughan was described vividly in the bill as a:

> man of wealth and power in the ... countie [who is] thereby imboldned to live in all licentiousnes and disorder, and making himelfe a common maintainer and countenancer of sundry his kinsmen, frendes and servants, beinge outlawes and malefactors [and] doth endveavour by all meanes possible to iniure, oppress and endanger [Richard Herbert] to the hazard of his lyfe.

Herbert went even further than most rhetorical flourishes in Star Chamber bills in his assertion that through the Vaughans' abuse of office as JPs, 'insolences, outrages and disorders in that parte of Wales doe more abound then in anie other parte of your kingdome'. Such allegations echo earlier complaints against Owen's father and speak to the intergenerational nature of feuding and family politics in this region, but also to its scale, disruptiveness and viciousness. A later Herbert brief described Owen as 'an adulterer & incestious liver … [and] a bolsterer of theeves & outlawes'.[47] In 1606 Richard Herbert brought yet another Star Chamber suit against Owen Vaughan and his allies, accusing them of orchestrating an unlawful assembly in the contested borough of Llanfyllin in 1602, protesting against the rights of Sir Edward Herbert's widow there.[48] These suits helped give rise to contemporary complaints about retaining and the maintenance of a network of kinsmen and allies by Welsh gentlemen, and of the troubles caused by private retinues who were willing to follow, and to fight for, their masters.[49] Retaining was not a practice that died out quickly in this part of the kingdom, however, and even in 1660 Edward Vaughan can be found sending men wearing his livery to support a local ally.[50] Family, retinues and lineages were crucial features in the landscape of Montgomeryshire's public politics in the Elizabethan and Jacobean periods, but it is part of this book's argument that their influence continued into the civil war era and beyond.

Factional division of the type outlined above was not easily quashed, but neither was the fuel which fed it inexhaustible. The death in quick succession of Sir Edward Herbert of Montgomery in 1593 and of his son, Richard (the victim of the Llanerfyl churchyard attack) in 1596, must have been a major shock to the dynasty. The successor at Montgomery Castle, Sir Edward Herbert, the future Lord Herbert of Cherbury, was not particularly interested in local affairs, preferring instead to focus on Court politics and foreign adventures.[51] The mantle of Herbert superiority in the region thus passed to the collateral branch of the Herberts of Powis Castle, under the leadership of Sir William Herbert, the future Lord Powis, who succeeded his father in 1595. Sir Edward Herbert, for example, gave up standing for the Montgomeryshire parliamentary seat in 1604, although the borough seat of Montgomery remained the preserve of his family and their nominees down to 1640.[52]

As we have seen, the Powis Castle Herberts at their entry into Montgomeryshire in 1587 clashed with the Vaughans over concealed lands, and an enmity between the two great families who resided uncomfortably cheek-by-jowl in the north of the county was never far below the surface. There was, moreover, an additional edge which had been brought to the traditional factional rivalries in the county: religion. The Powis Castle Herberts were crypto-Catholics while the Vaughans of Llwydiarth had become sturdy Protestants by the late sixteenth century. In June 1594 Edward Herbert's wife and five children were named to the county great sessions as recusants for not having attended services at Welshpool parish church.[53] Although their presentment was moved by the local minister and churchwardens, one wonders whether larger forces were at work. One of the children presented on this occasion was Edward's heir, William. In 1602, when William sought to be made Montgomeryshire's sheriff, a group headed by Owen Vaughan attempted to stop him with a petition to Elizabeth's chief secretary, Sir Robert Cecil. The first article that Vaughan enumerated against the candidate was that he 'is suspected to be backward in religion, althoughe he doth temporise to serve his owne turne; & his nowe wife [is] a knowne recusant & hath not received the holie communyon nor bine at church … for the space of two yeres'.[54] Vaughan also claimed that Herbert's first child was baptised by a 'jesuit or other popishe preist', and that when a bill of indictment for recusancy was preferred against his wife at the previous great sessions, Herbert had 'publikely reviled the preferrer & prosecutor', calling him a 'base fellowe', and had prevailed with the jury not to return her. It seems possible that the 'base fellowe' preferring this bill was Vaughan himself, but his petition against Herbert (who was not returned as sheriff) provides important evidence for the confessional element which came to play a prominent role in the Vaughan-Herbert confrontation later in the seventeenth century. It is not possible based on such thin evidence, of course, to determine whether Owen's use of Herbert's Catholic sympathies was simply instrumental, a means of carrying on a family feud by any means necessary, or whether he was animated principally by religious convictions. The truth was probably some combination of the two, but Owen must have been sufficiently secure in his own Protestantism to have considered crossing Herbert on these grounds.

Marriage, murder and suicide, 1606–17

Despite their history of confrontation, in the calculus of local politics around the turn of the seventeenth century Owen Vaughan seems to have concluded that it was better for him and his family to be at peace with the Protestant Herberts of Montgomery Castle, perhaps so that they might act as something of a counterweight to the Catholic Herberts of Powis Castle. He determined on an alternative policy to the feuding and fighting which had characterised the previous two decades and settled instead on allying with his one-time enemy. Thus it was that on 3 November 1606, Owen Vaughan's eldest son and prospective heir, John, was married to Margaret, Sir Edward Herbert of Montgomery's sister, with a 'greate and liberall porcion' of £1,000.[55] In his *Autobiography* Sir Edward wrote that through this match 'some former differences betwixt our house and that [of Vaughan] were appeased and reconciled'.[56] The match had settled some of the Vaughan estates on Margaret as jointure lands and, sadly, she needed access to them less than a decade after their marriage as her husband predeceased his father in March 1616.[57] Their short union nonetheless produced three daughters who, with their mother, demanded their share of the estate in an acrimonious lawsuit in the Court of Wards which ground on for several years before a settlement was reached in July 1622.[58] There was thus no male heir for the Vaughan family through this line.

After John's death Owen Vaughan modified the entail of his lands, constituting his next eldest son, Robert, as his heir. Matters then took a decidedly unexpected turn. In September 1616, Owen Vaughan attended a meeting of the Montgomeryshire great sessions court, 'thinkinge by his greate power there to save on[e] John Lloyd, his coozen, whoe was to bee then tryed for killinge a servant of the Lord Powis [that is, Sir William Herbert] & had formerly killd another'.[59] Lloyd was a partisan of the Vaughan family, and was actually Owen Vaughan's nephew rather than his cousin as this later account records. He was the brother of Charles Lloyd of Moel-y-Garth, a man who became a prosperous London draper and who will become a prominent character in Edward Vaughan's struggles during the 1620s and 1630s.

The encounter which resulted in the homicide is, in fact, very well documented among Montgomeryshire's great sessions records.[60] It involved a dispute between Lloyd and Thomas Jones, the Herbert family servant. The precise origins of their differences are unclear, but Lloyd was evidently upset by some remarks Jones had made, saying 'He [Jones] had wronged me, and I could not endure him'. Jones's brother claimed that he had to accompany Thomas on the streets of Welshpool when he stayed late in the town, 'lest any should lye in awayte for him ... by the procurement of John Lloyd'. On the night of 22 January 1616, following an altercation in a Welshpool alehouse, the two men met by a bridge in the town. Lloyd claimed they had fallen into an argument about an old rent dispute and had begun to grapple, and that it was during this struggle that Jones was accidentally killed. A surgeon (and, interestingly, his female associate, Ellen Bedoes) who viewed the deceased's body told a different story, however. They described a single sword or rapier thrust to the abdomen, 'soe that by reason therof his gutts and greasse dyd burste out, and upon better viewe of the ... body, that his neacke was broken and mightely abused by wrestinge and stranglinge of his throate'. In the depositions around the event, witnesses described a penumbra of friends and kinsman who lay behind and gave encouragement to the two protagonists. Although their outlines can only hazily be discerned, we can see traces of the wider factional groupings which these two men represented, and which had helped animate their confrontation.

After discovery of Jones's body, John Lloyd was taken into custody. Lloyd was an inveterate antagonist of the Herberts, and he would be found in the mid-1620s conspiring to murder the scion of the Herbert line who claimed title to Llwydiarth.[61] Independent evidence corroborates the fact that Owen Vaughan attempted to intercede on Lloyd's behalf at the assizes. Vaughan apparently requested that Sir William Herbert would 'prefer a light bill against his nephew', and also that he offered a good deal of money to the murdered man's wife 'if they would favor him with kindness'.[62] The bereaved woman replied that 'she would not sell the blood of ye father of her children'. Vaughan's entreaties were thus dismissed, and the suit was prosecuted vigorously by the Herberts, and John Lloyd was found guilty of the homicide. Dismayed by his inability to save his nephew from the rigours of Herbert justice, Owen Vaughan apparently 'went thence home & killd himself'.[63] John Lloyd, in fact, would walk free from the court in June 1617, after being convicted of the lesser charge of manslaughter, reading the 'neck verse', being branded on the thumb, and then set at liberty. A much later account had it that Owen Vaughan's son had complained frequently that it cost his father 'much money in sideing with John Lloyd ... aboute the killing of a man, almost to the overthrowe of his estate'.[64] Thus it may have been financial near ruin in supporting his kinsman's suit as much as reputational damage that brought Owen Vaughan to such a desperate pass.

The information about Owen Vaughan's startling suicide comes from a later legal document produced for Sir William Herbert and so should be considered suspect, although the basic outline of events is supported by the trial documents and by a family account from the turn of the eighteenth century. Among the Montgomeryshire great sessions records for the same June 1617 meeting of the great sessions which tried John Lloyd is the record of Owen Vaughan's inquest held before the county coroner David Blayney the previous October.[65] This records the inquest's finding that around 10 p.m. on 5 October 1616 Owen Vaughan died at Llwydiarth 'by the visitation of God'. This was something of a catch-all term employed by early modern inquests which does not necessarily rule out the possibility that Owen had taken his own life. Such a finding, however, was certainly not one of suicide and thus should have stopped any possibility of the suicide's goods escheating to the Crown.

There is one contemporary but undated letter which deals with the aftermath of Vaughan's death, but, unfortunately, it is so gnomic as to not cast much illumination on the matter.[66] It was written by Simon Parry to Owen Vaughan's son-in-law, William Salesbury of Rûg in Merioneth, who in 1612 had married Owen's daughter, Dorothy. Parry noted that 'Mr Vaughan', presumably Robert Vaughan the new Llwydiarth heir, was demanding that Parry accompany him to Llwydiarth, a journey that was much desired by 'all that love the bones of Owen Vauchan'. Parry added that Robert Vaughan now relied on his brother-in-law in all things. There is no reference to suicide or to the forfeiture of the Llwydiarth estates to Sir William Herbert, matters which surely would have come up in such a communication. One thing that the letter did mention, however, was that, since Robert's coming into his inheritance, Parry had heard of marriage propositions for the now highly desirable bachelor. It seems highly unlikely that such proposals would have been forthcoming had his estate fallen into the hands of the Powis Castle interest as the later Herbert legal brief suggested.

Reconciliation? The marriage of Sir Robert Vaughan and Katherine Herbert

This mention of marriage introduces a critical development for our narrative which followed Owen Vaughan's sudden death: Robert Vaughan's union with Katherine, daughter of Sir William Herbert of Powis Castle. This event shaped the legal brief that Herbert had drawn up in the 1630s, when it made sense for him to portray his actions in bringing Vaughan into the family as being driven by pity and compassion. The full story behind the suicide and subsequent developments remains murky, but there was indeed a marriage made between these traditional enemies of Montgomeryshire gentry politics on 29 May 1619. The match was clearly designed to seal up the breach which had run through local society since the late 1580s. In his later account, Herbert maintained that upon the marriage he provided the couple with a portion of some £1,000.[67] It certainly appears that Sir William was behind Robert Vaughan's advancement at Court, an arena in which the Vaughans had yet to feature. The Herberts would later describe the marriage as 'a greate advauncement to him [i.e. Sir Robert]'.[68] It is possible that the Llwydiarth man was the 'Sir' Robert Vaughan who was appointed to the prince of Wales's household in March 1617.[69] The confusion in identifying this individual with the Montgomeryshire Robert comes from the fact that he was not knighted at this time, although he did receive this honour at Windsor, in July 1619, only two months after his marriage.[70] He was first of his family to hold such a distinction, and it is certain that his association with Sir William Herbert had greased the wheels necessary to achieve his dubbing by King James I.

Despite his advancement, however, Sir Robert did not readily relinquish the Vaughan enmity to the Herbert clan. Around the time of his dubbing, Lord Herbert of Cherbury, head of the Montgomery family, was at the Inner Temple, where he encountered Sir Robert Vaughan who was probably visiting his younger brother Edward, who was then about his studies and whom we shall discuss more in a moment. As Herbert later recorded in his *Autobiography*, 'some harsh words past betwixt us, which occasioned him [Vaughan], at the persuasion of others … to send me a challenge'.[71] The matter of their disagreement was almost certainly Sir Robert's poor treatment of Herbert's sister and nieces, the widow and children of John Vaughan, from whom Sir Robert was withholding dowry money, and for which they were pursuing him in the courts.[72] We may wonder whether the 'others' who encouraged him to duel included his younger brother Edward. Sir Robert employed the Radnorshire man, Sir Charles Price of Pilleth to deliver his challenge to Herbert; Price was also to be his second in the duel. As Lord Herbert told it, however, Sir Robert never appeared at their rendezvous in Chelsea, and the following day, having got wind of the intended fight, the king ordered that the duel be stopped, and so, Herbert reminisced, 'without much ado … ended the business betwixt Sir Robert Vaughan and myself'.[73]

Apart from individual encounters arising from particular grievances such as this, the marriage of Sir Robert Vaughan and Katherine Herbert was meant to pour oil on the troubled waters of Montgomeryshire gentry politics. The uniting of Llwydiarth and Powis Castle should have promised a harmonious dynastic future. This was not to be, however, for the marriage was short, as Sir Robert died in 1624, and the struggle over his legacy forms much of the essential framework within which the rest of this book develops. Before we discuss the collapse of the Herbert-Vaughan alliance, however, we should introduce the individual who emerges as leader of the Llwydiarth clan following his brother's demise, and who is the main subject of this volume: Edward Vaughan.

Introducing Edward Vaughan

Owen Vaughan's marriage with Catherine Moris produced the greatest wealth that an early modern gentleman could wish for: a surfeit of sons.[74] Catherine bore seven sons in all, although, astonishingly, this line would not produce a male heir to inherit the vast Llwydiarth estates past this generation, save for a much-contested period in the 1620s and 1630s. The sons were John (who died in March 1616), Sir Robert, Charles, Roger, Edward, Celynin (who died in March 1619) and Rowland.[75] Edward Vaughan was thus the fifth-born son, but because of early mortality among his siblings, he was third in line of succession following John's death.[76] However, his elder brother Charles seems to have suffered from some form of cognitive impairment, being described variously as 'weake in ... understanding' and a 'foole', and so, it was argued, was incapable of running an estate. He did, however, marry the co-heiress of Edward Pryce of Eglwysegle in Denbighshire around 1615, but only a few years later the couple separated and Charles became embroiled in legal difficulties (including with Edward Vaughan himself) which appear to have reinforced the impression that he was not sufficiently competent to possess his own estate.[77] Being this low down in the pecking order of a gentry family meant that Edward Vaughan would never have expected to inherit the patrimony and so would need make his own way in the world. In this period many younger sons entered the Church, but many others, like Edward Vaughan himself, turned instead to make good in the profession of the law. It is critical for understanding Edward Vaughan's actions and perspectives as they are enumerated in this book, to remember that he was a lawyer by training and, it seems, by disposition and inclination also.

Although there is some uncertainty (much of it fostered by Edward himself) over the exact date of his birth, it seems that he was born at Llwydiarth in 1596, some eight years after his parents' marriage.[78] It is likely that he went to Shrewsbury grammar school given its proximity to the Welsh borders; some Montgomeryshire gentlemen later deposed that they knew him 'since hee was at schoole', which suggests that he attended an institution convenient for the gentry of the Welsh Marches, and Shrewsbury seems the obvious place.[79] From his grammar school

Edward went on to the Inner Temple in London in 1618 when he was aged twenty-two; it does not seem that he attended university. His entry was comparatively late, and this might suggest that he toured the continent for a period or that he did indeed enter university, but we have no record of his matriculation. Edward's great uncle, Howell Vaughan, was a member of Clement's Inn, the Inn of Chancery attached to the Inner Temple, and this lineage may help explain the decision for him to attend this institution.[80] Vaughan was trained in the law in the later 1610s and early 1620s but was not called to the bar until 1635; this was a long intervening period, but becoming a barrister was not, of course, any necessary impediment to practising the law in the interim.[81] It seems likely, however, that the delay between his entering the Inner Temple and his elevation to the bar was occasioned by Edward's preoccupation with the crisis over his estate which consumed his time and resources. We know, however, that he kept a chamber at the Inner Temple in this period, which was where his brother Sir Robert was visiting in 1619, and he probably felt at home among London's legal community. Later developments would also reveal not only that was Vaughan constantly involved in litigation in the 1620s and 1630s, but also that he was an unscrupulous and creative exploiter of the law who was not above fabrication and sharp practice.

And this, in sum, is all we know about Edward Vaughan's early life. The scarcity of our knowledge reflects his relatively lowly status and comparative obscurity before his involvement in the disputes over Llwydiarth. His humble profile, along with his position as a younger son, make his bold actions in confronting the power of Sir William Herbert in the coming decades even more surprising and, in some ways, more impressive.

Sir Robert Vaughan's death and the contest for Llwydiarth, 1624–25

Even Edward Vaughan's opponents acknowledged that Sir Robert 'did affect him [Edward] before his other brothers', an impression which seems confirmed by the fact that Sir Robert entrusted his baby daughter,

Eleanor's, education to him. Later testimony also suggested, however, that he wished Edward to raise his child because he was worried that she might otherwise be brought up in her mother's Catholic faith.[82] Edward Vaughan was a solid Protestant, and his moderately reformist religious leanings would become apparent in the 1640s. According to Edward, however, his brother ran into debt soon after his marriage, with one report describing him as 'being in great suits in lawe and standing in want of much money'.[83] Edward himself claimed that his brother owed him some £500, while other creditors claimed nearly £6,000.[84] The stresses such money problems brought with them may have contributed to a difficult atmosphere at Llwydiarth House, for some reports claimed that Sir Robert and his wife became estranged, although she fell pregnant again by the autumn of 1623. Edward Vaughan's supporters, however, maintained that Sir Robert had asserted that 'if the lady was with child, yt was none of his, and noe child of hers should inherit his lands'.[85] In June 1624, Sir Robert fell ill with a 'deade palsey' at his property at Llangedwyn in Denbighshire, where he was attended by his heavily pregnant wife.[86] With blood streaming uncontrollably from his nose, as it had for some twelve hours, Sir Robert died on 2 July. Then all hell broke loose.

As improbable as it might seem, mortality and issues of mental competence meant that Edward as the fifth-born son, was now the effective leader of the Vaughan dynasty and the man who could plausibly claim an inheritance of the estate: but for the child in his sister-in-law's belly that is. Aware of the high stakes game which he now found himself playing, Edward Vaughan, along with his brothers Charles and Rowland, hurried to Llangedwyn and removed all the horses so that Dame Katherine could not readily leave the property. He then moved on the main estate of Llwydiarth with some 200 followers, many of whom were armed.[87] The forms of retainership and maintenance seen in the Elizabethan and early Jacobean disputes with the Herbert interest were clearly once again in evidence serving the cause of Montgomeryshire factional politics. Vaughan occupied Llwydiarth ('after a subtile manner' according to Lady Katherine) and also took possession of the young Eleanor Vaughan, who had not accompanied her mother to Llangedwyn. He also seized the deeds and legal papers in Sir Robert's study at Llwydiarth and, allegedly, some £6,000 in plate, jewels and money.[88]

At this point Edward Vaughan held lots of important cards in the dangerous game of securing his family's lands, particularly possession of the property itself. However, Sir William Herbert, the widow's father, would not stand idly by while his daughter and grandchild's inheritance were imperilled. Using his contacts as a Gentleman of the Privy Chamber, Herbert informed the Privy Council about the outrage of his daughter, who was 'great with child', and his young granddaughter being ousted by Sir Robert's brothers.[89] He described how Edward Vaughan, along with his brother Charles, 'by force and great numbers of men maintaine their possession' of the estate, despite the fact that the women were 'next heires at common lawe'. Such outrages, he said, were compounded by the fact that the brothers also kept his granddaughter, Eleanor Vaughan, prisoner. As a result of Sir William's information, on 11 July 1624 the Privy Council wrote to the lord president of Wales asking that he be 'very carefull and sencible of such violent and unlawfull procedings happening within the limits of your gouverment', and that he 'have speciall care of this businesse', and see Eleanor returned safely to her mother. That Sir William Herbert's son, the Catholic Sir Percy Herbert, was appointed as a deputy lieutenant for the county at the end of August was a telling indication of where central favour and patronage lay at this point.[90]

With plausible forms of authorisation from the Privy Council and the lord president of Wales secured, Sir William Herbert and an enormous body of some 2,000 men moved on Llwydiarth in October 1624 determined to oust the upstart lawyer from the property.[91] Edward Vaughan had it that Sir William with 'a great number of armed men in his companie' came to the property 'in violent, forcible & warlike manner … without collor of right' to oust him and his allies.[92] The confrontation between the Vaughan supporters occupying the house and the Herbert forces that had come to remove them turned violent: several individuals were wounded, and one of Herbert's followers, Cadwalader ap Griffith, was killed. Unsurprisingly given his mobilisation of superior numbers of men, Herbert managed to oust the Vaughan occupiers, and some forty-three of them, including Edward's brothers Charles and Rowland, were committed to the county gaol; Charles was held on suspicion of murder.[93] There the Vaughan associates languished 'to their greate & intollerable charges and many of them in greate want and myserie', for thirteen weeks.[94] In January 1625 they petitioned the president of the Council in the Marches of Wales, the earl of Northampton, for bail, which was granted after the case had been referred to the local assize justices.[95] Edward Vaughan himself had gone to London, presumably preparing for the legal battles which Herbert's move would now provoke. The court of Star Chamber demanded that the case be turned over to its jurisdiction, doubtless with Sir William Herbert requesting that the matter be removed from a local arena (the great sessions) where the Vaughans could exert influence; but here the paper trail on the case against the Vaughan adherents goes cold.[96]

Nothing daunted by these reverses, Edward Vaughan asserted that he had a legal claim to Llwydiarth and its extensive estates through his brother's will but also through an entail which, he said, Sir Robert had drawn up on 2 February 1622. This entail turned over all of the Llwydiarth estates to Edward Vaughan and then, successively, to Charles and Rowland Vaughan and disinherited Sir Robert's wife and children.[97] Sir Robert's will, meanwhile, provided £1,500 for his daughter Eleanor, and appointed 'my deare & loving brother' Edward to be her 'sole tutor & gardian, & of ye speciall trust and confidence I repose in him, [I] doe desire him to see her vertiously & religiously brought up'.[98] She was to receive £500 when she reached the age of sixteen (which would become the basis for a major prosecution in 1637), but only 12d if she or 'her friends' initiated suit against Edward Vaughan over the Llwydiarth lands. Sir Robert's will (or at least the version that Edward Vaughan later promulgated) contained no mention of, or bequest to, his wife. It was almost as if the will had been written by Edward Vaughan himself; many, in fact, suspected that it was. Katherine Vaughan had gone to her family at Powis Castle after being removed from Llwydiarth. There, on 30 July 1624, three weeks after her husband's death, she gave birth to a son, Herbert Vaughan, the forename standing as a rebuke to the surname.[99] This posthumous heir stood to inherit the Llwydiarth estate when he came of age as long as the courts were not minded to enforce the suspect entail and his father's will; in the interim, however, Herbert Vaughan's powerful grandfather would act as his guardian and seek to protect his interests. This meant defending him from Edward Vaughan's attempts to recover his patrimony, an effort which would dominate the lawyer's life for the next decade and a half.

Conclusion

The history of the Vaughan family in the later sixteenth and early seventeenth centuries was one of faction, conflict and confrontation. Even in a period when disputes among the Welsh gentry were common, the Vaughan-Herbert feud was particularly intense, bitter and protracted. The politics of entourage and the mobilisation of family and kin networks was a notable characteristic of their rivalry, which on occasion resembled feuds from the Elizabethan and Jacobean stage. From the Vaughan side, we can see the signal importance of lineage, name, blood and affinity as animating forces in their confrontations with the Herberts. Although peace occasionally broke out, it was fragile, and enmity was often close to the surface. The marriages that were concluded between the Vaughans and the Herberts in 1606 and 1619 were attempts to heal the rift between the two factions, but they tended instead to produce problems of their own and to enhance rather than to ameliorate the bitterness between the two clans. These dissentions were not merely matters of local and familial significance; they influenced appointments to county office and were factors in the region's electoral politics. The Council in the Marches of Wales and the Privy Council were also drawn to intervene in Montgomeryshire affairs because of its dysfunctional gentry politics. At the heart of these disputes was land and influence. Llwydiarth was a key estate which ran from northern Montgomeryshire into Merioneth and Denbighshire, and a presence across three counties provided an important regional dimension to these gentry dynamics. But the Vaughan-Herbert feud was not simply a struggle over money and resources. Land and patrimony were intimately tied to notions of gentility, lineage and honour. Edward Vaughan, the unlikely claimant to the Llwydiarth inheritance in 1624, was an individual who was deeply invested in concepts of kinship and in the prestige of the Vaughan name. He would never have expected to inherit the estate, but when the opportunity presented itself he seized his chance, and he would use his legal training, along with every trick he could think of, to make good his claim. The next chapter considers how Edward's struggle to control Llwydiarth, and thus to defend the very existence of the Vaughan lineage in its ancestral patrimony, unfolded in the courts down to the early 1630s.

CHAPTER 2

A Labyrinth of Lawsuits: Contesting the Llwydiarth Inheritance, 1622–1631

T he struggle for the Llwydiarth inheritance becomes something of a *cause célèbre* in the 1620s and 1630s. The protracted dispute took place in at least eleven different legal jurisdictions including the Council in the Marches of Wales, Star Chamber, the Court of Wards, Chancery, the Exchequer, the Court of Delegates, King's Bench, the High Court of Chivalry, the great sessions, the assizes and parliament. It thus becomes an excellent case study not only for examining the means by which provincial elites before the civil wars used the law as an instrument in familial disputes, but also for exploring the complex and interlocking legal and political strategies adopted by the respective sides both in seeking an advantage and in undermining their opponent's case.[1] The records produced by this lengthy struggle also afford us insights into the social histories of the Welsh gentry and the networks of alliance and affinity upon which they drew as a fundamental resource in the battle to control their localities.

The principal arena for the fight over Llwydiarth would be Star Chamber. Something of a 'gentleman's court', this was not infrequently the venue in which major gentry contests played out in this period. Richard Cust has shown how the status of the court's judges (who were the leading statesmen of the realm) made it an appropriate place for adjudicating major disputes such as that over Llwydiarth.[2] Another important venue for the case was the Court of Wards, the body that oversaw the granting and administration of lands of minors who had come into their inheritance; individuals such as the infant Herbert Vaughan. This chapter contributes to the historiography of these bodies which remain somewhat under-explored, in the case of Star Chamber particularly because of the loss of its records for the Caroline era, but we fortunately have quite extensive reports of proceedings in this suit, albeit not the original bill, answer and depositions.[3] It is also the case that tracing the history of this dispute through these various jurisdictions throws a light on that anxious inflection moment among early modern gentry families of death and inheritance and the means by which title was to be demonstrated and defended thereafter.[4] The authority and authenticity of conveyance documents become key points at issue in the Vaughan case and, at moments, the evidence, in Star Chamber in particular, devolves into a form of forensic graphology. Forgery and deceit rather than the mobilisation of family retinues were the strategies and the points at issue in these legal battles.[5] This chapter also reveals Edward Vaughan's unscrupulous exploitation of any means necessary to secure a hold on the ancestral estate which now lay in the possession of his family's bitterest enemy. Without these estates Edward Vaughan was nothing but a younger son and a provincial lawyer. With them he was the powerful representative of an ancient family born to hold sway over a considerable swathe of north Wales.

Entails and elections

In September 1624, soon after Sir William Herbert had secured Llwydiarth, his widowed daughter Dame Katherine Vaughan prosecuted Edward Vaughan in the court of the Council in the Marches of Wales for forcible entry on the property.[6] For his part, Vaughan defended his actions, as he would until his death, on the basis of the entail of 2 February 1622 which, he asserted, assured his title to the property. The Council court, however, adjudicated that the infant Herbert Vaughan (via his guardian, of course) should have interim possession of the estate. Edward Vaughan responded with a countersuit in King's Bench by which he managed to secure a stay of the Council's order. After legal arguments were had on both sides, however, King's Bench reversed its decision, asserting that the common law right to Llwydiarth should reside in the male heir, and, in October 1624, it affirmed Herbert Vaughan's possession. Edward responded with a bill in Chancery against his sister-in-law and nephew, describing how he had been kept from Llwydiarth by 'divers and sundry forcible entries', and reflected that Katherine had commenced several suits in the country, 'where … Lady Vaughan, having great alliance, hath great power and frends'.[7] A critical issue in these suits, of course, was the validity of the will and the entail through which Edward Vaughan asserted his title. Katherine Vaughan was soon challenging the will in the Court of Delegates, the suspicious entail in Star Chamber and Edward's seizure of Sir Robert's personal goods in the Court of Wards.[8]

The Llwydiarth case thus rapidly became a complex and bewildering beast with simultaneous actions being brought in multiple jurisdictions that crossed one another and dealt confusingly with different aspects of the same case.[9] Most of these suits were initiated by the Herbert interest in a deliberate strategy to vex, weary and ultimately to bankrupt Vaughan by using the courts as weapons of attrition as much as instruments of justice. Ejected from possession of Llwydiarth, Vaughan claimed he had only a small estate of leased lands at his disposal as well as an £80 annuity from his father upon which he now relied (although there was also, perhaps, the large sums in plate and money he spirited away from Llwydiarth in 1624); he was thus rather outgunned in the courts.[10] Lady Katherine had not only Llwydiarth's resources but also those of Powis Castle, and in addition could utilise her father's contacts in Ludlow, London and at Court. The change of regime with the death of James I in March 1625 might momentarily have troubled the Herberts, but Sir William managed to retain his positions of power and influence both at Court, where he continued as a Gentleman of the Privy Chamber, and in the country, where he remained chief magistrate of the Montgomeryshire commission of the peace and also member of the powerful Council in the Marches.[11] In this situation, Simon Healey, the author of an excellent parliamentary biography of Edward Vaughan, believes that he probably sought a seat in the 1625 parliament where he might launch a private bill designed to recover the Llwydiarth lands or, more likely, where he could frustrate any effort by Sir William Herbert to have his family's title confirmed through legislation.[12] It is Healey's belief that Vaughan may have contested the Montgomeryshire seat with Sir William Herbert for the first parliament of Charles I's reign in May 1625, and that he perhaps also sought the Merioneth seat where he could rely on the backing of his brother-in-law William Salesbury of Rûg.[13] If this was the case, he was unsuccessful in both attempts, but the brief and abortive assembly, which met at Oxford because of an outbreak of plague in London, achieved little and there was no possibility of prosecuting such private business there.

Another opportunity to pursue parliamentary influence in the Llwydiarth case arose soon afterwards, however, for King Charles I announced plans for another assembly in late 1625, which would meet in early February 1626. Sir William Herbert's power and patronage in Montgomeryshire and Sir Edward Herbert's dominant presence in the borough seat meant that these were not viable options for Edward Vaughan. He thus looked to Merioneth where he enjoyed good relationships with influential figures such as Salesbury.[14] Henry Wynn of Rhiwgoch, who entered the Inner Temple only a month after Vaughan in 1618, had been chosen as Merioneth's knight in 1625, and he declared in September of that year his 'desire to hould the same place I have done afore', while in December his brother William asked their father Sir John Wynn to 'use what meanes yow may betimes for my brother Harrye to serve for the countie of Merionith'.[15] Given the interest of multiple candidates in a constituency with only one seat, the election would clearly be somewhat fraught, and in February 1626, shortly before the election, one London correspondent described the 'great bustlinge in Meyrionethshire' to secure the seat.[16] It seems likely that some negotiation among the interested parties sought to settle on a candidate, and Edward Vaughan was ultimately elected. The indenture returning him was witnessed prominently by William Salesbury while Edward Vaughan's close relation John Vaughan of Caergai, along with many other leading gentlemen of the shire, also endorsed him.[17] His return demonstrates that, despite the reverses he had suffered at the hands of his Herbert opponents since the summer of 1624, Vaughan could draw on the support of a wider affinity in north Wales and overcome some quite powerful opposition and secure a parliamentary seat. This was no mean feat, but his election also indicates that there were influential elements among the north Wales gentry who were willing to recognise him as the rightful heir to Llwydiarth; his endorsement must have represented a significant boost for Vaughan in some very trying times. As a counterbalance to this, however, Vaughan was removed from his place on the Montgomeryshire commission of the peace in April 1626, a position he had held since claiming the Llwydiarth inheritance in 1624.[18] This probably represented retribution effected by Sir William Herbert through his Court contacts for Vaughan's securing a seat in parliament. The Powis Castle interest ensured that Vaughan remained excluded from the Montgomeryshire bench until the early 1640s.

Any hopes that Vaughan may have had to press a private bill to secure title to Llwydiarth in the 1626 parliament were frustrated as this assembly was dominated by efforts to impeach Charles I's favourite, the duke of Buckingham. Vaughan was able to attack the Herberts by introducing into the Commons on 3 May a 'formal presentment from Montgomeryshire against Sir William and Sir John [*vice* Percy] Herbert [Sir William's heir]' as Catholic officeholders in the county.[19] There is little sign that this was indeed a formal expression of county sentiment or anything beyond a private initiative to damage Sir William's position and reputation. However, the attempt did not wound the Powis Castle magnate as much as Vaughan hoped, for the House failed to respond positively to the initiative. Herbert enjoyed the backing of the powerful courtier the earl of Pembroke, his kinsman, and it was probably through his agency that Herbert's name was removed from the list of recusant officeholders in Montgomeryshire which was eventually presented to parliament later in the session. With contacts such as Pembroke, Herbert's religious inclinations could, for the most part, politely be ignored in everyday politics.

Herbert's connection with Pembroke may also have been instrumental in another development before the parliament ended which was significant for the Llwydiarth case. In June 1626 Sir Robert

Vaughan's widow, Dame Katherine, married James Palmer, a courtier who had once been a servant to the earl of Montgomery, Pembroke's brother, and who was also, like Sir William Herbert, a member of the royal household.[20] Palmer was a talented painter who produced portraits of James I and the royal favourite the duke of Buckingham. Sir Henry Herbert, a scion of the Montgomery Castle family, wrote that Palmer, 'like an excellen[t] painter hath taken the face of my Lady Vaughan, the dainty widowe, so longe that now he hath taken her heart & is maryed to her, wherein she hath deceived all her frends and many sutors'.[21] Palmer was an MP in the 1626 parliament who sat there through Montgomery's graces, and who probably helped frustrate any effort by Vaughan against his father-in-law in the Commons chamber.[22] Indeed, Herbert and Palmer, and also Katherine Vaughan, seem to have been connected before 1626. One deponent in a Star Chamber case claimed that in Sir Robert Vaughan's final illness, Sir William Herbert wrote a letter to Palmer noting that if the Llwydiarth squire should die then 'he [Palmer] should have his wife'.[23]

The 1626 parliament broke up inconclusively in late June, and it seems possible that Vaughan mounted another challenge to Sir William Herbert at the Montgomeryshire election for the 1628 parliament, although, if he did so, he was defeated.[24] Vaughan was unable to land a telling blow against his enemies in these parliaments, and his failure must have seemed compounded by Sir William Herbert's continued favour at Court, and his elevation to the aristocracy as Lord Powis in April 1629.[25] His new status seems to have emboldened him to place his own bill in Star Chamber against Edward Vaughan.[26] Vaughan probably remained in London where he was facing down these legal challenges. The principal arenas in which he was forced to defend himself from the legal onslaught by Lord Powis and his daughter, and the courts in which he tried to overturn their possession of Llwydiarth, were Star Chamber, the Court of Wards and the court of the Council in the Marches of Wales. An examination of these parallel cases forms the focus of the following section, and it tells an extraordinary story involving allegations of attempted child murder, forgery, deception and a conspiracy to defame Herbert Vaughan as a changeling.

The first *Star Chamber* case: *Attorney General* versus Vaughan, 1624–28

The case in Star Chamber between Lord Powis and his daughter Katherine Vaughan on the one hand, and Edward Vaughan on the other, is particularly valuable because this court's records have effectively vanished for King Charles's reign. We are fortunate, however, that this 'grand cause', as one contemporary called it, generated a fairly substantial body of records which we can follow through Edward Vaughan's own archive and reports surviving among the state papers. A suit was initiated against Edward on 4 November 1624 by Dame Katherine Vaughan, in the name of the Attorney General.[27] Katherine maintained that this action was intended to prove that the 2 February 1622 entail by which Edward asserted possession of Llwydiarth was 'a false and forged deede'.[28] We know that Edward Vaughan had put his answer into the court by January 1625, but Star Chamber was a legal venue in which cases often proceeded slowly, and there were several hearings of the cause between 1626 and 1628, with depositions being taken from witnesses on both sides, but the matter remaining undetermined.[29] In June 1628, Lord Powis commenced an action against one of Edward Vaughan's alleged co-conspirators, which was designed to shore up the Attorney General's case against Vaughan.[30] This latter suit concerned allegations that Edward had defamed Herbert Vaughan, and, after lengthy debate in the court, in November 1629 it was decided that this case and that initiated by Dame Katherine would proceed together, something a contemporary legal commentator described as 'sans president'.[31]

The Star Chamber suit brought by Dame Katherine (with her father a palpable presence behind the scenes) against Edward Vaughan in 1624 focused on three interrelated elements of the case: (1) the alleged forgery of the deed of entail of 2 February 1622 by which Edward Vaughan claimed Llwydiarth; (2) the alleged forgery of Sir Robert Vaughan's will which supported the deed's provisions; and (3) the 'fowle and insolent ryotts comitted at Lloydiard … to possesse Edward Vaughan of theise lands according to the false deed'.[32] A number of defendants were named along with Vaughan in these supposed offences, most of whom were said to rely on him as servants or associates. The deed of entail became a key focus of the case. All parties concurred that Sir Robert Vaughan had indeed made a conveyance in February 1622, but they disputed whether the deed which Edward Vaughan had taken from Llwydiarth House after being ousted by Sir William Herbert was, in fact, the same as that signed by his dead brother. The Herbert interest maintained that the copy Vaughan promulgated was a fake, asserting that it had been Sir Robert's 'undoubted intention to uphold his name & familie, first in the issues males of his owne bodie, if God should send him any'. They further argued for the 'improbabillitie & almost impossibillitie that he would dissente his owne issues [i.e. children] without some extraordinary occasion to move him thereto'.[33]

A key witness in the debate over the entail's validity was an intimate of Sir Robert Vaughan, the clergyman Richard Lewis who wrote the 2 February 1622 deed in the buttery at Llwydiarth House. In the Star Chamber case Lewis deposed that the deed he transcribed, before Sir Robert had any male heir of course, conveyed the estates to Edward Vaughan and then to his two brothers, Rowland and Charles, successively. Lewis recalled that after initially writing the deed, he drew Sir Robert's attention to the fact that the conveyance omitted reference to any heirs which he might have, and Sir Robert asked him to include a clause to this effect, noting that he was following the example of his own grandfather, John Owen Vaughan, in producing this document because he had no legal counsel present to advise him.[34] There was thus an interlineation on the original deed which conveyed Llwydiarth to Sir Robert's 'heires males of his bodie lawfully begotten and to be begotten', before the remainder to Edward Vaughan, and then to his brothers.[35] The deed was then sealed with a memorandum on its dorse in the presence of ten witnesses before being turned over for safekeeping to Griffith Kyffin, one of Sir Robert's servants.

When confronted with Edward Vaughan's copy of the entail in court, however, Lewis told a striking story. He maintained that shortly after Sir Robert's death, Edward Vaughan requested that he draw up a version of the deed on parchment and provided Lewis with notes as to what he wanted included.[36] In some versions of this story, it seems that

Edward duped Richard Lewis by suggesting that he was only making a copy of the deed for his own reference rather than deviously involving him in a conspiracy. Crucially, this new deed entailed the estates on Sir Robert's brothers, but it omitted any reference to Sir Robert's potential male heirs. Its effect would be to entail Llwydiarth on Edward Vaughan and to exclude the infant Herbert Vaughan from the estate. The deed produced in evidence, Lewis maintained, was indeed in his writing, but it was composed after Sir Robert's death; he also asserted that his signature and that of Sir Robert's had been added to the document in another hand. Lewis further deposed that Edward Vaughan had also required him to draw up three copies of Sir Robert's will, all of which were made in conformity with the entail, and Lewis noted further that these 'were dictated by Ed[ward Vaughan] and ye deede as was prescribed by a copie of Ed[ward] V[aughan]'.[37] For doing this, Edward Vaughan supposedly offered Lewis £100 and the expectation of 'preferments and greate promises'.[38] As a contemporary notetaker of the Star Chamber proceedings had it when reviewing the case, 'There must be forgerie in Ed: Vaughan or perjurie in [Richard] Lewys.'[39]

Edward Vaughan's actions immediately before and after the drawing up of the deed were cast as deeply suspicious by his Star Chamber prosecutors. In September 1623, Vaughan was in discussions about marrying a daughter of Sir Walter Pye, an influential local gentleman who was chief justice of the Brecon circuit. Vaughan's opponents pointed out that in September 1623 Sir Robert Vaughan had made a conveyance to settle his Merionethshire lands on Edward as a jointure settlement to help advance his prospects in the marriage negotiations. The Herberts reasonably asked why Sir Robert would have done this when the pretended deed of 2 February 1622 had supposedly already made Edward a much more attractive marriage prospect than was suggested by this jointure settlement: 'suerlie Sir Robert wold have made a better bargaine with Sir Walter Pie whoe noe doubt would have geven far more for a certenty of such an estate then for a remote possibility for want of issue male'.[40] Moreover, the September 1623 jointure conveyance apparently settled the larger Llwydiarth estate on Sir Robert for life, then his male heirs, and only in the absence of any such progeny on Edward, an arrangement that argued strongly against the existence of the deed which Edward Vaughan now brought before the courts.[41]

The Vaughan defence strategy focused on demonstrating the validity of the entail and on emphasising the discord which he claimed had existed between Sir Robert and Lady Katherine in the last years of his life. This marital strife, he argued, helped explain Sir Robert's desire to leave his estate to his brother rather than to his wife, but it also helped to cast into some doubt Herbert Vaughan's legitimacy. This latter point would be developed as another strand in Edward Vaughan's campaign to recover Llwydiarth and is discussed further below. Edward focused his fire on the clerical scribe Richard Lewis, whom he described as 'the greatest instrument to mayntayne the ... information touching the pretended forgerye', but who, he claimed, had long been dependent on the Herberts and was acting only as their puppet.[42] Vaughan also produced seven witnesses who attested to the entail's validity and discredited Lewis's narrative of its production. These seven individuals, one contemporary noted, avow the deed 'most expresslye [and] acknowledg their hands, [and] sweare they sett their hands to noe other deed of entale'.[43] Most of these individuals were also witnesses to Sir Robert's will which had been proved by the Prerogative Court of Canterbury; therefore, as one observer reasoned, if the credit of the witnesses was endorsed by the verdict of that court, so they should be acknowledged as credible with relation to their attestation of the entail in Star Chamber.[44]

In addition to upholding the deed's legitimacy, Vaughan and his supporters also told a narrative that helped explain why Sir Robert would want to exclude his wife from his will and disinherit his son. Their account focused on allegations of marital breakdown at Llwydiarth in the early 1620s.[45] Gaynor Lloyd deposed that Katherine Vaughan had assaulted her husband and that she had to be restrained, while another witness testified that 'there was much unbefitting cariage' on Katherine's part at Llwydiarth. One Robert Pierce alleged that Sir Robert had grown so tired of his wife's behaviour that he had retired to Llangedwyn 'to be quiet', while Thomas Powell, a servant at Llwydiarth, reported that Lady Katherine 'unjustly quarrelled and fell out with [Sir Robert]

... when she came home unto him from the Redd Castle, the house of her grandmother ... [telling him] that she loved him not nor ever would'.[46] Witnesses also pointed to the provision in Sir Robert's will which entrusted his daughter Eleanor's education to Edward Vaughan's care, a move that not only suggested concern for her religious education, but also an anxiety regarding his children's wardship after his death. Such concerns were highlighted by the Denbighshire gentleman Simon Thelwall the elder, who had recently married Edward Vaughan's aunt, and who testified that Sir Robert Vaughan had told him that he intended to make his brother his heir even if he had a son, because 'he would not have the education of him and administracion of his estate so long to his wifes kindred'. In this telling of Sir Robert's last months, the old enmity between the Herberts and Vaughans appeared to have penetrated the marriage like dry rot, undermining its foundations and causing a breakdown in relations.

In their testimony to Star Chamber commissioners, Edward Vaughan's supporters also darkly suggested that the breakdown in Sir Robert's marriage meant that it was impossible that Herbert Vaughan was, in fact, his son. Watkin Kyffin maintained that Sir Robert had called his wife 'little virgin', while a midwife named Anne Lourt said that Sir Robert had told her that Lady Katherine was, in fact, not with child, and that 'nothing had passed betwixt them [for] a yeare before'. The idea was thus introduced into the court that the putative heir of Llwydiarth was, in fact, nothing of the sort and certainly not of the Vaughan bloodline. Mary Price of Vaynor, Sir Robert and Edward Vaughan's sister, claimed that Katherine Vaughan 'counterfaited herself to be with child', while another deponent described the pregnancy as a 'fiction'. Margaret Kynerton endorsed this notion, stating that Sir Robert was so displeased with his wife's conduct that he resolved to settle Llwydiarth on Edward Vaughan 'fearing lest there should be some supposed child, yt therefore he would marrie his brother into some goode house'. This idea of a changeling, a 'supposititious' child who was not of Sir Robert Vaughan's blood, would be the subject of much bitter controversy across the next decade. In fact, the suggestion had already been raised by Edward Vaughan in a suit at the Court of Wards, and it became a central thread in Sir William Herbert's second Star Chamber action. A final incendiary submission from Vaughan's witnesses came from one Anne Lloyd, who testified that she had seen a letter sent from Sir William Herbert to Sir James Palmer, which had indicated that if Sir Robert Vaughan died, then 'he [Palmer] should have his wife', something that, of course, did indeed transpire in June 1626.[47]

For their part, the Herbert interest sought to rebut all these points and to undermine the credibility of the defence witnesses.[48] They asserted, for example, that Richard Lewis was effectively a servant of Edward Vaughan rather than of Sir William Herbert as their opponents had alleged. They explained away the lack of a bequest to Dame Katherine in the will and Sir Robert's constituting Edward as his executor by pointing out that the widow already possessed a handsome dowry settlement, and that she could also expect half of Sir Robert's personal estate following the 'custom of Wales'.[49] They also noted tellingly that Edward Vaughan had received no legacy by the will either. The Herbert counsel painted as deeply partial the witnesses who had appeared on Edward Vaughan's behalf: they pointed out that Mary Price was his sister and 'the bonfire of the cause'; John Vaughan was a kinsman but also only a 'meane serving man'; Simon Thelwall, meanwhile, they claimed 'has a bad memory'. Those who testified to witnessing Vaughan's 'pretended deed' were also criticised for their naked partiality and lowborn status. Several of them were Vaughan's kinsmen; Lewis Vaughan was apparently Edward's bastard brother; Evan Lloyd was his servant; Thomas Powell was 'an alehowse keeper & tobecco man'; Evan ap Morris Griffith was 'a ploughman that can neither write nor reade'. The plaintiff's counsel also argued that these witnesses' answers on points of detail regarding the deed were hopelessly inadequate. And on the points regarding Sir Robert's troubled marriage and the letter to Sir James Palmer, the Herbert interest concluded that, 'the truth is, when they saw the Lady [Katherine] married to Sir James Palmer [in June 1626], then they put all this in the forge against the honour of the Lady which they could noe way touch'.

The second Star Chamber case: *Powis* versus *Gilbert*, 1628–30

Such was the substance of the first Star Chamber case as it made its stately progress through the court from 1624 until it was combined with the suit initiated by Sir William Herbert in mid-1628, much to Vaughan's dismay and chagrin.[50] This latter action focused on the 'devylish practize', in which Vaughan was intimately involved, to murder the infant Herbert Vaughan, and to spread rumours that he was a changeling who had been swapped at birth. The action named several defendants including Edward Vaughan himself, his brothers-in-law, Arthur Price of Vaynor and William Salesbury of Rûg, his younger brother Rowland, his cousin John Lloyd (the same man who had killed a Herbert servant in 1616 triggering the chain of events that culminated in Owen Vaughan's suicide) and one of his servants, Gilbert Watkin. In addition to this close circle of Vaughan associates, the bill also named a poor woman, Eleanor Gilbert, who became ensnared in the web of intrigue and deceit that swirled around Powis Castle and Llwydiarth in the summer of 1626.[51]

Sir William Herbert's information in Star Chamber was a startling one.[52] He claimed that Edward Vaughan had forged the 2 February 1622 entail, but because this undertaking had failed to deliver him Llwydiarth, he had confederated together with John Lloyd and William Salesbury in an alternative scheme: 'by some wicked and devilish meanes to take away the life of … Herbert Vaughan'. Herbert's narrative ran that, shortly after Herbert Vaughan's birth, John Lloyd had enquired of Elizabeth Dale, a midwife at Powis Castle, whether Lady Vaughan was delivered of a boy. On being told that she was but that the child was born prematurely and was 'weake', Lloyd supposedly asked Dale that she 'doe not thy best ye childe should live, and I will doe my best yt Ed[ward] V[aughan] shall reward you'. He then allegedly offered her £60 to either kill the baby or to see it die of neglect.[53] Elizabeth Dale refused to become part of this horrific scheme, however, and so, according to Herbert's information, the confederates were driven to find some new instrument for their nefarious designs. This materialised in the shape of Eleanor Gilbert, who is described in the documents as the wife of John Corfield, although there is no clear

explanation for why she has a different surname to her husband. Eleanor
Gilbert's answer to Sir William Herbert's Star Chamber information is
one of the more striking narratives to be found among that court's rich
archives, and is worth relating in some detail.[54] That it closely aligns
with Sir William Herbert's bill suggests either that this was a collusive
action against Vaughan, or that the Powis Castle magnate had managed
to overawe her and could depend on her ready cooperation in his cause.[55]

Gilbert described herself as a 'poore woman' and she related how
in late 1624 she was travelling in Dyffryn in Radnorshire when she was
'greatlie payned in her papes or brest, and sate downe on the ground
to milke her breste for hir ease'. In another source, it was reported that
Gilbert had been committed to gaol on suspicion of committing a felony
and had been released, but that she had a child while in custody.[56] Bishop
William Laud described her as 'a queane', and so she may have been in gaol
for prostitution.[57] Gilbert said that while she was by the side of the road,
one of John Lloyd's servants, a man named Gilbert Watkin, saw her in this
sorry state and said, 'I see you are poore and reiected by your friends, yet
it lyeth in your power greatlie to pleasure gentlemen of worth and frinds
of myne'. He informed her that there were 'great suits' between Edward
Vaughan and the Herbert family touching lands of considerable value,
and said that it would 'much availe ... Edward Vaughan to bastardize ...
Herbert Vaughan and to lay an ymputacion or scandale upon the Ladie
his mother'. Watkin promised Eleanor that she would be compensated
with £60 and a small plot of land if she agreed to help with their scheme.
Initially Watkin rehearsed a variation on the plot suggested by his master
John Lloyd to Elizabeth Dale: he asked Eleanor Gilbert to obtain entry to
the nursery at Powis Castle and 'give him [Herbert Vaughan] sucke and
... there upon ... minister some poyson unto [him] ... thereby to distroye
him and bereave him of his liefe'. Like Dale before her, however, Eleanor
Gilbert refused to countenance the plan, but by Watkin's 'extraordinary
ymporunitie', she consented to spread the disinformation that Herbert
Vaughan was, in fact, her own child. The story which Watkin fed her and
asked her to disperse was that in June 1624 Eleanor had delivered her own
infant boy to Lady Vaughan's servants, and that she had received in return
a baby girl who was handed over in a basket. Gilbert now spread this story

'publiquelie' throughout north Wales and Shropshire, receiving some thirty-two shillings from Watkin at three separate meetings in Welshpool. Gilbert told the court that at each rendezvous Watkin encouraged her to 'continew in speeches of scandall'. Additionally, she claimed that William Salesbury of Rûg and his wife, Dorothy (Edward Vaughan's sister), had also given her small amounts of silver and gold. Beside these inducements, however, came 'indigestible threates', with Watkin telling her that if ever she disclosed the truth of the business, 'that then shee ... should bee kild'.

We should be wary of accepting this extraordinary tale at face value, but it is a plausible narrative, and one that a relatively impoverished abandoned mother would have been unlikely to devise independently. It is suspect in that it tracks Sir William Herbert's information closely, but there are divergences from his information too. In his submission, Sir William alleged that the conspirators had attempted to get Eleanor to divulge that it was he who had made her pregnant, and thus that it was his own impostor son who stood to inherit Llwydiarth. He had claimed that in return for her baby boy Eleanor was to communicate that she had received from Lady Katherine a dead child rather than a daughter. He also alleged that she was promised £100 for her part in the conspiracy rather than the £60 to which she admitted in her answer. Moreover, independent witnesses also testified that Gilbert had admitted to spreading the rumour.[58] One witness, Mabel Rogers, told the court that she had heard Gilbert confess to these schemes, and described how Watkin had given the latter gold and silver and 'lay uppon ye grownd with his face downeward because he might [later] sweare he saw her not'. In a pitiful reflection of the power dynamics at play in these exchanges, one reporter of the cause made a marginal note that 'she deserves to be hanged', but remained silent regarding the powerful gentry figures who had manipulated her.

Edward Vaughan submitted an answer to these charges in July 1628. He claimed Sir William's bill was intended to cross his daughter's earlier action and 'give occation to stirr upp some examinacion or question touching' the deed.[59] In one defence brief, Vaughan's counsel queried why the cause was being raised now and that the matter was not reported at the hearing on the first Star Chamber cause.[60] Thus Vaughan asserted that this action was an attempt to dredge up 'supplementall & extraiudicyall' proof regarding the forgery case and so resolved not to provide an answer while that cause was under consideration. His alleged confederates were similarly tight-lipped, with John Lloyd alleging that Herbert's bill was preferred 'of meere spleene and malice', while William Salesbury gave the pithy response that 'there is never a true worde that concerneth [him in the bill] but his name'.[61] Edward Vaughan was examined regarding the cause in October 1628, when he bullishly described himself as 'of Lloydearth'.[62] He provided a Trumpian set of responses in which he asserted that he did not know Eleanor Gilbert and had been in London when some of the rumours were circulating, including one that Herbert Vaughan 'never tumbled in the Ladie Vaughans belly'. He refused to respond to the question as to whether he himself had reported that Gilbert was the child's true mother, however, maintaining that he was not charged in the bill with publishing any such report. The silence of Vaughan and his associates seems eloquent on the matter of the conspiracy to spread the rumours, however, and we know that Vaughan maintained in a simultaneous suit in the Court of Wards that Herbert Vaughan was an impostor and not Katherine Vaughan's legitimate child.[63] As one commentator on the Star Chamber cause had it, in these proceedings Edward Vaughan sought to support 'a false deede in place of a true one: now a true child calumniated for a false one'.[64] Nevertheless, the prominence of John Lloyd and Gilbert Watkin in these allegations tended to leave Vaughan operating only as a shadowy figure behind the scenes: there was no evidence tying him directly to Eleanor Gilbert or the circulation of rumours. As William Laud, then bishop of London and one of the justices considering the case in Star Chamber, put it at the time, there was 'noe shadowe of proofe against Ed[ward] Va[ughan]'.[65] His lawyerly slipperiness seems to have served him well.

A verdict (of sorts): Star Chamber, 1630

After it was decided in November 1629 that these two bills would proceed together, the Star Chamber case eventually came to a hearing on 28

May 1630.[66] The complexity of the matter was noted at the hearing's opening, when Secretary of State Sir John Coke 'had in some seven sheetes of paper full writt with a small hand, collected all depositions of witnesses and all allegacions of councell on both parties in both causes, having imploid a full hower at least in reading thereof'.[67] Vaughan would later claim in a petition to the king that at this hearing the entail and Sir Robert's will were 'made good by the opinion of all the judges', but this was not quite the case.[68] Indeed, Sir William Herbert would later assert that the court's determination had proven that the deed was a forgery![69] It is fair to say that the court did not produce an unequivocal verdict. The opinions of some fifteen judges, many of them privy councillors, were recorded, and some, such as the earl of Portland and Richard Neile, bishop of Winchester, determined that the deed was, in fact, forged.[70] The latter in particular supported the Herbert line, arguing that the taking of Llwydiarth was 'violent and riotous' and that 'those who have wronged ye Lady [Vaughan] should make publique acknowledgement'. William Laud, bishop of London, who would again be involved in this case later in the decade, was not convinced by two of Herbert's witnesses, describing Richard Lewis as 'variable', and he was in favour of the will and the deed. Yet although there were few who believed that the threshold to prove forgery had been met, there was very little enthusiasm for the suspect deed. Secretary John Coke, for example, believed that there was 'not proofe sufficient' to find Vaughan guilty of forging the document, but believed that it was 'not a fitt deede to carrie away such an inheritance'. Chief Justice Richardson concurred that proving forgery required a high level of proof which was not met in the case, but dismissed the deed as *non liquet*, or 'not clear'. The other judges' opinions followed a similar line: that they were not minded to declare the deed as a forgery, but neither were they prepared to rule that it was sufficiently robust to disinherit Edward Vaughan's nephew. Laud wrote 'I doe not denie anye thinge upon proofe of mouth or force enough to disinherit hime [Herbert Vaughan]'.[71]

The court thus gave a more ambiguous ruling on the case than Edward Vaughan later implied: it left the entail as a 'suspected deed' and referred the case to trial at common law.[72] As the endorsement to a report on the opinions collected among the State Papers put it, 'The sence of the

Starchamber against ye deed. The sentence not for it'.[73] Interestingly, none of the judges were disposed to adjudicate on Herbert Vaughan's paternity, and all wanted this case dismissed. Bishop Laud was moved to note that there was 'no culler it should be a suppositious childe', and in his private notes on the case he wrote, 'I am in mye heart as tender for ye heire as can be', and there was a general sense that Lady Katherine's honour should be cleared.[74] It is understandable that the court did not wish to decide on this delicate business if they could avoid doing so. Laud wrote that 'the whole cause is but one against another in the 2 necessarye things', meaning the entail and the will. 'All ye rest', he wrote, 'is throwinge of durt'.[75]

For his part, Sir William Herbert, who became Lord Powis in April 1629, was particularly disappointed with the court's failure to punish Vaughan for calumniating his daughter. He averred that Eleanor Gilbert's answer was suppressed because of a confusion over her surname, being the wife of John Corfield. Powis later gave an interesting explanation for his failure to win an outright victory in this long-running case. He argued that Vaughan had used:

> indirecte meanes by great rewards & otherwise to cumpase his ... purpose and cunningly insinuated himselfe into the favoure of persons then in great power, pretendinge to marrie one of their kin[d]red and thereby gayned a great partie in Court and elsewhere under cullor that your peticioner [i.e. Powis] did oppresse him ... [and] Edward & his confederats escaped ponishment.[76]

We know that Vaughan had been talking of marriage into the Buckingham dynasty in the 1620s, and this seems to be the suggestion Powis was promoting here, although the great duke was dead by the time of the Star Chamber judgment. As is discussed in the final chapter, Edward Vaughan was indeed involved in a potential clandestine marriage, but this was in the mid-1630s and certainly did not involve Court politics. As this was a submission from early 1641, however, it is quite possible that Powis was simply trying to stir up trouble and insinuation without much basis in fact. There might even be some wounded pride mixed in with his memories of this event, and his inability to finish off Vaughan's claim to the estate when, as we shall see in the next chapter, this effort was now bearing such fruit under the aegis of the Long Parliament.

The Court of Wards: Katherine and Herbert Vaughan versus Edward Vaughan, 1624–31

So Star Chamber made no clear determination of the case in May 1630 and the matter of the 1622 entail was turned over to common law. There was, however, a concurrent case which had been making its own slow progress through another prerogative jurisdiction, that of the Court of Wards. Katherine Vaughan placed a bill against Edward Vaughan into the court in November 1624, which focused particularly on the £6,000 of Sir Robert's personal estate which she claimed had been spirited away from Llwydiarth.[77] In February 1628 another bill was submitted by Sir William Herbert on behalf of his grandson, Herbert Vaughan. This action alleged that Edward Vaughan had taken Llwydiarth's deeds and evidences from the house in 1624, and that this had meant that no inquisition of the deceased Sir Robert's lands could be taken. An inquisition would discover what rights and revenues were due to the Crown from the estate but would also, more crucially, make a determination regarding the rightful heir.[78] It was in his May 1628 answer to this bill that Edward Vaughan introduced the claim that Herbert was not Sir Robert's son but rather the child of Eleanor (or 'Ellen') Gilbert.[79] He asked that the court examine the truth of his assertion so that he 'may bee noe further vexed with the suppositiouse yssue of Sir Robert Vaughans body', adding that he was 'confident that noe jury can finde ... Herbert Vaughan to be the sonne and heire of ... Sir Robert Vaughan'. Edward's answer also rehearsed his arguments about the contested entail, noting that this had been questioned in Star Chamber but 'noe way impeached by the judgement of that court'. This was, again, a piece of lawyerly legerdemain rather than an accurate representation of the court's findings.

It seems that the Court of Wards did not wish to prejudge issues which were then under review in Star Chamber, but with the (rather indeterminate) judgment of May 1630, the case was revived in the former jurisdiction. The court issued a commission to take depositions in the country regarding tenures on Llwydiarth lands since 1624. These were taken at Llanfyllin on 5 January 1631, and involved a very large number of witnesses who described the rents and duties they had paid to Lady Katherine Vaughan (now Lady Palmer) since Sir Robert's death.[80] The logjam of the actions over the inheritance was breaking since the Star Chamber referral, however, as Edward Vaughan now had to contest the supposed entail at common law. However, the Herbert interest obtained an injunction on any such proceedings by asking the Court of Wards to adjudicate.[81] In early September 1631, Dame Katherine, or perhaps more likely Lord Powis, managed to have a writ issued out of Wards for the holding of the much-delayed inquisition post-mortem into Sir Robert's lands. The importance of this inquest to the balance of local power is indicated by the powerful commissioners who attended. These included Sir John Bridgeman, chief justice of Chester, Sir Marmaduke Lloyd, second justice of Chester, Richard Newport, the Shropshire MP, Sir Andrew Corbet, another Shropshire MP, and Richard Hopton, a future chief justice of north Wales.[82] These four men were also, however, members of the Council in the Marches, the body of which Lord Powis was also a member and which had ruled in his favour in 1624. Vaughan asserted that some of them were the judges who had issued the order ejecting him from Llwydiarth in 1624, and that their efforts were 'partiall', 'unindifferent' and were moved largely by the desire to uphold their former ruling.[83] The inquisition was held over a remarkably long four days, 'during the greatest parte of which time the principal matter insisted upon in evidence' was whether the much-contested February 1622 entail was a forgery or not.[84] Clearly, then, this was a far from straightforward process, and it is evident that Edward Vaughan, or his agents, were seeking to re-run the arguments before the inquest that had been aired in Star Chamber. In a later action brought in the Court of Wards, Edward Vaughan claimed that Sir Marmaduke Lloyd had given a direction to the inquisition jury in which he informed them that the emperor Justinian had insisted that the word of a priest held especial weight and credibility, and that it 'was to be taken for truth against 10. I [*vice* 'Aye'] against 1,000 witnesses'.[85] Thus, Lloyd directed the jury to rely particularly on the testimony of

Richard Lewis, the cleric who had sworn in Star Chamber that the entail was a forgery.[86] In another review of the case, Vaughan asserted that the commissioners 'did direct the jury to finde against theire evidence', and to ignore the entail which was to be tried at common law.[87] Given such direction, then, it was perhaps unsurprising that the jury determined that Herbert Vaughan was Sir Robert's heir, a finding that effectively stymied Edward Vaughan's efforts to bring further suits in the court.[88]

This was a disastrous result for Edward who tried to challenge the decision with several bills in the court against the finding, the process and the conduct of the judges, but each effort was denied as the court maintained that a determination had been made. Vaughan argued that he was thus 'denied the ordinary course of iustice'.[89] On 20 November 1631, only a few short months after the inquisition returned its verdict finding that Herbert Vaughan was Llwydiarth's heir and ward of the Crown, Lord Powis swooped in and purchased his grandson's wardship for the sum of £1,000 (although he only ever paid £500) and £200 per year rent, most of which he never paid.[90] This was seen as something of a bargain, however, as he had convinced the court that the property was burdened with £8,000 of debt, although this was largely an amount of his own invention.[91] Llwydiarth now lay squarely and securely in Herbert hands. Edward Vaughan was particularly outraged as the inquest had found the inheritance in Montgomeryshire only, but that possession of the lands in Denbighshire and Merioneth were evidently comprehended under the order. The court gave Vaughan no scope to challenge the ward's possession in any part of the estate.[92] This would become a chink in the legal ruling that he would try and exploit in the early months of the Long Parliament's sitting.

Conclusion

This had been a bruising decade for Edward Vaughan. In the early 1620s he had hopes of inheriting his brother's estate and its thousands of pounds in annual revenues. Sir Robert Vaughan only had a daughter, was estranged from his wife and had written a will that favoured his younger brother. A decade later and Edward Vaughan was on the wrong end of a marathon set of lawsuits. Although his brother was dead, Edward had been ejected from Llwydiarth by the Council in the Marches of Wales and was denied a route to recovery by an intransigent Court of Wards. His nemesis, Sir William Herbert, had been elevated to the aristocracy as Baron Powis, and he had orchestrated a skilful campaign to seize control of his ward's Llwydiarth lands which now considerably augmented his own, already extensive, landed presence in north Wales.

Having experienced, however briefly, the heady thrill of being Llwydiarth's owner, however, this younger son was not prepared to readily accept his position as a defeated claimant. Vaughan was nothing if not determined, and he would continue to press his claims to the lands in the 1630s until his entreaties began to fall on receptive ears. He was frequently in London while these efforts were in train, probably residing at his chambers in the Inner Temple. He certainly could not claim Llwydiarth as his residence, and, when in Wales, he lived at Celynog in Montgomeryshire, a property belonging to the Phillips family of Llanddewi in Radnorshire which we know Vaughan leased at this time.[93] As we will see in chapter 10, this was the home he shared in the later 1630s with his secret wife who was one of the Phillipses of Radnorshire. Vaughan had only a small income at this time, and we know that he relied in part on the support of his kinsman, the London draper Charles Lloyd. Lloyd would later claim that during Edward Vaughan's 'troubles in suites of lawe, [he] being putt out of his estate', Lloyd had loaned him 'great somes of money as his occasions called for it ... for the space of about ten yeares together'. Lloyd estimated that he had loaned him around £1,000, adding that Vaughan would have 'of necessity ... sunke under the burthen of those troubles and suites' without his help.[94] Despite this support, Vaughan needed to augment his income and he probably undertook legal work to help pay the bills.[95] He was called to the bar in November 1635, perhaps thinking of making the law his principal area of operations should he fail in his efforts to regain his patrimony.[96] But the tenacious Edward Vaughan would not give up the fight quite yet, and his continued efforts to recover Llwydiarth would have significant ramifications, not just for his own power and prosperity, but for the very existence of the courts that had found against him. This is the subject of the following chapter.

CHAPTER 3

Powis *versus* Vaughan and the Downfall of Prerogative Justice, 1631-1642

During the early 1630s an uneasy truce seems to have prevailed in relations between Edward Vaughan and his Herbert antagonists. Vaughan was licking his wounds after the bruising judgment of the Court of Wards which had barred him from pursuing the Llwydiarth inheritance. He effectively falls off the documentary radar for the first half of the decade, a fact that testifies to the importance of his controlling the family estate for possessing any kind of public profile or local power. The appearance of tranquillity was deceptive, however, and old resentments bubbled close beneath the surface. When the opportunity arose for Vaughan to go on the offensive in the later 1630s, he seized it with both hands. In so doing, he aligned himself with reformist elements that sought to denude or eradicate the power of the king's prerogative courts; courts that had provided a powerbase for Lord Powis.

This chapter explores how Vaughan's personal ambitions came to assume a more general, indeed constitutional, significance as part of a wider campaign against the Council in the Marches of Wales in particular, but also against prerogative justice more generally. Vaughan venerated the legal scholar and MP John Selden, and, like Selden, this period would see him forge an alliance with the Archbishop of Canterbury but also attack the prerogative courts as arbitrary bodies that impeded the king's subjects from enjoying impartial justice.[1] During the decade of Personal Rule in the 1630s, then, Vaughan endured further assaults by Lord Powis in the

Council in the Marches and in the High Court of Chivalry, but these were jurisdictions that came under attack with the collapse of Charles I's government and the calling of the Long Parliament. As this chapter shows, Vaughan's arguments for his ill-treatment at the hands of the prerogative courts received a sympathetic hearing from the House of Commons. In addition to tearing down the edifice of prerogative justice which had been Lord Powis's main source of authority in occupying Llwydiarth, the Long Parliament also gave Vaughan the opportunity to assert his title to his ancestral estates and to overturn what it portrayed as the 'arbitrary' judgments against him from the 1620s and 1630s. This chapter explores Vaughan's experiences as a fascinating case study of the overturning of old certainties with the advent of the Long Parliament, and of the way an individual could, if so minded, harness the reformist impulses of that body for their own ends. It is also an examination of the foundations upon which Vaughan's later parliamentarianism would rest. Although his political allegiance in the civil wars was not simply a pragmatic position designed merely to defeat his royalist antagonist, this chapter will chart his remarkable reversal of fortunes, something for which the Long Parliament was almost entirely responsible.

The Council in the Marches, Archbishop Laud and the Vaughan legacy dispute, 1637–40

Although the legal battles between Vaughan and the Herbert interest entered something of a hiatus after the 1631 Court of Wards resolution, by 1635 antagonism between the Montgomeryshire's key power blocs was once more disturbing the political quiet of the Welsh Marches. One occasion for this was the selection of Montgomeryshire's sheriff. The shrievalty was an important, though often burdensome, office, whose holder functioned as the Crown's representative in the locality. In 1635 the individual selected to fill this post was Thomas Ireland of Shrewsbury.[2] Word of Ireland's selection reached the ears of the Herbert interest, whereupon Lord Powis wrote to the man responsible for selecting sheriffs for the Crown, John Egerton, first earl of

Bridgewater and lord president of the Council in the Marches of Wales. Powis complained that 'there is a neere kindred between this Thomas Ireland and Edward Vaughan, gent., agaynst whom ther is divers suitts, and whoe doth prosecut many causes' in Montgomeryshire.[3] Because of Ireland's likely partiality in these cases, Powis asked to 'have Mr Ireland challenged from being sheeryffe of the countye of Mountgomerye'. Powis's anxiety over Ireland's selection was probably based on the fact that his mother was Mary Purcell, heiress of Vaynor, a line with close ties to the Vaughans of Llwydiarth.[4] The shrieval selections had apparently already been sent to the king by this time, so Powis was unsuccessful in his efforts to halt the appointment, but it seems that his concerns were misplaced and Ireland never materialises as a Vaughan partisan. However, Powis's reference to Vaughan prosecuting numerous suits, and the very fact that he tried to block Ireland's appointment, indicate that any impression of a cessation in the antagonism between the Herbert and Vaughan camps is probably a product of deficiencies in our sources rather than a true reflection of reality.

Lord Powis may have been seeking the selection of a sheriff amenable to the Powis Castle interest as he was about to launch a new legal offensive against Edward Vaughan, and a biddable individual in this post would have been to his advantage. The first shots in this new legal démarche were fired in late 1635 when Powis, acting on behalf of his grand-daughter, Eleanor Vaughan (Sir Robert's daughter and Herbert Vaughan's sister), exhibited a bill against Edward Vaughan in the Court of Wards.[5] The suit concerned Sir Robert's contentious will, of which Edward had been named executor, and which he had proved in the Prerogative Court of Canterbury in 1624. The will provided that Eleanor was to receive £500 from her father's estate when she turned sixteen. Powis maintained that Vaughan had taken thousands of pounds from Llwydiarth to cover such liabilities and so needed to pay the money to his niece. Vaughan submitted his answer into the Court of Wards and the business seems to have been making its way through that jurisdiction when, in October 1637, Powis introduced a second bill, which largely mirrored this action, into the court of the Council in the Marches of Wales.[6] Vaughan maintained that this second action was to do 'double vexacion in severall courts for one

and the same matter', but in his response to this new offensive he also
opened up a much more fundamental challenge to the suit by arguing
that the matter was 'properly determinable in the ecclesiastical court …
the jurisdiccion whereof such matters of legacy doe properlie belonge'.[7]
Lord Powis was hoping to add to the sum of Vaughan's misery by suing
him for Eleanor's legacy. However, his new suit had instead introduced
a thorny and potentially explosive issue, for Vaughan now sought not
simply to fight the case on its merits, but also to argue that the Council
in the Marches, a Herbert powerbase, had no jurisdiction in such actions.
Moreover, this was not a randomly chosen defence strategy on Vaughan's
part; rather he was aligning himself with powerful forces that were intent
on challenging the Council's ecclesiastical jurisdiction.

Vaughan's strategy was informed by Archbishop William Laud's
contemporaneous effort to augment and extend the authority of the
Established Church which he saw as having been denuded by secular
interests. The Council in the Marches of Wales possessed a jurisdiction
in ecclesiastical matters such as legacies because of the broad powers
given it by the royal instructions upon which the institution's authority
rested.[8] However, this jurisdiction constituted something of a chink in
the Council's armour which Vaughan looked to exploit, for complaints
had been voiced about the Marcher court exercising such a power since
at least the mid-1620s. During the 1624 parliament Archbishop Abbott
submitted a set of papers to the then lord president of Wales, the earl
of Northampton, which asserted that matters of legacies and the like
properly belonged to the ecclesiastical courts, but that the Council in
the Marches had 'taken … cognizance of divers causes of this nature,
contrarye to their instruccions, impeaching thereby the libertie of the
Churche'.[9] The submission constituted a fully developed set of arguments
against the Ludlow court for having encroached on the jurisdiction of
the church courts, particularly in matters of legacies. The paper claimed
that the Council in the Marches 'doth use to call such persons to inforce
them to pay legacies contrary to the law in that behalfe'. Although these
arguments were not taken up at this parliament, the Council's authority
over legacies remained contentious. Indeed, the most recent set of royal
instructions issued to the Council in 1633 acknowledged that, 'of late

certaine doubtes and questions have bine made touchinge the power of
the ... Councell to hould plea of suites touching legacies exceedinge the
value of fiftie pounds'.[10] Despite these complaints, the 1633 instructions
stressed that the Council's authority in this area was necessary to address
the needs of those who could not get relief in the ecclesiastical courts for
non-payment of legacies, 'to the greate ease and benifitt of his Maiesties
subiects within that whole jurisdiction'. Legacies were a small part of
the Council's business, but it was part of a competency in ecclesiastical
business which also comprehended questions of sexual immorality, and
these latter actions were, as Penry Williams observed, 'essential to ... [the
court's] existence, since they supplied a large proportion of its income
from fines'.[11] The lord president wrote in 1636 that if legacies and issues
of incontinency were taken away, 'there wilbe such a decay of the fines
that they will not support the charge of the house'.[12] The Vaughan case
thus represented a potentially ruinous breach in the Council's authority.

The issue of Ludlow's ecclesiastical jurisdiction had clearly been
challenged when the 1633 instructions were being devised, and in that
year Charles I selected William Laud to succeed George Abbott as
Archbishop of Canterbury. Laud was active in reasserting the Church's
rights and jurisdictions in areas where he believed it had lost ground
to secular interests. In the account of his archdiocese which Laud
presented to the king in 1636, he reflected that 'much more might
be done there [in Welsh dioceses] in a church-way, if they were not
overborne by the proceedings of the court of the marches'.[13] He reported
that his commissioners conducting the metropolitical visitation in the
principality had 'complain[ed] unto me, that the power which belongs
to my place hath been in them very much wronged and impeached by
that court'. Laud asked Charles for a hearing on these matters and the
king scribbled his intention to 'agree thease differences by my heering
of them'. In July 1637 Laud wrote to Sir John Bridgeman, a leading
member of the Council and a man who had been among the 'partiall'
commissioners at Sir Robert Vaughan's 1631 inquisition post-mortem,
complaining about churchwardens being brought up to the Council
for regulating church seating, a matter that should have been solely a
matter for church courts. He complained that if the petition he had

received on the issue was correct, then 'the Church power is cut very short by the Court of the Marches and the proceedings there'.[14] It may have been Laud's agitation to which one Council official referred when, in July 1636, he provided Lord President Bridgewater with 'a note of such answeres as I conceave fitt to be made to the obiections against the instructions concerning incontinencie & legacies'.[15] So the archbishop was already gunning for the Council when the case of Eleanor Vaughan's legacy raised its head in October 1637.

Thus it was that Edward Vaughan had an unlikely potential ally in defending his case in the person of the Archbishop of Canterbury. Laud knew of Vaughan's legal tribulations with Lord Powis: he had sat in judgment in Star Chamber in 1630 and took his own extensive notes on the matter.[16] He was apparently inclined to support Vaughan's position, finding Herbert witnesses such as Richard Lewis to be unreliable, and agreed that both Sir Robert's will and the 1622 entail were valid documents.[17] Laud was, of course, the man who helped determine the controversial religious policy of the Personal Rule which many took to be a backsliding towards a form of crypto-Catholicism.[18] We know that Edward Vaughan was a convinced Protestant who later demonstrated Presbyterian sympathies, so, although he was unsympathetic to the drift in church policy under Laud, he was willing to make a strategic alliance to undermine Lord Powis's case, but also to strike at the body which was an important source of his local authority. Thus it was that in the autumn of 1637 Vaughan launched an effort, with Laud's backing and assistance, to have the legacy case transferred through a legal writ called a prohibition to the ecclesiastical jurisdiction of the Prerogative Court of Canterbury, where Laud's influence would be determinative. Vaughan's attorneys were Charles Jones of Lincoln's Inn, originally a Caernarvonshire man, who had become London's deputy recorder, and Edward Henden of Gray's Inn, a serjeant-at-law.[19] These men 'very eager[ly]' moved for a writ of prohibition in King's Bench because the Powis action, they argued, was 'for ye determininge of ye legacy only, being no way mixed with any other circumstance of equity', and so it properly belonged in the Prerogative Court. Although they acknowledged that the 1633 royal instructions gave the Council a capacity to hear legacies, 'yett we conceave yt the same instruccions shall not deprive or devest ye ecclesiastical court, neither give ye Court of ye Marches a concurrent jurisdicion'.[20] They further maintained that, as the will had already been proved in the Prerogative Court, so the Council in the Marches could not question Vaughan's executorship without crossing that body's jurisdiction.[21] Henden added that the ecclesiastical court's 'prerogative jurisdiction cannot be taken away generall by instructions' such as those which underpinned the Council's authority.[22] Vaughan was actively involved in these legal arguments in London, moving between his counsels and the attorney for the Council in the Marches, Roger Holland, in his efforts to have the matter removed from the Marches court.[23]

The day before this action commenced, Laud's secretary William Dell wrote a revealing letter to Sir John Lambe, Dean of the Arches, the official who presided over the Prerogative Court of Canterbury. Dell wrote that:

> My Lords Grace hath taken such care of Mr Vaughans busines (or rather indeed of his owne jurisdicion), that he hath moved his Majesty about it, who assumes all ye differences betwixt the ecclesiasticall courtes and that of ye Marches to his owne hearing. And in ye meane tyme hath given command to my Lord President [of Wales] for ye respiting all further proceedings there in businesses of this or the like nature. Soe yt I suppose Mr Vaughan will have noe great neede of his prohibicion whether he obtayne it or not. I pray faile not to send him [Vaughan] to my Lord, soe soone as you can for he desires to speake with him.[24]

It is fascinating to see Vaughan operating here in tandem with Laud when a decade later the Llwydiarth squire would be supporting a moderate Presbyterian Church settlement. However, one element of Vaughan's life and career which recurs throughout this book is his flexibility and adaptability when the prize of securing Llwydiarth and its riches was on the table. Moreover, we might be mistaken to read his later politics too readily into his position in 1637. Vaughan may not have found Laudianism as obnoxious as many and might have been happy to yoke the archbishop's authority to his own cause and leverage it for his own ends.

Certainly, the convergence of his and Laud's interests deeply worried the Council's lord president.

The precedent which Vaughan's challenge could set for the Council's business would threaten not only legacy cases but also those of sexual incontinency. On the same day that Dell wrote to Lambe, Bridgewater drafted a letter to Sir John Bridgeman discussing the Vaughan case. He forwarded some documents concerning the matter, noting 'you may perceave by thenclosed to what height the storme is growne', and adding that they needed quickly to devise a strategy for meeting this challenge.[25] He continued that the decision in Vaughan's case would 'either adde muche luster to the Court or very much dam & blemishe it ... if the fines [for sexual incontinency] be lessened, I scarcely knowe howe the house will subsist'. He was aware, too, that the case would open up fissures elsewhere within the Council's authority, particularly in its jurisdiction over the four English border shires where there had been a long-standing agitation to remove the Council's jurisdiction over them.[26] Dilating on the challenge presented by Vaughan's case, Bridgewater reflected:

> if the foure [English] countyes have not bene yett of power to doe more harme unto it [the Council] then to grinne & shewe their teethe, I should be very sory to finde it nowe so bitten & crushed that it shoulde not be hable to breathe or move within the limits of its jurisdicion.

The legacy case emerging out of the wider confrontation between Powis and Vaughan thus began to take on important constitutional as well as legal dimensions. This was no longer simply a battle between powerful gentlemen over wills and entails: it had become a confrontation in which the very jurisdiction of the courts determining these matters was brought into question. The wider forces at play also emerged from a confrontation between common law jurisdictions and those whose authority was based in the royal prerogative. Writs of prohibition, such as that Vaughan was employing in this case, had been used by common lawyers to challenge prerogative jurisdictions such as those of the Council in the Marches. Indeed, when drawing up the most recent set of instructions for the Council, lawyers had spent some time considering how to deal with prohibitions designed to remove cases out of the Ludlow court and into common law courts.[27] The chief justice of south Wales, Timothy Tourneur, discussing the Vaughan case with Bridgewater, believed that 'there wilbe no dowbt of the patronage of this cause by the kings councell at lawe', while Bridgewater himself reflected 'I doubt wee shall scarcely have any of the kinges councell to help maintaine his majestyes instruccions & our proceedings thereupon'.[28] The Vaughan legacy case and its attack on the Council in the Marches, then, saw a strange conjunction of interests, with Laud whose rule and authority supported the prerogative rights of 'Thorough' during the 1630s, siding with common lawyers who wished to clip the wings of prerogative justice.

The matter had become sufficiently important that the king himself took it into his consideration. On 21 November 1637, Lord President Bridgewater attended an audience with Charles I and there he:

> receaved direccions from his [the king's] owne mouth, that I should write to you of his Counsel in the Marches of Wales to lett you knowe that he would not have any farther proceeding to be had there in the case of legacye betweene Vaughan & Vaughan, until suche time as he had hearde the differences between the Prerogative Courte & that his counsell upon the article concerning legacyes.[29]

Powis's suit had indeed become an incendiary one, but not for the reasons he might have anticipated. Now a matter of royal interest, the cause had come to threaten the very existence of the Council in the Marches of Wales and the court's supporters scrambled to meet the challenge. Timothy Tourneur received the King's Bench's prohibition on 2 December 1637 and requested that Bridgewater direct Lord Powis to excavate legal precedents among Chancery decrees which 'maybe of use to answer their obiection that personall legacies are particular to the jurisdiccion of ecclesiasticall courts & not pleadable elswhere'.[30] Tourneur was confident that they had a strong legal case grounded in the Council's royal instructions, and believed that the arguments made by Edward Vaughan's counsel 'are soe feeble that I conceave them to arise rather from too much boldnesse to question the iurisdiccion [rather] then reason'. Although Bridgewater initially seemed hopeful that the king's stay of ecclesiastical business ruling applied only to Vaughan's case rather than more generally, a ruling from King's Bench on Vaughan's writ of prohibition meant a suspension of all such proceedings until the following legal term. This suspension did not endure, however, and the council seems to have resumed hearings on matters of legacies and incontinency soon thereafter.[31]

Although other cases might have been heard, the Vaughan suit was halted by express order pending the king's determination, but nothing seems to have been done in the matter by the summer of 1638 and the case remained in limbo.[32] Vaughan recognised that the king's oversight of his case had potentially opened a new avenue for him to bring pressure on Lord Powis. Thus it was that at some point in 1637, probably timed to coincide with his writ of prohibition, Edward Vaughan addressed a petition to King Charles I.[33] The petition rehearsed his narrative of being ejected from Llwydiarth in 1624, and he attempted to make the deeply contentious claim that the 1622 entail and his brother's will had been endorsed by the 1630 Star Chamber judgment. Vaughan complained that he was barred from pursuing the matter in Wards by an injunction and that he had been 'enforced' to attend the 1631 inquisition on the Llwydiarth lands which was conducted by 'unindifferent' commissioners and 'illiterate' jurors.[34] Despite his efforts to have a hearing in Wards or at common law, he had been frustrated at every turn and would now be barred from bringing the matter to trial until Herbert Vaughan reached his majority. He had, moreover, been 'vexed with suits' in a multiplicity of courts despite his much-reduced means, and so, 'dispossest of all', he now faced the legacy claim from Eleanor Vaughan. Doubtless hoping to break any hold which the Council in the Marches might have over the case, he asked for the king to grant him leave to demonstrate his title at common law 'while his witnesses are livinge'. Accompanying the petition was a set of reasons as to why Vaughan should be allowed to pursue his case to have the 1622 entail proven and enforced.[35] The document rehearsed the points outlined in the petition in a little more detail including Vaughan's argument that the 'ordinarie course of justice being denied, it is proper to appeale to his Majestie who is the fountaine of justice'. He also slyly introduced his allegations about the ward's legitimacy, claiming that there was a 'stronge presumption' at the Star Chamber hearing that Herbert Vaughan was not Sir Robert's legitimate offspring.

Although these arguments did not move the king to make a determination in the matter, they continued to apply pressure in the case, and his appeal encompassed the compelling image of a man being denied the basic right of having his case heard by a conspiracy of powerful actors. To rule against Vaughan would be for the king openly to side with a crypto-Catholic in a high-profile case which could initiate a wider assault on one of his prerogative courts. In the circumstances, it probably seemed best to let the matter rest without a resolution for as long as possible. This result, however, must have angered and exasperated Lord Powis whose efforts to attack Vaughan in Wards and the Council in the Marches had been frustrated. As a result of this, Powis turned to another prerogative jurisdiction as a means of bringing Vaughan low: the High Court of Chivalry.

Powis versus *Vaughan in the High Court of Chivalry, 1638–39*

The High Court of Chivalry, also known as the Earl Marshal's Court, was a jurisdiction whose origins reached back to the fourteenth century, and which sat in judgment on individual cases of aristocratic honour. It had largely fallen into disuse by the early seventeenth century, but in 1634 Charles I revived the court to adjudicate in matters of honour among the gentry and aristocracy.[36] The court became a popular venue for gentlemen who claimed that their public honour had been impugned, and it had a good record of upholding the claims of gentle and aristocratic litigants and of imposing swingeing fines. As the leading historian of the court has noted, rulings in the High Court of Chivalry demonstrated a 'determination … to "get tough" with anyone challenging a peer and provided a ready means of repairing his honour'.[37] This was a jurisdiction, moreover, where the odds would have been stacked in Lord Powis's favour and where he could expect a sympathetic and favourable hearing. So it was that on 28 November 1638 Powis introduced a bill (or 'libel') into the Court of Chivalry against Edward Vaughan.[38] In this document he asserted that since 1627 Vaughan had 'within the cittyes of London and Westminster and other places' given out that Herbert Vaughan was an illegitimate child. Moreover, he claimed that in his 1628 answer to Powis's bill in the Court of Wards, which was discussed above, Vaughan had repeated these assertions, giving out that 'Sir Robert had noe sonne'. In line with the court's protocols to stop violence among the elite, he finished by declaring that such actions were likely to provoke a duel, and so requested restitution of his family's honour.[39]

A week later Vaughan submitted his answer (or 'plea and demurrer'), which was crafted with a decidedly lawyerly hand. His response invoked the Jacobean statute for limitations of actions, which was principally concerned with remedies for debts arising out of contracts, but which specified that actions for cases upon slanderous words needed to be brought within two years of the words being spoken.[40] As Powis alleged these words against Herbert Vaughan were first spoken in 1627, so Edward claimed that the 'time thereby limited for the suing thereof is long since elapsed and run out'. Vaughan also asked who was prosecuting here? The alleged words concerned Herbert Vaughan but Lord Powis was bringing the case in his own name. As for the substance of the matter, Vaughan asserted that the allegation that Herbert Vaughan was the child of Eleanor Gilbert and not Sir Robert Vaughan was a matter of fact then under adjudication in the Court of Wards and was 'very proper and pertinent to be put in issue' there. It is relevant to note that Vaughan's counsel in the matter was Dr William Meyrick, a civil lawyer of Welsh extraction who was later appointed a judge of the Prerogative Court of Canterbury by none other than William Laud.[41] Although we have no evidence that Laud was backing Vaughan's case, the conjunction of personalities is at the very least noteworthy.

On 21 February 1639 the court appointed a commission to take witness testimony in the case. Some of the questions which Vaughan wished to ask deponents have survived, and they implied that evidence against Vaughan was being rendered by servants and lackeys of the Powis Castle interest. One interrogatory, for instance, asked, 'Was the witness related to Lord Powis, and to which party would he give the victory?' The case caught the attention of the newsletter writer Edward Rossingham, who discussed it at some length in a dispatch he wrote to the Herefordshire gentleman John Scudamore on 5 March 1639.[42] He related that a private hearing on the case had been held in the Council Chamber before the chief justices of Common Pleas (Sir John Finch) and King's Bench (Sir John Bramston), along with the Lord Privy Seal (the earl of Manchester) and the judge Sir Henry Marten. Rossingham reported that their discussions concerned Vaughan who 'call'd his nephewe 12 years since a bastard'. The parties had debated the statute of limitations issue and some of the judges were sympathetic to the case that, because of the time which had elapsed since the alleged words were spoken, the matter could not now be heard. Powis's counsel, however, argued that the cause remained determinable, and the most important figure present, the court's leading official, the earl of Arundel, agreed, noting that the court had never 'bine strictly tyed in matters of honour either to the common or the civill lawe'. Thus the cause would move forward, but Rossingham's own comment on the case is striking: 'the truth is Vaughan, the uncle, is maliciously guilty of many fowle aspertions against his nephewe, besides that by these aspertions he hath designe to deprive him of his patrimony of his birth right'.

It is evident, then, that Vaughan had not been circumspect in voicing his doubts about Herbert Vaughan's legitimacy, and the case represented a serious threat to him. The fines in the High Court of Chivalry could be substantial and would have caused serious problems for a man like Vaughan who was without a significant income. It was generally felt that right was on Powis's side, but we do not have any record of a sentence being given in the matter, perhaps because Vaughan successfully managed to postpone proceedings until the court fell victim to the Long Parliament's axe in December 1640. The lawsuits kept on piling up, nevertheless, with a new Chancery action initiated by Powis in the autumn of 1639, which Vaughan dismissed as a vexatious suit prosecuted 'for some … private & sinister ends', and he accused Powis of trying to ruin him by getting Sir Robert's creditors to sue him for debts as Llwydiarth's executor even though he had no access to its resources.[43] He lamented that the Herberts had 'continually vexed him for … fifteene yeares together by … suites prosecuted against him in all or most of his majesties courts of justice in England', leaving him only with 'the bare title of an executor'.

The collapse of Personal Rule

As the controversy over the Llwydiarth inheritance and over Vaughan's malicious tactics continued to swirl, however, the wider political landscape was rapidly being transformed. A political crisis initiated by King Charles I's efforts to enforce a Laudian prayer book in Scotland in 1637 had precipitated a national rising north of the border as the 'Covenanters' mobilised to protect their church from what they saw as the malign and creeping forces of popery. As Vaughan was answering yet another Powis bill in Chancery, so the king was contemplating summoning a parliament to assist him in raising an army against his rebellious northern kingdom. This would be the first time in over a decade that an assembly had been called, and a decade's worth of grievances and frustrations had built up which would shape its brief proceedings. In Montgomeryshire Sir Richard Herbert of Montgomery Castle, the heir of Edward Herbert, Lord Cherbury, moved to hold the county seat at this election. Lord Powis could not stand as a member of the peerage, while his son, Sir Percy Herbert, was effectively barred from seeking the place because he had converted to Catholicism. It does not appear that Edward Vaughan stood on this occasion, although he almost certainly supported the candidate who challenged Herbert for the knightship, Sir John Price of Newton, who was his cousin.[44] Price was a long-standing opponent of the Powis Castle interest, and it was probably because of Herbert influence that, despite his social standing, Price had been excluded from the Montgomeryshire commission of the peace since 1629.[45] Sir Richard Herbert prevailed on this occasion, although it does not appear that there was a contest on election day. This was not necessarily a 'defeat' for Vaughan, however. We should remember that the Herberts of Montgomery Castle were a distinct interest from Vaughan's antagonists at Powis Castle; indeed, the successful candidate at this hustings, Sir Richard Herbert, had challenged Lord Powis's heir, Sir Percy Herbert, to a duel in 1630.[46]

The parliament which assembled in April 1640 would prove abortive, as the strong desire to address the pressing religious, fiscal and political grievances which had built up since the assembly's last meeting in 1629 saw it clash with King Charles who believed parliament's role was to vote him monies for meeting the Scottish challenge. The dissolution of this assembly and the subsequent defeat of the king's army at the hands of the Covenanters in August 1640 precipitated an unprecedented political crisis. Charles's efforts to rule without parliament had failed disastrously. The king was forced to convene a new assembly that would meet on 3 November 1640 and would become known to history as the Long Parliament. The reformist spirit which animated this body was fired by a desire to address abuses of the king's prerogative and the drift towards crypto-Catholicism in the Laudian church: such an atmosphere did not bode well for the Herberts of Powis Castle. In the Montgomeryshire elections to this assembly, this shift in the political tides can be seen in the election of Sir John Price, the man defeated in April, to the county seat at a hustings held at Machynlleth on 17 October 1640. He was returned on a heavily subscribed election indenture that was not endorsed by any representative from the Herbert family, but on which four individuals named 'Vaughan' subscribed their names.[47] It is possible that Edward Vaughan also witnessed the document, but the indenture is damaged and some names have been lost. We can, however, see on this return several figures who would become Vaughan's political allies during the 1640s, including George Devereux, Gabriel Wynne, William Kyffin and Charles Lloyd. This was something of a political breakthrough in the county: a breaking of the Herbert stranglehold on parliamentary representation, which was further confirmed by Sir John Price's re-admittance to the county's commission of the peace soon after his election.[48] The impression is of a group with which Vaughan had ties, and which had been marginalised during the 1630s by the Powis Castle interest, now gaining the political initiative; and Vaughan was doubtless thrilled. We see in the election indenture the hazy contours of the parliamentary interest in the county that would coalesce around Vaughan in the mid-1640s. Also present on the document, and another man returning to the commission of the peace after a period in the wilderness, was Lloyd Pierce of Maesmawr. He was another member of the anti-Herbert interest who followed parliament's banner; he would, however, also become Vaughan's nemesis in an internecine parliamentary feud during the 1640s, which is discussed in detail in chapters 5 and 6.

Edward Vaughan had been battling a storm of lawsuits for a decade and a half. Ejected from his family's estates, he had made use of limited resources to defend his position against a much wealthier and more potent adversary. The calling of the Long Parliament helped transform not only the local political balance in Montgomeryshire, but also the wider context within which Vaughan's legal struggles took place. Powis as a Catholic sympathiser was increasingly marginalised in the new atmosphere of aggressive anti-popery. Parliament was also committed to investigating and reforming the unpopular institutions that had bolstered the 'arbitrary' policies of the Personal Rule, and particular targets were courts whose authority lay in the king's prerogative rather than the common law. These were jurisdictions such as Star Chamber, the Court of Wards, the High Court of Chivalry and the Council in the Marches of Wales. In other words, they were the very venues in which Vaughan had been principally embroiled since 1624, and which had delivered rulings that ejected him from Llwydiarth and had enriched and empowered the magnate of Powis Castle. The time was ripe for a reckoning.

Edward Vaughan, the Council in the Marches, and the parliamentary committee for Courts of Justice, 1640–41

The new parliament witnessed a rush of petitioners and supplicants who wished to have their grievances addressed, and these often involved what were seen as unjust decisions in the prerogative courts. Agitation against the Council in the Marches was already on foot during the April 1640 assembly, while on 23 November 1640, Lord President Bridgewater's secretary, Edward Martyn, wrote to his master 'ther is much talk & some feare of the parlement proceeding against the jurisdiccion of this courte'.[49] On 26 November 1640 the Lords established a new committee to 'examine abuses in matters of imprisonment and all other abuses in courts of justice', although its jurisdiction overlapped with the already-established Committee for Petitions.[50] Edward Vaughan tacked adroitly to the new political winds and in December 1640 appealed to parliament for a ruling in his case: one that had passed through several of the jurisdictions which were now in the cross-hairs of a parliamentary movement for judicial reform.[51] The committee for courts of justice considered Edward Vaughan's submission on 12 March 1641.[52] A report of proceedings indicates that he rehearsed the prehistory of the case for the committee, claiming that Llwydiarth had been settled on him by the 2 February 1622 entail, but that 2,000 of Powis's men seized the property after placing a bill in the Council in the Marches.[53] Vaughan claimed that 'the [Council in the] Marches had noe jurisdiction of this businesse', and argued that the 'order for [Powis's] possession was naught'. He maintained that the Court of Wards would not admit him to challenge its findings at the 1631 inquisition 'because the judges and jury were of soe good quallity', and that, although he had put in a bill against the commissioners (such as Sir Marmaduke Lloyd) into the court, this had been 'cast out'.

Lord Powis did not remain idle as these matters were under review. At the same time as the case was being heard in committee, he submitted a petition to his fellow lordships in the name of his grandson.[54] The petition provided his partial take on events across the last two decades, emphasising Vaughan's perfidiousness in, for example, taking away the horses at Llangedwyn after Sir Robert Vaughan's death so that his heavily pregnant wife could not make it back to Llwydiarth to challenge Edward's occupancy. Powis's submission told a story of theft, forgery and deceit, maintaining that Vaughan and his accomplices were 'notoriouse & infamouse' for their 'scandalouse proceedings' in trying to defame the Herbert name, and he described them colourfully as 'the most comon practisers in that cuntrey of conspiracies'. Powis thus requested that the peers enquire into Vaughan's sharp practices 'soe cunninglye continued to the scandale & disinherisione of the ... infant and his posteritie'. He was effectively warming over the arguments used in the High Court of Chivalry action, and was hoping that a jury of his peers in the Lords would see a fellow noble being calumniated and abused by a commoner and rush to his defence. A problem was, however, that the High Court of Chivalry had been abolished by parliament as a bastion of 'arbitrary' prerogative justice on 4 December 1640, and that Powis, as a crypto-Catholic who had relied on such jurisdictions throughout the 1630s, was now standing on very uncertain ground. He was a difficult individual, and his was a difficult case, to defend at this moment in time. And there is no sign that any serious resistance to Vaughan's requests for redress materialised in either House.

On 19 March 1641, a week after its initial hearing, Vaughan's case received a ruling from the parliamentary committee which had momentous implications for Edward Vaughan and, ultimately, for the complexion of gentry politics in eastern Wales over the next two decades, and perhaps we might even say the next two centuries. The matter was listed as Edward Vaughan against Lord Powis, but also against Sir John Bridgeman and Sir Marmaduke Lloyd, the commissioners who oversaw Sir Robert's 1631 inquisition.[55] This hearing considered the idea of the 'suppositious child', and the parliamentary diarist Sir Simonds D'Ewes noted that Katherine Vaughan had 'fained her selfe to bee brought to bedd of a sonne (which was thought shee gott from some poore bodie) and named him Harbert'.[56] Acknowledging the length and complexity of the case, D'Ewes summarised that, having married Sir James Palmer, Katherine had secured Herbert Vaughan's wardship and the Llwydiarth lands:

> and have ever since by the power of the Lorde Powys kept the possession
> of the same, and the saied Mr Edward Vahan could never have justice
> either in the Court of the Marches of Wales[,] in the Starrechamber or
> the Court of Wardes in England.

Having reviewed the evidence, the committee ruled that the Council in the Marches had 'done iniustice & illegallity in theire proceedings against Mr Vaughan', while the courts of Star Chamber and Wards had done 'iniustice & greivance' against him.[57] Finally, it resolved that Vaughan should be 'relieved' and restored to possession of the Llwydiarth lands in Merioneth and Denbighshire and be allowed to traverse, that is to say, to formally dispute, ownership of the Montgomeryshire estates. The resolution concluded with a resounding endorsement that its findings be reported to the Commons, 'it being consistent with the honour and justice of the house, in regard the said Vaughan hath these 17 yeares beene unjustly kept out of his estate by the injustice of other courts'. When the ruling was handed down, Vaughan immediately sent word into the country that he had recovered these lands and he 'caused the bells to be ronge in diverse places there'.[58]

This was a remarkable reversal of fortunes, albeit not a complete victory. Vaughan could now sue to enter his family estates in Denbighshire and Merioneth, but there remained work to do to confirm his title to the majority of the estate which lay in Montgomeryshire. Still, he was vindicated by this ruling, one that he would return to constantly throughout the complex and contested terrain of the next twenty years. To bolster his claims to the Montgomeryshire lands, and perhaps also to publicise the committee's decision, Vaughan had a broadside printed, *Mr Edward Vaughans Case*, which he could distribute in parliament and perhaps also around the law courts.[59] This told a familiar narrative about his illegal ejection from Llwydiarth and Lord Powis's barring him from legal redress, but he could now speak with a degree of parliamentary sanction about the 'multitude of vexatious suits brought against him, of purpose to oppress and ruine him'. This text also hints at the next steps Vaughan had in mind. He had been barred from his inheritance worth £2,000 per annum for seventeen years; Vaughan believed he was owed more than £34,000 by the grasping Herberts.[60] It did not seem to matter that most of these arrears arose from the Montgomeryshire lands which parliament had not granted to him. The broadside concluded by reproducing in full the committee's decision of 19 March 1641 as something of an authorising warrant.

Edward Vaughan Rediviva: *anti-Catholicism and the Herberts, 1641*

Vaughan was now coming after the Herbert family, and the public politics of 1641 demonstrates how vulnerable they had become. In the Long

Parliament's hearings against one of Charles I's most trusted ministers, Thomas Wentworth, earl of Strafford, one allegation was that he had been willing to levy a Catholic force, ostensibly to suppress the Covenanters in Scotland, but in reality, so said his accusers, to move against the king's opponents in England and Wales. This accusation was part of a wider 'popish conspiracy' which leading figures in the Commons, such as John Pym, argued could explain the challenges that the Church and state had faced over the past decade. The investigation into Strafford, however, revealed a Welsh dimension of this 'conspiracy' as MPs discussed how the Catholic earl of Worcester in Monmouthshire had received a secret military commission from the king in 1638. In a Commons debate of 29 January 1641, Sir John Price, Montgomeryshire's MP and Vaughan's cousin, rose to assert that, after news about Worcester's military commission had been received in the country, Lord Powis's eldest son, Sir Percy Herbert, had bought up corn from the farms on his lands in Montgomeryshire. Price also informed the House that, although also a recusant, Herbert had received a military commission from Worcester, and that upon this authority he had taken custody of the county's magazine and arms and moved it into Powis Castle. As a result of these revelations, the Commons ordered that Sir Percy be sent for as a delinquent.[61] Sir Percy came to London for his examination by parliament in early June 1641, and refused to take the oaths of supremacy and allegiance.[62]

The parliamentary attacks on the Herberts bolstered Edward Vaughan's position at home. With Lord Powis and his son being investigated as potentially dangerous Catholics, it must have felt particularly good to Vaughan to be named as one of parliament's commissioners for disarming Montgomeryshire's recusants in August 1641.[63] Although we do not have clear evidence about how he may have discharged his role, anxiety about the Catholic influence in the county transformed into something akin to panic in the wake of the Irish Rebellion of October 1641. Control of the county armoury now became a central focus of concern, and on 16 November 1641 parliament ordered that Montgomeryshire's magazine be moved to Sir John Price's borough of Newtown, hoping that this would put it beyond the Herberts' reach.[64] A Herefordshire correspondent wrote darkly a few days after this order was issued that 'the rumour is here that loads of munition goe by night to ye Red Castle [Powis Castle]'.[65]

The tensions within the county which had principally revolved about inheritance, land and power, and which had constellations of kin affinities and familial links that stretched back generations, were becoming increasingly inflected by a much more potent ideological dimension as the rift between parliament and the king grew. Vaughan doubtless hoped to use his position as a commissioner for disarming recusants to good effect, but he was also keen to use the leverage of the 19 March committee ruling to recover his family's landed power, something that parliament would have welcomed as a counterbalance to the baleful Lord Powis. In the autumn of 1641, Vaughan came into north Wales and entered his ancestral lands in Denbighshire and Merioneth. He sent two tenants who refused to pay their rents to him to gaol as an example, prevailing on two JPs who were his kinsmen to assist him.[66] Vaughan averred that he had obtained verdicts of title to the Merioneth and Denbighshire lands in August 1642 at the Merioneth great sessions, although opponents asserted that this was only for a 'poor cottage', and that the 'verdicts' were made while Lord Powis was absent and could not contest the claim, so 'the whole cownty cried "shame" in the proceedings'.[67] For his part, Vaughan maintained that 'all ye tenants in Merioneth & Denbigh' attorned to him.[68]

One correspondent wrote from Bala in Merioneth in late December 1641 that 'Mr Edward Vaughan the laste weeke was amongst the tennants of Llwydiarth to have them atturne tennants unto him, and some did & those that did not he entred & will bringe accions against them the nexte terme'.[69] Indeed, he had journeyed into his home county to try and secure the prize of his Montgomeryshire estates. Vaughan attended Llanfihangel-yng-Ngwynfa church (where he had not worshipped for some sixteen years) on 9 January 1642.[70] He was accompanied by a group of men 'of ill reputacion' who 'caried themselves very rudly', and proceeded to enter Herbert Vaughan's pew in the church. In occupying the armorial Vaughan pew, Edward was making a very public symbolic statement about the ownership of Llwydiarth and his position as the rightful head of the bloodline which ruled there. On 26 January he and his followers broke into a property where manorial courts were held for Llwydiarth and proceeded to hold their own court in Edward Vaughan's name. Vaughan returned to Llanfihangel church on the following Sunday, 30 January 1642, along with around twenty followers. There they assaulted and harassed Herbert Vaughan and his followers, and a witness claimed that one of Edward's servants, Richard Wynn, 'with his naked sword willfully ranne and thrust at … Herbert Vaughan and would then have killed [him]', but for the intervention of the latter's servants. Another individual claimed that the assembly at the church was 'a plott layed by … Edward Vaughan to take away the life' of his nephew. Edward does not seem to have followed up on these broils, however, as further proceedings and hearings were held in the Court of Wards over the matter, and he may have been counselled not to be too bold in ignoring the court's proceedings. Nevertheless, the Herberts were clearly on the defensive, and Edward Vaughan was emboldened and empowered by his success in the Commons to press his claims to the Montgomeryshire estates with renewed vigour.

At the moment of his triumph, however, Vaughan's prize began to recede before his eyes. The court sessions of August 1642 in Merioneth and Denbighshire were held against the backdrop of preparations for civil war, and any verdicts in his favour would mean little amidst the violence and upheaval which sundered the country over the next five years. Parliament had given Edward Vaughan his strongest grip on his ancestral home in nearly two decades, and it had also, albeit briefly, brought his main rival low. How he would repay the favour they had done him is the subject of the following three chapters.

PART TWO:

POLITICS AND PATRIMONY DURING THE BRITISH CIVIL WARS

CHAPTER 4

Civil War, Conquest and Committees, 1642-1645

The political shockwaves of the breakdown between king and parliament in 1641–2 propagated out through the provinces. There remains a good deal of truth in John Morrill's observation that, in the 1640s, each locality was 'unique, subject to different pressures working through different power structures, and that the interaction of national and local events was inevitably complex'.[1] And it is in exploring this *interaction*, between centre and locality that historians can provide a dynamic picture of provincial politics in the mid-seventeenth century which captures both its particularism but also its participation in a rapidly developing national political culture. This and the following chapters contribute to that historiographical endeavour by considering Edward Vaughan's fortunes during the 1640s and 1650s.

The approach adopted here organises our perspective on the complex politics of the period through a series of interlocking spatial frameworks. First, we have the individual or personal study: that of Edward Vaughan himself and the politics of family and inheritance which has already underpinned the discussion in previous chapters. Secondly, we explore the county politics of Montgomeryshire. This was not a 'county community' in the sense of being an isolated or autonomous administrative or political area, and indeed it never had been.[2] We see a deep interpenetration of its gentry politics in the 1640s with that of neighbouring Shropshire, for example. Yet Montgomeryshire was also an important site for political action and for identity formation among the county's gentry. Thirdly, the history of the 1640s and 1650s in this area is also one that needs to encompass a politics of north Wales, of the armies and regional bodies which were instituted to subdue and then to govern the region during the civil wars and the republic. In some ways the Llwydiarth estate mirrors this amorphous but important regional dimension of our analysis, straddling as it did three shires in north Wales. Fourth and finally, there is the national dimension of the relationship between the locality and the political centre, particularly with parliament, which is critical to understanding the political dynamics of these decades. This study, then, looks to use Edward Vaughan's experiences as a means of exploring these distinct but inextricably interconnected locales. Although much of the discussion revolves around the Llwydiarth inheritance, the struggles to secure this prize cannot be understood in any kind of localist isolation. Vaughan had to negotiate these various spheres of social and political activity to try and secure his hold on the family estate and thus on local power.

So this and the following chapters examine how Vaughan's personal ambitions and his local feuds became enmeshed in the peculiar dynamics of parliamentarian conquest in north Wales under the generals Sir Thomas Myddelton and his successor Thomas Mytton. These chapters provide new evidence about parliament's establishing of committees and an apparatus for governing its reconquered territories in north Wales; about the recruiter elections to parliament in 1647; and about the ways in which established and newly forged personal and factional divisions in Montgomeryshire and north Wales mapped onto the 'Independent' and 'Presbyterian' political positions as these developed from the mid-1640s. Money and accounting were weaponised by both factions in these struggles, and an analysis of Edward Vaughan's chairmanship of the Montgomeryshire sub-committee of accounts contributes to an expanding literature on the role of civil war finances and audit in shaping the contours of local parliamentarian politics.[3] Shadowing this entire narrative, of course, is the less ideologically freighted issue which has held our focus to this point, and which speaks to the continued significance of local feuds and faction and the force of raw gentry power dynamics in the provinces during the mid-1640s: the struggle to possess Llwydiarth.

Although Montgomeryshire's civil war narrative needs to be understood in the context of wider national political and military developments, it must also be told partly through Edward Vaughan's efforts to gain local supremacy by securing his title. Even though we can often bring this discussion back to his landed ambitions, the Montgomeryshire inheritance case was not simply of local importance. The county's divisions undermined parliament's efforts to secure and control the royalist redoubt of north Wales, and Vaughan became involved in a power struggle with both Myddelton and later Mytton and their allies and satraps who were installed as the region's administrators.

Vaughan represents the moderate Presbyterian voice in north Wales which was eclipsed by the end of the 1640s by the republican soldiers and radical clerics who established themselves in the wake of parliament's conquest. Montgomeryshire was the first Welsh county recovered from the royalists, and it was also among the first in which a parliamentary administration was established. This precedence saw it pulled into the arena of parliamentary divisions in the mid-1640s in a manner that other Welsh counties were not. Histories of the localities remain thin on the ground for civil war Wales, and examining the twists and turns of the factional struggles in Montgomeryshire suggests some of the rich territory which might yet be explored.[4]

The current chapter examines how Vaughan's hopes of recovering Llwydiarth turned to ashes in the initial stages of the civil wars. It is unsurprising that he became a parliamentarian given the Long Parliament's qualified authorisation of his claim to Llwydiarth, and the fact that the Herbert interest became committed supporters of the royalist cause. Vaughan's political allegiance, however, saw him exiled from north Wales, where royalist sentiment dominated, and seek refuge in London. This chapter does not detail the narrative of the civil wars in the region, but it does explore the complex politics surrounding Montgomeryshire's reconquest under Sir Thomas Myddelton and Thomas Mytton. Vaughan returned to Wales in the spring of 1645, establishing his own garrison in northern Montgomeryshire, but also floating his own proposals for the settlement of north Wales. The following sections examine these proposals and the way they crossed army interests in the region.

The chapter considers what these proposals reveal about Vaughan's moderate Presbyterianism and also about his antipathy to the army establishment. This is the first work to discuss the establishing of both the Montgomeryshire committee in late 1644, and the Committee for North Wales in late 1645. These bodies would become the institutional bases for the more radical Independent parliamentary interests in the later 1640s, and thus for Vaughan's sworn enemies. Parliament's recovery of Montgomeryshire shattered the Herbert's control and allowed Vaughan to claim back Llwydiarth. The question was whether his parliamentarian enemies would let him keep it.

Edward Vaughan and questions of allegiance, 1642

In the autumn of 1641 Edward Vaughan would have been buoyant. Parliament had agreed that he could recover his estates in Merioneth and Denbigh, and it was harassing his inveterate enemies at Powis Castle because of their Catholic sympathies. He had made significant strides towards regaining his estates not only in Merioneth and Denbighshire, but also in Montgomeryshire where he and his allies confronted Herbert Vaughan at Llanfihangel-yng-Ngwynfa between November 1641 and January 1642. Yet while these successes must have been gratifying, the political breakdown between king and parliament, particularly after the Irish Rebellion of October 1641, profoundly destabilised local society and threatened to set Vaughan's recent successes at nought.

Montgomeryshire became a focus of parliamentary concern, particularly because of the efforts by Lord Powis and his son to secure the county magazine.[5] In the spring and summer of 1642 fundamental fractures were appearing in the gentry communities of north Wales, as elsewhere, as the choice to support king or parliament operated upon, and sometimes reconfigured, pre-existing factional, political and religious interests. By August 1642 troops were being raised for the king in Montgomeryshire.[6] Charles visited the Welsh borders in late 1642 to encourage recruitment, and a later account described how his army grew slowly in the north of England, 'but when he was come to Shrewsbury, the

Welch-men came running downe the mountaines in such multitudes that their example did much animate the English'.[7]

So in Montgomeryshire, as elsewhere, sides were being taken and difficult decisions of allegiance were being made. There was little question, however, which way the Herberts of Powis Castle would jump. Courtiers and Catholic sympathisers who had already fallen foul of parliament's investigations, they were seemingly destined to fly to King Charles's banner. But what of their great adversary, Edward Vaughan? Lord Powis doubtless had a line to the king, and when Charles I issued a list of commissioners of array for the county who would raise forces on his behalf, it is unsurprising that Vaughan's name was omitted.[8] But there were political as well as personal reasons for this omission: by the summer of 1642 Vaughan had become one of the most high-profile parliamentary supporters in north Wales.

In many ways Edward Vaughan was caught on the horns of a dilemma: the estate which he had laboured to recover for so long was in a region where royalist sentiment was strong; but standing at the forefront of this royalism, and in some ways emblematic of it, was his most potent adversary. Vaughan had been granted a route to possessing his ancestral home by parliament; but parliament was effectively excluded from the area by his enemies. We cannot say that it was inevitable that Edward Vaughan would support parliament, or that his support, when it came, was merely instrumental and based on self-interest. We must treat Professor Dodd's judgement that Vaughan 'supported parliament merely to secure the Llwydiarth estate against his popish [*sic*] nephew [Herbert Vaughan], who fought for the other side' as simplistic and suspect.[9] It is the 'merely' in this sentence that does so much damage to our understanding of the complexity of such key political decisions, and which robs Vaughan of any agency. Nevertheless, as Dodd acknowledged, it is difficult to imagine that Vaughan would have followed the king and jeopardised his parliamentary-endorsed claim to (at least some of) the Llwydiarth estates, or failed to recognise how a victorious assembly would potentially reward those who had helped it meet the Catholic threat in the provinces; a threat that was particularly potent in Montgomeryshire. Indeed, some contemporaries also saw his parliamentarianism in simply personal terms, with Sir James Palmer describing how Vaughan would be 'glad to have these private ends [of Llwydiarth's possession] under publicke pretences'.[10] It is also the case that portraying Vaughan's allegiance as simply opportunistic was a position which served his family's purposes during the Restoration. His younger brother Rowland in 1663, for example, described how Edward Vaughan 'did soe farr comply with the last Longe Parliament as to counterballance his adversaries and thereby regayne ... the estate, but further could not digest their later wayes and proceedings against his late Majesty'.[11] There was clearly a significant element of truth in such an account, as we shall see, Vaughan recoiled from the regicide, but we should not think that it was the whole truth of his decision to support parliament.

We know that in the summer of 1642 Edward Vaughan was in Merioneth obtaining verdicts of title in the great sessions there, as parliament had allowed.[12] As the political temperature rose, he began to demonstrate public support for parliament's cause. He met with Sir Thomas Myddelton and 'divers gentlemen well affected to the parliament of Denbighshire' at Myddelton's home of Chirk Castle, where they discussed how to 'oppose the illegall comission of array which then the enimy was about to sett on foote in that countie'.[13] In July 1642 he attended a major meeting of the Denbighshire and Flintshire gentry at Ruthin which had been called to implement the array.[14] A self-exculpatory account penned by Vaughan (or by someone on his behalf) around 1646 describes what occurred.[15] Among the local gentlemen present at the meeting were Sir Richard Lloyd of Esclus, a leading royalist and the king's attorney general in north Wales, Sir Thomas Salusbury of Lleweni, who would shortly raise a regiment for the king, and also William Salesbury of Rûg, Vaughan's brother-in-law and the man who had assisted him in the campaign involving Eleanor Gilbert in the 1620s. Vaughan's account had it that he attended the meeting with 'sundry others of his frends' who held estates in the county, where, 'upon debate', Vaughan 'affirme[d] publiquely' that the array was 'illegall'. Thereupon, he alleged, there 'grewe a hot contest' between himself and Sir Richard Lloyd. Vaughan contended that, because of his own intervention, the array was not implemented at this time.

We must be cautious about this retrospective account which was designed to cast Vaughan's actions in the best light. However, his allies endorsed this story, maintaining that he 'did appear in person in publique for the parliament against the commission of array, and did declare in publique that it was illegal'.[16] Moreover, his account has the merit of being partly corroborated by a near-contemporary set of royalist articles presented against Vaughan which are discussed below.[17] Another hostile source also told a similar story. In what appears to be a response by Sir James Palmer to a Vaughan petition while the latter was defending himself at Oxford in early 1643, Palmer observed that around August 1642, Lord Powis instructed the local commissioners of array to seize the arms of any suspected person, and he believed 'Mr Vaughan was as ill affected as … Sir Thomas Middleton … [and] Mr [Thomas] Glynne, [William] Lloyd & [Griffith] Bodurda [who] were apprehended upon smaller grounds then could be iustly alleged & proved against … Vaughan'.[18] Palmer also mentioned the 'complaints of most men of quality in the cowntry of Denbeigh against Mr Vaughan as the most notorious hinderer of his Majesties service'. It does indeed appear, then, that from the very early stages of the civil war Vaughan was willing to stand against the prevailing tide of this deeply royalist area.[19] The degree to which his parliamentarianism was a product of his landed interests or of ideological commitment is impossible to answer. We can say, however, that this was a bold, unpopular and dangerous position to adopt in north Wales. According to Vaughan's own account, around September 1642, after the array was executed and while troops were being levied for Sir Thomas Salusbury's regiment, Vaughan sought out the other parliamentarian magnate of the region, Sir Thomas Myddelton, who would become a major figure in Vaughan's civil war life, and they discussed 'what was to be don for preservation of themselves and that county'.[20] The two men would fall out in the mid-1640s, and this account was partly designed to undermine Myddelton's public reputation. We must, then, treat as problematic Vaughan's claim that he told Myddelton to hold his castle home against local royalists and that 'if he [Myddelton] were not willing to ingage in it, that he [Vaughan] and his freinds … would undertake the defence thereof against the kings forces (which were then not farr of)'.[21]

Nevertheless, their association at this time and Vaughan's public support for parliament indicates that he had nailed his political colours to the mast in the autumn of 1642, and in so doing, he had placed himself in serious jeopardy.

A visit to Oxford, 1643

When King Charles I was in Shrewsbury in September 1642, Sir Richard Lloyd, the man with whom Vaughan had clashed at the Ruthin meeting in July, requested that Vaughan be secured 'for offences capital and for divers most notorious crymes against his majestie'.[22] Nothing was done on this occasion because some of Vaughan's associates had supposedly indicated to Lloyd that he would submit to the king. Ultimately, however, Vaughan refused to do so, leaving Lloyd to conclude that 'Mr Vaughan was the fittest man to be made an example of the kings justice in all Wales'. The situation in Denbighshire was becoming too uncomfortable for Vaughan and Myddelton to remain. After leaving Shrewsbury, the king journeyed to Wrexham in the county on 27 September 1642 where the local population rallied to him in considerable numbers.[23] Myddelton probably left the county shortly beforehand; certainly he was back in the Commons by late October.[24] From this point, Vaughan maintained forty or fifty musketeers 'at his owne house for the security of his person'. This would not have been Llwydiarth, which was held by Katherine Palmer,[25] and at this point Vaughan seems to have resided at Celynog which lay at the extreme northern end of Montgomeryshire close to the border with Denbighshire.[26] This was a useful strategic position from which he could oversee the northern Llwydiarth estates, but it was also deep in hostile royalist territory: Vaughan probably needed his phalanx of musketeers.

Once the king had settled in his capital at Oxford in early 1643, the Herbert forces mobilised their resources to try and destroy the Llwydiarth claimant. On 5 February 1643 a warrant against Vaughan was issued to the sheriffs of Montgomeryshire and Denbighshire, for 'sundry notorious insolences and outrages' Vaughan had countenanced and committed, intending to 'alienate the hartes of good subiects in those partes'.[27] The warrant was procured by Sir James Palmer, Lord Powis's son-in-law. According to his own narrative, when Edward Vaughan received notice of the warrant in March 1643, he fled Wales and made for London, dodging royalist garrisons on the Anglo-Welsh border where he was 'often in daunger of his lyfe'.[28] Indeed, he would later claim that the warrant to secure him was actually a cover to try and have him killed; something the Herbert interest denied as 'meere invension'.[29] Vaughan claimed that, after leaving Wales, he came to Oxford en route to London, but 'was taken noatise of and for a time restrayned' in the city. This seems an unlikely scenario. For a parliamentarian 'outlaw' against whom a royalist warrant had been issued, a brief sojourn in the royalist capital while making for London was not an obvious move. It is much more likely that he attended the Court to address the charges against him and perhaps to test the standing of his claim to the estate with the king. The offer of some kind of royalist support on his part, or perhaps even a studied neutrality, might have seemed like a possible bargaining chip. Influence across three counties of north Wales was something the king might have traded for full title to his estates. The problem was that the king already had de facto control of the estate through his trusted agents. For whatever reasons he did it, Vaughan rode into the lions' den when he rode into Oxford, and on his arrival articles of high treason were levied against him.

As we shall see in the following chapters, Vaughan's trip to Oxford would haunt him as he tried to rise in parliament's favour. It gave plenty of opportunity for his enemies to tar him as a delinquent for having visited the king's capital, apparently remaining there for more than a month.[30] In his opponents' account, Vaughan went to Oxford to petition the king against Powis and Sir James Palmer, who, he said, were withholding from the monarch large amounts of money from the Llwydiarth estates.[31] Vaughan supposedly expressed his readiness to serve the king and asked that his claims to Llwydiarth be referred to Denbighshire's commissioners of array for adjudication, appealing to the judgement of Sir Richard Lloyd in the matter. This is a deeply tendentious and polemical narrative of Vaughan's actions at Oxford, put together later by enemies who had little reason to know what went on in the royalist capital. The idea that Vaughan would appeal to the Denbighshire commissioners of array or Sir Richard

Lloyd is unconvincing, indeed outlandish. Yet for all its problems such an account probably does contain a kernel of truth. It does seem likely that if Vaughan was at Oxford, under restraint or not, then he would try to barter for his inheritance. His promises of support to the royalists may have been strategic, but any opportunity he was offered to undermine Powis would be taken. Yet the broader narrative in which Vaughan visited Oxford to declare his allegiance to the king's side as a determined royalist is unpersuasive, particularly given the fact that there was a royal warrant out for his arrest, and that he had articles presented against him while there.

Vaughan and his allies told a very different story about his Oxford sojourn. His appearance in the city, they said, was to answer the warrant for his arrest and to petition the king for a fair hearing, fearing that if the warrant was executed by his enemies in Wales, then he might be murdered or 'debarred from his liberty and legall tryall'.[32] While Vaughan was in Oxford, articles of treason were exhibited against him on 21 May 1643, presumably at the instigation of Palmer and Powis. These articles, later submitted in evidence to the Committee for Accounts by Vaughan's associate, the lawyer Owen Andrewes,[33] detailed Vaughan's opposition to the execution of array in Denbighshire in July 1642; his efforts to persuade people in north Wales that the array was illegal; his protection of a man who had spoken treasonable words about the king; and his calling a neighbour 'traitor' for contributing monies for the king's service. They also alleged that when Lord Powis nominated the royalist Montgomery MP Richard Herbert (disabled by parliament in September 1642) to find an office of Herbert Vaughan's lands, Vaughan had excepted against him as a 'malignant [because] … hee was for the kinge and against the parliment'.[34] These articles confirm the impression of Vaughan's early and public parliamentarian activism, but the point about using Richard Herbert to find an office (that is, to determine rightful ownership of land) is also noteworthy. Clearly, Powis was using the disruption to parliament's authority in the area to reinstate the Court of Wards' 1631 findings regarding the Llwydiarth estate in Merioneth and Denbighshire. Thus, the articles provide a vivid illustration of the complex intertwining of the personal and the political in Vaughan's calculations during the early years of the conflict.

Faced with these charges, Vaughan's own later account described how he entered into a recognisance of £3,000 before the king's Lord Chief Justice, Sir Robert Heath, and promised to appear to answer the allegations and 'in the meane tyme not to adhere to the rebells and traytors at Westminster'. Shortly afterwards the king, being further 'inscenced' against Vaughan, was dissatisfied with the recognisance and wished him placed under more stringent conditions.[35] Vaughan, having notice of the king's displeasure, managed to procure a ticket to pass the guards at Oxford which he did, disguised as David Matthews, Owen Andrewes's servant. Vaughan concluded his account by claiming that Andrewes had helped smuggle him out of the city, and that the pair had then fled to London.[36] There is doubtless a good deal of half-truth and embellishment in this tale of derring-do, but the warrant for his arrest and the articles of treason are all attested to by independent evidence. Moreover, in June 1643, the king wrote to Caernarvonshire's commissioners of array noting that Edward Vaughan had 'withdrawn himself from Oxford contrary to our express command', and the monarch asked them to do their utmost to apprehend him.[37] Contrary to his opponents' account of the Oxford episode, then, this seems like a case of bridges burned rather than one of an opportunity missed. We cannot recover Vaughan's motivations for his Oxford visit, but he was probably driven partly by a desire to answer the warrant for his arrest and partly by the hope that he might gain some royal concessions over Llwydiarth. Given his known parliamentarian sympathies and the hostility towards him from the royalist administration in north Wales, it does seem reasonable that he would fear the local execution of the warrant against him. The Oxford journey would leave him with the taint of a possible royalist sympathiser, however, and it would hang over his head in the later 1640s.

Exile: London, 1643–45

Doubtless chastened by his Oxford experience, Vaughan moved to the refuge of parliamentarian London. There he likely resided at his lodgings at the Inner Temple and, according to his own testimony, he subsisted 'by his frendes affecion and his profession', presumably meaning that he practised law.[38] Owen Andrewes was probably one of these 'frendes' as a fellow lawyer who worked with north Wales clients. Andrewes was later to become one of the surveyors for the sequestered estates of Lord Powis in 1650, perhaps upon Vaughan's recommendation.[39] Vaughan could not access the income from his lands, not even his father's small annuity of £80, and so these were straitened times for the man who claimed to own one of the largest estates in north Wales. Unfortunately, and probably because of his present need to work, for the next two years Vaughan effectively goes to earth and the documentary record on his activities dries up. He was presumably untroubled in the capital as a parliamentarian supporter, but he had few close ties with the parliamentarian leadership over and above his connection with the Denbigh MP Simon Thelwall the younger.[40] Vaughan later averred that during this period he frequently offered his services to parliament and 'propose[d] some faire offers of assistance for the reduction of Northwales', but that these were not taken up.[41] He made this assertion in a self-justifying narrative in 1646. This claim cannot be independently verified, but if this was indeed the case, the likely reason for his rejection was the intervention of parliament's most influential grandee in north Wales and the commander of its army there, Sir Thomas Myddelton. The following section discusses Vaughan's re-emergence into Welsh parliamentary politics from the summer of 1645, but it also begins to trace how an acrimonious feud with Myddelton developed, and how this became a critical element in the post-war politics of Montgomeryshire and north Wales. The chapter also casts new light on the parliamentary administrative apparatus that was established in the wake of Montgomeryshire's reconquest, and on how local committees become the new political battleground for Llwydiarth's heir.

Parliamentarian reconquest: Sir Thomas Myddelton and the Montgomeryshire sequestration committee, 1644

Vaughan did not return to Montgomeryshire while the Powis Castle interest held sway. Royalist control in the county endured down to the

Battle of Montgomery in September 1644, when Sir Thomas Myddelton, as parliamentarian commander in north Wales, achieved a victory which proved critical in breaking the king's control of mid Wales. The captured Lord Powis was sent to London where he remained under house arrest for the rest of the war. Myddelton's victory provided parliament with a critical bridgehead in Wales, but historians have not sufficiently recognised the unusually extensive autonomy parliament gave him to fashion the administrative apparatus of those areas he recovered, including Montgomeryshire.[42] The ordinance of February 1644 appointing Myddelton as sergeant major general of north Wales empowered him to implement all ordinances for raising money and sequestering delinquents, and also to appoint all local officers required to execute these ordinances. Those so appointed were to have 'full power and authority ... as if they were named by the two Houses of Parliament'.[43] Myddelton thus had remarkable latitude and discretion in moulding the committee apparatus in the areas he secured from the enemy: what one opponent later described as 'all power both militarie and civill ... [which laid] a ground for his owne ambition and greatnes'.[44] However, these powers kept his nominees from being routinely listed in our usual sources such as the journals of both Houses or Firth and Rait's *Acts and Ordinances*. As a result, our knowledge of these men and their activities has been at best sketchy and Myddelton's role in helping to determine the character of early parliamentarian administration in Wales has not received the attention it deserves. Suffice it to say here, that in royalist Wales Myddelton had a shallow pool from which to draw such officials beyond those who had supported him or fought in his campaigns. The early parliamentary bureaucracy in places like Montgomeryshire was thus restricted in number, comparatively humble in social origins, and often military in character.

Shortly after the Battle of Montgomey, then, 'asoone as the countrey was reduced', a committee was established at Powis Castle (usually called 'Red Castle') which was generally referred to as a 'committee for sequestrations'. Its first recorded meeting was on 11 November 1644 before Myddelton himself, along with Captain (later Colonel) Hugh Price, Lloyd Pierce, George Devereux and Gabriel Wynne, although it appears that it began operating a month previously.[45] One of first parliamentary committees to be established in Wales, this body effectively functioned as the executive county committee for Montgomeryshire.[46] It not only formed the nucleus of the county's administration down to the 1650s, but also provided an administrative proving ground for other important parliamentarian figures in north Wales including John Jones of Maesygarnedd, the future regicide.[47] Its operations were not confined to Montgomeryshire but reached into the wider region, as is attested by a certificate from Rhayader hundred in Radnorshire which recalled that, in July 1645, the local constables had received a directive to raise assessments 'from the comittee of sequestracion ... then residinge at Red Castle, beinge the first warrant that was directed into this hundred by any havinge aucthority under the parliament'.[48] A later attack on the Montgomeryshire committee claimed that Myddelton nominated other local gentry to sit on the body, but that they had declined the service 'in regard sundry comanders and officers who had noe estate in that countie were made comittee men and over voted them ... with whom they held it not safe to joyne'.[49] The truth of this allegation is unclear, but it gives a flavour of how controversial the body was to become. Indeed, as early as April 1645, its principal official, Lloyd Pierce, was complaining about the 'scorne & contempt' the committee was encountering as it tried to discharge its business.[50]

It is worth taking a moment to introduce the individuals present at this meeting as they will loom large in our narrative and become important as, respectively, Edward Vaughan's allies and antagonists. Hugh Price of Gwern-y-go had a relatively modest background, his only clear role in public administration before the civil wars being his appointment as bailiff of Llanidloes hundred in 1633.[51] Price became a radical puritan, but his service in the army was the making of him. It is possible that he was the captain of that name who appears in the forces raised to fight in Ireland in the spring of 1642, but his military record is obscure.[52] It does not appear that he was an officer in Myddelton's army as his name is absent from its officer lists and payment docquets, although the major general evidently trusted Price and appointed him as Powis Castle's governor following its capture in October 1644. Price also became a diligent committeeman and a vocal opponent of Edward Vaughan.

The most active member of the sequestration committee, however, and the man who would become Vaughan's bête noire was Lloyd Pierce of Maesmawr. The son of a Shropshire barrister and the heiress of Maesmawr, Pierce appeared on the county bench in 1625 and served as Montgomeryshire's ship money sheriff in 1637.[53] He was another man whose civil war service was obscure, with some suggesting that he had been a commissioner of array and royalist officer under Lord Capel. Although not necessarily a convinced parliamentarian, then, he changed colours in sufficient time to win Myddelton's favour, who appointed him as treasurer of the Montgomery committee at its establishment.[54] Pierce quickly became the committee's effective leader and continued as a diligent and active local administrator into the interregnum. Price and Pierce would also become leading figures in the emergent radical parliamentarian group in the county which, in due course, we can characterise as the 'Independents'.

Lloyd Pierce and Hugh Price would become Edward Vaughan's most determined opponents after 1646, while the other two individuals who were present at the committee's first known meeting would become some of his staunchest supporters. Gabriel Wynne of Dolarddyn in Castell Caereinion was another obscure individual with little track record in local government. He was Lloyd Pierce's brother-in-law but was also related to the Vaughans of Llwydiarth through his mother, and in 1657 he appointed 'my welbeloved Edward Vaughan' as overseer of his will.[55] George Devereux was a Warwickshire man but in 1633 he married Bridget, daughter and heiress of Arthur Price of Vaynor, who was also Edward Vaughan's niece.[56] Devereux later testified that he had known Vaughan since the time of his marriage.[57] Devereux dallied with royalism, to his cost as we shall see in chapter 6, but upon Myddelton's coming to Montgomeryshire, he raised a troop of horse and a company of foot for parliament and maintained them at his own charge, a service which helped convince Myddelton to nominate him to the sequestration committee.[58] In February 1645, almost certainly through the intervention of his kinsman and the man who then led parliament's forces, the earl of Essex, Devereux was appointed a Montgomeryshire deputy lieutenant and was also commissioned as a colonel of foot and captain of horse.[59]

Edward Vaughan's return to Wales and the garrison at Abermarchant, June 1645

Although Myddelton's victory at Montgomery and the establishing of the committee at Powis Castle consolidated a parliamentary enclave in north Wales, most of the surrounding country remained firmly in royalist hands and parliamentarian control was often tenuous. Nevertheless, the ground had been laid for Edward Vaughan to return home and to attempt to make good on his claim to Llwydiarth, particularly now that the Herberts' power in the shire had been shattered. Thus it was that, in June 1645, Vaughan entered Montgomeryshire which, he claimed, 'was so infested by the enemy that there was noe safety for any but such as lived in garrisons', and so, he raised a troop of horse and foot at his own expense, and established a garrison at Abermarchant in Llanwddyn parish which lay close to Llwydiarth.[60] Lloyd Pierce wrote a cryptic line in a letter of July 1645 mentioning 'the expectation of some whose taedious coming-down puts us into some distress', which seems to be a reference to Vaughan's arrival and his potentially destabilising presence in the county.[61] Although Vaughan would go on to detail the actions he and his troop undertook on parliament's behalf, 'whereby for a long time he much preserved that part of ye countrey & often met with the enemy doeing good service against them', suspicions arose that his garrison was simply ensuring the security of his title to Llwydiarth.[62] Indeed, one newsbook observed that Vaughan raised his troops to defend himself from royalist forces in Merioneth 'which in a short time might prove prejudiciall to himselfe and to his owne house, which he had garrisoned for the safetie of himselfe and the service of the parliament'.[63] It was clearly difficult to separate private and public interest in Vaughan's military activities.

Llwydiarth sequestered (or not?): April–October 1645

Despite Llwydiarth having been abandoned by his adversaries, Edward Vaughan could not assume control as the property had been sequestered by the local committee in April 1645 as a result of Sir James Palmer and Herbert Vaughan's delinquency.[64] In late July or early August 1645 Edward Vaughan challenged those tenants who paid their rents to the state because of this sequestration and appealed that parliament had granted him title in March 1641.[65] This was not quite true, of course, as parliament had only given him leave to sue for the Montgomeryshire estates – it had not placed him in possession. Vaughan's case for ownership was supported by a warrant issued by two local committee members, George Devereux and Matthew Morgan, as well as Vaughan's cousin, the side-changing county MP, Sir John Price of Newtown, who was then installed as governor of Montgomery Castle.[66] A later account of the case, which was hostile to Vaughan, maintained that he, 'pretending himselfe to be a frind to parliament, and having many frinds on the committee, procured an order to be tenant of the estate'.[67] Although initially minded, on the advice of John Bradshaw, solicitor to the central sequestration committee, to continue the estate in the sequestrators' hands, the Montgomeryshire committee at its meeting on 25 September 1645 ordered that Vaughan be allowed to have possession of the estate for a year, having first satisfied any outstanding debts due to the state.[68] This order was, however, reviewed by the central sequestration committee the following month, supposedly on account of a proviso added by Lloyd Pierce, whose actions in having Vaughan's case reviewed contributed significantly to, if they were not in fact the origin of, Vaughan and Pierce's blistering feud in the coming months.[69]

As a result of its review, the central sequestration committee at Goldsmiths' Hall ruled that Vaughan should, in fact, not be admitted as tenant because he was currently involved in a legal dispute over the property, and so his title was unproven.[70] Information from a later (anonymous) account of the Llwydiarth estate is revealing: it claimed that it was 'some friends of Herbert Vaughan [who] moved the committee of Lords and Commons that Edward Vaughan might not be tenant to the estate, in regard he claimed a title thereto'.[71] Unfortunately, the account is silent on who these 'friends' might be, but doubtless Herbert Vaughan's grandfather, Lord Powis, was able to pull some strings in London to frustrate Edward Vaughan's efforts. However, taking advantage of the ambiguities of these somewhat contradictory orders from the local and central sequestration bodies, Edward Vaughan decided to ignore the central committee's decision of October 1645 and to act instead on the local committee's directive of September, entering the vast and lucrative Llwydiarth estates and receiving its rents. In so doing, he helped destabilise parliament's administrative apparatus in the county and in north Wales more generally, and began a decade of wrangling for supremacy and control of this tactically significant estate.

Military reorganisation, Thomas Mytton and Edward Vaughan's 'Propositions', May–November 1645

Vaughan's return to Montgomeryshire coincided, perhaps not coincidentally, with the military reorganisation which attended the Self-Denying Ordinance and the new modelling of the army. In north Wales this saw Sir Thomas Myddelton recalled to Westminster and the appointment of Thomas Mytton, Myddelton's brother-in-law, as the new commander-in-chief of parliament's forces there; this change was accompanied by the establishing of a new military association of north Wales, a body that was to have its own executive committee.[72] Mytton assumed command on 13 June 1645,[73] and it is likely that Vaughan saw this as something of an opportunity for his personal advancement: certainly there was little love lost between him and Myddelton and it was unlikely that he would flourish during the latter's tenure as north Wales's commander. As we saw earlier in this chapter, Vaughan claimed that Myddelton had effectively abandoned parliament's cause in north Wales in the summer of 1642 and had failed to back Vaughan in his opposition to the array there. Given Vaughan's proclivity for sharing his low opinions of his enemies in and around London, one can speculate that he may well have spread damaging rumours about Myddelton and his military capabilities in the capital. Certainly, it seems that the two men had been antagonists since early in the war.[74] It seems likely, then, that Myddelton backed the Montgomeryshire committee's sequestration of Llwydiarth, and that this helped exacerbate and intensify his split with Vaughan. It was Myddelton who, in September 1645, passed on a letter from Lloyd Pierce and Hugh Price to the Goldsmith's Hall committee that resulted in the initial order not to turn Llwydiarth over to Vaughan, and Myddelton continued to demonstrate an interest in the case into 1646.[75]

Vaughan, meanwhile, was asking to be permitted to contribute to the parliamentarian military effort in north Wales. In November 1645, now with the resources of Llwydiarth (albeit somewhat problematically) back in his hands, he approached parliament's executive body for running the war, the Committee of Both Kingdoms, with a proposal for raising 500 horse and foot, mostly upon his own charge, to defend Montgomeryshire. The committee waited for the endorsements of Sir Thomas Myddelton and then also of Thomas Mytton before proceeding in the matter, but the initiative came to nothing.[76] A surviving copy of a justification for Vaughan's 'Propositions' (as he described this initiative) indicates why the two commanders were unenthusiastic about the proposal.[77] This text described Vaughan as having 'the greatest interest of any man in that countie [Montgomeryshire] ... eyther in regard of his estate, kindred or affections of the people', and also lauded his 'integritie and faythfullnesse to the parliament'. It continued that this proposal would preserve the county from plundering by troops of either side (a hot topic in north Wales at the time) and, significantly, argued that it would be 'abundantly satisfactorye for the natives to bee comaunded by a person of knowne worth and interest in theire owne country' for whom they would willingly fight, while 'from strangers & such that have noe interest in the countrey, persones of meane qualitie, they cannot rayse to themselves any such grounds of confidence and assureance as, of late, they have often experienced'. This was a barb aimed at the previous and perhaps also the current military disposition in north Wales, and may have been directed at the relatively humble-born English officers who accompanied Myddelton into north Wales, such as the Yorkshireman George Twistleton or Buckinghamshire's

John Carter, who were commanding Montgomeryshire's horse and foot by late 1645. There is the suggestion, however, that Vaughan had an even bigger target in his sights with his proposal for establishing an independent military commend in the north of the county: the new major general, Thomas Mytton himself.

Among a bundle of Vaughan papers is a document entitled 'Certaine reasons whereby it appears that if Collonel Mitton be employed as commander in chiefe for reducing of ye 6 Counties of North Wales it will much prejudice yt service'.[78] The document, which must have been produced around the time that Mytton was gazetted on 12 May 1645, dilated on his shortcomings, including his damaging (and ongoing) feud with the Shropshire county committee.[79] This paper dovetailed with Vaughan's 'Propositions' in its emphasis on the need for a local individual of worth and integrity to be appointed as north Wales's commander-in-chief. The document counselled that 'some gentleman of interest in ye said counties' be appointed so that 'they may have an honest, able & well experienced soldier'. While Vaughan was not an 'experienced soldier', he was a local man of considerable means, as his 'Propositions' had maintained, who had commanded his own garrison. Although it might be going too far to suggest that in these proposals Vaughan was vying to replace Myddelton and to cross Mytton by assuming military command of north Wales himself, the presence of this document among his papers argues that his November 'Propositions' was part of a plan to consolidate his parliamentarian credentials by contributing to the reduction of north Wales. As ever, his interests vis-à-vis Llwydiarth were likely connected to this wider effort, for his capacity to assist and support the reconquest of north Wales rested on his claim to possess 'the greatest interest of any man in that countie', and this would, of course, need him to be unquestioned master of his ancestral estate. Given the self-aggrandising nature of the 'Propositions' and the fact that the Committee of Both Kingdoms requested the scheme's endorsement by both Myddelton and Mytton, it is small wonder that Vaughan's proposal disappeared into the aether.

Reforming local bureaucracy: anti-army sentiment and the 'draft ordinance' for associating north Wales, c.April 1645

As Vaughan floated his 'Propositions', so reform of the local bureaucracy which accompanied the military re-organisation in north Wales was taking shape. At Mytton's appointment in May 1645, a committee for north Wales 'to order and direct' the war there was discussed in parliament, but its nomination was postponed 'at the desire of the gentlemen of that country', presumably referring to the few local MPs who remained in the Commons such as Vaughan's kinsman Simon Thelwall the younger, Sir John Trevor and John Glynne.[80] It seems possible, however, that even here Vaughan was trying to interpose himself and modify the proposed settlement to his advantage. Among Vaughan's papers survive two partial drafts of an ordinance for associating north Wales which can be dated to this period.[81] They evidently originate from discussions taking place around this time as one draft describes how the 'worke of reducing ye said counties [of north Wales] is not yet completed: five of ye 6 counties being wholy in ye enemies power', and it also mentions the ongoing threat from Irish forces landing in north Wales. The provenance of these drafts is uncertain, but their presence among Vaughan's archive suggests his close interest and involvement with them, as does the centrality of Montgomeryshire and Vaughan's allies in the proposed settlement that they outlined. Vaughan's hand is also suggested by the drafts' subtle digs at Myddelton's legacy: one paper, for example, notes that after 'much expence of tyme and treasure there yet remaynes the same pressing necessity of perfecting ye reducement of the said countyes'. The draft seemed to be posing a question that Vaughan would later articulate more fully: given all the resources with which Myddelton had been provided, why had he been so singularly unsuccessful in securing north Wales for parliament?[82] In connecting Vaughan's interests with these drafts, it is also worth emphasising how the administrative settlement of north Wales they envisaged was centred particularly on Montgomeryshire. One of them noted that, despite its reduction, the county remained 'infested with ye continuall inroads of ye enemy', and that locals were forced to pay both royalist and parliamentarian levies. Vaughan had given similar reasons as justifications for his maintaining a garrison at Abermarchant. The draft also justifies its provisions as taking into consideration 'ye present condicion of Northwales in generall and of ye county of Mountgomery in particular'. Moreover, and as is discussed further below, the personnel appointed to implement this settlement would be drawn disproportionately from that county. It appears from a petition of January 1646, which is discussed in chapter 5, that an ordinance along the lines sketched here had been introduced to parliament but that it remained undiscussed at that time.

In their proposals for conquering north Wales, these drafts outlined plans for raising a body of 1,000 foot and 300 horse which would be maintained by loans, weekly assessments and the sequestration of delinquents' estates. The committee that parliament had envisaged as a coordinating body for such forces is at the heart of these documents. However, rather than being the creature of the army, as the actual Committee for North Wales would eventually become, the committee proposed in these drafts would have oversight and control of these forces. It would be empowered to appoint all major officers and to issue commissions to the individual whom parliament appointed commander-in-chief of the north Wales forces. Importantly, one draft provides the names of a suggested committee. While it included many whom one might expect to find in such a document, such as the officer Roger Sontley (who would later support Vaughan's Llwydiarth claim), Thomas Myddelton (son of the parliamentarian commander) and any MP with estates in north Wales, the body was stuffed with Vaughan allies, drawn mostly from Montgomeryshire. Many of these were obscure men with no public profile and no right to be on such a powerful body: individuals like Matthew Morgan, Gabriel Wynne and Richard Harries. Edward Vaughan himself was among the proposed nominees, of course, as was his local opponent Lloyd Pierce, but perhaps one of the most striking elements about this proposal was its thoroughly civilian character. This chimes with Vaughan's distaste for military rule which he would articulate on several occasions, and it stands in stark contrast to the body that ultimately did emerge in north Wales, and which was dominated by the military. A final noteworthy aspect of the proposed settlement was its religious dimension.

The draft ordinance empowered the committee to call before it all clergy and schoolmasters 'that are scandalous in theire lives, ill affected to the parliament or fomenters of this unnaturall warr', or who resisted parliament's ordinances. Witnesses could be produced against such men and the committee could, with the consent and advice of 'godly' divines, eject these individuals and nominate others in their place. This was of a piece with a general recognition that the royalist ministry had been a mainstay of the king's cause in Wales and was a body in desperate need of reform and remodelling. Such opinions had been articulated from before the meeting of the Long Parliament by the most influential puritan figure in the Welsh Marches, Sir Robert Harley of Brampton Bryan in Herefordshire.[83] Harley was described in 1646 as one of 'Gods champions … and instruments of his glory' in Wales, and he supported reforms for purging the Welsh church of its allegedly corrupted members and replacing them with a godly preaching ministry.[84] While such provisions for reforming the ministry found in these drafts might call to mind the work of the Commission for the Propagation of the Gospel in Wales which functioned between 1650 and 1653, it would be a mistake to see this and the proposed committee of spring 1645 as cut from the same cloth. The propagation commission was a breeding ground for radical Independency, and its leading lights such as Morgan Llwyd and Vavasor Powell were already operating in the Welsh Marches in 1645. By contrast, Vaughan, like Harley, was a religious Presbyterian who wanted a sober further reformation secured by settling orthodox ministers within a national church structure. He was, moreover, anxious about the religious disruption that the war had already caused in Montgomeryshire. We can see this Presbyterian impulse in the proposed ordinance among Vaughan's papers which empowered the committee to minister oaths to military officers and to exclude any that refused the National Covenant or the Vow and Covenant, shibboleths of the Presbyterian cause. Moreover, the committee was authorised to administer the National Covenant to any individual in north Wales. Such provisions were anathema to the more forward religious reformers among the Welsh Independents and would simultaneously have been a strike against such opinions that had been gaining ground in the army, among figures such as John Jones and

Hugh Price who sat on the Montgomeryshire sequestration committee, for example. This fascinating proposal, then, gives us a glimpse at the road not taken in the political and religious life of civil war Wales: the possibility of a Presbyterian settlement in which men like Vaughan and Harley held the reins of authority rather than Llwyd and Powell.[85]

The Committee for North Wales

The draft ordinances remained just drafts, however, and parliament failed to appoint its anticipated committee for north Wales, probably because of disputes between the emerging Presbyterian and Independent factions in the area over who should be nominated. However, despite the lack of any official appointments to the body proposed at Mytton's nomination in May 1645, an executive body was nonetheless constituted and is first mentioned in a note of the Committee of Both Kingdoms of 3 December 1645 as 'the Committee of North Wales', and again by a local commander in the same terms four days later, when the body was sitting at Dodleston on the Flintshire-Cheshire border.[86] It is thus incorrect to suggest, as did A. H. Dodd in his classic study of civil war committees and as did the author of a recent article on the 'Wrexham committee', that parliamentarian administration here only really began in early 1647.[87] The new committee's members were drawn from the army and included the Commander-in-Chief Mytton himself along with John Jones, Roger Sontley, Thomas Ball and Roger Pope. Jones and Pope would also be appointed to the Montgomeryshire sequestration committee and later became involved in its disputes with Vaughan. Jones, a future regicide, had long been associated with Sir Thomas Myddelton's father and stepmother, and had been in Myddelton's service in London before the war. He became treasurer of Myddelton's brigade and had recently been appointed a colonel under Mytton.[88] Pope, meanwhile, was a Shropshire man who also owned lands in Montgomeryshire. Pope had been Sir Thomas Myddelton's ward after his father's death in 1637, and he had also recently become Mytton's son-in-law.[89] He served under the latter in his campaigns in the Welsh Marches and rose to become, like John Jones, a colonel in the north Wales army in November 1645.[90] The Committee for North Wales, then, was wholly military in origin; indeed, one observer later claimed that the power to nominate such committees had lapsed with Myddelton's command, and thus that there was no true committee there 'but all things [are] acted by the souldiery'.[91] In the absence of an alternative bureaucracy established by parliamentary ordinances, however, the Committee for North Wales assumed the role of superior executive body in the association and was populated by figures who supported their sister (sequestration) committee in Montgomeryshire; they also became resolute opponents of Edward Vaughan and his designs.

* * *

The Red Castle committee's decision in October 1645 to continue Llwydiarth's sequestration placed them on a collision course with Edward Vaughan and the civilian interest he was cultivating in the county. Having failed to insinuate himself into the military dispensation in north Wales as it took shape from mid-1645, Vaughan lacked any kind of institutional power base from which he might defend his precarious hold on Llwydiarth, and thus on his political power in the county. However, in late December 1645 a new committee was established in Montgomeryshire which was to become the foundation of Vaughan's authority and the instrument of his ambitions.[92] This was the county's sub-committee of the central Committee for Taking the Accounts of the Kingdom. The central committee was established in 1643 to oversee military spending and had become a partisan body closely associated with the Presbyterian effort to clip the wings of the army, moderate the ambitions of radicals and help achieve a moderate settlement with the king.[93] Such priorities meshed with those of Edward Vaughan, particularly opposing the military-backed committees (which were not supportive of his claim to Llwydiarth), but they also aligned with his moderate political and religious Presbyterianism.

It is unclear who moved for the establishing of the sub-committee, but it is quite possible that Vaughan reached out to the Presbyterian leaders at Westminster, such as William Prynne or Herefordshire's Sir Robert Harley, arguing that the county, and perhaps north Wales more generally, was being lost to the radical soldiery, and pressing for assistance in curbing their designs. Whatever the mechanisms behind its establishment, the Montgomeryshire sub-committee began its work in early 1646 by demanding an audit of the sequestration committee's accounts.[94] Their request was extremely detailed and extensive, probably deliberately so in an attempt to catch and confound the sequestrators. Moreover, the demand was personal rather than general, being directed to Lloyd Pierce, because:

> we finde you have bin a constant commissioner without those whose order nothinge hath bin acted concerninge the receipte and disburstments of money and dispachis of all kindes thorough the countie, and likewise because you have bin treasurer for all the receipts of all natures in this county and adiacent parts to who all inferior officers have or ought to have accompted.[95]

The stage was set for an epic battle of wills between Vaughan and Pierce, which was simultaneously a clash between ideological positions within the parliamentary phalanx and also a confrontation between local civilian and military administrators. This clash forms the centrepiece of the next chapter.

Edward Vaughan, the Governance of North Wales and the Struggle over Accounts, January–October 1646

E dward Vaughan's chairmanship of Montgomeryshire's sub-committee for accounts provided him with an institutional authority that he could wield to protect his occupation of Llwydiarth. It also, however, plugged him directly into a component of the parliamentary administrative machine which reflected his political priorities. The Montgomeryshire sub-committee became the powerbase of the Presbyterian interest in the county, and it also drew in figures from neighbouring Shropshire. Vaughan and his allies thus represented an important, but largely neglected, strain of moderate parliamentarianism on the Anglo-Welsh border. This chapter is the first attempt fully to explore this body's work and Vaughan's role as its chair. It is also the first extended discussion of the local politics of parliamentary reconquest in north Wales and of the feuds and factions which emerged within parliament's ranks as part of that recovery effort. This chapter, then, investigates the vicious feuds that arose between Vaughan and the accounts sub-committee on the one hand, and Lloyd Pierce, and his allies on the Montgomeryshire sequestration committee and the Committee for North Wales on the other. The chapter argues that much which was opaque and unclear about the factional differences within the parliamentarian phalanx becomes clearer when viewed through Vaughan's archive and the papers of the central Accounts Committee. This and the following chapter, then, offer a new analysis of political dynamics in north Wales between 1645 and 1648. It is a novel discussion of the emergence and growth of factional politics within north Wales, but also of the manner in which personality and self-interest coloured the clash between Presbyterian and Independent in civil war Wales.

The Montgomeryshire sub-committee of accounts

Edward Vaughan assumed the chairmanship of the Montgomeryshire sub-committee of accounts and was its guiding light. However, he was accompanied by a group of men who became important actors in its clashes with the county's sequestration committee and with the military establishment of north Wales. In many ways, the struggle between Montgomeryshire's sequestration and accounts committees was a battle between two castles: the former at Red (or Powis) Castle, and the latter at Montgomery Castle.[1] The most prominent individual alongside Vaughan in the earliest iteration of the sub-committee was Samuel More, who had been appointed governor of Montgomery Castle in May 1645.[2] More was a Shropshire native whose father was a noted puritan sympathiser. Samuel himself became a captain in the parliamentary army and was known for his resolute, although doomed, defence of Hopton Castle in early 1644.[3] He was also a member of the Shropshire county committee, and, although it does not seem that he was prominent in its opposition to Thomas Mytton in 1644–5, he would by 1646 turn on his former commanding officer.[4] It was More, along with Lieutenant Colonel James Till, who led the bloodless action which took Montgomery Castle for parliament on 10 September 1644.[5]

The remainder of the Montgomeryshire sub-committeemen were comparatively obscure men, although this is perhaps not surprising as the personnel of accounts sub-committees were intended to be individuals who did not already hold military posts or positions involved with raising revenue (it seems likely that More was appointable on the technicality that his posts were held in Shropshire rather than in Montgomeryshire). Thus we find along with Vaughan and More individuals such as Matthew Morgan of Aberhafesb, Richard Harries, Richard Griffith of Mathrafal and Robert Lloyd of Castellmoch, minor gentlemen all with little record of parliamentarian commitment. Indeed, the convention that sub-committeemen were not current holders of other public offices meant that, in many instances, these were men who had questionable records of parliamentarian commitment and were often suspected of being royalists or 'neuters'; such suspicions were particularly prevalent in solidly royalist areas like eastern Wales. It is also worth mentioning that some of these men had close connections to Vaughan before appearing alongside him on the sub-committee. Robert Lloyd, for example, had acted as Vaughan's steward, been one of the officers in his Abermarchant garrison, would subsequently operate as his agent in Merioneth, and later claimed that he 'for divers yeares together [did] follow and sollicite ... Edward Vaughans law suites'.[6] These, then, were figures who we will encounter from the mid-1640s alongside Edward Vaughan as his political associates and allies; and he would need their support in the stormy months ahead.

Edward Vaughan, opposition to the army and the Montgomeryshire petition of January 1646

The Montgomeryshire accounts sub-committee quickly became a vehicle for civilian opposition to the military establishment in north Wales as it took shape from mid-1645.[7] Vaughan was the effective leader of this movement and, from early 1646 onwards, we see what might be characterised as a moderate, civilian Presbyterian mobilisation against army personnel and their Independent-aligned allies emerge in the Montgomeryshire-Shropshire area. Such mobilisations by Presbyterian-allied accounts sub-committees against more Independent-leaning county committees can be witnessed in several other places such as Warwickshire, Lincolnshire and Somersetshire.[8] In Montgomeryshire, the more moderate parliamentarian caucus broke cover with a petition to the Commons in the name of the gentry, ministers and freeholders of the county in January 1646, a document that has not previously been discussed by historians.[9] Our surviving copy of the petition is to be found among Vaughan's papers and includes seventy-nine signatures (some eighteen of which are original, the remainder being scribal copies) of individuals from the 'parishe of Llanvihangell', presumably Llanfihangel-yng-Ngwynfa, in which Llwydiarth was situated. This suggests that, in common with petitionary practice of this sort found elsewhere, the document was circulated throughout the county parish by parish, accumulating signatures and acquiring legitimacy and a claim to represent majority opinion. Such an approach was important in maintaining the position that this was the corporate voice of the political community. We shall return to these signatories in a moment.

The county petition began by noting that the unusual powers for settling civil and military authority inherent in Sir Thomas Myddelton's commission had been discontinued by the Self-Denying Ordinance and that they had not been conferred on another appointee, 'allthough an ordinance hath longe depended in this honourable house for the supplie of that defect'. This was evidently a reference to the draft ordinance for establishing a Committee for North Wales which was discussed in the previous chapter. As a result of the failure to address this lapse of 'legitimate' parliamentarian authority in the county, the petition continued, there was now no 'lawfull magistrate for the preservacion of the publique peace', nor any individual who could 'setle able and conscionable preachers in such churches as were diserted by the malignant ministers'. It was indeed true that, following the collapse of royalist control, no local bench of justices was appointed and no law courts sat in the county until March 1648; the sequestration committee at Powis Castle was the main organ of local government and justice down to this point.[10] The petition did not pull its punches in its assertions that the failure to settle proper forms of civil and religious authority in Montgomeryshire had 'much hindred' parliament's service and resulted in 'many unwarrantable proceedinges tendinge to the enslavinge of many well affected persons', despite the fact that the county had been under parliamentarian control for fifteen months. Such language overlapped with emerging anti-committee sentiment in the kingdom at large which was expressed principally by Presbyterian sympathisers. This discourse was articulated forcefully by the MP Clement Walker, who argued that if there was 'any intention to restore our laws and liberties … it is fit that these committees and all [military] associations be laid down … and that the old form of government by sheriffs, justices of the peace, & c be re-established'.[11]

In order to address the core problems it identified, the petition requested that the ordinance which was currently in parliamentary limbo be passed, 'thereby enablinge men of integritie & interest in the said counties to redresse the ... greevances' so that Montgomeryshire would have 'the same lawe to walke by as other counties have'. It was also the case that Montgomeryshire now had no parliamentary representative: the borough member Richard Herbert was disabled in 1642, while the county MP, Sir John Price, had fallen foul of Sir Thomas Myddelton (an event mentioned in the petition) when he changed sides to support the royalists once again in early 1645, and had been disabled from sitting in the Commons in October.[12] Perhaps as a means to remedy this lack of representation in parliament, the petition also requested that the Commons appoint a sheriff in the county. Importantly, this would be the official who could authorise and oversee new elections for the shire's vacant constituencies, a process which had begun elsewhere in the country in the autumn of 1645.[13] Indeed, on 21 October 1645, soon after Price was disabled, the leader of parliamentarian forces besieging Chester, Sir William Brereton, when discussing 'elections in these parts', asked his associate in the Commons, William Ashhurst, to see 'if you could bring it about to have a sheriff pricked for Montgom[eryshire] and a writ [for electing an MP] speedily sent down, [so] a good man might be procured'.[14] The prospect of appointing a sheriff and securing elections to the vacant Montgomeryshire seat, then, were very much on the minds of parliamentarian supporters in the Welsh Marches at this time, although a sheriff would not be nominated in Montgomeryshire for another year and an election would only take place in November 1646.[15] The petition concluded by acknowledging parliament's 'undefatigable paines' on the petitioners' behalf, and the signatories pledged their lives and fortunes to 'advaunce that blessed reformacion soe happily begin in Church and common wealth'.

This is a fascinating text which operated as a critique of the current parliamentary administration in the county, and by extension the rest of the North Wales Association, and which overlapped with the priorities found in the 'draught of that ordinance in the house of Commons' which was discussed in the previous chapter. Perhaps the petition's most striking claim was that the county's 'well affected' were being 'enslaved' by the 'unwarrantable proceedinges' in the county. This was clearly an accusation levelled against Lloyd Pierce and the sequestration committee, but it doubtless also comprehended its associated body, the Committee for North Wales, which was operating without any explicit parliamentary authorisation. The argument that the sequestration committee's authority had lapsed with Myddleton's ordinance, while the Committee for North Wales had never received official sanction, played into the developing anti-committee rhetoric elsewhere in the country that these were extra-legal bodies that were operating arbitrarily and without sufficient oversight.[16] Also in line with the emergent (and often Presbyterian-inspired) campaign against county committees elsewhere, the petition articulated a social critique of parliament's local governors and a desire for the return to established forms of local rule. The document's reference to men of 'integritie & interest' returning to office echoed Vaughan's language in his 'Propositions', but it also suggested that those currently exercising power in the county were low-born individuals lacking the requisite qualities to govern. It also implied, of course, that such men lacked integrity and were thus potentially corrupt, a line which, as we shall see shortly, Vaughan's accounts sub-committee was simultaneously developing against the Red Castle cadre. Also striking, however, and once more suggesting a degree of overlap with the stalled ordinance in parliament, is the petition's emphasis on religious reformation and the need to replace ejected ministers with orthodox preachers. While not as explicitly Presbyterian as the draft ordinance, the petition nonetheless occupied similar ideological territory, with an emphasis on revivifying the damaged church and the orderly replacement of malignant preachers with a reformed preaching ministry.

The January 1646 petition, then, was a clear attack on parliament's current governors in Montgomeryshire, with Lloyd Pierce and his sequestration committee being particular targets. As mentioned above, it seems that the document was circulated among local parishes to obtain signatures and support, and these signatures repay some further analysis. As befits his role as the moving force behind the document, Edward

Vaughan's name is prominent in first position beneath the petition's text. However, this was not simply a personal vendetta: the petition was a mobilisation by the incipient Presbyterian group in the county which found its institutional expression in the sub-committee of accounts. Thus we find alongside Vaughan the signatures of his fellow members on that body, Matthew Morgan, Richard Harries, Richard Griffith and Samuel More, as well as two individuals who had recently joined them, George Devereux and Robert Griffith. Devereux had initially been appointed to the county's sequestration committee but clearly felt that he was not among like-minded individuals there and managed to switch horses in late 1645.[17] Devereux would become Edward Vaughan's closest ally on the sub-committee and would act as something like his second-in-command in their campaign against Lloyd Pierce and his allies. Robert Griffith was a less prominent figure, but, like Devereux, he too was a 'defector' from the sequestration committee, having been appointed as its solicitor in 1644, but he only served for six months or so.[18]

The petition's other signatories were not on the accounts sub-committee but were nonetheless clearly within Edward Vaughan's orbit. John Vaughan, for example, was possibly the lawyer of Cefnbodig whom Edward Vaughan would support in the contested 1654 Merioneth election.[19] William Kyffin of Bodfach (Llanfyllin) was Vaughan's steward who held manorial courts for him at Llwydiarth in the autumn of 1641 and again from 1644.[20] Kyffin was also one of those named to the prospective committee for north Wales found in Vaughan's 1645 draft ordinance, and he would go on to assist Vaughan in his confrontation with Pierce and Hugh Price during the early Commonwealth.[21] The original signatures of Cornet Owen Vaughan and his brother Captain Evan are also noteworthy: these were two soldiers who would assist Edward Vaughan in his attacks on the military competency of their former commanding officer, Sir Thomas Myddelton.[22] Other signatories included Robert Vaughan, a squire who appeared in the ranks of Edward Vaughan's supporters and allies in the 1650s,[23] and also the local clergyman, Maurice Morgan, who presumably would have helped drum up support for the petition among his parishioners. And there were many more signatories, although in the absence of robust parish data it is impossible to identify these individuals or to say much more about them, although the comparative frequency of patronymics suggests that these were comparatively humble men drawn from the yeoman and husbandman classes.

There is no record that this county petition was received by the Commons which may leave us to wonder whether this effort amounted to anything. However, in a letter of February 1646, Vaughan and his fellow sub-committeemen spoke of the need for a 'generall settlement in this county' adding that it had been 'long expected and now also petitioned for by this county'.[24] This suggests that the petition had indeed been submitted or, possibly, that this effort was still ongoing. The letter also confirms the close ties between the petitionary effort and the accounts sub-committee personnel: all of those who signed the February 1646 letter had also witnessed the Llanfihangel petition. Further evidence that the petition was indeed submitted, or at the very least that it was seen as a genuine threat, can be seen in the fact that it elicited a backlash from Lloyd Pierce and his supporters among the army and the sequestration committee.

Retaliation: Thomas Mytton, Sir Thomas Myddelton and the attack on Edward Vaughan, February–March 1646

In parallel with the county petition, Vaughan and his colleagues on the sub-committee were pressing for an accounting from the Red Castle (sequestration) committee for its activities over the previous year or so, but their efforts had been frustrated. As a result, in early February 1646 the accountants sent a report of their proceedings to their parent body, the Committee for Taking the Accounts of the Kingdom, which sat at Cornhill in London.[25] In this letter they observed that Lloyd Pierce had provided only a partial reckoning of his committee's finances, and that Vaughan and his fellow accountants were in no way satisfied. They claimed that Pierce should have accounted for some £40,000 of revenue but had only produced documentation for a little more than £4,000. He had also refused to hand over his committee's records and the sub-committee had fined him £100 for his contempt. The Montgomeryshire accountants were wary of proceeding further in the business without the advice of the Cornhill body. In addition to reporting their frustrations with Pierce, the sub-committeemen also asked that Esay (or 'Esai' or 'Isiah') Thomas of Bishop's Castle, Shropshire, 'a person well known unto us', be appointed as their treasurer, a request to which the central committee acceded.[26] Thomas was elected to parliament for Bishop's Castle around the time this letter was penned and, as we shall see, he fitted well into the sub-committee's political and religious profile. Their letter concluded darkly, 'we omit to informe you what discouragements we finde in this worke … by under-hand practises … and onely intimate this much to obtain your furtherance in that particular'. They also alluded to the need for a 'generall settlement' in Montgomeryshire which had also been the aim of Vaughan's January petition.

The accountants' investigative efforts helped touch off a concerted fightback from Montgomeryshire's sequestration committee and its allies among the military establishment in north Wales. Fighting off the attempt to probe further into his committee's activities, Lloyd Pierce appealed to the Committee for North Wales. Its members were disposed to assist Pierce and his associates with whom they had close ties and whose broader political and ideological aims they shared. Moreover, it seems likely that the Committee for North Wales was stung by Vaughan's January petition and its claims that the current disposition of parliamentary authority in north Wales was arbitrary and lacking in legislative foundation. Thus it was that, on 18 February 1646, Major General Thomas Mytton and his fellow committeemen wrote from Ruthin in Denbighshire to the Commons Speaker William Lenthall, noting that they were finding it difficult to obtain money and supplies for their forces.[27] Whereas the whole association should have been pulling together to support their work in recovering the royalist north, the committee complained that in Montgomeryshire, 'the only settled county in all the associacion', Colonel Hugh Price and Lloyd Pierce ('being two of this committee resideing in that county') had informed them that Edward Vaughan had violently taken contribution money from local constables and 'disswaded the people' from paying their assessments, 'alleadging that Sir Thomas Middleton had noe power to ympose a monthly contribucion upon the county and that neither hee nor his tenants would pay unlesse they were distrayned'.[28]

Pierce and Price were seeking to stymie Vaughan's investigation into their finances but also to bolster the Red Castle committee's position as the principal authority in Montgomeryshire. Moreover, the claim that Vaughan was querying the legitimacy of the committees raising taxes for the army has clear resonances with the county petition that may still have been gathering signatures when Mytton and his colleagues sent their letter.[29] It is also evident that Pierce and Price were speaking from experience: Vaughan did indeed complain elsewhere that the power to nominate committees had lapsed with Myddelton's command.[30] With the county petition and his resistance to military taxes, Vaughan evidently felt emboldened by his recent elevation as chairman of the only accounts sub-committee in north Wales, a post whose brief was explicitly to act as an overseer of the army. However, he was antagonising forces that had become powerful in the region since the military tide had swung decisively against the royalists and since the parliamentarian military presence established itself as a working bureaucracy rather than simply as an invading force using ad hoc administrative expedients.

In an apparently co-ordinated effort, Mytton's letter was accompanied by an attack on the Montgomeryshire accounts sub-committee from Sir Thomas Myddelton, Mytton's brother-in-law, who had returned to Westminster as MP for Denbighshire after relinquishing his military command. Thus it was that in mid-February a series of 'exceptions' taken by 'Sir Thomas Myddelton and others' to Vaughan and other members of the Montgomeryshire sub-committee being 'accomptants & comanders, and soe disabled to take accompts' was drawn up and submitted to the central Committee for Taking the Accounts of the Kingdom.[31] It is worth pausing for a moment to examine Myddelton's role in initiating this attack. Although he was no longer commander of the military in north Wales, Myddelton remained an important strategic lynchpin for the reconquest efforts in parliament. He also remained, of course, a close ally of Mytton, the officers he had led in his Welsh campaigns such as his one-time servant Colonel John Jones, and the committeemen he had installed in places like Montgomeryshire such as Lloyd Pierce. Indeed, it seems telling that even in April 1647, many months after he had resigned his military command, contemporaries continued to refer to these north Wales bodies as 'Sir Thomas Middletons committees'.[32] Myddelton's involvement with the parliamentary conquest of north Wales did not cease with his return to parliament, then, and on 4 February 1646 he, along with the remaining MPs from north Wales, who included Sir John Trevor, Simon Thelwall the younger and John Glynne, were appointed to a Commons committee to consider the means for reducing the area. This committee had been established after receipt of a dispatch from Mytton lamenting that 'we cannot raise one penny towards the payment of my soldiers'.[33] As Mytton's letter to Speaker Lenthall made clear, Edward Vaughan was proving a serious obstacle to collecting money for his forces, and it seems likely that Myddelton, and perhaps other members of this parliamentary committee, saw removing Vaughan and his allies from the scene as an important means of furthering Mytton's objectives. Myddelton's 'exceptions' against the Montgomeryshire accounts sub-committee thus emerges from a close concern with the fortunes of the North Wales Association in parliament and was almost certainly coordinated with Mytton and his allies on the Committee for North Wales.

We are fortunate that a copy of Myddelton's 'exceptions' against the Montgomeryshire sub-committee's members has survived; these help establish the basic grounds upon which much of the opposition to Vaughan and his local allies would rest for the next several years.[34] As might be expected, Edward Vaughan headed the list of the sub-committee's malefactors. Myddelton's paper alleged that it had been acknowledged before the Committee of Both Kingdoms that Vaughan had visited Oxford when it was the king's garrison in March 1643. The 'exceptions' continued that Vaughan had never supported parliament in person or through financial contributions until Montgomeryshire was wholly reduced, and it was only then that he returned and established his Abermarchant garrison 'without comission from parliament or consent of the comittee'. The accusation was designed to portray Vaughan as a loose cannon acting only from personal rather than public interest, a position which was strengthened by the assertion that he had received the sequestered rents of the Llwydiarth estates without order and in contempt of a prohibition from the central sequestration committee. Moreover, Myddelton maintained that Vaughan had forced his tenants to pay their rents to him rather than to the state, and that he had refused to provide an accounting of his receipts before Mytton or the Committee for North Wales. It was further alleged that many of the soldiers in Vaughan's garrison had been cashiered by Myddelton for plundering in north Wales, and also that they had taken contribution monies in Merionethshire which should have been directed towards supporting the siege of Chester.[35] The document argued that it was Vaughan who should be providing an account to the state for the monies he had seized and that on this basis he should be disabled from being an auditor of public revenue. This was a comprehensive set of charges which cumulatively portrayed Vaughan as tainted with royalism, only acting out of self-interest and responsible for undermining the war effort in north Wales. Many of these allegations would be rehearsed and repeated in the coming months. The charges are suggestive of close local knowledge, and it seems highly likely that Lloyd Pierce and his colleagues on the Montgomeryshire sequestration committee had furnished Myddelton with details of Vaughan's supposed misdeeds.

Vaughan was not the only target of Myddelton's campaign, however. The whole accounts sub-committee was presented as being tainted with dubious royalist pasts, or as having current public employments which rendered them incapable of serving as auditors. Samuel More, for example, was said to be unable to act on the sub-committee as he was captain of a horse troop and governor of Montgomery Castle and 'therby accomptable'. John Price and Matthew Morgan were alleged to have taken Lord Capel's royalist oath in 1643, to have raised forces for him and, when nominated to the sequestration committee for the county by Sir Thomas Myddelton in 1644, it was alleged that they 'did slite and neglecte it'. This is an interesting allegation which suggests that, from its inception, the Red Castle committee was seen by some sections of local society as a partisan body. The 'exceptions' concluded by noting that several members of the sub-committee – William Wynne, Cadwaladr Meredith, Robert Lloyd and Henry Thomas – were 'such inconsiderable men as [are] not known in the ... county, or ever as wee heard bare office or of the quality of gentlemen, who wee are assured never appeare[d] for the parliament or fitt to be entrusted with such a power'. This charge was an attempt to counter the suggestions of Vaughan's January 1646 petition that government by social inferiors was a problem exclusive to the Montgomeryshire sequestration committee. These 'inconsiderable men', who were evidently nominated to the sub-committee but rarely appear on any of its surviving orders or correspondence, provide some striking evidence of the degree to which the body was a creature of the Vaughan interest. Wynne and Lloyd were soldiers under Vaughan's command in the Abermarchant garrison and had not appeared in parliamentary lists beforehand. Henry Thomas, meanwhile, was described as Edward Vaughan's 'servant' in the garrison, and, when he deposed before the central Accounts Committee on Vaughan's behalf, he acknowledged that he 'belong[ed]' to Vaughan.[36]

The 'exceptions', along with Mytton's letter to Lenthall demonstrate that Myddelton, Mytton and the Red Castle committee had launched a concerted and apparently coordinated effort to torpedo the accountants' work and to nullify Edward Vaughan's influence. The attack was predicated upon differences in political, religious and military priorities. Vaughan and his allies were looking to moderate the parliamentary conquest of north Wales, and to negate or at least to restrain the influence of figures such as Hugh Price and Lloyd Pierce who supported a vigorous prosecution of the war, and who were more comfortable with the radical religious ideas that were infiltrating the army and local society at this time. As is discussed below, the garrison at Red Castle was already being exposed to the radical preaching of Morgan Llwyd, while men like Hugh Price would go on to support the extreme puritan Vavasor Powell and the Fifth Monarchy Men. By contrast, Vaughan and his allies were political and religious moderates who craved a negotiated settlement with the king, a national church and a return to government by known forms and traditional gentry families. We should not, however, consider these as rigid political and ideological blocs as the divisions between Presbyterians and Independents remained fluid, especially while the war continued. Thus we have some potentially uncomfortable bedfellows in these respective 'camps', like the Presbyterian Sir Thomas Myddelton and the radical Independent Hugh

Price, who, although occupying different political and religious worlds by 1649, were united in 1646 in their conviction that the army in north Wales needed concerted support to complete its reconquest. Nonetheless, these emergent 'Independent' and 'Presbyterian' ideological positions were structuring elements of the developing feud between Myddelton, Mytton and the Montgomeryshire sequestration committee on the one hand, and Edward Vaughan and the accounts sub-committee on the other.

Myddelton's 'exceptions' were submitted to the Committee for Taking the Accounts of the Kingdom in London which, consequently, took a series of depositions in late February and early March 1646. Although these examinations were designed to show that the Cornhill committee was investigating Myddelton's allegations seriously, they were also clearly an effort by that body to support (and to exonerate) their placemen in Montgomeryshire.[37] On 24 February 1646, two Gray's Inn lawyers, Owen Andrewes and Simon Vaughan, as well as Edward Vaughan's servant and a target of Myddelton's paper, Henry Thomas, all gave evidence verifying Vaughan's parliamentarian bona fides. Also noteworthy is a set of interrogatories among the committee's papers which were designed to exonerate Samuel More, John Price and Matthew Morgan.[38] In a letter of 16 March 1646, the central Accounts Committee wrote to its Montgomeryshire officers providing their full-throated support.[39] The committee's bullish chairman, the Presbyterian grandee William Prynne, was clearly satisfied that the testimony of these witnesses had exonerated their sub-committeemen, and he backed Vaughan and his associates to the hilt in their confrontation with Lloyd Pierce.[40] Prynne ordered that if Pierce continued to defy their directions then he should be apprehended, his papers seized and that they should 'administer unto him what interrogatories yow thinke fitt'.

Edward Vaughan and the Committee for North Wales, March 1646

The investigation of Myddelton's 'exceptions' and the subsequent backing of the central Accounts Committee doubtless pleased Edward

Vaughan and fortified his local supporters. They declared themselves relieved that 'ye sinister practises against us tooke no effect with you [i.e. the Committee for Taking Accounts]'.[41] However, the failure of Myddelton's stratagem seems only to have strengthened the resolve of Vaughan's opponents to bring him low. Thus it was that on 18 March 1646 certificates were issued by Thomas Mytton and the Red Castle committee ordering that Vaughan be apprehended for seizing Llwydiarth contrary to the orders of the London sequestrators, and also that 'it be referred to the ... committees of Mountgomery, Denbigh and elswhere; to examine whether ... Edward Vaughan be a delinquent himself, by goeing to the kings quarters, viz. Chester or Oxford', adding that if he was found guilty of such charges, then he should be sequestered.[42] This move represented a serious threat, for Vaughan was indeed occupying Llwydiarth (and thus operating as a significant player in county politics) on the basis of ambiguities between the different sequestration orders issued the previous October. Llwydiarth was not a prize he could afford to give up, and the prospect of being named a delinquent, of course, would be ruinous. After receiving the warrant, Vaughan devised a paper which argued that he could never get justice before the local parliamentary administration, and which therefore shifted the focus from his particular case to an indictment of his enemies and the power structures in north Wales that supported and empowered them.[43]

The thrust of the paper was that Vaughan's delinquency or otherwise should not be referred to local committees. First, he argued that only two individuals, meaning Hugh Price and Lloyd Pierce, actually acted as committeemen in Montgomeryshire. In this, he seems to have been largely correct as the two men signed the majority of the committee's orders and were clearly the most active figures of a small rump working out of Powis Castle.[44] Vaughan also moved onto the offensive in the document, claiming that Pierce had been a commissioner of array who had taken Capel's royalist oath and had given money to his forces. These were the kinds of allegations that were relatively easy to throw in a county which had been under royal control for several years. However, as we shall see, some more substantial evidence supporting these allegations would soon turn up after a search of Pierce's home. As he had in the January petition,

Vaughan also played on the theme of low-born individuals assuming office, describing Hugh Price as 'a soldier ... [who] hath noe estate in ye county', and claiming that when Sir Thomas Myddelton nominated the committee in 1644, 'the rest of ye gentry' refused the service 'in regard sundry comanders and officers who had noe estate in yt countie were made committee men'. Vaughan continued that the accounts sub-committee had discovered 'a great summe of money', more than £20,000, lying in Lloyd Pierce's hands which remained unaccounted for. This, then, was more than just a personal defence, it was an attack on those who were slated to be Vaughan's judge and jury and an attempt to undermine their legitimacy as inquisitors.

Vaughan's paper also moved beyond personalities to deal with the wider structures of parliamentary rule in north Wales. The central sequestration committee's order had referred his case to the committees 'of Montgomery, Denbigh and elsewhere', and Vaughan drilled down into this construction to tease out some of its problems. In Denbighshire, for example, he noted that no committee had been nominated by Sir Thomas Myddelton when he was commander-in-chief. There was still 'noe committee there', and Mytton did not have the same powers of nomination granted by legislation that his predecessor had. As a result, Vaughan lamented, 'all things [are] acted by the souldiery'. Rule by the military carried with it the spectre of arbitrary and unaccountable authority at the point of the sword, and such arguments formed the basis of Presbyterian opposition to many county committees, the New Model Army and the Independent interest. Vaughan developed this critique in a section that is worth quoting at length, encompassing as it does some of the key ideas which drove his and his allies' ideological resistance to the army and its local avatars. He noted that the men acting as committees in both Montgomeryshire and Denbighshire were:

> commanders and officers ... taking upon them the powers of ceasing [i.e. assessing] and leavying what money they please upon ye countrey and inforceing the same oftentimes by sending troopes of horse, and they assuming to themselves the power of sequestrators. And all the moneyes soe raised being to pay themselves and their souldiers ... It will

be of dangerous consequence to make such men judges of other mens
delinquencie, especially of such as are to sift and bring them to accompt,
it being ye committees duetie soe to doe for the benefitt of ye state.

We must always remember that Vaughan's personal interest, indeed his
personal survival, was tied up with defending his claim to Llwydiarth,
but it is difficult to think that he was simply ventriloquising such anti-
army discourse merely as a front for private gain. The wider contours
of his and the accounts sub-committee's resistance to Mytton, the
North Wales Association and men like Hugh Price and Lloyd Pierce
are more clearly discerned in this paper. Parliament had taken up arms
to defend the people's liberties against arbitrary rule and the rights of
the subject; Vaughan himself had seen the bitter harvest of prerogative
courts where 'arbitrary' decisions overrode common law justice. Here,
however, Vaughan conjured the image of soldiers extracting their own
pay from the population through force and acting as judge and jury
over sub-committeemen like himself who had been appointed, in theory
at least, to ensure probity and fairness in the army's dealings with local
communities. Vaughan's discourse echoes closely that of Presbyterian
critics like Clement Walker who bemoaned the arbitrary conduct of
county committees working in league with an unaccountable army, and
who argued that 'if any man but speak of calling them [the army and
county committees] to give an account [for their revenues], they presently
vote him a delinquent and sequester him'.[45] Vaughan was claiming that
this was precisely what was happening in his case.

The surviving example of Vaughan's paper against the 18 March order
is a fair scribal copy, which suggests that he had submitted the original in
an effort to head off the case against him.[46] The whole thrust of this paper
was that it was impossible for Vaughan to obtain justice in north Wales, and
we know from a later account that he 'repayred in person' to the central
sequestration committee at Goldsmith's Hall in London to argue that he
should be admitted to trial at law for his possession of Llwydiarth.[47] While
legal title to the estate remained undecided, of course, Vaughan could not
be prosecuted for wrongfully entering the property. Nevertheless, on 24
April 1646 the central sequestration committee ordered that Vaughan

obey the committee's earlier order and restore to the state the rents he had
received since occupying the property in mid-1645; the case was then to
be referred to the Montgomeryshire sequestration committee who were
to examine proofs and witnesses on both sides.[48] This was a dire result for
Vaughan who petitioned the central committee five days later, rehearsing
the 19 March 1641 parliamentary orders regarding the Llwydiarth estate,
but also noting his fears that the Red Castle committee, to which the case
had been referred, were themselves being investigated by his own sub-
committee, 'soe that your petitioner feares that they are not indifferent'.
He also asked that any charge of delinquency against him be referred
to 'some indifferent committee' which 'are not parties subiect to iust
exceptions'.[49] Vaughan also submitted a similar petition to parliament
in which he recounted his labours on parliament's behalf in establishing
the Abermarchant garrison. In this petition, Vaughan argued that he had
possessed the Llwydiarth lands before they had been sequestered and that
he had spent any profits taken therefrom 'in the service of the publique
at ye often hazard of his life'.[50] He concluded by requesting that he be
allowed to continue in possession of the estate 'which he hath bene so
long uniustly kept from', and only be outed following a full trial at law '&
not by any committees orders who are ... debarred from intermeddling
betwixt party & party'.[51] These petitions do not seem to have changed
any minds at Westminster, however. This meant that Vaughan's claims to
Llwydiarth now lay in his enemies' hands. His response to this situation
was a spectacular escalation of his feud with the sequestration committee
and the exacerbation of an already significant rift in the parliamentary
phalanx in north Wales.

On 2 May 1646, probably soon after returning from London, Edward
Vaughan attended a meeting of the Montgomeryshire accounts sub-
committee. This meeting issued a warrant for Lloyd Pierce's arrest who,
the document stated, had 'most wilfully and contempteously disobeyed
our warrants' by refusing to produce his accounts and books of orders.[52]
The order noted that Pierce was then out of the county, and the sub-
committee later alleged that he had been tipped off and had fled to
London. In the meantime, the accountants demanded that Hugh Price,
as governor of Powis Castle, assist their agents in searching for the

sequestration committee's books and papers at the castle; Price refused to comply and the committee fined him £50 for contempt.[53]

In Pierce's absence, however, the sub-committee's agents searched his house at Maesmawr, where they found an incriminating document.[54] This was a cryptic text, but it seemed to indicate that Pierce had been an active royalist, or at least that he had pledged to support the royalist cause. The document seemed to be a representation to the king from a group of royalists in the county, of whom Pierce was one, complaining about the overweening power and arbitrary actions of royalist commanders in the region. Although the paper complained to the king that his subjects had been 'bought and sould like slaves' through the actions of the local army leadership, it nevertheless articulated a clear and resolute loyalty to the king's cause, 'beinge resolved to remayne noe lese, what calamity soever belafse us'. This paper was accompanied by another which concerned monies raised and disbursed in the royalist cause in Guilsfield parish in Montgomeryshire, and which was witnessed by Lloyd Pierce as 'unworthey accomptant'. The sub-committee gleefully sent up a copy to its parent body in early May, noting that Pierce appeared to be 'a more willing accomptant formerly to ye enemy: whose oath also we finde he hath taken, lent moneys and raysed forces upon occasion'. It was welcome ammunition in Vaughan's fight, but it was also relatively small beer: an ambiguous single paper taken from a man's house following a search of dubious legality was not the strongest basis upon which to be making serious accusations of a delinquent past. Rather more substantive, however, were the claims that Pierce and his sequestration committee had underrated delinquents' estates and that those who had gathered sequestered rents and taxes had fled the county while the sub-committee was investigating. The accountants asked their masters in London for advice as to how best to proceed, but the sub-committee was clearly moving onto the offensive, seeking to secure Lloyd Pierce's estate (worth £300 p.a.) as security for any shortfall in his accounts. Vaughan had committed to a strategy of harassment and intimidation which, while it may have rendered him a more effective agent of parliamentary oversight, also operated as a means of leverage against the Red Castle committee in their deliberations over Llwydiarth.

The intensifying confrontation between the two parliamentary committees in Montgomeryshire was making some individuals wary of serving on these bodies lest they get caught in the crossfire. In a letter to the central Accounts Committee on 7 May 1646, Edward Vaughan and his associates noted that some who had been nominated to their body had declined or were incapable of serving, so they requested the addition of three new committeemen, which the parent body granted. As two of them would become active sub-committeemen, it is worth considering them here. The first was Edward Owen of Woodhouse, Shropshire. His half-brother, Leighton, was an active member of the Shropshire county committee where he served alongside Samuel More. Owen was a minor figure in the local politics of the Anglo–Welsh border with little public profile to this point, although it is worth noting that he was one of those nominated to the proposed committee for north Wales under the draft ordinances of 1645, so was evidently considered a trusted member of the Vaughan circle. The second appointee was Samuel Bigg of Churchstoke, Shropshire.[55] Another minor county figure, his father, William, was connected to Samuel More's family who had owned his living at More in Shropshire. It is likely that Bigg and his father shared the Mores' puritan leanings before the civil wars.[56] Like Edward Owen, Bigg was also nominated to the proposed committee for north Wales in 1645. The sub-committee also nominated one Lewis Griffith but he remains an inconspicuous figure who does not appear to have taken up his position. Upon the recommendation of its treasurer, Esay Thomas, from the beginning of May 1646 the sub-committee also acquired a 'register', or secretary, in the person of William Barbour, a London scrivener.[57] A possible link here was Thomas Niccolls, the parliamentarian sheriff of Montgomeryshire in 1642, who was connected with the Barbour (or 'Barbor') family in Hertfordshire.[58] William Barbour was another committee figure closely associated with Vaughan, and he later testified to being employed as the Llwydiarth squire's 'sollicitor' who helped managed his affairs.[59]

It is worth noting at this point the number of 'out of county' men who were now members of the sub-committee. Devereux, More, Owen and Bigg, as well as Barbour and Esay Thomas hailed from places other than Montgomeryshire, many from Shropshire. This fact demonstrates the problematic nature of examining this period through the lens of the 'county community', as the realities of committee rule stretched readily across shire boundaries. However, the composition of the accounts sub-committee (and to a degree Montgomeryshire's sequestration committee) also testifies to the comparatively shallow pool of reliable parliamentarian candidates in such an ex-royalist county. Indeed, it was easy to portray the parliamentary administration of this region as fatally compromised by royalist pasts and continuing 'delinquent' sympathies.[60] Such tactics, as we have seen, were employed by the respective parties against one another in Montgomeryshire and were characteristic of a region where parliamentarian zeal was in short supply.

Escalation: Lloyd Pierce's arrest, May–September 1646

Lloyd Pierce soon returned to Maesmawr from London, and at this point the confrontation between himself and his committee and Edward Vaughan and his sub-committee became explosive.[61] Several agents arrived at Maesmawr on 18 May 1646 with a warrant for Pierce's arrest. Pierce allowed one of them inside his house and barred the doors against the agent's associates. Pierce then disarmed the man, avowing that 'he should not be his prisoner', and sent to Hugh Price at Powis Castle for assistance; he also rallied several neighbours to his aid. Edward Vaughan, who was then some two miles away, was informed of developments and raced to Maesmawr with two associates and had Pierce 'by force' arrested and secured in Montgomery Castle. For good measure, Pierce was fined £100 for his misconduct (on top of his earlier fine of £100 for contempt). The shadow of unaccountable rule by military force summoned up in some of Vaughan's earlier papers seemed to be taking on a disquieting solidity in Pierce's resistance. Indeed, the sub-committee alleged that Governor Hugh Price had sent three files of musketeers and a dozen horse to rescue Pierce, and also that Price 'suffered his souldiers to abuse our messengers in reviling terms as calling them spies, enemies, fidlers, traitors & c., and himselfe saying openly that Mr Vaughan had nothing to do with ye accompts'.[62] Vaughan and his colleagues requested the support of the Cornhill Accounts Committee, but also asked that it would 'vindicate your power, strooke at in so high a measure through our sides, and endeavoured to be overborne both by strength of hand and underhand practises against it & us'. It seems that the potential of this confrontation to destabilise the parliamentarian reconquest of north Wales was beginning to be recognised in London.

The battle over accounts, then, had become a test of wills, not only between the personalities of Vaughan and Pierce and the men arrayed behind them, but also between the ideological positions within the parliamentarian coalition which were becoming more concrete and bitterly opposed as 1646 progressed. As the Montgomeryshire dispute escalates, it becomes difficult to untangle the personal rivalries from the political differences, but it is probably artificial and unhelpful to attempt to do this too neatly in any event. As the sequestration committee and the sub-committee of accounts emerged as the forcing grounds for respectively Independent and Presbyterian authority in the area, so their ideological antagonism fed on the clash of personalities and vice-versa. Clearly, however, things had reached new heights with Pierce's incarceration and the snowballing fines meted out both to him and to Hugh Price. The two sides appealed to the political centre for assistance and attempted to draw on the resources of political patronage both in Westminster and in the Welsh Marches to gain the upper hand in what had become a violent struggle for local supremacy. Tracing the avenues, both local and national, through which this complex dispute developed over the next year can tell us much about the granular dynamics of local politics in the civil wars, and also about its particular complexion in Wales and the Marches.

Lloyd Pierce waited in confinement at Montgomery Castle, refusing to comply with the sub-committee's orders for production of all documents related to his committee's work. However, he and his allies were not idle. On 3 June 1646, a petition was read in the House of Lords which the journal records as coming from 'Lloyd Price', but this is a misreading for 'Lloyd Pierce'.[63] The garbled journal entry describes that the petition had requested bail for Herbert Vaughan, Edward Vaughan's nephew and principal rival for Llwydiarth. In fact, the petition was an application from Pierce himself to be bailed and to appear before the central sequestration committee, an application which was granted.[64]

It is worth noting that Pierce had petitioned the Lords, and the confused journal entry mentioning Herbert Vaughan might give us some insight into as to why. It later transpired that Pierce told the Lords he had been imprisoned by Edward Vaughan for trying to execute the sequestration committee's orders over possession of Llwydiarth. When the central sequestration committee had ruled on 18 March 1646 that Llwydiarth be removed from Edward Vaughan's control, the rents could not be paid to Herbert Vaughan who was a delinquent and a minor.[65] This being the case, they determined that the earl of Pembroke should receive the estate's revenues. Pembroke was a parliamentarian grandee with a considerable amount of land and influence in south Wales and the Marches, but he was also Herbert Vaughan's guardian and had apparently been involved on his ward's behalf in opposing Edward Vaughan's suits before the Council in the Marches of Wales.[66] Pembroke was present in the Lords when Pierce's petition was approved. Reading the runes of Pembroke's political machinations during the 1640s is a thankless task, but it is possible that he was a powerful figure at the political centre who could provide backing for Lloyd Pierce and the anti-Vaughan group. Pembroke was, in early 1646 at least, a supporter of the army and of the kinds of zealous local agents populating the Red Castle committee, and although his backing of Pierce and his allies in this case remains speculative, his connection with Llwydiarth does strengthen the possibility of his involvement on Pierce's behalf.[67]

On the same day as the Lords approved Pierce's application for bail, members of the sequestration committee at Red Castle composed a letter to the central Accounts Committee in London which portrayed Pierce's imprisonment as the product of personal animus rather than due process, reinforcing the narrative that Pierce described in his (now lost) petition to the Lords.[68] The sequestrators opened by resuscitating Sir Thomas Myddelton's 'exceptions' of mid-February. The suspect sub-committeemen, the letter then asserted, 'prosecute[d] the businesse with so much violence in pursuit of former grudges to particular persons, to the disturbance of the peace of this countie'. They argued that the sub-committee's actions were wholly disproportionate and driven by personal animus. The sequestrators made it clear, too, that by the sub-committee's actions, 'the publique service is hindered in this necessarie tyme, when neere 3,000 horse and foote are in service in these parts and to bee supplied partely from moneyes to be received by him [Pierce]'. Doubtless Vaughan would have answered that this was part of the problem – the interruption of normal government by the soldiery and the levying of taxation with menaces – but the seriousness of this dispute and its potential to undermine parliament's wider objectives in north Wales were made plain. As a result of their harmful influence, then, the Red Castle committee requested that those to whom they objected on the accounts sub-committee be removed and that Lloyd Pierce be released 'to follow his imployment for the supply of our armie'.

The use of Myddelton's 'exceptions' in this letter confirms the close working relationship between the Myddelton-Mytton military axis and the Montgomeryshire sequestration committee. This connection is further revealed when we examine the men who subscribed the letter. First among them, as might be expected, was Colonel Hugh Price, governor of Red Castle and veteran of Myddelton's military campaign.[69] However, he was now accompanied by Richard Price and Lodowick Myddelton. Richard Price came from Gunley in Montgomeryshire and was described by Lloyd Pierce as 'a true & reale friend of the Parliament'.[70] Richard Price's father, Edward, was an intimate of the Myddelton family before the war and also of their then servant, John Jones, addressing the future regicide in 1634 as 'my very loveing friend'.[71] His son, Richard, stood out as an early and active parliamentarian and had become a captain attached to Myddelton's forces by April 1644.[72] In April 1646 he assisted Mytton in taking Ruthin Castle and was involved in the clearing of north Wales's royalist garrisons and castles down to his appearance on the Montgomeryshire committee.[73] Price was also a member of the radical wing in the parliamentarian caucus, with no less a figure than Oliver Cromwell recommending him to parliament in 1649, noting how he was 'thoroughly acquainted with the sufferings of Capt. Richard Price for his affection to the parliament from the beginning ... being the only man in that county proclaimed rebel by the … king'.[74] Price also became an active member of the Fifth Monarchist Vavasor Powell's congregation. Lodowick Myddelton is a much less prominent figure but was probably a kinsman of his namesake Sir Thomas and possibly hailed from Churchstoke on the Montgomeryshire-Shropshire border. That he knew the major general is suggested by an entry in Sir Thomas's accounts of 1652 when he paid some men to go to Montgomeryshire with 'Mr Lodowicke Myddelton's son', to search for coal.[75]

That the dispute between Vaughan and Pierce was damaging wider parliamentarian aims is suggested by the fact that it seems to have registered in the national press. In early June 1646, the newsbook *Perfect Occurrences* related Thomas Mytton's successes in north Wales and the hopes that Flint Castle would soon surrender to parliament. However, the text then added that 'care is needfull to be had in Mountgomeryshire, that honest, tryed well affected men suffer not by camelions'.[76] This must have been a reference to the accounts sub-committee's 'persecution' of Pierce and his fellow committeemen. The reference to 'camelions' is telling, suggestive of those who changed colours when needed, and evidently referring to sometime royalist sympathisers who were now to be found among parliament's ranks. As Myddelton's 'exceptions' indicated, Edward Vaughan might be counted among such chameleonic politicians. It is also worth noting that *Perfect Occurrences* was produced by Henry Walker, an Independent supporter with connections to the New Model. Vaughan was exactly the kind of figure Walker would despise: a man of suspect political sympathies who was now harassing those who had been constant for the cause. It is intriguing to speculate whether Walker had noticed this case himself, or whether it had been fed to him by an interested party in London, perhaps by the earl of Pembroke. It is also worth noting that the Committee for North Wales in June 1646 was reporting, after the manner of Mytton's February letter, that Montgomeryshire was contributing little to the association's cause 'and will hereafter yeald us lesse if any at all', because Vaughan was 'opposeing the contribucions' of the county 'by informing and perswading the people that it is illegall and unwarrantable, although it bee not above halfe the contribucion which that county did pay to the enemy'.[77] Given this kind of 'support', it was perhaps small wonder that commentators might consider Vaughan as a dangerous 'camelion' in their fold.

The Montgomeryshire accounts sub-committee had been wrong-footed by the House of Lords' directive bailing Lloyd Pierce on 3 June. After receiving the order, its members wrote on 9 June to the central Accounts Committee describing how 'we are sought to be disenabled' and requested their advice and assistance.[78] They particularly asked that the central committee (a number of whom were MPs) 'disabuse ye House of Peeres and … represent thinges truly to their Lordships on our behalfe'. They clearly felt that the wool had been pulled over the Lords' eyes in the account they had received of Lloyd Pierce's case. Given the extent to which they had been misinformed, Vaughan, More and their fellow sub-committee members requested that the Lords be persuaded to rescind their order for Pierce's bail, 'which we conceive was indirectly gotten and may be prejudicially applied by Sir T[homas] Middletons commissioners heere (who consist for the most part of ye souldiers, persons of no visible fortunes in these parts and lyable to accompt)'. This was a nice summary not only of the sub-committee's objections to those of the sequestration committee, but also of the wider body of Presbyterian-inspired criticism focusing on county committees and military rule. In short, the accountants requested that their parent body 'vindicate us, who have done nothing heerein … but in pursuance of ye ordinance and of your directions'.

Reinforcing their message and evidently pursuing a comprehensive strategy, on the same day that they wrote to the central Accounts Committee, the sub-committeemen also addressed a letter to the Speaker of the House of Lords, the Presbyterian peer, the earl of Manchester.[79] They noted that Pierce had made it appear that he was imprisoned by Edward Vaughan for attempting to execute sequestration committee's order over title to Llwydiarth, rather than for problems related to the production of his accounts, but that 'there was noe grownd at all for that suggestion'. They referred to their request that the central accounts committee 'informe your Lordshipps rightly herin' and asked that the peers' order, 'so indirectly gotten', be recalled as otherwise 'such use be made therof as may preiudice the service wherewith we are intrusted'. The subscribers, Vaughan prominent among them, must have hoped that their use of the language of public service and probity would have some traction with the Lords who were, generally, minded to side against the Independent-leaning county committees. For all their invocation of the public interest, however, Edward Vaughan was surely desperate to stop Pierce testifying before the London sequestration committee about his own possession of Llwydiarth. Yet, even here, we should be wary of seeing matters simply in personal terms. If Pierce and his committee got their hands on Llwydiarth then the resources available for supporting the local military and their own authority would have been significantly augmented. Edward Vaughan's possession of Llwydiarth was not just good news for his own coffers, it also acted as a break on Independent-army power in the region and bolstered that of their moderate Presbyterian opponents.

The Vaughan–Pierce/accounts–sequestrations feud was swept up into the wider dynamics of factional politics at Westminster as the Montgomeryshire sequestration committee also wrote to the Lords about their efforts to execute the 3 June order.[80] They informed their lordships that they had taken sureties as high as £40,000 for Lloyd Pierce's appearance before the central sequestration committee and so had gone to Montgomery Castle requesting his release. However, the sub-committee's marshal, Howell Evans, was told not to hand him over unless he received an order from Edward Vaughan and the rest of the committee. Three sequestration committeemen, Hugh Price, Evan Lloyd and Lodowick Myddelton, then went to Montgomery themselves, 'declaring the want the Generall Colonel Mitton and the army under his command in north Wales were in, for want of the liberty of ... Lloyd Pierce ... concerning which the Gennerall & the rest of the Committee of North Wales residing with the army had written two letters ... unto ... Mr [Edward] Vaughan ... shewing them the bond of forty thousand pounds which they had taken'. Even after this show of strength, however, Vaughan and his colleagues refused to release Pierce, so the Red Castle committee requested the Lords' intervention to ensure the execution of their own order. The confluence of the Mytton-army-sequestration committee interest here is striking and underlines the way in which the battle lines drawn between the committees at Powis and Montgomery castles ramified into the wider region, into the war effort in north Wales and, ultimately, into Westminster itself.

On 20 June 1646, the House of Lords read the letters it had received from the two committees in Montgomeryshire concerning 'Mr Peire Floyd [*sic*] and Mr Vaughan'.[81] The House determined to turn the letters over to the central Committee of Accounts, asking them to examine the matter and make a report. Lloyd Pierce was disconcerted by his case being handed over to his enemies, and he requested an opportunity to 'answeare for myself before you', clearly fearing the narrative of recent events in Montgomeryshire that would be spun in his absence.[82] He also concluded his letter with an interesting construction, requesting to 'have my liberties (so much insisted upon by every free borne subject)'. While such formulations were not the preserve of the radical parliamentarian wing, they were nonetheless characteristic of the discourse associated with figures like John Lilburne in his struggles with the House of Lords. This may be a tantalising hint of the kind of radical language that was percolating through army-supporting networks and which had perhaps by now reached into eastern Wales.

The central Committee of Accounts adjudicated in an even-handed manner in the business on 30 June 1646.[83] They reported that Pierce had agreed to deliver his accounts over to Montgomery Castle and to meet any outstanding sums which might be found when his audit was concluded. He was to be released. They requested of their Montgomeryshire agents that 'yow mittigate his fine that soe your proceedings may not seeme violent and [so will] stop the mouthes of all those that clamour against yow here & elce where'. This is a fascinating indication that the case was generating public interest and, indeed, causing outrage, in London and beyond. This is intriguing because there are few traces of the controversy in print, the source material routinely used in current scholarship as a metric for gauging levels of political engagement and controversy. Rather, it seems, and as it was characterised in the committee's report, that the clamour was to be found in heated gossip and oral argument, and probably in the indignation vented in the corridors and committee rooms of Westminster. It would be enormously helpful to know who constituted Pierce's 'frends and agents' in London, but these remain shadowy figures, although Sir Thomas Myddelton might well be one candidate. The central committee's missive also suggests its own delicate role in these proceedings. While it was not necessarily afraid of controversy, rank partisanship and disproportionate, even excessive, targeting and punishment of individuals its agencies investigated, faction and personal interest rather than public accountability did not reflect well on its work. Moreover, it was difficult to make the case that county committees were acting arbitrarily and contrary to natural law and justice when one's own agents were meting out heavy fines and swift imprisonment and were failing to respect parliamentary orders.

The wrangling over Lloyd Pierce's accounts and his incarceration in Montgomery Castle dragged on into the summer of 1646. The Montgomeryshire accounts sub-committee contested that Pierce was not complying fully with their requests for information, while Pierce, for his part, maintained that his adversaries were refusing to comply with the directives that he be released.[84] Pierce wrote a series of stinging letters to the central Accounts Committee appealing for their intervention with a local body which he suggested had gone rogue.[85] In one missive he provided an intriguing account of the basis for his contest with the squire of Llwydiarth.[86] Pierce maintained that his poor treatment was:

> all by the malice (since I am first to speake it) of one man ever, Mr Vaughan, my profest enemy, who, being the chairman of the committee, the rest in truth noe other than his servants, who was pleased to utter even within his house as I am told, that for all my labour & appealing unto you, I should be as far from obteyning my libertie now as I was at first. The grownd of his malice towards me is but troublesome unto you to heare related, it being comon in every mans eare abroad the countrey, that not my accompts or contempts (which it greive me not a litle upon his misinformation I am sure to find presented in your letter(?) to the House of Lords) but former discourtesie had brought this trouble upon me.

Pierce requested their protection from 'such violent proceedings not to be paraleld againe in the kingdome', and asked for his enlargement by the agency of an 'indifferent man of the committee if it may be besids Mr Vaughan, or I beleeve your labour will be fruitles & my captivity endles'.

Despite Pierce's claim that the grounds of their dispute were in 'every mans eare', in fact the nature of this 'former discourtesie' between Pierce and Vaughan remains unclear even in the voluminous correspondence surrounding their case. It served Pierce's turn to present the contest as personal, grounded upon no more than individual malice and without any wider merit or substance. Yet it does seem that we are dealing with a clash of personalities which was grounded on older enmities. The pair's animosity might have been tied up with the matter of Lloyd Pierce's daughter, Deiley, who, in January 1641 married Andrew Phillips, son of Frances, Edward Vaughan's secret wife, by her first marriage. Deiley died in August 1643 leaving a daughter (technically Edward Vaughan's step-granddaughter), but by the terms of the marriage settlement, Pierce claimed he should have received £500 from the settlement's trustees, Frances, Simon Thelwall the elder and Edward Vaughan himself. However, they had taken possession of the deeds relating to this transaction and refused to hand over any of the money.[87] There is no clear evidence that this was indeed the source of Pierce and Vaughan's enmity, but it is noteworthy that the two men were transacting such family business on the eve of the civil wars, and that this had turned sour at a point when Edward Vaughan fled the county. Whatever the root of their antagonism, however, we should not see their civil war confrontation as emptied of wider ideological concerns. With the Powis Castle interest eclipsed, these were now the two most powerful men in the county who were using the agencies of state, their own committees, the standing committees in London, and parliament itself, in a struggle to exercise the new dispensation of parliamentary power in eastern Wales, but also to define and delimit the nature of that power and its ideological tenor. The stakes of their dispute were high indeed.

By the end of July Pierce was submitting his fourth appeal for freedom and the central Accounts Committee was getting queasy about the optics of the dispute. On 31 July 1646, they wrote to the Montgomeryshire sub-committee requesting that 'since the eye of the whole country is bent upon your proceedings in this cause and that there are many clamours against yow … of your hard dealings towards him, that yow would mitigate the rigor of your proceedings' and release Pierce.[88] Once again it seems that the public interest in this case was measured differently by these participants compared with those who wrote newsbooks, which are silent on the matter. Their letter is explicit, however, that there was widespread scrutiny of, and interest in, the damaging row in the county, and that this wider interest was making the Cornhill Committee deeply uncomfortable. It doubtless did not calm nerves in the Accounts Committee's meetings, then, that Vaughan and his associates replied to their request that they had 'put on a resolution to neglect clamour and calumny (whereof wee were since beforehand to have our share in ye discharge of our trust we might have been long since induced to desist from our duties)'.[89] Controversy was evidently also swirling in the locality, then, but the sub-committee presented itself as determined to press on with its mission in a spirit of public duty. They clearly felt that larger forces were at work than simply Pierce's accounting practices, and saw this as a test case for their authority in the area. As we shall see in a moment, they may have had in mind contemporary discussions in parliament which were then considering reforming the government of north Wales and which seemed designed to undermine the authority of committees such as theirs. They resolved to send their registrar, William Barbour, to London to give the central committee a full narrative of the matter, to address the duplicity of Pierce and of those 'yt abbett him', which meant that the central Accounts Committee 'seem not to discover so well as we could wish' that they were being hoodwinked. Clearly the sub-committee considered Pierce's case as key to their supervisory authority not just over the Montgomeryshire situation, but also over the wider military effort in north Wales. The idea that there were shadowy figures assisting Pierce, and wider problems of deception and malfeasance in the north Wales army which were being hidden from them, suggests a conspiratorial mindset among Vaughan and his colleagues which heightened their paranoia and made them unwilling to yield up the lynchpin that could unlock the wider machinery of corruption in the military establishment.

The central Accounts Committee's patience was running out, however. On 3 August, they once again requested that Pierce be bailed and his fine remitted, adding 'if you shall faile in the executing of the premisses to avoyde all further clamors, wee shall send upp for him hither and proceede with him according to the ordinances'.[90] Mindful of the obdurate resistance he was meeting in the county, in a letter which must have been penned shortly before the central committee's own dispatch arrived in the country, Pierce himself had actually requested that the central committee 'take my case into your owne hands', for he was sure that Vaughan's evasions would 'keepe me a prisoner here this twelve moneth'.[91]

As promised, the Montgomeryshire accounts sub-committee sent its registrar William Barbour to London, but it also provided the Central Accounts Committee with a lengthy narrative of the case regarding 'this troublesome buisnesse of Mr Lloyd Pierce', which was intended to act as a framework to help them better understand Barbour's presentation of the situation.[92] The work was also designed, the sub-committee averred, 'to vindicate us from a paper subscribed by some of Sir Thomas Midletons comissioners', which may refer to a version of the 'exceptions' that the sequestrators subscribed in February, or which might relate to a lost position paper circulated subsequently. Whatever the case, the construction of this opposition paper coming from 'Mideltons comissioners' underlines once more the close connection between the ex-major general and the agitation against Vaughan and his allies. The lengthy paper which accompanied Barbour to the central Accounts Committee may have been intended to elucidate matters in Montgomeryshire, but it was, in fact, a dense, elusive and tendentious narrative which attempted, rather unsuccessfully, to make Pierce's reluctance to accommodate the sub-committee's requests to examine sequestration records at their leisure in Montgomery Castle seem like an egregious evasion or breach of public trust. The sub-committee was also shaken by how much Pierce's 'storye of the divisions & factions of this countie' had 'found more credit with yow then is compatible with yt iust esteem and incouragement which our wary proceedings and faithfull endeavours in this buisiness ... we thought might deserve at your handes'.

The central committee now sent their agent down to the country in an effort to resolve the damaging impasse, and simultaneously dispatched further messages via Barbour repeating their order that Pierce be set at liberty.[93] Despite these initiatives, however, Pierce remained stuck in a kind of limbo at the mercy of his 'implacable adversaries' who manufactured delays and contrived excuses to keep him prisoner and stop him venturing up to the capital.[94] He was anxious about the 'sundry invectives pluckt up against me' by William Barbour in London, and the manner in which his adversaries sought to 'inflame the world against me', and he begged the central committee to 'beleeve no sinster reporte of me or my actions'. Pierce was concerned that 'the great distance of place & my present condition hath disabled me really to possess you with' the full details of his case and the justness of his cause. Questions of narrative, presentation, distance and perception were important in the conduct of this business, as the perceptual distance between London and Montgomeryshire meant that it was important to maintain lines of communication and to have an effective narrative to spin. This produced the intense exchange of letters between the parties in Wales and the central committee in London, and it is perhaps curious that no printed texts around this issue were produced to influence wider opinion and make pitches for supporting the partisan interpretations of recent events in Montgomeryshire.[95] Whatever the reason for this, the clash between the Montgomeryshire committees reminds us that serious disputes which were understood to be on a public stage, before the 'eye of the whole country', could be conducted in a realm that did not overly trouble the gushing presses of the 1640s.

In early September 1646, the Montgomeryshire sub-committee finally transmitted Lloyd Pierce to London.[96] His absence there saw the political temperature briefly drop in the country as he prepared two sets of accounts for scrutiny.[97] These accounts were transmitted back to Montgomeryshire, and the central committee invited Vaughan and his associates to produce any 'surcharge' they could find against him.[98] As we shall see in the next chapter, this would produce a whole new set of proceedings and confrontations when Pierce returned to the country. However, in the interim another breach had emerged between the Montgomeryshire sub-committee on the one hand and Colonel Thomas Mytton and his military establishment on the other.

Administrative reorganisation and tax resistance in north Wales, July–October 1646

This confrontation was, in fact, the continuation of the resistance by Edward Vaughan and his allies to the heavy taxes being levied by the Committee for North Wales to support the army. It was also a product of the administrative uncertainties which attended the parliamentarian government of north Wales after Sir Thomas Myddelton's return to Westminster. As we have seen, whereas Mytton felt that the Committee for North Wales had an executive role for the association, Vaughan and his allies saw it as an ad hoc body with no legitimacy, in thrall to the army and lacking legislative authority. These questions seem to have caused some pause for thought at Westminster. Thus it was that on 22 July 1646, John Glynne, London's recorder who hailed from Glynllifon in Caernarvonshire and who was an ally of the Myddelton-Mytton interest, was asked by the Commons 'to bring in an ordinance for the better establishing the affairs of North Wales, for putting the ordinances of parliament in execution, and for settling a preaching ministry there'.[99] It was also proposed to establish a standing committee of the House 'to take notice of, and overview the actions of, the several committees of those counties; and to consider of members of this House to go into those counties, and to prepare instructions for them'. Evidently some kind of administrative reorganisation was being envisaged for north Wales, which suggests a recognition that there were serious problems there which needed addressing. The newsbook *Perfect Diurnall* is helpful in clarifying things, noting that the House debated 'the government of Northwales and how all ordinances of parliament may be executed in those parts, and upon special reasons ordered that an ordinance should be brought in for constituting committees there, and one committee to supervise the rest'.[100] This report suggests that the criticisms of the current dispensation articulated by Vaughan and his associates may have had some resonance in Westminster, and the desire to manufacture a more integrated and coherent system of local administration seems to have been behind the initiative. The reference to a single supervisory committee, however, also suggests that this proposal may have been designed partly to give legitimacy to the de facto role of the Committee for North Wales as the supreme executive body of the North Wales Association, and to address criticism from army opponents, such as Vaughan and his allies, that it lacked legislative authority. The problem was, however, that this initiative came to nothing and no such ordinance appeared. Thus the ambiguous lines of parliamentary authority in north Wales continued, and the problem of contending factions and committees flared back into life with Mytton's money raising efforts in Montgomeryshire.

In August 1646, the Committee for North Wales had imposed a tax of £800 per month on Montgomeryshire to support the four current sieges and the nine garrisons that the army had in the field. The county's accounts sub-committee, however, had issued warrants prohibiting the assessment and payment of this money. As a result Thomas Mytton wrote to them so that there would be 'noe thuartinge [i.e. thwarting] amongst you nor any stopp made by yow which will exceedingly preiudice and indanger the publicke service'.[101] Mytton attempted to reassure them that he would 'ease the cuntrey of many of the unnesseary garrisons & reduce the charge to a farre lesse some with all possible speed', but exhorted the accountants to continue their support for the army 'for the reduceinge the rest of the association'. He added, somewhat threateningly, that he could provide three troops of horse to assist in levying money from those who proved refractory in the county. The continued burden of taxation for supporting the various parliamentarian forces was a significant cause of Presbyterian anger and resentment. As we shall see, this burden broke out into open mutiny and resistance in Montgomeryshire and other parts of Wales in early 1647, but it was clearly a cause of rancour and resentment long before then. This was, moreover, also bound up with the ideological fissures which separated the Independent and Presbyterian groups, and, in north Wales, was also connected to the administrative, jurisdictional and personal divisions which divided the Montgomeryshire sub-committee from the Committee for North Wales.[102]

The sub-committee's response was uncompromising.[103] They maintained that they had 'done both this poore countie and our selves but right' in 'freeing' the county of the £800 per month levied as part of the weekly assessment to this point. This tax, they claimed, had no 'legal warrant' beyond 'the exigencie of that tyme where in it was imposed', and was never to be continued so long than this 'apparent necessitie' and until other parts of the association could assist with contribution. This was not, however, simply an unwarranted burden, the Montgomeryshire men maintained, it was jurisdictional overreach by a body that had no legislative sanction. The sub-committee declared themselves unsatisfied as to the authority by which the sum was 'layed one this countie by the gentlemen of the Committee of Denbigh, soe wee must protest our dislike of such an act'. The sub-committee seemed to be taking advantage of the jurisdictional uncertainties of the parliamentary administration in north Wales, for the Committee for North Wales was only an expedient adopted under Mytton's command; that it sat in Denbighshire and was sometimes called the 'committee for Denbigh' only added to the confusion.

There was, however, a more fundamental point behind the sub-committee's position which overlapped with the stillborn parliamentary plans to pass an ordinance for north Wales. The basic question articulated by the sub-committee was: upon what authority did Mytton claim the right to impose taxes on Montgomeryshire when he had no legislative authority to do so? In their reply, the sub-committee continued bluntly that they would 'use noe arguments of performation or incurraigement to any to pay' the assessment, although they were careful to affirm that they would assist with collecting monies 'limited by the ordinance of parliament for the weekely asseassment'. The sub-committeemen noted that they had strained the county's resources to defeat the royalists when such arguments from necessity could be made, but that such reasoning no longer held as there was no 'necessary obligation upon the countrey still to beare yt'. They ended with a strident declaration of the burdens which Montgomeryshire had suffered in supporting the war as the first county in the region to come under parliament's authority, but also of their resistance to Mytton's continued calling on their purses:

> for the reduction of the whole association which, beeinge duly wayed
> by you, wee hope you will bee well advised upon what ground you levie
> moneyes by force of armes, and seriously consider whether you cane

> justifie a course of violence in this particular, beinge not warranted by
> any lawe or ordinance as wee conceave.

This was a reference to Mytton's offer of soldiers to assist in collecting of
taxes in Montgomeryshire, which summoned the image of unauthorised
and unregulated army power that could also be found in earlier papers
associated with Vaughan and the accountants. The sub-committeemen
declared themselves 'redie to serve all your reasonable desires', but their
reply was an uncompromising declaration of resistance to Mytton's
authority and to that of the Committee for North Wales. In some ways
this response was another aspect of the accountants' confrontation with
Lloyd Pierce and the sequestrators who had been conjured into being
by the army, and whose *raison d'être* was to support it with funds from
delinquents' estates.

The issue of local taxation was again present in another letter of
9 October 1646 from the Montgomeryshire accountants to the central
Accounts Committee.[104] Having received the directive to produce a
surcharge against Pierce, the usual problem of gaining access to records
in Red Castle had once again raised its head. The accountants had also
requested several other officers to appear before them, presumably
to attest to their accounts as part of Myddelton's forces, although
one, Lieutenant Lovingham, did not appear. When they attempted to
apprehend him, Lovingham was rescued by a party of horse 'and our
messenger abused'. The tensions between the accounts sub-committee
and the military were, then, very much in evidence, and this becomes
even more understandable when we learn that these forces had been sent
by Mytton to levy the £800 monthly assessment for his forces, which
the sub-committeemen had refused. Their letter complained about the
soldiers' presence, 'by what lawe or ordinance wee knowe not, and yt
by soldiers of noe visible fortunes, the said Loveingham being one of
them, there being as yet noe sherriff appointed for this countie and the
soldiers soe potent heere'. In this letter, then, Vaughan and his allies were
articulating concerns familiar from their January 1646 petition about the
lack of settlement in the county, the power of the soldiery, the uncertain
nature of parliamentary authority in north Wales and of the proper lines

of control, and the absence of a sheriff. The last point again suggested that Vaughan and his allies were looking to the possibility of gaining local superiority through an election to fill the vacant local seats in parliament. They probably knew that pressure for such a move was already being applied in parliament by their Presbyterian allies and the local tensions which have been described in this chapter morphed in a battle over the recruiter seats of Montgomeryshire and Montgomery Boroughs. It is this battle which forms the focus of the next chapter.

CHAPTER 6

The Army, Civilians and Parliamentary Elections, October 1646–April 1647

The previous chapter discussed how Edward Vaughan and his allies emerged as a significant political force in parliamentary politics in north Wales in the mid-1640s. Vaughan's role as chair of the sub-committee of accounts provided him with an institutional base for promoting a moderate Presbyterian settlement in the region, for crossing the interests of the army and its associated committees, and also for defending his claim to Llwydiarth. His confrontation with Myddelton, Mytton and Lloyd Pierce was something of a set piece in the developing hostilities between the Presbyterian and Independent groups as they emerged in the region although, as previously mentioned, these were not monolithic categories and each group's members did not share a single set of religious and political attitudes. Indeed, a figure like Myddelton was a political Presbyterian at Westminster, but in north Wales his personal connections and army connections meant that he could often be found associating with Independents such as his former servant John Jones.

The present chapter develops the themes introduced in the previous section by charting, for the first time, how such personal and ideological confrontations developed in north Wales between 1646 and 1647. It discusses in particular the efforts to secure parliamentary seats in Montgomeryshire in an effort to promote the respective political programmes of the two major parliamentarian factions. The chapter provides a comprehensive analysis of these elections, arguing that they demonstrate how the rancorous local politics of 1646 fed into clashes at the hustings in early 1647. Ultimately, Edward Vaughan and his Presbyterian and anti-army allies prevailed in these contests. These divisions transferred to Westminster, however, which became a new venue for the quarrel between Edward Vaughan and Sir Thomas Myddelton. The chapter explores these confrontations in the Commons and discusses how Vaughan managed to hang onto his seat in the face of attacks by old enemies, while his close ally George Devereux was removed from the House by his Independent antagonists.

Edward Vaughan, George Devereux and articles of delinquency, November 1646

The requests from Vaughan and his allies for the appointment of a sheriff in Montgomeryshire in both their January 1646 petition and their 9 October 1646 letter to the Committee for Taking the Accounts of the Kingdom, argue for a consistent effort to gain a voice in parliament and to restore a semblance of peacetime local government which could counterbalance the authority of the military-allied committees. It appears that the 9 October letter was adding momentum to a Westminster effort that was already in train, for on 24 October 1646 the Commons nominated Rowland Hunt of Shrewsbury as Montgomeryshire's sheriff, a nomination that the Lords endorsed a few days later.[1] Hunt's appointment was something of a victory for Vaughan and his Presbyterian associates. Rowland was the brother of Colonel Thomas Hunt, an active member of the Shropshire county committee alongside Vaughan associate Samuel More, and a man who, in October 1645, had himself been elected as the recruiter MP for Shrewsbury.[2] Thomas was a convinced religious Presbyterian who married the daughter of Edward Owen of Woodhouse, a member of the Montgomeryshire accounts sub-committee. The sheriff, Rowland, was a barrister who perhaps met Edward Vaughan in London's legal circles; he became Shrewsbury town clerk in November 1645.[3] Also noteworthy was the identity of Rowland Hunt's deputy as sheriff, Evan

Vaughan, who was a close ally of his namesake, Edward. Evan Vaughan had signed the January 1646 county petition; had submitted a deposition to the Montgomeryshire accounts sub-committee against Sir Thomas Myddelton's conduct after the Battle of Montgomery; was targeted by the Montgomeryshire sequestrators as a delinquent alongside Edward Vaughan in November 1646; and would appear as a material witness on Edward's behalf in a lawsuit during the Commonwealth.[4] These appointments were thus highly conducive to the prospective Presbyterian electoral interest in Montgomeryshire and represented a setback for the sequestrators and the pro-army faction.

Sensing that an important moment was approaching with a new election likely in the county, Lloyd Pierce gained leave from the central Accounts Committee and returned to Montgomeryshire at the end of October 1646. He was joined by new personnel on the sequestration committee, Colonels Roger Pope and John Jones.[5] Both military men had close ties with Thomas Mytton and his campaigns in north Wales, and both were also members of the Committee for North Wales.[6] In addition, Jones was an Independent and a convinced religious radical. Pope and Jones probably journeyed to Montgomeryshire to help bolster the sequestration faction in the forthcoming election and were doubtless accompanied by some of their military forces. The move against their local adversaries came soon after Lloyd Pierce's return from London, and, on 3 November 1646, the 'agent' or solicitor for the sequestration committee, Lewis Price, submitted articles of delinquency against Edward Vaughan and George Devereux.[7] Price had operated as the sequestration committee's agent since 1645, and it is likely that he was the squire of Pertheirin (Llanwnog) and the brother (or at least a close relation) of Hugh Price, Red Castle's governor.[8] The submission of these articles was something of a pre-emptive strike, as both of Price's targets would stand as candidates in the forthcoming parliamentary elections, but both would, of course, be disabled if they were found to be delinquents. Certainly, Edward Vaughan was convinced that 'adiudging him to be a delinquent was only a practise to prevent him to be chosen knight for the countie'.[9] It may also be worth noting that the death of the Presbyterian peer the earl of Essex in September 1646 may have emboldened the sequestrators to make such a move. Devereux in particular, of course, had family connections with Essex and the earl's death may have cleared a potential obstacle in moving against him.

Most of the charges against Vaughan were familiar from Myddelton's 'exceptions' of the previous February and, as we shall see, this was unsurprising as it seems that Myddelton was a moving force behind this new attack. Indeed, back in September 1646, Lewis Price had journeyed to London seeking guidance from the sequestration committee at Goldsmiths' Hall on delinquency cases in the county, and, while before them, he had queried whether his committee could move against Vaughan upon the basis of witness statements that had already been collected.[10] The central committee responded unequivocally that Vaughan should be proceeded against as a delinquent. In his charges of 3 November, Price accused Vaughan of residing at Oxford when it was the enemy's headquarters; of erecting a garrison in Montgomeryshire without any commission and illegally extracting money from the local population; and of disobeying the central sequestration committee's orders to yield Llwydiarth up to the state. An interesting charge among Price's list was that Vaughan, while at Oxford, had supposedly complained against Lord Powis and Sir James Palmer controlling Llwydiarth. Price claimed that as Powis was the earl of Pembroke's first cousin and Palmer was Pembroke's servant, so Vaughan had tried to persuade the king to endorse his own claim to the estate and thus free up its resources from the influence of the powerful parliamentarian peer. Bringing Pembroke into the equation in late 1646 is notable because, as we have seen, he was connected to Herbert Vaughan's wardship and was a potential ally of the war party in Montgomeryshire.[11] Moreover, just over a week before Price issued his delinquency charges, Pembroke had been nominated as Montgomeryshire's lord lieutenant in Essex's place.[12] Dragging Pembroke into the mix seems like a gambit designed to pit Vaughan's interests against one of the most powerful parliamentarian figures in Welsh politics, although we can only speculate as to whether this was done with Pembroke's knowledge or endorsement.

George Devereux had not been a target of Myddelton's 'exceptions' in February 1646 as he was not then a member of the accounts sub-committee. The delinquency charges of November were, nevertheless, cut from familiar cloth for such accusations in this region, and focused on allegations of royalist sympathies during the war. Devereux was accused of supporting the royalist cause and was said to have taken Lord Capel's 1643 royalist oath. He was also alleged to have received a commission from the king and to have railed against his kinsman, the earl of Essex, after the Battle of Edgehill in October 1642, 'calling him traytor and cuckold and using many other base reviling termes'. Price's charges even had Devereux supporting the king's cause after Montgomeryshire's reduction through his correspondence with royalist forces at Caus Castle in Shropshire. We have no independent corroboration for these charges, although depositions supporting them were submitted from a variety of ex-royalists who perhaps had been induced by promises of favourable dealing at the sequestration committee's hands to turn against Devereux.[13]

Vaughan and his allies did not tarry in returning fire. On 5 November 1646, Lewis Price was apprehended by the sub-committee's agents in Welshpool, supposedly for refusing to attest to his accounts, although Price argued that he had tried to finalise them on eight separate occasions but that the sub-committee had continually postponed their meetings.[14] For their part, the accountants accused Price of 'contemptiously neglect[ing] to appear', and they fined him £40 and put him in gaol.[15] Vaughan and his allies complained to the Cornhill Committee that the sequestrators had:

> with fource ... (upon ye same pretences formerly questioned and cleered
> before your selves upon a full debate of the buisnesse prosecuted by Sir
> Thomas Middleton and his agents) secured the estates of some of this
> committee, and soe by consequence, as much as in them lyes, indeavour
> to dashe our imployment.[16]

The sequestration agents, they added, openly defied their officers, 'which proves a great incouragement to ye rest of the soldiery to doe the like'.

Writs of election and factional confrontation, November 1646

Amidst this renewed skirmishing in the county the starting gun for the electoral contest was fired in earnest on 11 November 1646 when parliament issued warrants for new elections in both the vacant county and borough seats, with the writs being issued two days later.[17] These writs almost certainly came down to the country relatively quickly, although the sheriff was not sworn until 25 November. But here the advantage of having the sheriff as one's ally came into play, for the county election was then delayed for three months, while the borough contest would not be held until April 1647. Presumably after being sworn in as sheriff (by Edward Vaughan no less!) Rowland Hunt played a long game, waiting for the most advantageous moment for his associates in the factional melee which engulfed Montgomeryshire over the next few weeks.

A letter from Robert Poley (or 'Poole' or 'Pooley') of Welshpool written on 25 November 1646 provides a fascinating insight into the dynamics surrounding the electoral contest. Poley's connection with Montgomeryshire almost certainly derived from Sir James Palmer, whose mother was a Poley.[18] Poley's letter was addressed to the Cornish Presbyterian MP Francis Buller, who had inherited estates in Montgomeryshire in the 1630s. It seems that Poley acted as Buller's steward on the manor of Ystrad Marchell in Welshpool.[19] Poley informed Buller that 'many souldiers' were drawn to Welshpool 'to what purpose I know not, but heering great adoe about eleccion, Mr Ed[ward] Vaughan stands for knight & Mr Charles Lloyd for burgesse. I shall performe your direccons in this to the full; the sheriff is to be sworne today'.[20] It is notable that Poley described a 'great adoe' about the election, which indicates not only a degree of politicking, excitement and gossip about the event, but also the prospect of a contest. Importantly, he also confirms that Vaughan's candidacy for the shire seat was public knowledge and this frames our understanding of his adversaries' moves against him which were already in train at the time of Poley's writing. The prospective candidate for the borough seat, Charles Lloyd, was the squire of Moel-y-Garth and St Stephen's Walbrook in London. He was a wealthy merchant and Vaughan's kinsman, who had provided Vaughan with substantial financial assistance during his legal campaigns against the Herberts. It seems, however, that Poley was misinformed about the borough seat, or at least that the dynamics of the contest shifted after his writing, for it was soon understood that George Devereux and not Charles Lloyd was seeking the burgesship.

The fact that it was Devereux rather than Lloyd who was the likely Presbyterian candidate for the borough seat is indicated by the county sequestrators' efforts to imprison the former. Witnesses against Devereux were deposed between 13 and 16 November, among whose number was Lloyd Pierce himself.[21] On the basis of these examinations, Lloyd Pierce, Hugh Price, Roger Pope and John Jones (whom Devereux characterised as 'these 4 confederate commissioners') signed an order on 16 November to secure Devereux's house at Vaynor which was to be appraised for his sequestration.[22] At this point, and probably hoping to bolster his supporters and allies in the county after concluding the reduction of Conway,[23] Major General Thomas Mytton arrived in Montgomeryshire at the head of a substantial military force. Among Vaughan's muniments is an intriguing scrap of paper: an examination he took on 20 November 1646, acting as a Justice of the Peace, of one John Mottershed, a member of Captain Gerald Barbour's troop.[24] This brief but dramatic examination had Mottershed acknowledging that Mytton was expected to arrive at Powis Castle that evening accompanied by 500 foot and 300 horse 'to lay seige against the Castle of Mountgomery'. Mottershed refused to witness the examination, however, 'and saith hee will dye first'.[25] This, then, seems to be evidence taken from an unwilling witness about the use of unauthorised military force against the centre of Presbyterian power in the county. Although no such action came to pass, the examination nevertheless testifies to the tense atmosphere in the county following Mytton's arrival; a tension which seems to have blossomed into conspiracy and intrigue.

The hostilities between the two local factions were expressed more soberly in a letter Mytton wrote to the central Accounts Committee three days later.[26] This concerned the sub-committee's efforts to examine some of his soldiers, including Lieutenant Lovingham who was mentioned at the end of chapter 5.[27] Mytton asserted that he would be happy to make his men available for examination 'now it hath pleased God to bringe the worke of north Wales so neare unto an end'. However, he was determined that the central committee should hear the complaints being directed at their local agents regarding 'how they imprison men & fine them & will not suffer them to come to theire answere'. Mytton proceeded with an explicit denunciation of the sub-committee's wider agenda, maintaining that:

> under pretence of doinge the state service, they aime at the overthrow of my forces, unto which end the gentlemen of the comittee [at Red Castle] & my self cannot send anie to gather the weeklie paie, but they call them presentlie before them … That I cannot have money to discharge my souldiers … they forbid the countrey to paie anie more contribution.[28]

He concluded, 'all that I desire is that I maie keepe my forces together till I receive orders from the honourable howse of comons how to dispose of them', and that the 'hindrance of me & my soldiers' was seriously impeding him in his commission. This was a stark portrait of the breakdown in relations between the pro-military faction and their Presbyterian opponents, and provides a striking local manifestation of the wider ideological frictions which emerged with the prospect of an uncertain peace that was coming into view. The Welsh theatre of the war was unusual in that it continued for so long after arms had been laid down elsewhere: Mytton was still fighting many months after King Charles I had surrendered himself up to the Scots, for example. The military, then, remained an active part of the political landscape in north Wales when debates were moving on to settlement and negotiation in the rest of the kingdom. It is also the case that, although Mytton's army operated under Sir Thomas Fairfax's authority, it was a separate force from the New Model Army and had its own local dynamics and imperatives.

While Mytton and the sequestration committee were making sallies against their prospective electoral opponents, an unusual parliamentary initiative suggests that Vaughan was attempting a novel move of his own to outmanoeuvre them. On 21 November 1646, a motion was put in the House of Commons that 'Edward Vaughan shall stand in the committee for Mountgomeryshire'.[29] This motion immediately followed an unsuccessful effort to have Vaughan's relatives Simon Thelwall the elder, Edward Thelwall of Glantanat and Robert Wynne of Voylas added to the Denbighshire committee (perhaps referring to the Committee for North Wales). It is unfortunate that we do not know who sponsored these motions, but it was possibly Vaughan's relation Simon Thelwall the younger, although another candidate is Thomas More, Samuel's brother. It was clearly a Presbyterian effort to gain inroads into the army's powerbase in north Wales.

Whoever was responsible for the initiative, however, it appears that Vaughan was trying to get himself appointed to the very body that was investigating his own delinquency as well as his ownership of Llwydiarth! The Montgomeryshire committee was, however, small and usually only Lloyd Pierce and Hugh Price were its active members, although the recent appearance of John Jones and Robert Pope had changed these dynamics somewhat. Vaughan's appointment could thus have paralysed the committee's business as well as its support for Mytton's forces; perhaps Mytton's letter of 23 November was written with some awareness of Vaughan's parliamentary initiative in mind. The matter of Vaughan's appointment was put to the question in the House and was narrowly defeated, by 59 votes to 53. The rabidly partisan nature of this stratagem, however, can be read off from the tellers on either side of the division. The tellers supporting Vaughan's appointment were Anthony Nicoll, member for Bodmin and colleague of Francis Buller, who was impeached by the New Model as one of eleven Presbyterian members in July 1647, and 'Mr Bence', probably Alexander Bence, or possibly Squier Bence, who were both Presbyterians excluded at Pride's Purge in December 1648.[30] The tellers against Vaughan's appointment, however, were leading Independent hardliners, Sir Arthur Haselrig and no less a figure than Oliver Cromwell. This is a graphic illustration of the ideological divisions that had come to characterise the Montgomeryshire hostilities, but also of the way in which Vaughan's case was now a matter of national as well as 'simply' local concern, a matter which braided together personal imperatives and partisan parliamentary politics.

Edward Vaughan's arrest and imprisonment

Back in Montgomeryshire and bolstered by the presence of Mytton and his forces, on 24 November the Red Castle committee issued a warrant for the sequestration as delinquents of five members of the accounts sub-committee, including Edward Vaughan and George Devereux.[31] The warrant made the unusual provision that 'publicke notice' of the order was to be given in Llanfyllin on the next market day. On the same day as the sequestrators issued their warrant, a group of the accounts sub-committee, who confusingly now styled themselves 'the committee for sequestrations for the countie of Mountgomery', ordered George Devereux's discharge from sequestration.

What was happening here? It appears that those who signed this order – Matthew Morgan, Gabriel Wynne, Richard Griffith and Evan Lloyd – had all been appointed initially by Sir Thomas Myddelton to the county sequestration committee in late 1644 but had 'defected' to the accounts body. On this occasion, it seems, they 'rediscovered' their earlier appointments and tried to pass themselves off as the county's sequestration authority. This seems an extraordinary situation in which we have one set of committeemen literally impersonating a separate branch of the parliamentary state. Such a development suggests the confused, overlapping and sometimes slippery nature of parliamentary authority in places such as north Wales where political support for the king's opponents was thin on the ground.

The day after it issued its warrant, the 'legitimate' sequestration committee at Powis Castle arranged a meeting with Edward Vaughan and his colleagues 'to conferr about some particulars touching ye safety of this county'. It may be that this was viewed as an olive branch; a summit designed to lower the local political temperature. If so, it was a ruse, and one that worked.[32] The meeting was arranged at Welshpool, with Mytton's blessing, at which the respective parties were said to have 'much satisfied each other with divers particulars'. However, as Vaughan and his associates returned towards Montgomery, they were overtaken by one of Mytton's officers, Captain Gerald Barbour, a Wrexham associate of Morgan Llwyd, who rode at the head of some twenty horse.[33]

Barbour produced a warrant under the hands of Lloyd Pierce, Roger Pope and Hugh Price for Vaughan's arrest for his contempt in entering the sequestrated estate of Llwydiarth contrary to order.[34] Vaughan was taken under guard to Powis Castle where he was kept close prisoner. The rump of the accounts sub-commissioners, Matthew Morgan and Edward Owen, described these developments to their parent body as 'soe great a discuragement to us (Mr Vaughan being in ye chaire and best acquainted with ye imployment) that unles some course be taken for his inlargement, wee conceive ye buisinesse of accompts will be utterly retarded'.[35] The following day George Devereux, supposedly 'of his owne accord' came into the Red Castle garrison where he too was detained as 'an abettor unto Mr Vaughan in all his contempts', and a man who had 'opposed the payment of the contribucions of this county besides severall other acts of disquieting the peace of the county'.[36] Devereux, by contrast, maintained that he was incarcerated by Lloyd Pierce 'under false pretences … to prevent … his [Devereux's] eleccion'.[37]

The accounts sub-committee's two leading members were now under restraint in Powis Castle. It seems unlikely that the sheriff would proceed with any parliamentary election in this situation, and a wary standoff between the two sides prevailed for a time. The accountants were in limbo without their leading figures, however, and on 4 December 1646 the body's remaining members wrote to Hugh Price, governor of Powis Castle, complaining that Vaughan had been detained for over a week with no charge.[38] They emphasised Vaughan's importance as 'a person of qualitie and of great imployment, a justice of the peace and quorum [who] hath the records of the countie in his keepeinge in the vacancy [*recte* 'hacancy'] of a custos rotulor[um], the chayremen of the subcomittee of accompts … and is a comissioner to give the shereiffe his oath'. The emphasis on Vaughan's role (however nominal) as JP and acting *custos* is interesting. A commission of the peace was issued for the county which passed the Crown office in Chancery on 28 November 1645, and the original survives among Vaughan's papers.[39] As well as appointing Vaughan as a JP, the commission constituted Essex as the county's chief justice, which was a strong statement of the desire to return to a traditional form of local government and to move away from rule by committee.[40]

Vaughan filled the role of *custos* after the earl's death in September 1646, although the commission itself never functioned properly. In another letter of 4 December, the accounts sub-committee noted that Vaughan was 'the onlie man in this countie whoe acts as a justice of peace and indeavours to see the ordinances of Parliament duely executed'.[41] It is striking to see Vaughan as the only active JP, but this seems of a piece with his political Presbyterianism and opposition to the army, and by focusing on his activity as acting *custos*, the sub-committee's letter emphasised that there was an alternative thread to legitimate parliamentarian authority in the county which did not run through Powis Castle.

Montgomeryshire's accountants addressed the central Accounts Committee complaining of Vaughan's seizure 'in a warlike manner ... on the highway', and also lobbied allies in north Wales such as Captain Edward Thelwall, governor of Flint Castle.[42] They pressed Hugh Price and the sequestrators to release their colleagues, maintaining that their incarceration was 'without any legall authority tending to the destruction of the subiects liberty'.[43] Their requests and entreaties were met with a stony silence. On 4 December 1646, Vaughan and Devereux brought an action in Chancery against Pierce, Pope and Hugh Price, seeking a writ of habeas corpus for their release and to have the cause against them known. Significantly, their counsel in the matter was the Presbyterian chair of the central Accounts Committee, William Prynne.[44] Despite the court's issuing an order requiring Pierce and his allies to show cause in the matter, the request had to be repeated on 26 December as Pierce and his allies had failed to comply.[45] This finally brought a response from local sequestration officials, and on 2 January 1647, Hugh Price, Richard Griffith and George Twistleton (acting on behalf of the 'committee for sequestracions for North Wales', an interesting construction) directed their marshal to send Vaughan and Devereux to London along with the cause of their commitment.[46]

Vaughan's nemesis, Lloyd Pierce, was also on his way to the capital (one doubts the two men shared a coach) to appear once more before the central Accounts Committee. The Montgomeryshire sub-committeemen dispatched a missive to Cornhill which was probably designed to arrive around the same time as Pierce, complaining about his evasions and his unwillingness, in breach of former undertakings, to give them full access to his accounts. They described Pierce as 'protecting himselfe in Red Castle ... daily plotting to obstruct ye accompts ... which more eminently appeared in ye late injurious imprisonment of our chairman, contrived principally by himselfe'.[47] They also offered up a striking image of Pierce's alliance with the army and his extensive power in the county, complaining that:

> He hath soe over awed the countrey by the advantage of a place to exercise arbitrary power in the bringing in of soldiers to countenance his actions (whome alsoe he hath imployed to collect great summes, which he brings not into his owne accompt nor will they be brought to give anie) that ye countrey are deterred from charging either the one or the other, and some of our selves alsoe hath been attempted to be deterred from ye service by undue sequestration.

The action now moved to London where Lloyd Pierce was brought before the Cornhill Accounts Committee to answer the charges against him.[48] Vaughan and Devereux, meanwhile, appeared in Chancery and, upon giving bonds for their appearance upon notice, were released on 20 January 1647 by order of the speakers of both Houses.[49] It is worth noting the identity of the sureties they gave. One was Charles Lloyd, Vaughan's kinsman and ally who had been spoken of as a potential candidate for the borough seat; the other was Simon Vaughan of Gray's Inn, the man who had testified on Edward Vaughan's behalf before the central Committee of Accounts in its investigation of Sir Thomas Myddelton's 'exceptions'.[50] The two men then hurried back to Wales to hold the county election.

On 22 January 1647 the Cornhill Accounts committee provided a damaging assessment of Pierce's submission, stating that their sub-commissioners had taken 'iust exceptions to the ... generals and uncertentyes' in his accounts.[51] The same day, however, Pierce along with Hugh and Richard Price and George Twistleton, issued a new warrant for Vaughan and Devereux's arrest, alleging that they had made a 'wilful escape by night' from their confinement, out of London into Shrewsbury and thence to Montgomery.[52] Consequently, they directed officials to give notice 'in all markett townes, parishes, churches, chappells and all other places of publique resort' in the county, to search for them and the individuals who had abetted their 'escape'.[53] This unusual public declaration of a simple arrest warrant informed its auditors that they should not countenance 'or adheare' to Vaughan or Devereux 'in any of their wilfull and exhorbitant courses'. This was effectively a mechanism designed to stop either man from soliciting or receiving any support from freeholders in the forthcoming election. Devereux later described it as 'one of the strangest warrants that ever was heard of', and explicitly located it as part of a campaign to disrupt the county election.[54]

The claim that Vaughan and Devereux had unlawfully escaped custody was a fiction. On 30 January 1647 Vaughan and Samuel More directed a note to the constables of Deuddwr hundred in north-eastern Montgomeryshire, and probably to the constables of the county's other hundreds also, describing the 'scandalous paper ... in the forme of a warrant' tending to the 'defamacion' of himself and Devereux which was then circulating.[55] They warned that the paper 'may tend to the breach of the publicke peace of this county', and directed that if any such warrants came into their hands, they were to bring them to Montgomery Castle to 'receave directions'. Clearly the atmosphere in the county was becoming increasingly tense and volatile in the run-up to the county court where the parliamentary election would be held. In addition to the provocative warrant from the Red Castle committee, several companies of soldiers were also quartered in the county which must have added to the charged and uneasy atmosphere.

The Montgomeryshire recruiter election, 6 February 1647

The parliamentary election was held at Montgomery, a familiar site for the county poll but, significantly, now the stronghold of Vaughan and his sub-committee, on 6 February 1647. Vaughan recalled that his opponents had quartered soldiers near the town at the time of the election, 'threatning freeholders if they chose him'.[56] He also maintained that 'the commissioners' appeared in the election against him, by which he must have meant members of the Red Castle committee. Despite this intimidation, however, Vaughan in his own self-serving narrative, asserted that he was 'chosen with ye unanimous consent of all the freeholders'. While there is no other account of the election, a view of the indenture underlines the partisan nature of Vaughan's return and the victory it represented for himself and his allies.[57] It belies Vaughan's claim of a 'unanimous' choice by stating that he was elected by 'the greater part of the whole county', which indicates that there was a contest, although it is not clear as to whether there was another individual physically present to challenge him. The signatories witnessing the return also tell an eloquent story. They are headed by George Devereux, and they also include Vaughan's fellow sub-committeemen, supporters and family allies such as Matthew Morgan, Robert Griffiths, Samuel Bigg, Gabriel Wynne, Evan Lloyd, Edward Owen and Arthur Price of Vaynor.[58] Just as significant was the complete absence of any witness from the Red Castle faction or any of their army allies. As one hostile source later put it, Vaughan, 'by the healpe of those his friends & kindred caused himselfe to be elected knight of the shire for the ... county of Mountgomery'.[59]

The election was a victory carried out in the teeth of determined opposition and it represented a significant moment for Vaughan's personal ambitions as well as for those of the wider political Presbyterian interest in the county. Vaughan would now be able to defend his claim to Llwydiarth at Westminster, but he could also potentially draw on the influence of political allies like William Prynne to undermine Lloyd Pierce and the army establishment in north Wales. One commentator noted that, although the state's claim on Llwydiarth remained unresolved, Vaughan, 'sitting ... in the house as a Member of Parliament by his favourers there blasted & frustrated whatsoever the committee of the county did against him'.[60]

Emboldened by Vaughan's election and the backing of the Cornhill Committee in their dispute, the sub-committee at Montgomery Castle now once again imprisoned Lloyd Pierce for contempt.[61] Colonel John Jones headed the signatories to a letter from the county sequestrators to the Cornhill body requesting that good public servants not be punished for 'want of formality, or that publique authority should bee made use of to expresse private discontents'.[62] Pierce would, however, remain in confinement until early April 1647,[63] writing from prison to request an 'indifferent auditor', and complaining to the central accountants that matters in Montgomeryshire were 'clowded from your sight'.[64] He argued that, while in principle he supported the work of the sub-committee as necessary, 'I say & must make yt good, they intend nothing lesse but by the power of your comission to lengthen their authority what they can to raign over us'. Pierce was convinced that the sub-committeemen would never conclude their business because of their personal animosity towards him, and so he appealed to the Cornhill commissioners for 'the benefite of law to get out of this British-Inquisition'!

Hostilities at Westminster: Edward Vaughan and Sir Thomas Myddelton

As Pierce wrote his frustrated letters from confinement in Montgomery Castle, his chief adversary was making his way to Westminster where he was sworn as an MP on 15 February.[65] Despite Vaughan's election, however, there was to be no respite from the internecine politics of the parliamentarian party in north Wales. On 17 February 1647 an information against Vaughan was submitted to the Commons by his fellow MP and long-time adversary, Sir Thomas Myddelton.[66] The new member for Montgomeryshire must have known that such a manoeuvre was in the offing, however, for he immediately submitted his own set of counter-articles against Myddelton. The two papers were referred to a substantial committee of thirty-eight MPs which was empowered to send for parties, witnesses and records regarding the business. The committee was populated by several individuals who had a local or personal connection with the parties. Several Wiltshire members were also present on the committee, which suggests the likely interest of the earl of Pembroke whose electoral patronage in that county was considerable.

Vaughan's papers include several copies of Myddelton's 'information' against him.[67] The 'information' incorporated several charges from Myddelton's 'exceptions' of a year before along with some new allegations. Thus we have the claim that Vaughan stayed for an extended period in royalist Oxford; that he tried to levy £3,500 for the king but was hindered by the earl of Pembroke; that he had detained £3,000 of public money contrary to the central sequestration committee's ruling about his estate; and that he had been adjudged a 'delinquent', 'and now is chosen k[nigh]t of the shire although he be not discharged of his ... delinquencie'. The thread of Myddelton's opposition can be traced back at least to early 1646, and Vaughan also identified Myddelton as being behind some of the recent moves against him, claiming that the Red Castle committee's accusation of delinquency was 'only a practise to prevent him to be chosen knight for the countie, and, if chosen, to be ejected, Sir Thomas [Myddelton] his son in law standing for the place'. This was almost certainly Sir John Wittewronge who had married Myddelton's daughter, Mary.[68] Wittewronge was a parliamentarian colonel who had been involved, significantly along with John Jones, in mortgaging Welsh properties for his father-in-law before the civil wars.[69] At his mother's death on 17 January 1647, Wittewronge inherited the Montgomeryshire manor of Talerddig, giving him a notable landed interest in the county.[70] It seems likely, then, that the campaign against Vaughan since late 1646 was animated, at least in part, by Myddelton who wished to place Wittewronge into the Montgomeryshire seat.

For his part, Vaughan's submission against Myddelton was a lengthy, detailed and potentially ruinous assault on the most powerful parliamentarian grandee in north Wales.[71] He accused Myddelton of religious nonconformity through his obedience to Laudian directives in his chapel at Chirk in the 1630s. It is telling that the accusations stemmed from questions of religious conservatism rather than any current attachment to the radical figures in his own ranks, such as Morgan Llwyd or John Jones, for Myddelton had little time for their brand of fiery puritanism. Vaughan also presented Myddelton as a politique and a selfish opportunist who made a 'spetious shewe of pietie' at the outbreak of war and misrepresented the inhabitants of Wales as 'grosely ignorant' to obtain his commission as major general. The extensive powers granted him by parliamentary ordinance, Vaughan argued, laid the groundwork for 'his owne ambition and greatnes to the preiudice of the publique', and allowed him to reject offers of assistance from 'other gentlemen then in London of greater power and interest than himself in North Wales', a clear reference to Vaughan himself.

The articles also drew upon depositions Vaughan had taken in the county to tar Myddelton with the brush of military incompetence, cowardice and corruption. They suggested that, despite the large sums which had been raised to support Myddelton's forces, he had only brought some 300 men into the country, and 'had never beene able to enter Mountgomeryshire had not the well affected partie in that countie given him incouradgment to come in and ioyned with him'.[72] Moreover, Vaughan argued, large sums continued to be levied on the country, including the £800 monthly assessment, to support this small force, although, he claimed, little of this money found its way into the pockets of soldiers who continued to employ free quarter on Montgomeryshire's unfortunate inhabitants. Vaughan also turned the tables on allegations that John Jones (undoubtedly with Myddelton's connivance and blessing) had made against the parliamentarian commander Sir William Brereton in 1645, by claiming that Myddelton had neglected to pay his forces in north Wales and had allowed them to plunder the countryside. Myddelton was then alleged to have fled in the face of royalist Irish forces landing in north Wales, leaving parliament's supporters open to their depredations and rapine, something which 'hindered the countrey of Northwales from cominge in to the parliament'.[73] Brereton was a member of the committee considering these charges and he and his circle would probably have responded positively to the narrative that Vaughan attempted to spin here.

Finally, Vaughan turned his attention to Montgomeryshire where, he alleged, the major general had initially nominated committeemen 'who weere the men that first gave him footinge and broughte the countrey in unto him'. These, presumably, were individuals such as Samuel More and Gabriel Wynne whom, Vaughan, claimed were afterward rejected by Myddelton because they 'would not comply with his unlawfull purposes'. In their place, Vaughan asserted that Myddelton had 'nominated souldiers of noe fortune to bee commissioners and committee men, who used all manner of oppression and outrage against the people without controwle, havinge gott the pouer of the souldier to protect and assist them in their exorbitancies'. This charge provided a succinct summary of Vaughan and his allies' anger and frustration with the post-war settlement in Montgomeryshire, and it also encapsulated how such local realities came to overlap and combine with the Presbyterian interest's priorities in the kingdom more generally. Perhaps unsurprisingly, Vaughan's submission also protested that when the Montgomeryshire sequestrators were questioned by the accounts sub-committee, 'they graunted orders ... to sequester their estates and ... imprison their persons'.

This, then, was a fascinating Westminster clash between the principal parliamentarian factions that had emerged in north Wales. Vaughan and Myddelton were perhaps the two most powerful parliamentarian figures resident in the region and their opposition cannot but have had significant consequences for the dynamics of post-war politics there. Perhaps mindful of the gravity of their clash and the potential problems of taking sides in such a dispute when parliamentarian support in north Wales was thin and Westminster needed all the allies it could muster there, the Commons committee did not make any immediate ruling. Indeed, there was an order that their committee be revived on 6 April 1647, and, although it met and the parties 'wrangled to the purpose', still no resolution was forthcoming.[74] It was perhaps better to keep the matter in suspension than come to a decision in such a contentious case. That the committee was revived may suggest that one of the parties pressed for a decision; the fact that the day following the motion to revive the body an order was made to repeal the ordinance by which Myddelton had levied money in north Wales (and through which, presumably, Mytton continued to do so) might suggest that Vaughan felt he was in the ascendancy at this point.[75] The spring of 1647 saw the high watermark of Presbyterian power in parliament and the kingdom at large, and suspicion may have fallen on Myddelton from some Presbyterian members that he was too close to the army to sit comfortably within their group. Indeed, at this point we should turn our attention to the question of the army in north Wales and the election for the Montgomery Boroughs constituency which took place against a backdrop of restiveness and discontentment against the soldiery.

Anti-army sentiment and the Montgomery Boroughs election, April 1647

As we have seen, Edward Vaughan and his circle had, since at least mid-1646, been in the vanguard of opposing Thomas Mytton's forces and challenging the basis upon which he was levying heavy taxes in north Wales. Indeed, the region was burdened with additional army levies of questionable legality over and above authorised parliamentary assessments, a fact that provided substantive grounds for Vaughan's opposition.[76] The protracted effort to reduce north Wales took a heavy toll on the country, with the sieges of Chester, Denbigh, Ruthin, Holt, Harwarden, Flint and Rhuddlan consuming men, money and local goodwill as the populations had to feed and house many of these soldiers, often with the additional burdens of free quarter.[77] The war in north Wales dragged on and on, too, with Holt only surrendering in mid-January 1647, while Harlech held out until 15 March, its surrender effectively marking the end of military operations in north Wales some ten months after Charles I had given himself up to the Scottish Covenanters. Although army men themselves, figures like Thomas Mytton, Roger Pope and John Jones nevertheless were sensitive to the damaging effects that their forces were having in the region, and they described in a letter to William Lenthall of January 1647 the 'distressed condicion of this almost ruined countrey of Northwales'.[78] They went on to note, however, the 'continuall clamors of the soldery for want of pay (the countrey being soe much exhausted and impoverished that it is not able to contribute soe much as will discharge theire provision money)', and asked that a speedy course be taken either to pay the soldiers off and disband them, or to send them for service in Ireland, 'that they may bee no longer burthensome to the poore countrey either by contribucions or quarteringe'. They also asked to be informed 'for the better and speedyer disburtheninge and easeinge of the country', which garrisons (including perhaps that at Red Castle) should be dismantled as they 'have beene and still are verie chargeable'. Such problems were more pressing in places such as Denbighshire than in Montgomeryshire (although the latter's population had been contributing to the war effort much longer because of its early reduction), but the significant burden of taxation was shared throughout north Wales.

This letter encapsulated the dilemma facing the army and its Independent supporters: parliament's forces needed payment of their arrears to be disbanded, a process which would address problems of the kind articulated in this dispatch, but the Presbyterian majority in parliament in early 1647 meant that no reasonable settlement of arrears was on the table. Moreover, while the army remained on the ground it provided the Independents with a critical powerbase, but it was the army, along with the taxes needed to maintain it and the local committees that levied such contributions, which alienated many moderates and helped bolster Presbyterian support. From such tensions and contradictions arose the New Model's move against the Presbyterians in June 1647 which is discussed more fully in the next chapter.

Vaughan and his allies constituted one channel through which some of this antipathy towards the soldiery could be mobilised, partly through the tax strikes which they had spearheaded in Montgomeryshire throughout 1646. The soldiers themselves were restive and refractory because of lack of pay, and there was a substantial mutiny in Denbighshire in March 1647 when local soldiers heard of parliament's derisory offer of disbandment with one month's pay, upon which the troops imprisoned Colonels Jones, Twistleton and Sontley in Wrexham church for a time.[79] Although not as numerous as in places like Denbighshire, the soldiery nevertheless remained an important presence in Montgomeryshire in 1646–7, and featured as players in the parliamentary election for Montgomery Boroughs which took place in early April 1647.

Command of Montgomery Castle and its garrison had been placed in the hands of Samuel More, but a Commons order of 25 March 1647 returned control to its owner-occupier Lord Herbert of Cherbury.[80] Upon news of this change reaching the town, the soldiers garrisoned there, concerned that Herbert might disband them, 'began to crye out for their arreares, sayeinge they would not part before they had them, which weare greate'.[81] Herbert's bailiff, Richard Thompson, informed his patron that, in an effort to address this situation, he had managed to get £460 from Thomas Mytton who was in the area and was trying to influence the imminent election. Thompson was among a group that was fearful of these soldiers, and he informed Herbert that he wished to see them gone from the town, 'for they do nothinge but harbour Independents and Anabaptests and such lyke, which may happen to be dangerous if theare weare occasion'.[82] Thompson probably had in mind the radical Independent Morgan Llwyd who was then minister to the garrison and had been for some time.[83] That the famous Llwyd was the garrison's minister has not previously been known to historians, and it seems likely that he was important, along with Vavasor Powell and Ambrose Mostyn, in fomenting and sustaining the extreme strand of religious politics which would flourish in this area under their leadership in the coming decade.[84] Their brand of millenarian fervour, coupled with a discontented soldiery, was the face of extreme Independency which frightened mainstream puritans and moderate episcopalians alike, and it was from anxieties such as these that Vaughan and Devereux probably drew much of their support.

The Montgomery borough election took place on 6 April 1647, and new evidence has come to light which provides a fascinating insight into the contest. George Devereux of Vaynor, Vaughan's close ally, stood for the seat as a representative of what might be characterised as the anti-army Presbyterian interest in the county. On the other side, Thomas Mytton and his supporters promoted 'Mr Gerrard', who was possibly Gilbert Gerard of Crewood Hall in Cheshire, an associate of the parliamentarian commander Sir William Brereton, and a man who had served at the siege of Hawarden.[85] This attribution is not certain, but if it was this Gerard who stood for the seat, he was a low-born individual who had risen to a position of influence through the army and who became a convinced religious Independent. General Mytton was active in soliciting for his nominee, and on 3 April he wrote in this capacity to his 'cosen', 'Mrs Price' of Vaynor on Gerrard's behalf. This was Mary Price, the widow of Arthur, George Devereux's mother-in-law, and, importantly, Edward Vaughan's sister. Mytton's letter noted 'yt yow labor to make Mr Deverox burgesse for Mongomery', which was apparently contrary to her intimations to him in an earlier letter.[86] Mytton informed her that he had received a dispatch from the MP John Glynne suggesting, somewhat improbably, that her brother Edward Vaughan, then in Westminster of course, supported

Gerard for the place and had even written to several of his friends to this effect. This seems highly unlikely given the close bond between Devereux and Vaughan and their common front against the army interest, and it appears that Mytton was trying to pull the wool over his cousin's eyes. Mytton asked her to desist from supporting Devereux 'for I doe assure you it may doe more harme then you are aware of'. Two days later, on the eve of the election, Mytton wrote to Mary Price again, asking her 'to forbeare goeing on to make your sonne in law a parliament man'. This time, however, Mytton told her he had received assurances that 'there is proofe agaynst him that hee hathe taken an oath against ye parliament & done other thinges desinabling him to be a member of ye house'. This was a reference to Devereux having taken 'Capel's Oath', a charge which had been raised as one of Myddelton's 'exceptions' against him in February 1646. It seems that, just as Myddelton had moved against Vaughan at his appearance in the Commons, so he (or perhaps a proxy) was preparing to inform against Devereux if he was elected. The major general informed Mary Price that returning Devereux with such a stain on his record would 'much disadvantage my cosen Ed[ward] Vaughan', presumably because Vaughan also had Myddelton's charges pending against him in the House; if Devereux were disabled on similar grounds, then Vaughan's own case would doubtless look weaker. Mytton assured Mary that he was obliged to oppose the election of any individual who had carried himself openly against the cause, and concluded that 'instead of doeing hime [Devereux] good, it [his election] may fall oute otherwise in giving advantage to some yt doe not soe truly love & honor you'.

These revealing letters show a close network of connections working around the election which encompassed both local actors and regional representatives at Westminster. Mytton was no stranger to contested electoral politics, having himself served as sheriff in the disputed and controversial Shropshire election of August 1646.[87] The letters also present intriguing evidence of female involvement in the electoral process, with Mary Price, perhaps empowered by her status as a widow, lobbying interested parties on her son-in-law's behalf.

A full account of the Montgomery election was provided by bailiff Richard Thompson to Lord Herbert of Cherbury, although modern historians have not been aware of this material.[88] Thompson described Mytton as standing with 'Mr Gerarde' at the election but that 'all the burgesses' were against them, and he added that 'the country would not hear the General speake, but cried out for Devereux, whereupon he [Mytton] went out of the [town]hall very discontentedly, seeing the great disorder of the people'. At the election, Thompson, as bailiff, informed the burgesses that Gerard was recommended by Lord Herbert of Cherbury and Devereux 'by the country', and he asked the assembled crowd to make their choice between them, 'whereupon they cried out "Devereux", and not one voyce, as I could heare for Gerarde'. Thompson believed that the country would not countenance an individual of that name as their MP 'in regard they had so much mischiefe donne by Gerrarde on the king's side'. He was referring to the rapacious royalist general Charles Gerard whose brutal campaigns in Wales in 1644 and 1645 had alienated large swathes of the population from the king's cause. Thompson believed that Captain Edward Herbert's declaring his support for Devereux was important for the latter's securing of the seat and assisted with his popularity among the electors. Edward was Lord Herbert of Cherbury's second son, who evidently rebelled against his father's candidate in the election.[89] Lord Herbert had presumably supported Mytton's choice to keep on the right side of the general and the Red Castle committee in his quest to gain reparations for losses during the war. Captain Herbert's endorsement of Devereux perhaps suggests how the latter's election represented an alliance of royalist and Presbyterian interests as Edward had been active in the royalist cause alongside his elder brother, the disabled county MP, Richard.

In the election itself, it seems that the claim of the 'out boroughs' to participate in voting for the MP was revived: their voting rights had been denied in favour of Montgomery townsmen only in recent decades.[90] Certainly, Mytton sent some 350 foot to Welshpool the day after the election 'because the bailiffs shewed themsleves so far in this businesse', and the final vote tally reported by Thompson indicates the involvement of more than just Montgomery's own burgesses: Devereux, Thompson reported, had '703 votes of his side'. This was a very substantial figure and approaches the electorate estimated for the constituency in the early eighteenth century.[91] It is interesting to see the suggestion that Welshpool voters were important in this election as this borough was close to Llwydiarth. The election indenture itself only attests to the involvement of Montgomery voters with the identifiable signatories hailing from families who had long been associated with borough government.[92] An interesting addition to these local worthies was the handsome signature, as befits a scrivener, of William Barbour, register to the Montgomeryshire accounts sub-committee. As we might expect, there was no trace of an endorsement from figures associated with Mytton or the sequestration committee; this, like Edward Vaughan's, was a highly partisan election.

Unseating George Devereux

As Mytton had related to Mary Price, however, Devereux would, like Vaughan, come to Westminster with a cloud of suspicion over his head. A correspondent wrote to Mytton three days after the election, 'I … much feare theire will be noe prevencion of his coming into the house', which clearly indicates that discussions were already underway about how to stop Devereux taking up his seat.[93] Upon the Montgomery member's arrival in the Commons, on 15 April, when he had 'not sat many hours', proceedings were initiated against him upon 'great and grievous charges' of a 'high nature'. These included the allegations which Mytton had anticipated in his letter to Mary Price: that Devereux was a delinquent under sequestration and that he had taken Capel's royalist oath.[94] Copies of the depositions against Devereux taken by the Montgomeryshire sequestrators in November 1646 were now introduced as evidence against him.[95] Devereux maintained that the design to remove him was part of Lloyd Pierce's long anti-accounts campaign, and that 'by way of revenge, when hee could not prevent his eleccion, he endeavoured to [cause his] suspencion from and eiectment out of the howse'.[96]

The business was turned over to the same committee that was examining the charges against Edward Vaughan and Sir Thomas Myddelton. However, whereas this body was deadlocked over Vaughan's delinquency, the evidence against Devereux appears to have been more cut-and-dried, and his suspension was put to a vote: the Commons decided by a majority of sixty to forty-five to remove the Montgomery MP.[97] As with Vaughan's effort to be made a member of the Montgomeryshire sequestration committee the previous November, the tellers in this vote are instructive of the wider political interests operating here. Those supporting Devereux's exclusion were Sir William Brereton, the Cheshire commander and war party figure, and Sir Henry Mildmay, a prominent Independent who supported the attempted impeachment of eleven Presbyterian members in June 1647. The tellers who counted the votes for keeping Devereux in the House were Denzil Holles, Presbyterian grandee and one of those eleven members, and his associate Sir Edward Hungerford. As a result of the vote Devereux was suspended from the Commons and, although his case, along with Vaughan's, was referred in July 1647 to a committee chaired by John Bulkeley for considering complaints against members, Devereux lamented that its business was stalled.[98] He also maintained that Pierce's efforts against him were part of a 'plot' to secure his estate. He continued to proclaim his innocence and that, despite being 'duly elected and returned', as MPs, others 'both unduly elected and returned sitt there without suspencion notwithstanding peticions against theire eleccions, where as there is noe peticion at all against his eleccion or returne'.[99] Despite his efforts, Devereux was never readmitted to the House although it seems that he was never formally excluded either.

So Edward Vaughan would proceed as the only representative from Montgomeryshire in the Commons, and while there he would initially enjoy some support and success. He would be part of a wider Presbyterian 'mobilisation' in early 1647 which sought to curtail the power of the Independents both in the House and in the country more widely. The next chapter examines his activities in the Commons but also discusses how he suffered as part of the backlash against the Presbyterians, and how he ultimately fell victim to his Independent political enemies at Pride's Purge in December 1648.

CHAPTER 7:

Parliament Man? Edward Vaughan, Parliamentary Presbyterians and Pride's Purge, April 1647–February 1649

dward Vaughan had managed to secure a place in parliament as
Montgomeryshire's representative and had also weathered his
enemies' efforts to unseat him; his colleague George Devereux
was not so lucky. This chapter reviews Vaughan's activities as an MP from
his election down to his seclusion from the Commons in December 1648.
This section begins by reviewing other recruiter elections in north Wales
in the spring of 1647, locating Vaughan's (and indeed Devereux's) return
as part of a wider 'Presbyterian mobilisation' in the region between late
1646 and early 1647.[1] Attention then turns to Vaughan's involvement
with a neglected aspect of parliamentary politics in April 1647, the so-
called 'Committee for Wales' and its initiative to suspend sequestration
proceedings in the country. This is shown to be part of a Presbyterian
scheme to undermine the army presence in north Wales (although for
Vaughan, it also helped safeguard Llwydiarth). However, such initiatives
helped contribute to the Independent-army backlash of mid-1647 and
the ultimate fracturing of the parliamentarian alliance. The shattering of
the Presbyterians' superiority in London had serious ramifications for
Vaughan and his local allies, and this chapter traces the downfall of the
Montgomeryshire sub-committee of accounts and its inability to bring any
effective charges against its main target, Lloyd Pierce. Divisions among

Montgomeryshire's parliamentarians were subsumed briefly in the face of renewed royalist risings during the Second Civil War in the spring and summer of 1648. However, the ascendancy of the New Model and the Independents in the aftermath of the royalist defeat left parliamentarian moderates such as Vaughan highly vulnerable. This chapter discusses the revival of efforts by Vaughan's Independent-aligned enemies to challenge his possession of Llwydiarth, and it also discusses Vaughan's seclusion from parliament and imprisonment as a politically suspect individual.

Presbyterian mobilisation and recruiter elections in north Wales

The elections in Montgomeryshire in the spring of 1647 emerged from the county's visceral internecine parliamentarian politics. They were also, however, an expression of a broader Presbyterian mobilisation in Wales and the Marches in 1646–7 to secure seats at Westminster and to press for a moderate peace settlement centred around a negotiated treaty with the king, the reduction and eventual disbandment of the New Model and the securing of a religious settlement which would maintain orthodox religion and a national church.[2] The balance of power in the Commons shifted towards the Presbyterians in early 1647 partly as a result of these elections.[3] This is not to say that there was necessarily any formal coordination or collusion with Presbyterian grandees in Westminster, although this was the case in some parts of Wales. In the summer of 1647, army commentators would claim that 'malignants, neuters, knaves and fools like [George] Devereux and his adherents of the junto faction [that is, the Presbyterian MPs in parliament]', were elected in 1646–7 to 'obstruct the good proceedings of pious and public spirited persons'.[4] There is no evidence in the papers surrounding Devereux's return that there was, in fact, involvement from leading figures at Westminster in his election, although Mytton's reference to letters from the MPs John Glynne and Edward Vaughan, along with Denzil Holles's acting as a teller in the vote on Devereux's case in the Commons, means that we should not ignore the interest in, if not necessarily the active coordination from, grandees in parliament over these elections. It is interesting to see Devereux cited in the army dispatch as a particular example of Presbyterian electioneering, although the fact that his case seemed a clear instance of a delinquent entering parliament probably made it particularly attractive for their polemical case. Immediately after Devereux's suspension from the House, for example, one newsbook reflected that elections such as his were 'Welsh tricks', and this reflected a more general suspicion about recruiter elections in this formerly solidly royalist territory.[5]

Such concerns were articulated much more forcefully when the Independents gained ascendancy in parliament in mid-1647, with one editorial requesting that:

> the Houses may be speedily purged of such members as for their delinquency or for corruptions or abuse to the state or undue elections, ought not to sit there, whereof the late election in Cornwall [and] Wales … afford ill examples to the great prejudice of the peoples freedome in the said elections.[6]

Devereux's election and suspension was surely on the mind of such army authors. Another army paper from the latter half of 1647 identified a concerted effort by the Presbyterian grandees Sir Robert Harley and Sir William Lewis to make 'such creatures of their owne members of counteyes and shires to sitt in the House of Parliament' for constituencies in south Wales, adding that in all that region 'yow will hardly heare of a man there that serves in the House but have either bin made by delinquents or have bin commissioners of array or otherwise assisting the kinge in party … and alsoe your comittee men and justices of peace'.[7] There is certainly evidence that the political Presbyterians were effective in the recruiter elections in north Wales also, and that the Montgomeryshire elections were part of a wider electoral effort in the region.[8] In addition to Vaughan and Devereux's returns, for example, the Presbyterian grandees Sir John Trevor and Sir Thomas Myddelton had their sons and namesakes returned in December 1646 for the two seats available in Flintshire,[9] while Myddelton's son-in-law also took the Caernarvonshire seat, and a client of Presbyterian John Glynne took the county's borough place. In

Anglesey, the recruiter members were political moderates, one of whom was secluded at Pride's Purge as was the Cardiganshire recruiter Sir Richard Pryse.

The Montgomeryshire elections of 1647, then, were products of a unique set of local circumstances, but they fed into a wider picture of Welsh politics in this period which was largely conducive to the priorities and political concerns of men like Vaughan and Devereux rather than their ideological adversaries. However, Devereux's inability to hold on to his seat suggests the limits of their power and was also a troubling augury of the Independents' resurgence in the summer of 1647. Moreover, the electoral picture in north Wales was not uniformly positive for the Presbyterian interest. For example, the Montgomery sequestration committeeman Colonel Roger Pope managed to secure the Merioneth seat less than a fortnight after Devereux's suspension from the Commons, although there is the suggestion that Pope had by this time 'returned to his duty to the king' and aligned himself with the Presbyterians.[10] He was succeeded by his army colleague, the convinced Independent, Colonel John Jones. In August 1646, meanwhile, Cardigan boroughs also returned an Independent in the person of Thomas Wogan: he was a New Model officer who would go on to sign Charles I's death warrant. Despite these Independent victories, the political landscape of early 1647 both locally and nationally seemed conducive to the political priorities of Vaughan and of his Presbyterian allies.

The 'Committee for Wales', the suspension of sequestrations and the monthly assessment

The Welsh political Presbyterians were clearly not all of the same stripe. They were not a coherent group or party and possessed different backgrounds and priorities. Sir Thomas Myddelton and Edward Vaughan, for example, were both 'political Presbyterians', but the former was much closer to the army interest and, of course, the two had conducted a long-running feud in no small measure over the direction of parliamentary and army policy in the region. However, as 1647 progressed and the issues of settling the kingdom increasingly came to resolve into a confrontation between religious and political moderates and those who supported the New Model Army and a more radical political settlement encompassing far reaching religious reform, so such personal rivalries became somewhat sublimated into common concerns and aims. An important and largely unrecognised initiative which is of interest for our purposes was the Commons' reviving of the 'Committee for Wales' on 2 April 1647.[11] There had not been a Commons committee with a general remit for Wales before 1646, which was understandable, of course, because until that point most of the country lay beyond parliamentarian control. The Commons committee for Gloucester had informally assumed the role of a Westminster executive for south Wales between 1644 and 1646, and a 'Committee for North Wales' followed in 1646 as that region began to be reduced to parliament.[12] In June 1646 the Commons had nominated a committee to include all Welsh MPs, although many constituencies were yet to obtain representatives, of course, and a reference was made to the 'Committee for Wales' later that month.[13] This body seems to have fallen into abeyance, however, and the recruiter elections along with the final reduction of north Wales probably provided the impetus for reconstituting and reinvigorating this body in early April 1647.[14] It met on 3 April at the Queen's Court and present were Edward Vaughan, Sir William Lewis and John Glynne, two Presbyterian grandees who would be targeted specifically by the New Model in the summer of 1647. Also present were eight other Presbyterian MPs who represented constituencies in or who hailed from the region; among them was Sir Thomas Myddelton.[15]

The committee had been tasked by the Commons with considering 'proposicions of the settlinge and preservacion of Wales' and had resolved 'a way for effectinge the same', although its single surviving order does not specify what this was.[16] However, the report continued, because of the many weighty affairs requiring the Commons' attention their report would not readily be heard. As a result, and as an interim measure, they 'ordered that all committees for sequestracions bee desired to forbeare all proceedings … against all or any inhabitants of Wales, untill the sence and pleasures of the howse bee further declared therein'.[17] There were some exceptions to this suspension, including anyone exempted from pardons, Catholics who had been in arms, commissioners of array who did not voluntarily surrender and ex-MPs who had deserted the House. These orders were distributed to all sequestration committees in Wales 'whoe together with the soldiery there are desired to take notice hereof'. Shortly after this order was passed, a correspondent of Major General Mytton informed him that 'the members of the howse for north Wales have agreed that noe sequestration shal be of any but papist [*sic*] and excepted persons ... and they write their letters to the comittees and agents to this purpose'.[18] Later that month, the royalist colonel John Bodvel wrote that he had heard that the order was being obeyed by the committees of Merioneth, Flintshire, Denbighshire and Montgomeryshire 'and by Sir Tho[mas] Middletons committees there'.[19] This was an exceptional provision which has hardly been noticed in the scholarly literature. However, its implications were profound. It would, of course, cut off much needed supply and support for the army which was probably its intended effect, particularly as the weekly assessment, the mainstay of support for local forces elsewhere, was not being collected effectively in north Wales by this point.[20] The committee's order would also, of course, stop proceedings in the case of the Llwydiarth estate, and so had a particular importance for Edward Vaughan. The interruption of sequestration proceedings in Wales would give Vaughan some much needed breathing room in his ongoing battles over the estate and it would mean that he could focus on the business of being an MP and of furthering the political settlement he and his fellow Welsh Presbyterian MPs were pursuing.

A look at Vaughan's activities in the Commons is instructive in exploring his political sympathies and priorities at this point. His interest in reforming the ministry was evident in the January 1646 Montgomeryshire petition, and such concerns help explain his involvement in a Commons committee nominated on 22 March 1647 which considered an ordinance for excluding 'malignant ministers' from livings.[21] We can see Vaughan's concerns in this matter from around this time in a series of articles he preferred against the 'lewd life and evill behavioure' of Edmund Hall, the rector of Llansantffraid in north Montgomeryshire.[22] In this reformist vein, Vaughan was also nominated to a committee in late June 1647 to examine an ordinance designed to replace 'holy-dayes' for scholars and apprentices, which 'daies of recreation might be abused to the dishonour of God [and] scandal to religion', with 'more orderly' days of rest and respite.[23]

In addition to these religious interests, Vaughan was also, unsurprisingly, concerned with soldiers and the army. He was, for example, nominated on 10 May to the committee which was considering the ordinance for soldiers' indemnity.[24] More significantly, and also in May 1647, he was involved with the fallout from the army disturbances that had broken out in Montgomery, and which were part of a more general restiveness among the armed forces, particularly in provincial armies rather than the New Model, in the spring and summer of 1647.[25] In late April 1647, Lord Herbert of Cherbury wrote to Thomas Mytton about the 'discontented souldiers' of Montgomery whom the general had punitively quartered at Welshpool after that borough had supported Devereux in the recent election.[26] Herbert was worried that these men 'so neere mee, demanding pay', could not be supported from his own pocket, and so he requested that the money allowed to maintain a garrison there when the castle was under Samuel More's governorship be continued under his stewardship. As far back as August 1646 these soldiers were more than £250 in arrears, 'which the committee at Red Castle promised many times to satisfy', but had failed to do so, and doubtless this figure had grown since then.[27] Because of their desperate condition, on 6–7 May 1647 a serious disturbance broke out among these forces. The 300 foot quartered in Welshpool rose up in 'a new insurrection', and marched on Montgomery, seizing two members of the sequestration committee, Richard Griffiths of Sutton and Lodowick Myddelton, as well as Richard Thompson, the collector of sequestration money and Lord Herbert's bailiff.[28] Thompson was freed only on security that he return with £300 of the soldiers' pay. Another report had this narrative in its essentials but suggested a much lower figure of around sixty mutinous and 'desperate' soldiers who fired on Montgomery Castle demanding money, and noted that none in the castle garrison would assist in its defence unless they were paid first. The report's author, Lieutenant Edward Allen, head of the garrison and governor in Herbert's absence, said that he 'had not so much as meat' to give the twenty or so auxiliaries who assisted in the castle's defence.[29] A letter from the Montgomeryshire sequestration committee relating these events was read in the Commons on 12 May, and the matter was referred to the Derby House Committee.[30]

The Commons ordered Edward Vaughan to prepare a letter to Mytton communicating the intelligence they had received about these disturbances, to require him to suppress the disorders and to 'quarter such as are to go for Ireland … as may be … best for the content and ease of the county'. Vaughan's letter on the disturbances described them emotively as 'outrages'; he also emphasised the soldiers' tendency to plunder, and reported that when the mutineers had seized Griffiths, Myddelton and Thompson, they had also 'threatened to do the like with the rest of them and the committee of accompt for that town and their adherents'.[31] This seems to be some spice added to the narrative of events by the Llwydiarth squire, but it probably does also reflect the genuine animosity of the soldiery towards those local Presbyterian figures they deemed partly responsible for their lack of pay and poor conditions. Vaughan and his supporters doubtless welcomed such a disturbance, however, as it would have fanned anti-army feeling in the locality and would also draw unwelcome attention to the sequestration committee's shortcomings in supplying the soldiers. The lack of soldiers' pay and the inability to satisfy their arrears were not matters that would be resolved easily, although steps were taken by Mytton and the Committee for North Wales in response to Vaughan's letter to 'settle the distempers of the souldiers', by disbanding some foot regiments and preparing a regiment of between 700 and 1,000 men for shipping to Ireland.[32] However, 'severall troopes of horse & foote' remained in Montgomeryshire, and the burdens of the soldiery in the county were not resolved by these expedients and they remained an ongoing problem for the local population.[33]

It is unclear whether the Montgomeryshire sequestration committee's business fell victim to the 3 April order of the 'Committee of Wales', although John Bodvel's letter reported that it was indeed observing the injunction. There does seem to be something of a lull in its activity in April and May 1647, although the sequestration records for the county are fragmentary.[34] If there was a hiatus in sequestration business then this probably added to the problems with the local soldiery, and it seems that the Independents and pro-army figures were determined not to let the Welsh Presbyterian MPs' order undermine them. Consequently, on 20 May 1647 the Committee for North Wales issued its own directive, with Mytton as its leading signatory. This ordered that, in pursuance of directives from parliament, the sequestrators were immediately to secure in Powis Castle those Montgomeryshire men who had been in arms against the parliament (this potentially included George Devereux, of course), while local soldiers were directed to assist them in this business if necessary.[35] This order was a clear signal that sequestration business in north Wales was to continue, that men like Devereux were not safe, and that the military establishment was not content simply to follow directives of questionable legitimacy issued by the Welsh Presbyterians in Westminster.

The continued problems in north Wales of forces that needed supply and maintenance, of the costs of arrears and disbandment, of the need to prepare a force for Ireland and of the costs of putting a number of castles beyond use, required a regularised system of financial contribution above and beyond sequestration and the ad hoc expedients which had been relied upon in the region up to this point. As Wales had now been wholly reduced to parliamentary authority, so it was comprehended within the parliament's general taxation legislation. The efforts to implement the weekly assessment in north Wales were largely unsuccessful, if not stillborn, but this levy's replacement of July 1647, the monthly assessment, sought to remedy its failings. This was the first general assessment ordinance which included all Welsh counties, and the commissioners who were named for its implementation in Montgomeryshire provide an interesting snapshot of local power dynamics on the cusp of a decisive shift toward Independent and army rule in London and the provinces over the next few months.[36] The Montgomeryshire commissioners constituted an awkward conjunction of the local factions who had been at one another's throats for the past eighteen months.[37] Sir Thomas Myddelton and Sir John Wittewronge (Myddelton's potential candidate for the 1647 county election) were the most prestigious figures and were named first to the committee, although it is doubtful whether they actually acted in the county. The pro-army group on the commission was constituted from familiar sequestration committee figures including Thomas Mytton, Roger Pope, Richard Price, Lodowick Myddelton, and Lloyd and Richard Griffiths. To this group we can probably add the following: Rice Vaughan, a jurist and clerk to the central sequestrations committee who would become a coordinating figure in the attack on Edward Vaughan during the early Commonwealth;[38] and Brochwell Griffiths of Broniarth, sometime clerk of Montgomeryshire's quarter sessions and Myddelton's kinsman, who would also become a vocal opponent of Edward Vaughan.[39] It is noticeable, however, that these figures were outnumbered by their local opponents and that leading figures of the pro-army group, such as Lloyd Pierce and Hugh Price, were omitted. These points, and the fact that political Presbyterians had the upper hand in the other Welsh commissions named under this ordinance, suggest that the 'Committee of Wales' MPs may have been influential in determining the composition of these local bodies. The Montgomeryshire commission thus included Edward Vaughan himself as well as his allies and political fellow travellers including Charles Lloyd, Francis Buller, Esay ('Isaac') Thomas, John Price, Rowland Hunt, Matthew Morgan, Richard Harris, Edward Owen, Robert Griffith, Samuel Bigg, Thomas Hunt, Samuel More, Gabriel Wynne, Thomas Niccolls and Simon Thelwall, probably the elder of that name.

The New Model, the impeachment of the eleven members and the end of the Montgomeryshire sub-committee of accounts

The Montgomeryshire assessment commission was thus unlikely to be an assiduous collector of funds for the army, particularly as the shire was rated heavily compared with neighbouring counties.[40] Indeed, one tax collector wrote in August 1647 that Montgomeryshire was 'refractory but General Mitton's brigade of horse … is quartered there; else no payment of anything'.[41] However, the commission's business was overtaken by events at the political centre which would have profound consequences for Vaughan and for the local balance of power. In mid-June 1647, with a Presbyterian majority in parliament refusing to accommodate soldiers' grievances and pressing to conclude a soft peace with the king, the New Model drew up articles of impeachment against eleven prominent Presbyterian MPs. Elements of the impeachment articles are interesting for our purposes as they relate to recent Welsh elections and to the Committee of Wales's sequestration order of 3 April. One article asserted that this order was made without the authority of the House and was thus 'illegal'.[42] The order, it was claimed, freed many delinquents, ex-commissioners of array and malignant clergymen from investigation and punishment, so that the 'ill-affected gentry and ministry of that country are grown so high and insolent, that honest men dare scarce live amongst them'.[43] The army's charges focused particularly on the MPs John Glynne and Sir William Lewis who, it was alleged, had promoted ex-royalist friends and kinsmen to be JPs and committeemen.[44] In their response, Lewis and Glynne rather unconvincingly suggested that the 3 April order was 'only a report' to the Commons, and that it was supposed to relate to Carmarthenshire only, but that 'it came to pass the words were general'. They also denied any knowledge of how this 'report' was sent to every committee in Wales.[45] It seems likely that the army charge against Devereux as one of the 'malignants, neuters, knaves and fools ... adherents of the junto faction' who were elected to parliament was made at around this time. Vaughan was not among the eleven members, but he was a member of the committee which passed the 3 April order, and the army's mentioning of Devereux shows how close to his door retribution from the military came.

Vaughan remained in parliament during this tumultuous period which saw the eleven Presbyterian MPs absent themselves from the Commons for a period before a 'counter-revolution' by London Presbyterians returned them once more before, in a final reverse, the New Model marched on London and, ultimately, established the authority of the Independents. During this confused summer, Vaughan appeared in the House on 15 July 1647 as a committed Presbyterian supporter. On this date a division was called to consider action against members who had declared their royalist pasts. In this division, Vaughan was a teller for the noes, along with the Presbyterian John D'Oyly, whose side could

only marshal seventeen votes, while the leading Independents Sir Arthur
Haselrig and Sir John Evelyn counted seventy-seven votes in favour of
the motion.[46] This result points to the weakness of the Presbyterians in
the House at this time, but it is significant that Vaughan was willing to
put himself in the spotlight by standing as a teller in the division. Such a
heavy defeat for his 'side' and the febrile political atmosphere in London
seems to have taken its toll on Vaughan, however, for on 19 July he, along
with a number of other members, including Thomas More of Shrewsbury,
had leave to go into the country.[47] The Presbyterian 'counter-revolution'
in late July briefly made the Commons a more conducive place for men
like Vaughan, and on 2 August 1647 he was back investigating a 'tumult'
around the House.[48] However, when the army marched on London a few
days later, it is possible that Vaughan was one of those members who fled
the capital for fear of retribution as his parliamentary record falls silent for
several months. Although the events of the summer may have caused him
some anxiety over being too outspoken against the military establishment
and his Independent opponents, Vaughan nevertheless remained an MP.
On 23 December 1647 he, along with his ally the Denbigh member Simon
Thelwall, was sent into north Wales to assist the assessment commissioners
with disbanding supernumerary forces, something which is discussed in
more detail in the following chapter.[49]

The Presbyterians' problems at the political centre were mirrored in
Montgomeryshire by the travails of the sub-committee of accounts. The
difficulties of supplying the local soldiery seen in the Montgomery Castle
disturbances of early May 1647 as well as the struggles over sequestration
and tax collection cut across and took precedence over the ongoing
dispute between Lloyd Pierce and the county's accountants. This row,
which has framed so much of our discussion of the clash between the two
main political interests in the shire, was robbed of much of its energy and
momentum with the loss of the sub-committee's leading lights, especially
its chairman, who were absent in London for long periods. In April 1647,
Lloyd Pierce submitted to the central Accounts Committee some articles
of exception against the sub-committee, almost certainly a variation on the
theme of Sir Thomas Myddelton's 'exceptions' of February 1646.[50] The
charges were turned over to Edward Vaughan, now an MP of course, who

was to attend the committee and face some witnesses who were to prove Pierce's articles, although nothing concrete seems to have come of this meeting. As the business of investigating Pierce's accounts had dragged on, so it seems the central Cornhill Committee was losing interest in the matter. On 22 July 1647 it wrote to the Montgomeryshire body informing them that they needed to send in their promised surcharge against Pierce within two months.[51] They did not manage to do this, however, and the sub-committee effectively fell silent. This was in part because of the tumultuous national events of the summer of 1647 and the resurgent power of the army and the Independents which, in the localities, effectively meant that figures like Lloyd Pierce and Hugh Price could thumb their noses at their adversaries knowing that they would have little effective influence in Westminster to make any countermoves. In November 1647 the remaining sub-committee men wrote plaintively to their parent body:

> you maie perhapps wonder that yow have not had anie account of our proceedings of late; the truth is, wee have received at tymes soe manie discouragements through ye perverse carriage and practizes of some great accomptants that many of ye gentlemen who are in commission with us either forfeite or ... have refused alltogether to act with us, and some (even of those yt a while did act) have in a manner deserted ye employment ... By means whereof wee could not soe effectually of late goe forward with ye buisnesse of accompts as wee could have wished, and are at present reduced to soe slender a number that wee must be forced to desire some addition.[52]

This was a sorry state for the body which had been the Presbyterian powerhouse in the county. Their work effectively lapsed with the reorganisation of parliament's local administrative machinery in the later 1640s. After the Restoration, Lloyd Pierce could write that he attended the Cornhill Committee several times over the course of 1647 in anticipation of the promised surcharge against him. None was forthcoming, however, and from April 1648 he 'heard noe more from the ... committee'. He explained in 1662 that it was 'very unlikely that they who prosecuted [him] with such bitternes as they did should forbeare to exhibite a surharge against him if they had any, being soe often called upon for it by the grand committee & soe much time given them to prepar it'.[53]

The Second Civil War

The rising tide of discontent with the army's continued and burdensome presence, the ongoing problems of heavy taxation and rule by committee, the absence of a speedy peace settlement with the king and the rise of religious Independency generated a volatile and unstable politics throughout late 1647 and early 1648. This combustible atmosphere erupted into violence in the spring of 1648 with a series of local insurrections. Touched off in south Wales by the revolt of the Pembrokeshire ex-parliamentarian John Poyer which snowballed into a full-blown rebellion, these insurrections, combined with an invasion by the royalist-aligned Scottish Engagers, have become known to historians as the 'Second Civil War'.[54] Poyer's revolt saw large tracts of south Wales burst into open rebellion against parliament, rallying together around a rebel 'Declaration' which pledged its swearers to defend the king and Church against a rapacious and tyrannical parliament. Unsurprisingly, given its deep royalist attachments (it was less than a year in some places since royalist resistance had finally been snuffed out), north Wales also responded positively to the king's rallying call: as two parliamentarian officers from north Wales put it in June 1648, 'the sad distempers of these times ... [have] reached these countreyes in a great measure and threatened sad things to these parts'.[55]

The main episodes of resistance in north Wales were Sir John Owen's revolt in Caernarvonshire in May 1648 and Richard Bulkeley's uprising on Anglesey in September.[56] Montgomeryshire was not a centre of royalist activity, perhaps a reflection of the comparatively early defeat of the king's cause there in the First Civil War, but there can be no doubt that this fresh eruption of violence caused many parliamentarians in the county to fear that their own imminent destruction might be at hand. Some, following Poyer's example in the south, were probably tempted to turn their coats and join the royalist cause. Indeed, given Edward Vaughan's late appearance in parliamentarian colours, his clashes with army interests and his moderate political and religious priorities, we might wonder whether he was tempted to jump ship and join the rebels. He remained faithful to parliament, however, which is a testament perhaps to the sincerity of his initial parliamentarian support, although it is also the case that any royalist victory would have jeopardised his hold on Llwydiarth. One can imagine how Charles I's return to power would be accompanied by a triumphant Lord Powis and the restitution of Herbert Vaughan to his estates: a reward from a grateful king for their steadfast loyalty to his cause. Edward Vaughan's dilemma, however, was that a parliamentary victory which empowered his Independent adversaries would also probably put his estate in peril as their local allies would seek to sequester his patrimony and turn it over to the state. Such were the intractable problems thrown up by the rapid shifts of local and national politics in the later 1640s, and they presented a tricky balancing act for moderates like Vaughan. Nevertheless, despite the deeply divided nature of Montgomeryshire's warring parliamentarian factions, the 1648 uprising temporarily brought them together under a common banner of resistance.

On 20 May 1648, Edward Vaughan was at Montgomery where he subscribed an engagement of 'The gentlemen, ministers and well affected' of the county.[57] This document bound its subscribers to 'adhere (according to our Covenant) to the Parliament' against all enemies. Its signatories also associated together for the mutual defence of the county, agreed to raise forces and committed themselves to disarming 'all ill affected persons'. The list of subscribers is revealing of the way in which this moment of peril brought together the county's warring factions. The list was headed by Matthew Morgan as sheriff along with accounts sub-committee men like Vaughan, George Devereux, Samuel More, Edward Owen and Gabriel Wynne, but also present were Lloyd Pierce, Lodowick Myddelton, the officer Hercules Hannay (who had been pursued by the Montgomeryshire accountants),[58] along with the Independent preachers Ambrose Mostyn and Vavasor Powell.

Perhaps fortunately, given the inherent instability of this county coalition, Montgomeryshire's forces were not tested and the area did not become a major theatre for fighting. This is not to say, however, that there were not moments of considerable anxiety and concern during the spring and summer. Sir John Owen's abortive rising in Merioneth soon after the 20 May engagement, for example, saw Colonel George Twistleton send for forces out of Montgomeryshire to guard the 'passes' between the counties: the very area that Edward Vaughan had commanded with his Abermarchant garrison.[59] Indeed, Twistleton had received undertakings from Vaughan and Matthew Morgan, along with several other local gentlemen, 'that all the force they could make' would rendezvous at Llanfair to assist the colonel's forces in his pursuit of the rebels.[60] Sir John Owen's defeat by Twistleton at Y Dalar Hir in Caernarvonshire in early June removed the major royalist threat in north Wales, although Sir Henry Lingen's revolt in Herefordshire in August proved another moment for concern, although this too fizzled out harmlessly. This resurgence of military action in the area, however, served to strengthen the hand of Lloyd Pierce and his pro-army group. We can see a suggestion of this in the directions for defending Montgomery Castle which were issued on 20 April 1648 by the Red Castle committee. This order countermanded Lord Herbert of Cherbury's own directive that the townsmen be called in to secure the castle. The committee instead directed that 'a competent number of faithfull men' under direct military command be placed there, or that the leader of the army, Sir Thomas Fairfax, take some 'effectuall course' for the town's defence with New Model forces.[61] The signatories to this order were Lloyd Pierce, Hugh Price, Richard Price and Evan Lloyd: the sequestration cadre were empowered by the military emergency.

Independents ascendent, June–December 1648

Although he was present to assist Twistleton's efforts against Sir John Owen, by 1 June 1648 Edward Vaughan was back at Westminster, being nominated to a committee considering an ordinance for examining 'the accompts of the soldiery of the kingdom', an initiative which was of obvious interest to him.[62] A fortnight later he was appointed to a similar committee examining monies paid to soldiers and officers.[63] Although these nominations indicate his concern with the auditing of soldiers' accounts and possibly of opening a fresh line of attack against his local adversaries, it seems that the tide had decisively turned against Vaughan as the resurgence of military activity helped fuel a backlash against temporising moderates and ex-royalists who had been at the heart of the summer's rebellion. The defeat of the several insurrections in England and Wales and the vanquishing of the Engager forces at the Battle of Preston in mid-August delivered a major fillip for Independency and the New Model, and the new political landscape was hostile territory for moderate Presbyterians, even those who had stood firm for parliament in recent months.

It seems quite possible that Vaughan abandoned Westminster in the autumn to defend himself against new efforts by Lloyd Pierce and his allies to remove him from Llwydiarth. In mid-June 1648, a complaint brought to the central sequestration committee by these individuals demanded that Vaughan obey the central committee's directives of October 1645 and turn Llwydiarth over to the state.[64] Up to this point, the sequestrators alleged, Vaughan had 'by his favourers' in parliament 'blasted & frustrated' their efforts to enforce the state's claim to his properties.[65] According to one account, the central sequestration committee supported Pierce's complaint and required Vaughan to comply, although this is not corroborated by other sources.[66] There was, however, clearly a renewed and concerted effort to oust Vaughan from possession; a move that would likely be followed by an attempt to remove him from his parliamentary seat also. On 29 September 1648, Sir Thomas Fairfax penned a letter to those under his command noting that he had been informed of 'endeavours ... to gett some souldiers ... to dispossesse Edward Vaughan esq. a Member of the House of Commons of his howse (att Lloydiarth)'.[67] Fairfax noted that Vaughan had a writ of restitution from Montgomeryshire's commission of the peace (which, of course, was dominated by Vaughan and his allies) and the lord general required his forces not to involve themselves in the business, 'it being not proper for soldiers to meddle in matter of title betweene partye & partye'. Despite this order, on 25 October 1648 the Red Castle committee issued a certificate to sequestrators to take thirty soldiers from their garrison and secure Vaughan's lands.[68] This was a direct contravention of Fairfax's order, but it seems that the sequestrators believed that Vaughan's stock was falling quickly in the autumn of 1648 and that not too many questions would be asked if they moved against him. Although we lack evidence for what happened after the issuing of this certificate, Pierce and his associates were unable to make good on the order and Vaughan remained in possession; this was possibly because he kept armed men of his own at the property to defend it.

This renewed attack indicates that an important shift in local politics had accompanied the New Model's victory in the Second Civil War, and this seems confirmed by the fact that Montgomeryshire's next sheriff, pricked on 23 November 1648, was Evan Lloyd, a close associate of Lloyd Pierce, his fellow sequestration committeeman, sometime captain in Myddelton's brigade and a signatory of the October order to dispossess Vaughan.[69] This shift in local politics was not decisively towards the Independents, however: Vaughan remained the county MP and in August 1648 he, along with many accounts sub-committee colleagues, were named as commissioners to assist the North Wales Association in subduing Bulkley's Anglesey rising.[70] Moreover, on 2 December 1648, Vaughan was appointed a militia commissioner for both Merioneth and Montgomeryshire, although this would be his last appointment to local office for a lengthy period.[71]

Pride's Purge

The conclusion of the Second Civil War saw a bitter wave of recrimination sweep through army and Independent circles against those who had once again plunged the nation into war. Moreover, despite what these groups saw as the clear judgement of providence, many moderates were still willing to treat with King Charles I on modest terms in what seemed a betrayal of the army's many sacrifices for the cause. The Commons' willingness to continue negotiations with the king despite his evident double dealing and untrustworthiness brought a dramatic intervention from the New Model on 6 December 1648 in the episode which has become known as 'Pride's Purge'. Colonel Thomas Pride and his regiment marched on Westminster and excluded 140 MPs who had supported continued negotiation with the king and who were considered enemies of the army; some forty-five of these were also arrested, 'in a rude and ruffianly manner'.[72] Although there is some confusion as there were two 'Mr Vaughans' in the House (the other was Charles Vaughan, a Devonshire MP), it is clear that Edward Vaughan was not only secluded from sitting in the House, but that he was also arrested as one of those MPs considered most dangerous to the army's designs.[73] He was thus likely to have been among those who spent an uncomfortable night on 6 December under guard in a Westminster victualling house named *Hell*. Vaughan then joined fellow Presbyterian members such as Colonel Edward Harley of Herefordshire under house arrest, and probably only heard at second-hand about the momentous events at Westminster and Whitehall which saw the king placed on trial for his life before he was executed on 30 January 1649 and a republic declared.

Exclusion from the House was a defining moment in Vaughan's life and signalled the effective end of his political aspirations for a decade. Although a loyal parliamentarian, he had become a marked man, tainted by his moderate politics, his long-standing opposition to army interests and his willingness to hold out an olive branch to the king. On 16 January 1649, Vaughan and several other secluded members requested a licence to publish a response to an army pamphlet which had justified the purge.[74] The tract they targeted portrayed the secluded members as a corrupt and corrupting force within the House. The publication had especial contempt for those recruiter MPs like Vaughan who, it alleged, were 'self serving men united with the old royalists and new malignants and newters'.[75] By way of answer, this group produced a *Vindication* which was authored by Vaughan's old superior on the Accounts Committee, William Prynne. One section of this tract commented directly on by-election cases such as Vaughan's, asserting that those who had come into the House through this route were not 'neuters or malignants' as was alleged, but were rather men 'who either by their services as souldiers for the parliament, or in their committees ... or sufferings in their cause, gave a faithfulnesse to the parliament before they were elected'.[76] Vaughan was only released from his house arrest on 12 February 1649, a lengthy period which may suggest that he was considered particularly dangerous by the Commonwealth authorities or, perhaps more likely, that his local antagonists had useful agents operating on their behalf at Westminster who were able to ensure that Vaughan remained neutralised in London.[77] He had suffered a calamitous reverse. His 'cause' was in ruins and he himself was *persona non grata* in the new Commonwealth. Although still nominally an MP, he had few friends at the political centre who could help him in his travails. Even more troublingly, his enemies in the country were already circling, and they sought not just to neutralise Vaughan but to ruin him entirely by seizing his estate. The following chapter charts these struggles and Vaughan's desperate rearguard action to retain his hard-won hold on Llwydiarth.

PART THREE:

FROM REPUBLIC
TO RESTORATION

CHAPTER 8

Republican Revenge, 1648-1655

P ride's Purge was a climacteric in Edward Vaughan's life which saw him exiled to the margins of power and stripped of much of his influence. The revolution at the political centre was accompanied by something of a revolution in local politics, as allies of the religious radicals, the political Independents and of the New Model Army captured the apparatus of Montgomeryshire's government. This chapter examines Vaughan's struggles with his old adversaries from the Montgomeryshire sequestration committee who were empowered by the revolution and who sought to realise their ambition of sequestering Llwydiarth and ruining their longtime rival. This chapter draws on a wealth of unused evidence from the papers of the Committee for Compounding with Delinquents to tell an unusually detailed and textured story of Welsh political rivalries during the early Commonwealth. To do this, however, we must briefly look back to the later 1640s and to Edward Vaughan's role in disbanding north Wales's soldiery. His efforts in this regard provided material for the attack against him, which assumed a familiar form in Welsh public politics during this period – allegations of embezzlement and the misappropriation of public funds. The analysis offered here also brings to light important but hitherto unknown public appeals which Vaughan and his adversaries issued in 1649. These involved manuscript (and possibly printed) petitions and defences made in the name of the county, and these efforts provide us with some invaluable insights into the nature and conduct of local Welsh politics in the early Commonwealth. This is a period of Welsh history that is usually only examined through the lives of the 'Saints', of religious radicals such as Vavasor Powell who became such powerful figures in the Welsh Marches in the early 1650s. Although we should not neglect the critical role of these figures, Vaughan's struggles provide us with an alternative thread of moderate parliamentarian religion and politics during the Commonwealth. His case, then, offers a novel discussion from the perspective of a 'loser' in the mid-seventeenth-century revolution. This examination also provides further evidence of Vaughan's legal nous, guile and cunning which he needed to survive in the face of a cadre of local radicals bent upon his destruction.

Revenge: the controversy over disbandment

When Edward Vaughan returned to Llwydiarth after his bruising experiences in Westminster in late 1648 and early 1649, he came back to a new political world. We can see the nature of this change in the composition of Montgomeryshire's commission of the peace, which was issued on 30 March 1649.[1] Despite being the county's wealthiest parliamentarian and (nominally) chair of its accounts sub-committee, Vaughan's tenure as a JP was terminated. Some of his old associates managed to retain their places, but they were now joined by key Independents including Lloyd Pierce, Hugh and Richard Price, Richard Griffiths of Sutton and Evan Lloyd. There had been a decisive shift in power towards close allies of the New Model Army and Montgomeryshire's small cadre of radical parliamentarians. A similar pattern can be seen in the commissioners for collecting the general assessment who were appointed on 7 April 1649: Vaughan was omitted from this body also.[2]

The transformation wrought by the revolution in London emboldened Lloyd Pierce and his allies to move once more, and with renewed purpose, against the weakened and exposed Edward Vaughan. They devised a two-pronged attack, one part of which focused on the familiar allegations that Vaughan refused to turn over Llwydiarth to the state despite the orders of the central sequestration committee in 1644 and 1645. We will deal with this dimension of their charges in a moment. The other avenue of attack takes us back to late 1647 and early 1648 and to parliament's disbanding of north Wales's supernumerary forces (that is, those army companies which were not part of the New Model but were rather under the aegis of Thomas Mytton and the North Wales Association). This was part of the 'great disbandment' in which parliament shed nearly 20,000 of its provincial troops. As was discussed in chapters 6 and 7, the burdens of the soldiery were a constant refrain of complaint in north Wales in 1647, but in November there was hope that concrete steps towards disbandment would address the grievances of heavy taxation and free quarter. A meeting of the Committee for North Wales on 2 November 1647 had agreed to reduce the levels of taxation and to draw down Mytton's forces there.[3] On 23 December 1647, Edward Vaughan, along with his fellow MP Simon Thelwall, was ordered into north Wales by the Commons and the Committee of the Army to assist the commissioners for levying the monthly assessment in disbanding local forces; they were joined in this business by the other local members (who may have already been in north Wales), Sir Thomas Myddelton, Thomas Myddleton (the major general's son) and Colonel John Jones.[4] Disbandment was not a straightforward matter, however, and the various orders local gentlemen received from parliament, Sir Thomas Fairfax and the three MPs caused some confusion, as did the intricate system of loans and securities which was to provide the money for effecting the drawing down of local forces.[5]

Despite these issues, in Montgomeryshire Vaughan disbanded the five troops of horse which were costing the county some £800 per month, the kind of imposition that was described by one Caernarvonshire commentator in early 1648 as a 'cruel burthen upon the contrey', which would be 'eaten up to the verie bones ... and ruined for ever' if disbandment was not effected quickly.[6] However, according to the ordinance which parliament passed as Vaughan and his colleagues left Westminster, the troops required two months' pay immediately with the remainder of their arrears given in the form of debentures.[7] To obtain this sizeable sum, Vaughan proposed a scheme for the county to pay the £1,600 as a loan upon the security of monies assigned by the Army Committee out of assessments laid on Staffordshire.[8] His enemies would later claim that Vaughan took both Montgomeryshire's money and that from Staffordshire, but after disbanding the horse companies he never paid the advanced money back to the Montgomeryshire taxpayers but rather pocketed it himself.[9] The disbanding itself evidently went off peacefully,[10] but the imputation of financial malpractice during the process would hang over Vaughan's head for the next four years.

Revenge: the 'Montgomeryshire petition', April 1649

The allegations of financial malfeasance over disbandment would come to dog Vaughan from the spring of 1649, but the first rumblings of a renewed campaign against him following his seclusion from parliament was the revival of the efforts to eject him from Llwydiarth, efforts which had previously run out of steam in October 1647. The first warning shot was fired in a letter and a set of depositions that were submitted to the central sequestration committee at Goldsmiths' Hall on 1 March 1649 (an inauspicious St David's Day for Edward Vaughan!) by Hugh Price, Lloyd Pierce and Montgomeryshire's sheriff, Evan Lloyd.[11] The letter's signatories lamented their 'disability for want of assistance to take possession of ... Lloidiart, still kept by force & stronge hand from ye state by the agents of Mr Edward Vaughan'. The authors laid on pretty thickly the central committee's lack of support in enforcing their earlier order to take possession and averred that because of this failure Llwydiarth's tenants were refusing to pay a third of their rents to Lady Katherine Palmer for her jointure settlement. Moreover, the tenants claimed that they had been 'threatned by Mr Vaughans agents & servants' that if they did pay her rents, then these agents would quickly make them pay once more to Vaughan. Pierce and his associates concluded forebodingly that if the situation over the estate was not quickly addressed it 'will breed a sleighteing of your honours power & authority in these partes'. The depositions that accompanied the letter substantiated the story which the local sequestrators told, with individuals like Cadwalader Morris swearing that he would not pay rents to Lady Palmer as 'for feare of Mr Vaughans agents, servants and frends he dare not'.[12]

It does not appear that the Goldsmiths' Hall committee was disposed to move quickly on these allegations, however, perhaps because it was wary of tackling an MP, albeit one who had been secluded from the House. However, a more organised and concerted campaign against Vaughan began on 18 April 1649 with a petition submitted to parliament in the name of Montgomeryshire's inhabitants. One news-sheet recorded that this petition 'was … presented to the House, complaining of Edward Vaughan … [and] charging him with many things of high nature'.[13] The Leveller-aligned newsbook *The Moderate* asked whether leave was now given to inform against members of the Commons, adding that 'if so, this Member would not be a phenix', which is to say, that they believed the charges against him were such that he would not rise from the ashes of his seclusion to have a future political career.[14]

The county petition against Vaughan was organised by Lloyd Pierce. Although it was presented in the name of Montgomeryshire's inhabitants, Vaughan questioned its legitimacy, arguing that it did not appear in parliament's files (the Commons' clerk Henry Scobell agreed that this was the case), 'the originall … is not to be found', and also that the document was presented without the knowledge of the county's population, even though it purported to articulate their wishes.[15] Vaughan's supporters in Montgomeryshire similarly claimed that his 'malicious prosecutors' had wronged him by 'feighning a petition against him in ye name of ye countie'.[16] Vaughan himself alleged that Pierce had the petition printed and sent into the country and that he had it published 'in ye diurnall for yt week'. However, while no trace of the original petition can indeed be found, which helps corroborate Vaughan's claims that it was improperly presented to parliament, no printed copy or republication of the petition in the newsbooks for this period has been located either.[17] Despite the fact that this text has apparently not survived, it is interesting to see Pierce apparently venturing into the realm of print at this point, the first evidence we have of recourse to the press in the long history of his acrimonious dispute with Vaughan. This development suggests Pierce's recognition of the need to bring in a wider public interest, probably centred on Independent circles in London, which would help add momentum to his campaign. Recent scholarship has been very clear that the civil war changed the rules of public politics in a fundamental manner through the enormous expansion of the printed sphere which attended and inflamed so many of the bitter confrontations of the 1640s and 1650s.[18] Faced with this public relations campaign against him, Vaughan reacted in kind by mobilising his supporters behind a 'Vindication' of his own position, a document which garnered nearly 2,000 subscriptions in the county.[19]

Although no copy of Pierce's original petition survives, it is clear that it focused on Vaughan's role in disbanding the Montgomeryshire horse in the spring of 1648 and on his unwillingness to turn over possession of Llwydiarth to the state. On 18 April 1649 the Commons referred the business to the Committee for the Advance of Money at Haberdashers' Hall, which was empowered to examine the complaint against Vaughan; to take his accounts for the public monies he had received; and to transmit this evidence to the Montgomeryshire sequestration committee for further investigation.[20] On 27 April the Haberdashers' Hall committee summoned Vaughan and ordered the serjeant-at-arms to bring him up in custody.[21] A day later Kyffin Lloyd of Welshpool submitted to the committee a certificate that in 1648 he had been appointed by the commissioners for the monthly assessment to be treasurer for the monies involved in disbanding the supernumerary forces, and that he was happy to provide 'a iust & true accoumpt' when required.[22] The witnesses to his certificate give a good indication of Lloyd's allegiances: they included George Devereux and William Barbour.[23] Vaughan, however, was evidently less keen to accommodate his accusers and to meet this reckoning, for the 27 April order had to be repeated on 18 May when Hugh Price and George Twistleton as governors of Powis Castle and Denbigh were ordered to assist in bringing him before the Committee for the Advance of Money.[24] Vaughan evidently did make his way to the capital in June 1649, where he was presented with the charges and, at the end of the month, was discharged from custody after having provided the committee with his answer.[25]

So what were the charges against him and how did Vaughan respond? It is worth noting, before we examine these documents, that they were apparently presented by Thomas Pierce of Maesmawr, Lloyd Pierce's son.[26] This manoeuvre may simply have been the product of Lloyd Pierce's indisposition, but it may also have reflected an attempt by Lloyd to distance himself from the charge so that he might be involved in the subsequent investigation of the matter. One charge concerned the business of disbandment and was signed by a group of some fourteen individuals 'in the name of our selves and others subscribers of the late peticion against ... Mr Vaughan to the honourable House of Parliament'.[27] It described Vaughan as 'late a Member of the House of Commons', suggesting that his seclusion from the Commons in December 1648 had terminated his tenure of office (it had not). Such a tactic was probably a means of conveying that the signatories no longer considered him to be the county's legitimate representative and, indeed, to publicise the fact that they felt that they had effectively lost their voice at Westminster through his seclusion. Among the signatories to this document were the usual suspects – Lloyd Pierce and Hugh Price – who were undoubtedly the organising figures behind this attempt to bring down the county's MP. Alongside them were some new figures in local politics. One was James Mytton of Pontyscowrid (Meifod), a lawyer and kinsman of Thomas Mytton, who also sat on the Shropshire bench. Other signatories included Pierce's brother-in-law, Edward Maurice of Pen-y-bont and Richard Owen, an undistinguished official who became sheriff in 1653.[28] These were truly obscure individuals, particularly compared with local officeholders before the civil wars, and their presence suggests the way the foundations of county politics had slipped down the social scale since the revolution and regicide.[29] The document they subscribed was simple, brief and straightforward. It claimed that the money required to disband the county's forces in early 1648 was £1,967 12s. 0d but that Vaughan and his 'agents' had received some £3,751 9s. 0d for the service. There thus remained £1,783 17s. 0d on his hands unaccounted for.[30]

The second charge against Vaughan submitted to Haberdashers' Hall also focused on his improper withholding of public money, but this concerned Llwydiarth's sequestration.[31] This document was signed by the 'big three' among Vaughan's local opponents – Lloyd Pierce, Hugh Price and Richard Price – who, they said, constituted 'the committee of ... the county of Mountgomery'. The paper told a familiar narrative: that Herbert Vaughan, Llwydiarth's Catholic owner, was sequestered in 1644 and that Edward Vaughan had obtained a lease of the property in September 1645, but this had been negated a month later by the central sequestration committee because Vaughan was a party claiming title to the property. Notwithstanding this directive, Vaughan continued in possession of the estate, and so he was accountable for the rents he had received in the interim which were, in fact, the state's property. The signatories enumerated the amounts that they believed Vaughan owed: £1,000 at least from Montgomeryshire; £400 for four years from Denbighshire (£1,600); and £200 for four years from Merioneth (£800). This made a total of £3,400, a crippling sum in 'back taxes' which would have ruined Vaughan, particularly as their design would be to prise the estate from his hands and leave him with no resources with which he might meet these obligations.

These submissions represented the most dangerous moment for Edward Vaughan since his seclusion from the Commons; perhaps since he had fled Oxford six years before. The charges were being examined not before a committee in Montgomeryshire where he held resources of patronage and a body of supporters, or before the central Accounts Committee which was sympathetic to his cause. Rather the hearing was in the hostile environment of republican London where his adversaries were boosted by their long-standing support of the army and the Independent cause. The charges constituted an existential threat to Vaughan's capacity to retain his estates, support his local interests and defend himself from financial ruin and possible imprisonment. As long experience had showed, however, he was an indefatigable adversary when it came to Llwydiarth and a man who would use any tactic to defend his claim. Pierce and the two Prices must have known that he would not lie down in the face of their accusations, and he did indeed come out fighting with a pair of 'Defences' for wider circulation that sought to rebut the submissions made against him.

Response: Edward Vaughan's 'Defences' and 'Vindication'

In the first 'Defence' (which certainly did not to venture into Miltonic territory), Vaughan pointedly described himself as 'a Member of Parliament' and began with a bullish statement that it 'is ye undoubted privilege of anie Member of Parliament not to be impleaded before a committee without speciall order from the Howse', and that, knowing this, Lloyd Pierce had framed the suspect petition in the name of Montgomeryshire's inhabitants to haul Vaughan before them.[32] Indeed, he was pointed in upbraiding Pierce for 'termeing him late Member of the Howse of Commons'. It is notable, then, that Vaughan continued to claim the privileges of being an MP even though he no longer sat in the Rump Parliament (that part of the Long Parliament which remained following Pride's Purge). Indeed, he averred that parliament's order bringing him before the committee was 'a way of proceeding never used against anie person whatsoever where noe contempt [of parliament] is made'. Vaughan was indeed correct in asserting his parliamentary privileges as he was not disabled as a member and no new election had been called for his seat. It was effectively impossible for him to invoke these privileges, however, as to do so would have demonstrated his belief that the Rump was a legitimate body despite the coup which had ejected him and his fellow Presbyterians: Vaughan was willing to invoke parliamentary privilege, but only to make a rhetorical point rather than a practical one.

In his 'Defence', Vaughan rubbished the accounting of Pierce's submission regarding the costs of disbandment and went on the attack by suggesting that the efforts against him were motivated by his position as chair of the accounts sub-committee. Pierce was eager to 'abridge him', Vaughan said, because, as the county's sole treasurer since 1644, Pierce was accountable for £50,000 of public money 'which accompt he knew noe ready way to avoyd then by removeing Mr Vaughan from those parts and endeavoureing to make him an acomptant and soe consequently uncapable to act as chaireman for accompts'. So Vaughan sought to drag this business back into the politics of civil war Montgomeryshire, and to suggest that the claims against him were motivated solely by personal interest. The reasoning behind his defence was distinctly shaky, however, particularly given the fact that the accounts sub-committee was defunct. Vaughan took issue with the framing of the petition against him, maintaining that it was 'soe generally disliked' by the county's inhabitants that, in defence of themselves and of Vaughan, 'whome they had chosen knight of the shire of their countie', they had circulated a vindication 'subscribed by above two thowsand handes'. Vaughan submitted his

'Vindication' to the committee, although this document, like Pierce's original petition, has unfortunately not survived.

After stating his objections to the nature of the proceedings, Vaughan went on to provide what he described as a 'cleere satisfaction' to the committee, although it fell far short of a forensic accounting. Instead, he simply argued that he 'acted nothing of himselfe' in the disbanding service, but worked in concert with Simon Thelwall and Colonel John Jones, and that any monies that they as commissioners received for the service went to treasurers who would be happy to account for the same: he must have known that Kyffin Lloyd had given just such an undertaking to the committee some weeks before. And that was about it. Vaughan went into no further details about the business but rather declared himself 'ill requited for ye good service he therein did ye countrey', a service which he claimed had cost him £500, and he concluded by decrying the 'abuse offered to him as a member ... thus highly injur'd'.

Vaughan's other paper addressed the claims relating to Llwydiarth's sequestration and, unsurprisingly, was just as unyielding as his submission over disbandment monies.[33] In fact, he had already been preparing the ground for his defence on this subject. He informed the Committee for the Advance of Money that 'for better quieting' his title, on 30 May 1649 he had procured an order signed by three governors of castles in north Wales along with 'all of the comittee of sequestracions of north Wales', to suspend proceedings over Llwydiarth upon a promise that Vaughan would repay all rents due to Herbert Vaughan from the lands and 'not intermedle with the proffitts till he cleere his clayme thereunto'. In addition to this order, he secured a further paper dated 2 June 1649 which was submitted to the Haberdashers' committee in the name of the 'Committee of Sequestrations for Northwales'.[34] However, this was a body that did not exist at this point, but which seems to have been confected as a proxy for the Committee for North Wales (although, in practice, even this institution should have fallen into abeyance with the dissolution of the North Wales Association, and its civil jurisdiction should have devolved to individual county committees). The so-called committee's paper was essentially a narrative supporting Vaughan's claims to Llwydiarth based on 'proofes and records' with which the signatories had been provided. It endorsed the validity of Sir Robert Vaughan's 1622 entail and the supportive court verdicts that Vaughan had received in Merioneth and Denbighshire in August 1642. It further testified that Vaughan had owned Llwydiarth in July 1644 'and doth now likewise possesse ye same'. This was a powerful and timely vindication of Vaughan's title; and it was problematic for these very reasons.

Sequestration committees, real and invented, June 1650– January 1651

A glance at the signatories of the 'Committee of Sequestrations for North Wales' indicates why we should be suspicious about the submission, for it was filled with Vaughan allies from the Montgomeryshire sub-committee of accounts including George Devereux, Samuel More, Matthew Morgan, Gabriel Wynne, Richard Griffith and William Kyffin. While these men may nominally have been sequestrators appointed by Sir Thomas Myddelton in 1644, they had long since stopped acting in that capacity; although, as we have seen, they revived such claims when it suited them to do so.[35] There was also an impressive roster of military figures signing this document who constituted the backbone of government during the interregnum in counties like Denbighshire. These included John Alderley, Thomas Ball, Roger Sontley and Luke Lloyd, most of whom had close ties with Sir Thomas Myddelton. While their appearance on this paper may simply reflect their support for Vaughan as a former parliamentarian officer, it might equally be an indication of a rapprochement between Myddelton and Vaughan. There is evidence that Myddelton joined Vaughan as one of those secluded at Pride's Purge, and the former major general was certainly no fan of the New Model or of the radical political and religious agendas which now seemed set to steer the nation's course.[36] It is plausible, then, that Myddelton had come to recognise in Vaughan a fellow political Presbyterian who might act as a moderating force against the more radical elements of republican north Wales, many of which, ironically, Myddelton had once sponsored and promoted. One way to balance the power of figures like Richard Price, the supporter of the radical preacher Vavasor Powell, for example, would be to ensure that the influence of a major landed estate such as Llwydiarth remained in the hands of a political moderate. Other signatories to the paper were Thomas Ravenscroft, Flintshire's sheriff and, surprisingly, Evan Lloyd, his counterpart in Montgomeryshire. Lloyd's presence is inexplicable given his ties to Lloyd Pierce and further research is required to explain it.

The 2 June 1649 paper echoed and endorsed Vaughan's narrative about his possession of Llwydiarth which can be found in his second answer to the Haberdashers' committee.[37] This answer upheld Vaughan's claim to the property through his brother's entail, the 1630 Star Chamber decision, the votes of the Committee for Justice in March 1641 and the country verdicts of August 1642, which, taken together, he argued, meant that Herbert Vaughan was not in possession of Llwydiarth in 1644 and thus the estate could not be sequestered on account of his delinquency. Vaughan further asserted that the central sequestrations committee was only a 'committee of appeals', and as no appeal was made regarding the estate, their orders were 'only directorie to ye committee belowe' in Wales, and thus only constituted a requirement to execute parliament's ordinances. In any event, he asserted, these sequestration orders were all procured by Lloyd Pierce on 'untrue certificates', and Vaughan was 'neither partie nor privye' to the local committee's proceedings. He decried the 'practizes of … Mr Pierce and his adharents' and argued that the 'committee in Northwales' were the 'propper judges thereof' rather than the local sequestrators or the Haberdashers' committee. This was the point in his answer at which he brought in the certificate, 'signed by fourtene of the … comittee', which endorsed his version of events, and which he was happy to produce for his judges. Arguing that, on the basis of these submissions, no rents were due to the state, Vaughan requested a dismissal of the complaint against him but also reparations as would seem appropriate 'to a Member of Parliament thus wronged'.

On 4 July 1649 the Haberdashers' committee ordered that Pierce and the other prosecutors receive copies of Vaughan's answers and be given leave to take exceptions to them. This they did, and in the next couple of weeks Pierce and his associates submitted a robust response of

their own to the Committee for the Advance of Money which described
Vaughan's answers as 'either frivolous, false, impertinent, irratinal [*sic*]
or scandalous'.[38] This paper defended the county petition and denied
that Lloyd Pierce was an organising force, arguing rather that he was
only involved 'as a private person'. On the point of parliamentary
privilege, the text was eager to stress that Vaughan had been questioned
before a parliamentary committee on the basis of the petition, but they
also cheerfully reached back into February 1647 when Vaughan was
'questioned for a delinquent within 3 or 4 dayes after his comeinge to
the parliament house', where, it was alleged, a number of witnesses gave
evidence against him, although his case was not yet reported back to the
House. The paper brushed off the charges against Lloyd Pierce as simply
'impertinent', and driven largely by Pierce's own faithfulness to the state
in endeavouring to prove Vaughan a delinquent. This new submission was
dismissive of Vaughan's 'Vindication' (his response to the county petition
of April 1649), which Pierce claimed had been unduly procured as:

> most of those that subscribed it never heard it read, but weare forced
> to subscribe by Mr Vaughan and his agents … He lickwise threatned
> some of those that put theire hands to the peticion against him and used
> terrifying language … threatning that hee would make them repent it.

Pierce and his fellow authors also made the explosive allegation that
Vaughan, having disbanded the supernumerary troops, employed
the arms which came into his possession for raising a troop of horse,
pretending it to be for the service of the public, but, in fact, using it to
defend Llwydiarth from the sequestrators' attentions. They charged that
his 'expediting that service was more for his owne interest in wrongfully
possessinge another mans estate then the publique good'. To a nervous
fledgling republic that was painfully aware of the thin foundation of
public support upon which it rested, particularly in areas like Wales, the
image of a potentially delinquent major landholder employing his own
military forces was a troubling one. There is no independent evidence that
Vaughan had indeed used disbanded soldiers in this way, but he certainly
'had form' in his garrisoning of Abermarchant, and this was a well-chosen

image if one wanted to portray a bogeyman who was a potential threat to the state and needed speedy neutralising. To this end, Pierce and his allies requested that the business be referred back to them as the county committee, in part because it would be very expensive to bring so many witnesses up to London.

Having considered this submission, on 20 July 1649 the Committee for the Advance of Money ordered, as Pierce had requested, that the case papers be transmitted to the Montgomeryshire sequestration committee which was to 'examine the whole state of the charge', take witness depositions and report back.[39] This was potentially a calamitous development for Vaughan, of course, for his case would now be largely determined by his bitterest local enemies. As a result, he made a counter-motion that 'his accusers might not be his judges', and, after some wrangling, the Committee for the Advance of Money concurred, ordering that Lloyd Pierce, Hugh Price and Richard Price be exempted from any formal role in the business and that only the remainder of the Montgomeryshire sequestration committee examine the case – although it is doubtful whether they realised that this this would be only two people![40] This order frustrated Thomas Pierce who had presented the prosecutors' case in London, and he attempted to get his father and his two close colleagues reinstated through the agency of a figure who will loom large in our discussions of the early 1650s, the lawyer and jurist Rice Vaughan of Gray's Inn.

Rice (or 'Rhys'/'Rees') Vaughan originally hailed from Machynlleth, and was the clerk for the central sequestration committee until its abolition in 1649.[41] He was thus a committed parliamentarian and a man who had already been named to the first parliamentary committee established in Wales – that of Pembrokeshire in 1644 – and who would also be named to the highly influential Commission for the Propagation of the Gospel in February 1650.[42] In this case, Rice Vaughan argued forcefully before the Haberdashers' committee for the inclusion of the original prosecutors in the investigation of Edward Vaughan's finances, but he was crossed in these arguments by William Barbour, sometime clerk to the Montgomeryshire accounts sub-committee. Following their respective oral arguments, a scuffle broke out in which Rice Vaughan called Barbour 'rogue, and said if he were not of that place he would kick him [Barbour] and swore hee [Rice Vaughan] wold spend all the money he was worth but he would have ye order of 25 July ... reversed', and pledged that he would also have Barbour branded a delinquent.[43] After Barbour reproved him, Rice Vaughan, upon the committee's rising, drew his sword in the committee chamber, while Barbour claimed he was defenceless, holding 'but his papers and hatt in his hands'.[44] This incident suggests the passions which were inflamed by the Llwydiarth case and also speaks to the wider significance of both the personalities and the local power politics which lay behind the effort to bring Edward Vaughan down. It is certainly the case that Rice Vaughan was one to bear a grudge, and he and Edward Vaughan's men would clash spectacularly over the 1654 election in Merioneth, an incident which is discussed in the following chapter. Despite Rice's arguments (and his anger), the committee's order to exclude the original prosecutors stood.

Notwithstanding their efforts with the Haberdashers' committee, Pierce and his allies simultaneously resuscitated their attempt to enforce the original sequestration decision of October 1645 and obtained an order to that effect from the central sequestration committee on 25 June 1649.[45] However, before this could be executed, Vaughan managed to obtain another certificate from the 'committee of sequestrations for Montgomeryshire and Denbighshire', a body that had never formally existed and which, moreover, had been superseded by a general sequestration committee for north Wales.[46] Indeed, the collection of figures on this certificate was described by Lloyd Pierce as a mixture of 'most of the old and new committees for North Wales'.[47] This certificate, like that of 2 June, endorsed Edward Vaughan's title to Llwydiarth and also concluded that any challengers to his title could only proceed through recourse to law rather than through the sequestration process.[48] Pierce and Hugh Price later took issue with this document, describing it as a 'private order' which was 'grounded uppon noe publique debate of the cause, nor entred into any publique register that wee cane finde, but obtayned by secret labourings of hands from house to house (as wee are informed) purporting that they weare satisfied in Mr Vaughans title'.[49] Like the 2 June certificate, its signatories betray Vaughan's influence for they included figures like George Devereux and Matthew Morgan, while prominent army men including John Peck, Thomas Critchley and Thomas Ball were also prevailed upon to sign. In a letter reflecting on their efforts to enforce the state's interest in this matter, Pierce and Hugh Price lamented how their labours had been frustrated and 'that the Comonwealth (wheareunto wee are sworne to bee faithfull) hath of late beene much dampnified by the timidity or (which we are loth to say) partiallitie rather of some of our associates'.[50] They doubtless had in mind men like Devereux who were nominally sequestrators, but who had worked to obstruct and impede sequestration business, and the letter's authors reflected angrily on the 'backwardnes of some of the committees' properly to pursue Llwydiarth's sequestration.

Edward Vaughan had thus pulled off something of a coup by playing fast and loose with the various incarnations of the committees that had sprouted up under parliamentary rule in north Wales, fabricating a sequestration committee to obtain a certificate which provided him, effectively, with a stay of proceedings against his estate. Indeed, it seems upon the basis of later testimony that in late 1649 he began a new campaign of threatening those Llwydiarth tenants who paid their rents to the sequestrators and evicting some who did so by force of arms.[51] Despite the fillip the committee orders gave his cause, however, there remained the investigation proceeding under the seal of the Committee for the Advance of Money, and Vaughan's adversaries probably spent the summer and early autumn of 1649 gathering materials for their case against him, At this point, however, Vaughan manufactured a bravura piece of political theatre, deception and sheer effrontery which speaks to his bold inventiveness when it came to legal and procedural business connected with his estate.

A series of depositions were taken on 6 September 1649 at Glanhafren near Welshpool in response to the Haberdashers' committee order of 20 July. However, the commissioners running this hearing were hardly the individuals authorised to execute these proceedings and were certainly not a group that would back Pierce's campaign or, indeed, provide a vigorous and searching examination of the matter. They were Vaughan's close allies Matthew Morgan, Gabriel Wynne and William Kyffin of Bodfach. Moreover, this hearing was kept secret until the last minute and notice of its taking place was given to the prosecutors Lloyd Pierce and Hugh Price only the day before, while Richard Price was only told of its happening on the morning the commissioners met while he was still in bed![52] The commissioners claimed that they had invited the three prosecutors to the hearing 'who have all three refused to come though timely somoned'.[53] Pierce and his colleagues were livid at the fact that the hearing was held at all, but they were also incensed at the gall of their opponent in manufacturing such a political spectacle.

The deponents at this hearing look very much as if they had been handpicked by Edward Vaughan. The first, for example, was William Barbour.[54] In addition to being register to the county accounts sub-committee, Vaughan had also employed Barbour as an agent for stating the account and providing debentures in the disbandment process in early 1648. In what one official later described as a 'large narrative of Mr Vaughans good services for the country and the undue proceedings against him',[55] Barbour told a story of the disbandment in which Vaughan had received neither the £1,500 assigned from Staffordshire nor the £1,600 expected from Montgomeryshire; eventually only £600 from the latter was obtained.[56] Despite this lack of funds, Vaughan had managed to disband the horse troops carefully and quickly, although the means by which he did this and the funds which underwrote it remained vague in Barbour's account. In his deposition Barbour rounded on the origins of this investigation, stating that a petition was 'pretended' to have been submitted to parliament on the county's behalf, but that there was no formal record of it. He also recorded the story described above about Rice Vaughan's attack on him at Haberdashers' Hall, probably in an effort to portray Vaughan's prosecutors as violently prejudiced against him and driven by considerations other than the public interest. Other deponents at the Glanhafren hearing included Vaughan's disbandment treasurer, Kyffin Lloyd, Evan Lloyd of Bodyddon (not the county sheriff) who, like another deponent, Thomas Powell of Llanrhaeadr-ym-Mochnant, were witnesses who had testified as to the validity of Sir Robert Vaughan's 1622 entail.[57] These deponents all supported Vaughan's title to Llwydiarth and his version of events regarding the finances and processes of disbandment.

The commissioners brought the depositional material together and forwarded it to the Committee for the Advance of Money with a letter in which they claimed it was impossible for Vaughan to account for the disbanding money as he had acted jointly in the business, but also because the matter should properly be considered by the Committee of the Army.[58] They similarly dismissed the charges relating to Llwydiarth's sequestration, noting that Edward Vaughan was in possession by virtue of the 1622 entail. They concluded forcefully that Vaughan was:

> grossly abused by his malicious prosecutors whoe have verie highly wronged both him & this countie in feighning a peticion against him in ye name of ye countie, which petiticon is disavowed by a vindication of ye inhabitants to ye number of 1754 and upwards nowe readie to be produced ... and was likewise much injur'd by his prosecutors.[59]

In addition to the three commissioners who witnessed the deponents' statements, the letter was signed by Vaughan loyalist George Devereux and two men who had signed the 2 June 1649 certificate on Vaughan's behalf, Thomas Ravenscroft of Pickhill and Colonel John Alderley. The letter is endorsed by a recipient at Haberdashers' Hall 'discharge' but, as we might expect, Lloyd Pierce and his colleagues would not allow this parody of an investigation to be the last word on the matter.

Pierce personally drafted an account, on behalf of himself and Hugh and Richard Price, of what he described as the 'undue proceedings of Mr Edw. Vaughan & his adherents' at Glanhafren for the Committee for the Advance of Money.[60] His submission, unsurprisingly, throws a very different light on the events of 6 September. Pierce argued that Evan Lloyd of Plasaduon and Richard Griffiths of Sutton were the only commissioners enabled under Sir Thomas Myddelton's original sequestration appointments who were able to execute the committee's order because the prosecutors had been exempted. He maintained that, on 1 September, Edward Vaughan had asked them to convene shortly at Glanhafren for a hearing, but the prosecutors requested more time and asked that the venue be moved because, they argued, Glanhafren 'was a notorious alehouse for bowling, gaming & resort of cavaliers; not beseeming their gravitie or the cause in hand'. It is telling that Vaughan would wish the hearing to take place in such a venue which was clearly hostile to his pro-republican accusers. Pierce further claimed that the prosecutors were presented with an unsigned paper on 5 September calling on them to attend the execution of the order the day following ('their constant bowling day') but, Pierce noted, where neither Evan Lloyd nor Richard Griffiths would be in attendance. On 10 September Pierce and Hugh Price informed Lloyd and Griffiths that they were 'ready to prosecute for the countrey', but the two commissioners answered that 'the buysnes was finished already without them' by Devereux, Morgan, Wynne and Kyffin, 'but by what authority he [Pierce] knew not'. Vaughan then supposedly compelled Lloyd and Griffiths to subscribe a paper indicating that they had been ill and so could not attend the Glanhafren meeting.

In his account Pierce invited the Haberdashers' committee to consider 'how illegall, illusory & dangerous such proceedings are, if permitted in a peaceable Commonwealth'. He pointed out that he and his fellow prosecutors had been excluded but that those who subscribed Vaughan's petition were now allowed to be judges for the country, 'whoe cannot be thought will act anything against their owne subscriptions'. He also maintained that it was dangerous to permit individuals who were not committeemen, either appointed through Sir Thomas Myddelton's authority or under the recent sequestration ordinance for north Wales, to presume to administer oaths and examine witnesses 'in contempt of the power of … the lawes & constitutions of this present commonwealth'. He finished by asking rhetorically what these individuals would not 'dare to certifie for their owne defence be yt never so scandalous & impertinent against the prosecutors of their uniust proceedings'. Pierce also dismissed the actors as 'Mr Vaughans nere kinsemen' who illegally shared the county's money with him, and who had laboured a petition (that is, Vaughan's 'Vindication') subscribed by 'so many ignorant people & schoole boyes … that they hoped to escape the better with their prey in such a crowd undiscovered'. He requested that the 6 September depositions be suppressed and those involved be punished as an example to others; he also requested that 'indifferent men & none interested in the cause' be appointed to take Vaughan's account on the state's behalf.

This, then, is a remarkable incident which suggests just how intensely divided Montgomeryshire's politics remained in the early republic. It is unusual, if not unique, to see factional divisions degenerating into one side effectively impersonating local commissioners to provide a set of partisan depositions. Yet the case provides further evidence of just how important Edward Vaughan remained in north Wales politics even after his seclusion from parliament and his effective blackballing from local offices. It also highlights how the battles over accounting and over Llwydiarth itself were not simply personal and private tussles but, because of the power that the extensive estate conferred, also involved wider political concerns and affiliations. The essential factional configuration revealed by these struggles is familiar from the battles between the Montgomeryshire sequestration and the accounts committees of the mid-1640s, but the appearance of army figures such as John Alderley and of men such as Thomas Ravenscroft from Flintshire perhaps suggests how regional networks of Presbyterians and Independents were being drawn into this dispute. The mass petitions ('mass' for a relatively sparsely populated part of Wales, that is) which accompanied Vaughan's prosecution and his defence are also noteworthy, indicating that the respective factions were adopting some of the mechanisms of public politics which are familiar from other parts of the country.

It seems that the Committee for Advance of Money took heed of Pierce's complaint, and on 14 September 1649 it directed that three gentlemen appointed by them and three appointed by Vaughan examine his accounts and that the case be heard the following law term.[61] There was little movement thereafter, however, as the case was referred to counsel to report the proceedings in May and June 1650. Pierce and his fellow 'prosecutors' lamented in January 1650 that the Committee for the Advance of Money 'by access of buysnes of neerer concernment (as yt seems) tooke not that notize thereof as wee hoped'.[62] Moreover, in May 1650, Hugh and Lewis Price wrote to the Committee for Compounding that they 'have byne so busey and employed in publique buissines' that they were only now returning to sequestration matters.[63] In the spring of 1650 there was also confusion over who was to act as sequestration commissioners in Montgomeryshire after a reorganisation of the administrative apparatus there, and this also caused delays.[64]

Despite these delays, however, the Price brothers and Lloyd Pierce, who in 1650 was made Montgomeryshire sheriff, were not going to give up in their efforts to bring Vaughan down. In 1650, the Committee for the Advance of Money was effectively folded into the Committee for Compounding with Delinquents which sat at Goldsmiths' Hall, and on 21 January 1650 the three 'prosecutors', as they were referred to in some documents, wrote to this body to take on the case.[65] Once again, Pierce drafted their submission, which began with a flourish and is worth quoting in full:

> As it is the dutie of all those that wish well to the present government carefully to informe their faithfull pilots of the lets & impediments that may probably hinder them to anchor their hopes in the long desired haven of rest & safetie; even soe, it is the studie of all those that looke upon the present establishment with an evill eye, secretly to undermine, since they cannot forcibly overthrow, the foundation of yt by encroaching upon the landes & with houlding from the publique treasurie the rents & profits due unto the state, thereby enforcing yt to contynue unwillingly those heavy taxations upon the nation, for want of yts owne meanes remaining in private hands, to maynteyne those armies at home & abroade with out which we cannot long expect to enioy our liberties & freedome or any thing els that we possess in peace & tranquillitie.[66]

This represents something of a shift in tone in the campaign against Vaughan, which figured him not simply as a wayward accountant or errant landholder, but rather as an active threat to the Commonwealth and something approaching an enemy of the state. This perhaps reflects the change in political discourse as Welsh radicals were empowered by the moves to establish the Commission for the Propagation of the Gospel in Wales (of which both Hugh and Richard Price would be members) a month after this submission was written, but also perhaps a growing confidence on the part of those committed Independents who were now the face of republican politics in counties like Montgomeryshire. This letter asked for the Compounding Committee to take the case, which it did. Pierce made a compelling case in his submission that Vaughan's estate was a potentially plum prize for the state to secure. The Goldsmiths' committee appear to have received this letter on 13 March 1650 and two days later it ordered Llwydiarth to be sequestered, a careful account to be rendered and for Vaughan to appear before them.[67] It remains unclear whether Vaughan was indeed quickly secured as no record of further proceedings are extant until September 1650.

In the interim, however, an event occurred which changed many of these calculations and which had enormous implications for Edward Vaughan. On 22 February 1650, aged only twenty-five, the putative owner of Llwydiarth, Herbert Vaughan, died in Douglas on the Isle of Man apparently when returning from Ireland; news of his demise only reached Montgomeryshire in mid-July. In many ways, of course, this was wonderful news for Edward Vaughan. The state's case was constructed around the premise of an ousted owner who was sequestered both for his royalist activism and for his Catholicism. The removal of this dispossessed owner, critically, without an heir who might continue to fight for possession, only made it possible to sustain a retrospective case against Edward Vaughan: that he had unlawfully detained rents from the state for five years. Although having Vaughan declared as a delinquent may have removed Llwydiarth from his grasp, the events of the mid-1640s had shown that proving such a case would be difficult. There was no rival claimant besides Herbert's mother, Katherine Palmer, who could only realistically sue for arrears of her jointure rights.[68] A possible rival might be Lord Powis, Herbert's grandfather, but he was effectively removed from the scene, under house arrest in London with his own property in parliament's hands and himself only allowed a pension of £4 per week.[69] After nearly thirty years of legal battles, Edward Vaughan's title to Llwydiarth seemed secure, although there remained the challenge of those who wanted to squeeze him for significant sums which they claimed they were owed from the estate. Although he might now be the undisputed owner of Llwydiarth, Vaughan would still face severe financial penalties, even ruin, if his enemies managed to prevail.

The Committee for Compounding with Delinquents, 1650–55

Although Edward Vaughan must have been relieved at Herbert Vaughan's unexpected demise, he could certainly not rest easy as his adversaries gained in confidence, empowered as they were by the radical turn in politics and religion. On 9 August 1650, three Prices concerned with sequestrations business in Montgomeryshire – Hugh, Richard and Lewis – submitted to the Committee for Compounding a paper purporting to set out the 'true estate' of Herbert Vaughan's sequestered lands which were being forcibly detained from the state.[70] They related a history in which Edward Vaughan, a delinquent, kept Llwydiarth by force, ignored the orders of the local committee, sponsored factionalism by his powers of patronage and spurned the directives from the central sequestrators to hand the property over to the state. However, 'by his potencie in those parts', Vaughan had procured the order of 23 August 1649 endorsed by many of north Wales's sequestration committeemen and commissioners who, the authors maintained, 'had nothing to doe therein, but serveing by the multitude of hands to terrify the poore tenants to pay him theyr rents'. This 'illegall order' had ever since underwritten Vaughan's possession and the sequestration commissioners were unable to remedy the situation 'in regarde he [Vaughan] keeps a great number of men & armes in ye mansion house of Lloydiart (being a strong house) having with us noe sufficient force in the county to inforce his obedience unto the order of parliament'. The commissioners helpfully added that Rice Vaughan, the sequestration committee clerk who had crossed Vaughan and William Barbour the year before, could provide the central sequestrators with 'a full accompt of this busines from first to last', and could also produce the original committee orders.[71]

The spectre of Vaughan as the well-armed delinquent resisting the orders of the state was again raised in this submission and, perhaps with the colourful narrative of Rice Vaughan echoing in their ears, on 15 August 1650 the Committee for Compounding ordered that Vaughan appear before them. His antagonists were taking no chances on his non-appearance so, on 13 September 1650, Lieutenant Whitehead and thirty troops came to Llwydiarth and, acting on a warrant signed by Hugh

Price, Richard Price and Evan Lloyd as militia commissioners, secured Vaughan and his arms (some fifteen muskets and fowling pieces) and took him as a prisoner to Powis Castle.[72] They refused him bail, with Hugh Price telling Vaughan that he should obtain an order for his release from the Council of State 'for otherwise hee should not take notice of any order from any comittee'; the debacle of the 23 August 1649 certificate was probably uppermost in his mind as he said this. Vaughan probably did indeed approach the Council of State, for within a week that body wrote to the Montgomeryshire militia commissioners 'to certifie what those dangerous suspicions are for which they have have secured Edw[ard] Vaughan ... [and that they] will bee carefull to find out the armes they mention'.[73] Vaughan was evidently brought up to London, and in October he entered into a recognisance of £4,000 for good behaviour to cover his journey to the capital.[74] His surety for this huge sum was the man who had also acted as his guarantor in 1647, the wealthy merchant Charles Lloyd.[75] These developments provide a graphic illustration of how far Edward Vaughan's star had fallen in local and national politics. He was still nominally Montgomeryshire's MP, but he found himself imprisoned in Powis Castle and having to enter into enormous bonds to the state for his good behaviour simply to journey to London. He was being treated as a potential, if not an active, enemy of the Commonwealth.

On 17 October 1650 the Haberdashers' committee informed the local sequestrators that they were to seize Llwydiarth for the state.[76] However, Vaughan probably maintained that his case had not received a full hearing, and on 20 December the central committee's standing legal counsel, John Reading, produced a narrative of the case for his masters, a move which shows that the matter remained under consideration. No adjudication had been made as to whether Vaughan's answers to the charges against him were sufficient and, moreover, no witnesses had been produced on the Commonwealth's behalf in the proceedings.[77] The committee reviewed this report and on 2 January 1651 ordered that the depositions gathered at Glanhafren the previous September were to be considered void because they were '*coram non judice*', or not made before a judge with competent jurisdiction. The committee required that Vaughan put in a fresh answer to the disbanding charges and also render an account of the £3,751 he had received for the service. On the matter of Llwydiarth's sequestration, meanwhile, the committee wanted more time to navigate the thicket of proceedings which had grown up around the case and to ascertain who was in possession of the property when it was sequestered.[78] Eight days after this order Vaughan submitted his answer to the disbandment charge, but was given further time to produce his response to the question of sequestration.[79] As in many lawsuits, so in this case before the Compounding Committee, delay, debates about points of procedure and the stretching out of proceedings served a useful purpose for the defendant. The case was already complex and technical: the matters under review were extending into the receding past while important points of detail were easily lost in the welter of paper which landed on the desks of already over-burdened committeemen in London. Time was Vaughan's ally in this case, and he was a canny lawyer who had half a lifetime's training in using the courts as an obdurate tool of resistance.

The sequestrators in north Wales sought to move the case forward by taking fresh depositions at Wrexham in February and May 1651.[80] Ten witnesses were examined for the state, several of whom testified that they had paid their rents to agents for Herbert Vaughan until he (and his mother) fled before parliament's advance in 1644. A number indicated that they paid money to local sequestration agents thereafter until Edward Vaughan, emboldened by his certificate from the north Wales commissioners of August 1649, forced them to pay the monies to him or turned the recalcitrant off their lands. Contrariwise, some seventeen witnesses appeared on Vaughan's behalf (including his political associates Samuel More and Robert Lloyd), testifying that they believed that he was in possession of Llwydiarth when the sequestration order was made. The depositional evidence makes it evident that the disruption of war in 1644–5 and the contradictory orders issued by the local and central sequestrators produced a confused situation in which contemporaries were not wholly sure as to who owned Llwydiarth at the point of its sequestration.

Such inconclusive hearings were to Vaughan's advantage, and he was happy to keep proceedings moving at a snail's pace with foot-dragging and reluctant compliance.[81] Logistical problems also slowed down matters as many witnesses in the case lived in Montgomeryshire and could not be 'compelled to travaile out of the ... county' to attend the north Wales sequestration commissioners in places like Wrexham.[82] Charles II's invasion at the head of a Scottish army and the Battle of Worcester in September 1651 also interfered with the prosecution of the matter which fell into abeyance, with little activity for nearly a year. Efforts were made to restart business in September 1652 by the clerk to the north Wales sequestrators, Benjamin Rodenhurst.[83] He informed the central committee that the case remained in limbo because 'the number of commissioners which were to performe yt service, which must be 5 by your order, whoe live soe remote that they can hardly bee got soe many together'. However, he also alluded to another problem: that some of the Compounding Committee's orders had ended up in Vaughan's hands and, as a result, he had not delivered them to the local commissioners until the time for the orders' execution had nearly elapsed. Rodenhurst's letter seems to have produced a directive that further depositions were to be taken on the state's behalf, but it was not until February 1653 that these statements were sent to London.[84]

Thereafter the Llwydiarth case continued to be batted back and forth between the Compounding Committee who kept authorising the hearing of more witnesses, and Vaughan and his associates who kept finding problems with the process. The business rumbled on into 1654 and a dangerous moment for Vaughan came with the Compounding Committee's decision on 16 May of that year, after hearing counsel for both sides, that Llwydiarth had been duly sequestered in October 1644, and that Vaughan was responsible for the profits subsequently lost to the state: an enormous sum of around £9,000.[85] Such a fine would have ruined Vaughan, of course, but, as had so often been the case in this matter, execution of the decision was postponed to give Vaughan leave to appeal.[86] True to form, Vaughan delayed and prevaricated, petitioning in June 1654 that the witnesses he required to prove title were 'very aged'.[87] However, the man who in the early 1650s took Lloyd Pierce's place as Vaughan's bête noire, Rice Vaughan, had had enough of Vaughan's tactics, and asked the committee to ignore his pleas. Rice informed the committee that Edward Vaughan's witnesses were, in fact, 'very strong and able to travell', adding that if they were allowed to be examined in the country 'there may be suspition of undue endeavours by Mr Edward Vaughan in yt behaulfe as former experience hath manifested'.[88] This submission was the prelude to a very public clash between Rice and Edward Vaughan over the former's candidacy for election as the county MP for Merioneth in August 1654. This incident is discussed further in the next chapter, but it is relevant to note here that Edward Vaughan had asked Rice to get the sequestration proceedings against him at Haberdashers' Hall dropped, promising that if he did so, then Edward would manufacture his rival's unopposed election.[89] Rice Vaughan refused the offer and consequently lost the seat. This disappointment sharpened Rice's thirst for revenge, and in November 1654 he brought a charge of corruption against three witnesses who had proved a deed by which Edward Vaughan had claimed title to Llwydiarth in 1653.[90]

Despite the value of the property being disputed in the sequestration proceedings, it seems that fatigue was setting in with the Haberdashers' Hall committee and, although new orders were issued for fresh examinations in the case in early 1655, appetite for pursuing Edward Vaughan was evidently waning. This may partly have been the result of the shift to a somewhat less zealous regime from 1654 as Oliver Cromwell's Protectorate pursued a policy of 'healing and settling' and moved away from the more persecutory aspects of local government which had been seen during the Commonwealth. Vaughan was still a potent force in north Wales and, although he had been brought to London in 1649 under heavy clouds of suspicion, he had made no gestures towards resisting the republic and did not, on the face of it, seem to be an individual who posed a threat to the regime. The authorities perhaps calculated that such a moderate parliamentarian was a useful asset in a part of the country that was still viewed with suspicion because of its pervasive royalism. As is discussed in the following chapter, this is far from the whole picture of Vaughan's politics in the 1650s, but such an attitude on the authorities' part might help account for the diminishing interest in the case against him. The north Wales sequestrators' clerk John Reading produced another lengthy narrative of the case on 13 February 1655,[91] but on 1 March 1655 the matter was delayed until the following term and the local county committee was ordered not to levy arrears on Vaughan until a final order was forthcoming. The Compounding Committee indicated that this would be in May, but the order never materialised. In May 1656 a report from the Treasury Commissioners about Llwydiarth's sequestration was presented to the Council of State.[92] This was referred to a small group of councillors, but there is no indication that they produced any report. No mention of the case in the state's records appears after this point, and Vaughan continued in possession of Llwydiarth, apparently untroubled, down to his death.[93]

* * *

The pursuit of Edward Vaughan from April 1649 until March 1655 reveals some interesting aspects of north Wales politics during the early republic, elements of which are discussed further in the following chapter. The case against him shows a good degree of continuity with Vaughan's adversaries of the mid-1640s, but also demonstrates some significant elements of change in personalities too. Vaughan's great adversary Lloyd Pierce was a moving force in the initial assaults against the Montgomeryshire MP in 1649–50, but he fades into the background thereafter. The evidence suggests that Pierce's republicanism may have been instrumental rather than ideological and only ran as far as his opposition to Edward Vaughan would take it. For example, Pierce was not included as a sequestrator under the act for a general composition of north Wales of August 1649, and his omission from the county bench in July 1653, along with his absence from that body for the remainder of the 1650s argues for a withdrawal from republican politics and, consequently, from the pursuit of Edward Vaughan.[94] The fact that he only appears on local commissions down to 1652 tends to strengthen this impression, although it is relevant to note that from 1654 his son, Thomas, appeared on the bench and may have picked up the torch of local office from his father.[95] Pierce's disappearance from the local political scene robbed the campaign against Vaughan of some of its personal animus and impetus. However, the baton of investigator-in-chief passed to Rice Vaughan, although he appears to have been outraged by Vaughan's contempt for justice and due process as much as anything else. The republican true believers Richard and Hugh

Price remain a constant presence among the cast of Vaughan's antagonists. Sequestrators since 1644, they in some ways embodied the institutional memory of local radicals against the politically suspect and congenitally devious Edward Vaughan.

The effort to bring Vaughan down also brings into relief the presence in north Wales politics of those military personnel, a number of whom had come into the area with Sir Thomas Myddelton, who were now critical figures of influence and authority in the region.[96] Vaughan evidently had connections among these men and was able to get individuals like John Peck, Thomas Critchley and Thomas Ball to endorse his dubious certificates that testified to his possession of Llwydiarth prior to the orders for its sequestration. However, these individuals also complained about his delaying tactics and sought to discharge the fiat of the Compounding Committee as best they could; Vaughan was on thin ice with them. Sir Thomas Myddelton and Thomas Mytton, Vaughan's enemies from the 1640s, did not participate in the efforts against him in the 1650s. Their absence perhaps reflected how the shock of regicide had caused both these Presbyterians to withdraw from the cut and thrust of local politics. Indeed, Myddelton was suspected by the Commonwealth of royalist sympathies and was implicated in the earl of Derby's rising in 1651.[97]

The protracted campaign against Vaughan during the early republic also suggests his continued importance to the political scene in Montgomeryshire (and to an extent in Denbighshire and Merioneth also) during this period, but also the degree to which his influence had been reduced and his authority undercut after Pride's Purge. Although soon after Pierce's initial county petition against him Vaughan invoked parliamentary privilege and some righteous outrage about his treatment as an MP, the fact of the matter was that he was a secluded member and the Rump wanted nothing to do with him. In the early 1650s Vaughan was not without allies but he was without office and without official avenues of influence and patronage. His removal from Montgomeryshire's commission of the peace in March 1649 was testimony of this political emasculation, and this was the last local office he was to hold for nearly a decade. As long as he retained Llwydiarth Vaughan was a force to be reckoned with in terms of his wealth and social influence, but politically he was *persona non grata* until the late stages of the republic.

It was a tricky business to hold on to Llwydiarth in this hostile political environment, and our evidence reveals that Vaughan's propensity for evasiveness, legal chicanery and downright deception, which he had shown since the 1620s, was undiminished. It was important for his efforts to cling to Llwydiarth that Vaughan retained allies like Samuel More and Robert Lloyd, but his own capacity for delay, dissimulation and deceit was impressive and, ultimately, effective in retaining his estate. However, his opportunities to employ such tactics were encouraged by the comparatively lax oversight of the central committees involved in his prosecution between 1649 and 1655, as well as by the relatively small parliamentary bureaucracy in north Wales that was committed to taking this fight forward. The logistical problems facing his accusers were also an issue: the sequestrators wrote on several occasions of the difficulties they faced in bringing witnesses from an area of dispersed settlement together; of finding convenient times in which the required five commissioners from north Wales could be assembled to discharge this business; of acting swiftly on orders from the political centre; and of transmitting information and expertise about this case across a range of committees over a period of years. The two lengthy narratives of the case produced by John Reading disclose an interest on the part of the Committee for Compounding, but they equally speak to the problems of organising knowledge about a complex case across a lengthy period of time. One gets the impression that the central authorities too frequently came to Vaughan's case anew, and with something of a knowledge deficit that the defendant could use to his advantage. This chapter has sketched out some of the wider contexts within which Vaughan's various defences were situated. However, a fuller discussion of religious and political developments in north Wales during the republic, and of Vaughan's positioning within and against them, is also important if we are to fully understand his story, and this will constitute the focus of the following chapter.

CHAPTER 9

Religion, Politics and
Rehabilitation, 1650–1661

As was discussed in the previous chapter, Edward Vaughan faced a difficult and challenging period in the half decade following his seclusion from parliament. His antagonists of the mid-1640s were empowered by the revolution and doggedly pursued him. Employing his capacity for enduring protracted legal campaigns, as well as drawing on his connections among the north Wales gentry, Vaughan managed to survive their attacks. Although his defence of Llwydiarth consumed much of his time and resources, this was not the sum of his activities during the republic. The present chapter explores other dimensions of his life during this period, including some intriguing evidence regarding his religious attitudes. Political matters command much of our attention, however, and critical here were two episodes which demonstrate that, while Vaughan may have endured ongoing attacks from republican opponents, he was far from a spent force. These two instances both concern the lawyer Rice Vaughan, the man who took up the sequestration effort against Edward Vaughan from Lloyd Pierce. The first episode concerns a disturbance in the borough of Llanfyllin in October 1653, which provides intriguing evidence about the continuing (if surreptitious) influence of the Powis Castle Herberts in local politics, but also of Edward Vaughan's continued capacity to command local support. The 'riot' on this occasion concerned the election of borough officials and saw the Llwydiarth squire defeat Rice Vaughan's efforts to install his own men in the corporation's government. The second episode revolves around the Merioneth county election of July 1654, and provides arresting evidence of Edward Vaughan's ongoing ability to rally political backing and influence electoral politics in north Wales.

If the previous chapter traced Edward Vaughan's political eclipse between 1649 and 1653, this chapter charts how his star began to rise as the 1650s progressed. Critical in this, of course, was the fact that he had effectively secured title to Llwydiarth by 1655. As the more moderate Protectorate regime allowed the return to power and influence of political Presbyterians such as Vaughan and his allies, so we can plot his political recovery and return to public office. This rehabilitation can be seen in his selection as Denbighshire's sheriff in 1658, but most strikingly in his election to parliament as county member to Richard Cromwell's parliament in 1659. The chapter concludes by examining how Vaughan successfully managed to negotiate the Restoration and discusses perhaps the crowning achievement of his political career: his election as Montgomeryshire MP to the Cavalier Parliament. The narrative offered here, then, is an unusual one in historical studies of republican Wales. Instead of focusing on the frustrated ambitions of radical millenarians like Vavasor Powell or Morgan Llwyd, we can instead map the political rehabilitation of a parliamentarian moderate across the 1650s.

The Commission for the Propagation of the Gospel in Wales and religious attitudes

The campaign against Vaughan in the early 1650s coincided with the introduction of the Commission for the Propagation of the Gospel in Wales which was established by ordinance on 22 February 1650. The commission was a radical initiative which sought nothing less than the political and religious re-education of Wales, a country that was seen by most republicans as corrupted by royalism and religious ignorance. It was established partly in response to a petition from the 'well affected' of north Wales in December 1649, a group likely centred around Morgan Llwyd, and whose number probably included Richard Price of Gunley, who 'with much affection and fidelity ... have adhered to your honours [parliament] and served you in severall places and callings without baulking, byassing or back-sliding'.[1] The commission was an immensely powerful body which some historians have argued constituted the 'real' government of Wales down to its dissolution in 1653, although even after this point, those empowered by the commission remained highly influential in local politics.[2] Several of Vaughan's most potent enemies were appointed as commissioners, including Hugh Price, Richard Price, Lewis Price, Evan Lloyd and Rice Vaughan, although their number also included his allies William Barbour, Edward Owen and Robert Griffith. The Montgomeryshire area was a particular focus for the commission, in no small measure because of the attentions of one of its most influential leading lights, Vavasor Powell, who hailed from neighbouring Radnorshire, and whose itinerant ministry was especially intense in the Welsh Marches. Even when Powell moved into opposition against the Protectorate, his associates' influence in the area remained considerable: in March 1654 Gabriel Lloyd from Welshpool could write that the 'faction' around Powell, Morgan Llwyd and Thomas Harrison 'is in power, and in all commissions in the countrie; so that they rule the roast, and give life to the faction'.[3]

Confusion has reigned over Edward Vaughan's relationship to the propagation commission and to various other organs of the local state in the 1650s. Thomas Richards, for example, places Edward Vaughan as one of the north Wales solicitors for the propagation commission and as its Montgomeryshire agent.[4] This Edward Vaughan was also was added to the local commission of the peace in October 1653.[5] A. H. Dodd, meanwhile, believes that Vaughan was a sequestration commissioner in Montgomeryshire helping Richard Price of Gunley take 'punitive measures' against his neighbours: a remarkable volte-face if this was indeed the case.[6] It was not. In fact, the man appointed to all these posts was Edward Vaughan of Tirymynach in Guilsfield, Montgomeryshire, a very minor gentleman who, on account of his lowly status (one satirical manuscript described him as 'the spider cacher'[7]) would have had no opportunity to participate in local government before the civil wars. Critically, however, this Edward Vaughan was a convinced Independent, and a man whom Hugh and Lewis Price could laud as 'active & faithfull'

(Hugh appointed him overseer of his will), and was someone who staunchly supported Vavasor Powell and the propagation commission when it came under attack in 1652–4.[8] Edward Vaughan of Llwydiarth was of a quite different character, however, and was likely to be agitating against rather than supporting the propagation commission. It is significant, for example, that a Montgomeryshire grand jury presentment of 1 April 1652 described the 'most generall and allmost universall compaint' about the lack of able ministers in the county following the propagators' attentions there. The presentment focused on the forty-seven ministers who had been ejected and replaced with 'a few illiterate poor tradesmen', so that, as a result, the gospel was 'so farr from being visibly propagated among us … that it is much feared … it is rather in a way of declining'. The two foremen of the jury presenting this indictment of the propagators' work were Edward Vaughan's old associates Gabriel Wynne and William Kyffin of Bodfach.[9] Although we cannot simply read off his attitudes from his colleagues' activity, it is surely the case that Vaughan would have supported their position. It may also be significant that a petition in the name of 'many thousands of the six counties of Northwales' against the propagation commission was being organised around the time this grand jury presentment was made, suggesting that it may have been part of an organised lobbying effort.[10]

Although Vaughan had shown sympathy with the cause of reforming the ministry and ejecting unworthy ministers during the 1640s, we may be sure that he had no truck with the kind of millenarian excesses associated with the propagation commission. As we saw in the January 1646 Montgomeryshire petition, he supported the settling of reformed ministers within a national church structure rather than any kind of congregational system. He was, then, a religious moderate and an interesting piece of evidence for his religious attitudes during the republic comes from the era of the propagation commission's activity. In January 1653, Richard Jones, a Church of England minister who had been ejected by the propagators from his living at Llanfair Caereinion in Montgomeryshire in June 1650, produced a volume entitled *Testûn Testament Newydd*.[11] This was a summary in Welsh verse of every chapter of the Bible, and was designed to assist in advancing knowledge of the

Scriptures among humble parishioners. It was the sort of initiative deemed necessary in some quarters as a response to the kinds of spiritual abandonment which had been articulated by the Montgomeryshire grand jury nine months before. A university-educated cleric of moderate views, Jones was the kind of individual whom many individuals thought should be respected within the Church rather than ejected. It is significant, then, that Jones dedicated his volume 'to the famous, esteemed gentleman Edward Vaughan of Llwydiarth' ('At yr enwog urddasol bendefig Edward Vaughan o Lwydiart'). In his dedication Jones praised Vaughan's many laudable qualities, noting particularly his patience and forbearance in the face of difficulty and adversity. Jones reflected that he knew of few others in the state who had faced more difficulties than Vaughan, who had often encountered tribulations, contentions ('terfyscau') and danger from his own nation, doubtless a reference to his struggles with the likes of Lloyd Pierce, Hugh Price and Rice Vaughan. Written during a period of relative quiet in the sequestrators' case against Vaughan, Jones somewhat prematurely praised Vaughan's patience in securing his freedom and the peaceful possession of his ancestors' legitimate patrimony ('ei steddle gartrefol cyfreithlon dreftafaeth eich henafiaid'). Following this conceit of Vaughan's patience in times of challenge, Jones offered his dedicatee up as a model for himself and others to follow. Jones presented the volume as a New Year's gift, the first fruits of an afflicted spirit, in thanks for Vaughan's many kindnesses. Jones referred to Vaughan's 'shield of love for the ministers of the gospel' ('darian y cariad sydd gennych tuag at weinidogion yr Efengil') and signed himself as 'your faithful minister' ('eich ffydd-llongar weinidog').

The dedication is clear evidence that Vaughan, while sympathetic to moderate reformers in the Church, was also a protector of ejected 'Anglican' ministers and was probably one of those who gave such individuals succour and support during the wilderness years of the 1650s.[12] He was clearly also someone who opposed the aims, methods and personnel of the propagation commission, but the ongoing assault on his possession of Llwydiarth, along with the potency of figures associated with the commission in his locality, made it difficult and dangerous for Vaughan to break cover and articulate such opposition openly. Given the nature of our evidence, it is impossible to provide much in the way of detail regarding Vaughan's probable opposition to the Commonwealth, but this dedication from an ejected minister provides a useful proxy for assessing his religious attitudes and, to a degree, his political positions also.

Opposing Rice Vaughan (I): the Llanfyllin 'riot', October 1653

Although Edward Vaughan was not prepared to demonstrate any open opposition to the republic, he was willing to challenge local adversaries who were prominent republicans, and two incidents involving Rice Vaughan, the man who pushed the state's sequestration case against him, offer some revealing evidence in this regard. The first of these involves the selection of town officials at the town of Llanfyllin on Saturday, 8 October 1653. Llanfyllin was a borough which claimed contributory rights in Montgomery's parliamentary elections.[13] The borough was governed by two bailiffs chosen annually: one by the lord of the manor and the other by the fifteen capital burgesses. This, then, was a town of significance in the county and the court being held in October 1653 was the first under new lords of the manor: Sir George Whitmore and his two sons, who, two months before, had purchased Llanfyllin as part of the lordship of Powis from parliamentary trustees following the property's sequestration for Sir Percy Herbert's delinquency.[14] This sale was something of a smokescreen, however, for Whitmore had discharged business for the Powis interest before the wars, while Sir Percy Herbert's wife, Elizabeth, was Whitmore's niece.[15] It thus seems that the Whitmores bought the manor as surrogates for Sir Percy Herbert and his family. It is worth noting in this context that Rice Vaughan (along with a Whitmore once again, this time Sir George's son Charles) assisted Sir Percy and his wife with their efforts to secure properties in Hendon, Middlesex, which were at risk from sequestration.[16] Although Llanfyllin was thus 'under new management', it seems that it was, in fact, still under Herbert control. Llanfyllin lay at some distance from the Herbert centres of control at

Welshpool and Montgomery and was closer to Llwydiarth's sphere of influence. Indeed, the dispute between the Herberts and Vaughans over borough government had a lengthy pedigree, with some major set piece confrontations between the two houses in the early seventeenth century, when Edward Vaughan's father and grandfather had attempted to disrupt the choice of new bailiffs by the Herbert steward of the manor.[17]

Sir George Whitmore, or more likely the Herbert interest, installed Rice Vaughan as Llanfyllin's steward and Humphrey Jones as its town clerk.[18] Jones asked Rice Vaughan to be present at the election of the new bailiffs, partly because Jones feared trouble at the election, but also, as he informed Sir Percy Herbert's son, because it was 'our first entrance on ye parliaments score'.[19] Jones also alluded to 'unwarrantable & extra iudiciall proccedings [in Llanfyllin] acted against our privileges hitherto unquestioned'. There had thus already been efforts to encroach on the Herberts' control of Llanfyllin, and the fact that the two current bailiffs were Edward Vaughan's nominees indicates that he was behind these 'extra iudiciall' efforts. In fact, Rice Vaughan was told before his journey to the town that it was not safe to hold the Llanfyllin court, 'by reason of Mr [Edward] Vaughans power & of ye lawless cariage of ye inhabitants whoe had formerly wounded & beaten severall parliament soldiers'. It seems, then, that Edward Vaughan was challenging the veneer of legitimacy under which the Powis Castle Herberts sought to retain control over the borough following Sir Percy's sequestration, and also that he wished to capitalise on the anti-republican sentiments which bubbled close to the surface there.

On election day, Humphrey Jones collected the Herbert nominee for bailiff, Cadwalader Oliver, on his way to the town and waited for Lady Katherine Palmer, Sir Percy's sister and Edward Vaughan's one-time sister-in-law, to appear. In the meantime, Edward Vaughan arrived at Llanfyllin with two namesakes, Howell Vaughan of Glanllyn in Merioneth, a cousin whose family would ultimately inherit Llwydiarth, and John Vaughan of Cefnbodig, also in Merioneth, a lawyer and a distant relation whom Edward would support in the forthcoming Merioneth election. Edward Vaughan was also accompanied by sixteen armed horsemen and had sent his cook and a store of venison before him so that he was 'greatly attended' in the town. In a letter to William Herbert, Sir Percy's son, written a few days after these events, Humphrey Jones detailed how his party's plans had been 'to name our bayliffe & in case of non acceptance, to disolve ye court & suffer them to agrevate their offence'. Interestingly, Jones noted that his 'cousen Mytton' had argued against this course as he himself had been opposed in an election to the Llanfyllin bailiff's place. Although it is not specified, it seems likely that this was a relative of the ex-major general of north Wales, perhaps James Mytton of Pontyscowrid who was a Montgomeryshire JP at this time, which suggests that old battle lines against Vaughan were being refashioned with new personalities.[20] Mytton and Rice Vaughan, both lawyers, counselled that the Herbert party should introduce their choice for bailiff and if any opposed, then to swear both bailiffs, but that whatever occurred, they should make their best efforts to assert their rights in the borough. They argued that only in the event of violent resistance should the court be dissolved and that, if this happened, then they would make all those who opposed them 'parties to ye abuse'.

When the Herbert interest arrived at Llanfyllin town hall, they found the jury to be composed of 'Mr Ed[war]d Va[ugha]ns freinds & servants'. Rice Vaughan nevertheless gave the charge, informing the jury of Sir George Whitmore's right to name a bailiff, and that in Whitmore's name he nominated Cadwalader Oliver and directed the jury to approve him. The court adjourned and the jury and the incumbent bailiffs went to Edward Vaughan's house for dinner. The jury delayed their return to court until it was dark 'that tyme being most seasonable for them to execute ye designe of ye great mover of ye wheele [that is, Edward Vaughan]'. The jury then presented Howell Evans, Edward Vaughan's servant who had also been messenger for the sub-committee of accounts in the 1640s,[21] and Robert Price, presumably another Vaughan ally, as their choices for bailiffs, ignoring the steward's directive. When Rice Vaughan attempted to oppose this move by directing Jones to swear in Oliver, as the latter's hand was laid on the Bible to take his oath of office, Edward Vaughan's followers snatched the volume away. Humphrey Jones himself was manhandled by the outgoing bailiffs, William and Charles Kyffin, individuals described as Vaughan's 'attendants', and both long-standing Vaughan allies.[22] After Cadwalader Oliver's swearing in had been prevented, Edward

Vaughan's supporters leapt onto the table and commanded Jones to dissolve the court. In the ensuing tumult, the candles in the town hall were extinguished, halberds were brandished, 'murther cryed & Cad[wala]d[er] Oliver beaten'. In addition to William and Charles Kyffin, also prominent among Vaughan's supporters in this 'hurliburly' were Robert Lloyd of Castellmoch, a notable Vaughan supporter since the mid-1640s, and Philip Weaver who described himself as a 'servant' or 'agent' for the Llwydiarth squire.[23]

Rice Vaughan wished to remain in Llanfyllin and not depart upon 'such disonorable tearmes', but his party was outnumbered and outgunned, with 'the towne ... all in an uproare', and they left the hall. Seeing this, Edward Vaughan's followers, whom Jones described as 'ryotters', swore in their new bailiffs 'crying & shouting "hay for Vaughan"'. Jones believed that the mob's main target had been Rice Vaughan himself, but that they had 'missed in their designe' to bring him down. The town clerk concluded, however, that it would be unsafe for him to venture back to Llanfyllin. In his report on the debacle, Jones urged William Herbert to prosecute Edward Vaughan and the rioters 'for it concearnes yow so much'. He counselled that Herbert would not meet with a better opportunity to bring suit and that to neglect doing so might discourage Rice Vaughan, 'who is your freind & now suffitiently netled' to employ 'his interest' to assist in the case. Rice Vaughan had also told Jones that 'what I can prove at [Haber]Dashers Hall against Edward Vaughan is upon record'.

The Herbert interest, via the Whitmores, did initiate legal proceedings against William and Charles Kyffin, Howell Evans, Robert Price and others for obstructions in holding the manor court, but did not mention Edward Vaughan.[24] However, there is no clear evidence that the case made any progress; certainly, no suit troubled Vaughan. The Llanfyllin election is significant for our purposes as it shows Vaughan still taking up the cudgels against his old Herbert adversaries (and vice-versa), and demonstrates that, despite his problems with the Llwydiarth sequestration case, he remained an active and influential force in local politics. It is also interesting to see him rallying a network of familiar allies and supporters from the 1640s, and it seems clear that the Vaughan political network was still functioning despite its setbacks during the early republic. The reference to the Llanfyllin townsmen aligned with Vaughan having beaten parliamentary soldiers is also worth noting. Although the connections are not clear or obvious and the evidence is polemical, it is natural that he should keep company with groups opposed to the army; such an attitude fits well with his history since 1646. Friction with convinced republican supporters is also clear in the Llanfyllin exchanges, of course, especially in his crossing swords with Rice Vaughan, although here questions of Rice's instrumental role in the sequestration effort against Llwydiarth were also significant. As is so often the case, it is hard, and perhaps impossible, to distinguish Edward Vaughan's personal interests from his political ones. This rivalry between the two Vaughans would burst into public view once more with the elections to the first Protectorate parliament some ten months after the Llanfyllin clash.

Opposing Rice Vaughan (II): the Merioneth parliamentary election, July 1654

The only parliamentary 'elections' in north Wales since the swathe of 'recruiter' returns in 1646–7 were the unusual nominations of six members to sit in 'Barebones Parliament', more properly called the Nominated Assembly, in mid-1653. The assembly has often been seen as the high point of republican radicalism in which millenarian and Fifth Monarchist opinion and radicals like Vavasor Powell, Morgan Llwyd and Major General Thomas Harrison were particularly influential.[25] Among those members chosen for north Wales was Richard Price of Gunley, an inveterate opponent of Edward Vaughan, who was nominated on Powell and Harrison's recommendation.[26] That assembly's dissolution and the inauguration of Oliver Cromwell's Protectorate was a decisive moment for Powell and his associates, who considered the move a betrayal of the 'true' godly cause. Powell moved into open opposition to the Protector with his vehement denunciation *A Word for God* in the autumn of 1655, a document which Richard Price presented personally to Cromwell.[27] The establishing of the Protectorate represented a retreat from more radical courses in religion and politics and opened up spaces in many regions for the return of political moderates. We can see some of these shifts in Welsh elections to the first Protectorate parliament in the summer of 1654. These were the first to be held under the reformed franchise (which probably reduced the electorate in Wales) which had been determined by the Instrument of Government: the written constitution adopted in 1653, which also added an additional seat in some county constituencies, including Montgomeryshire.[28] It appears that Vaughan's troubled parliamentary background may have precluded him from seeking a seat. The Council of State could now scrutinise election returns and exclude those whom they considered politically suspect. As Vaughan continued to labour under the cloud that he had defrauded the state of many thousands of pounds, he probably concluded that it was prudent not to draw attention to himself by standing for election. These considerations did not stop him from exercising his influence in the elections, however.

The change in the political temperature from the Nominated Assembly to the first Protectorate parliament can be seen in the two MPs who were returned for Montgomeryshire. One place was taken by the old side-changer Sir John Price, although he was excluded from sitting by the Council of State for his questionable political record.[29] The other seat was filled by Vaughan's close ally Charles Lloyd, the man who had supported him financially when he battled the Herbert interest before the civil wars. That Vaughan was involved in the elections of these two moderates is demonstrated by Rice Vaughan's petition over the Merioneth election, discussed further in a moment, in which he stated that the poll in Merioneth was delayed because Edward Vaughan went 'towards Montgomerysheir to promote ye election of two kinsmen of his for that county'.[30] Elections in Denbighshire, where Vaughan had a significant estate, were also conducive to his personal and political interests. Here another old Presbyterian supporter and Vaughan ally, Simon Thelwall the younger, was elected, alongside Colonel John Carter, a man who had endorsed Vaughan's dubious certificate of May 1649 freeing Llwydiarth from sequestration. In the other county where Vaughan held estates, however, the candidacy of Rice Vaughan for the single Merioneth seat would have been far less acceptable to him.

Edward Vaughan had taken the Merioneth knightship back in 1626 and his estate in the county amounted to around 1,000 acres. He was also connected by marriage to the influential Salesbury family of Rûg and so had several social, economic and political levers to pull when it came to electoral patronage in the area. Rice Vaughan was a county native who, in June 1653, had been appointed to the prestigious office of prothonotary for the great sessions of Montgomeryshire and Denbighshire, a post he had sought since 1646.[31] His candidacy for the Merioneth seat posed a particular threat to Edward Vaughan for Rice would be much better placed to make headway with the Llwydiarth sequestration effort as an MP than he would simply as a local official. As a result, Vaughan began to make plans to cross Rice's candidacy some two months before the election writ was issued.[32] He allegedly organised his campaign in concert with some Merioneth gentlemen who had been commissioners of array, and who probably included his brother-in-law, William Salesbury of Rûg.[33] Moreover, we know that Simon Thelwall the younger also lent his support to Rice Vaughan's opponents, in what seems to be something of a resurgence of political Presbyterians in north Wales in the mid-1650s.[34]

Rice Vaughan's opponent was John Vaughan of Cefnbodig, Merioneth, the lawyer who had accompanied Edward Vaughan to Llanfyllin the year before.[35] He may also have been the witness who in 1646 had attempted to defend Edward Vaughan's presence in royalist Oxford three years previously.[36] It seems clear, then, that John Vaughan was a long-standing associate of the Llwydiarth squire, and they were also kinsmen: Edward's grandmother and John's father were siblings, making the men second cousins.[37] John's will of 1671 asked the ultimate inheritor of Llwydiarth to distribute to his grandchildren the £500 due to him out of the estate, for the 'service I did his uncle [Edward] Vaughan of Lloydiarth'.[38]

In his later account of the 1654 election, Rice alleged that Edward Vaughan colluded with the sheriff, Morris Lewis, to have the election moved from its usual venue of Harlech to Bala which was 'very incommodious', but importantly was closer to Edward Vaughan's estates. Rice's petition also asserted that Lewis delayed the election so that Edward Vaughan could lend his support to his candidates in Montgomeryshire. The Merioneth contest was eventually held between 12 and 14 July 1654, but before the meeting, Rice Vaughan claimed that several of John Vaughan's supporters offered to allow Rice an unopposed return if he agreed to stop Edward Vaughan's prosecution at Haberdashers' Hall. Edward Vaughan arrived at Bala from Montgomeryshire around midday on 13 July attended by some forty men, most of them non-residents of Merionethshire and thus precluded from participating in proceedings.[39] Armed with swords and pistols, these Vaughan dependents were 'entertained with a continued shout of neer halfe an hower long by ye rude rabble' of Bala. This observation demonstrates that Edward Vaughan continued to be able to animate significant support in north Wales in the mid-1650s, and also, perhaps, that the divisions between old Presbyterians like himself and the popular royalism which had characterised communities such as those of this region in the 1640s had diminished after the experience of regicide, propagation and Commonwealth. Indeed, one account of the election has John Vaughan supported by William Price of Rhiwlas, a royalist who had been disabled from sitting in the Long Parliament, and also by the translator into Welsh of the king's *Eikon Basilike* (and the man who composed a commendatory poem to Edward Vaughan two years previously), Rowland Vaughan of Caergai.[40] Other supporters at the hustings included Edward Vaughan's close kinsman Howell Vaughan of Glanllyn and his legal counsel John Lloyd of Maesypandy, two men whom he would constitute as trustees of his estate a year later.[41] Rice Vaughan also mentioned that four of those accompanying Edward Vaughan to the election were men he had personally indicted for riot, which surely refers to the disturbances at Llanfyllin, and indicates that figures like William and Charles Kyffin and Howell Evans were probably present in his entourage.

We also know from a later Exchequer case that Vaughan had also undertaken some legal legerdemain to improve his candidate's chances.[42] He had sent for all his tenants and associates in the county to attend the election and had threatened those who would not vote for John Vaughan with ejection from their lands. In addition, Edward Vaughan had at least fourteen of his tenants enter large bonds or securities of £200 with his steward, Robert Lloyd. He did this so they could plausibly claim to meet the franchise threshold established by the Instrument of Government and vote in the election, even though most of them possessed only tiny estates.

Vaughan had also brought in a number of Montgomeryshire men to Bala who now masqueraded as Merioneth freeholders.

As the sheriff began the county court, Edward Vaughan attempted to have Rice removed, asking facetiously whether he (Rice Vaughan) was the sheriff's clerk. The prothonotary stood his ground, however, replying patiently that he would have 'legall satisfaction' for any attempt to remove (or, as he put it, 'assault') him. Evan so, proceedings were drawn out by the sheriff, stretching into a third day, with Rice Vaughan maintaining that his supporters were jostled, derided and some of them even taken into custody. Rice Vaughan himself was denounced in terms which are revealing of the political and religious positions at play here, as the prothonotary was called 'a lyar, a rogue, a seictary, a man against their Church & c'. Rice Vaughan's serving as a propagation commissioner clearly placed him squarely against the religious moderation of Edward Vaughan and his allies. The mention of 'their Church' also recalls Edward Vaughan's protection and patronage for ejected ministers like Richard Jones. Despite this kind of opposition, Rice Vaughan nonetheless asserted that he polled the greater number of votes in the election, but that the partial sheriff returned John Vaughan as the county knight 'in a private & obscure place' and had refused to allow anyone a view of the electors' names on his tally. This was a tightly fought battle, however, and witnesses later recalled that John Vaughan only carried the day 'by three or fower votes and ... noe more', and that if Edward had not created voters through his dubious sealing of bonds, then 'they would had [*sic*] lost the election'.[43] Following Rice Vaughan's complaints, the Council of State considered the miscarriages in the election but does not seem to have overturned the result.[44]

Political rehabilitation and knight of the shire

Although we should not read too much into a single contest, the Merioneth election nevertheless indicates that by the autumn of 1654 Edward Vaughan was back on the road to influence in local politics. Although he did not stand for election himself, and although the sequestration case against him continued to pose a serious threat, he was still able to mobilise a significant degree of support in Merioneth and to face down a trusted agent of the Independent interest in north Wales. Almost certainly because of his enemies' continuing influence and his own capacity to alienate Independent opinion, Vaughan remained outside the political tent, but the elections at Llanfyllin and in Merionethshire are signs of his return to local influence, and such signs would become more plentiful as the sequestration case against him ran aground. There was certainly no headlong rush back into the forefront of county politics, but his inclusion on an assessment commission for Montgomeryshire in June 1657 was an important moment.[45] Alongside him on this body were some familiar faces including George Devereux, Matthew Morgan, Robert Griffith, Samuel Bigg and Gabriel Wynne. All of these were Presbyterian colleagues from the accounts sub-committee, and their presence suggests that the political climate in north Wales under the later Protectorate had become much more conducive to moderate parliamentarian opinion.

This drift away from 'propagation politics' worried many in the army who saw north Wales as a repository of barely suppressed royalist sentiment. Reports flew in March 1655, for example, of 'a considerable party of old cavaliers risen in arms in Mountgomerishire', with one commentator concluding that 'they cannot leave their old tricks, and honest men cannot forget their old malice'.[46] A response to threats of royalist insurrection at this time was Cromwell's initiative of instituting direct military rule through the major generals. The individual who oversaw Wales and the Marches between August 1655 and January 1657, Major General James Berry, was sympathetic to the Welsh, but recognised his region as riddled with royalist sentiment.[47] Berry discussed the importance of maintaining a garrison at Powis Castle in July 1656, describing north Wales as a place 'where men will rule, if they be not ruled'. He acknowledged that many would like the castle rendered unserviceable, but argued against such proposals, maintaining that Governor Hugh Price's military presence should be augmented, adding that 'though the mountains of Wales be somewhat smooth, yet it may not be amisse to keepe it from being quite levelled, and to that end here and there a castle will doe well'.[48] Indeed, Edward Vaughan himself was drifting some distance from the parliamentarian fold in this period. In addition to supporting his candidate at the Merioneth election, the thoroughgoing ex-royalist Rowland Vaughan penned a laudatory ode to Edward in 1652, addressing him in glowing terms as a learned man of the law running an ancient estate.[49] It was also later reported, however, that Vaughan had been heard several times 'call[ing] the Protector a murtherer & a rebell'.[50] Although such hearsay evidence produced many years after the fact is problematic, it does seem likely that Vaughan's support for the republic was a veneer, and that his moderate parliamentarianism had turned to a cautious royalism in the face of revolution.

Stephen Roberts in his recent biography of Edward Vaughan for the History of Parliament, discovered that his political rehabilitation in this period may have owed something to his connections with the powerful parliamentarian lawyer and ambassador, Bulstrode Whitelocke.[51] Vaughan had become familiar with Whitelocke by 1655/6, probably through the agency of Sir Richard Pryse of Gogerddan in Cardiganshire who had married Whitelocke's daughter in 1653.[52] In December 1656 Whitelocke noted that Vaughan was being kind to his son, William, while soon after Vaughan's nomination to the Montgomeryshire assessment commission, Whitelocke recorded that Vaughan might make William his heir as the Llwydiarth squire had no children of his own.[53] In the later 1650s inheritance was much on Vaughan's mind, and at this time he reflected that his father 'as soone as hee hadd ended his troubles, dyed', that the same had happened to his brother Sir Robert, and that Vaughan himself, 'having then made an end of great troubles that lay upon him, hee beleeved hee should not live longe … and that hee had one foote in the grave'.[54] The sequestration case was clearly the 'great troubles' referred to here, and we know that Vaughan was dangling the prospect of inheriting his estates in front of several possible candidates. Indeed, in later testimony, several individuals mentioned Whitelocke as a potential heir in this regard, so there is good reason to believe that Whitelocke's report is genuine.[55] Whitelocke was a Cromwellian intimate who had power and influence at the political centre, but he was also a slippery and devious individual who refashioned his involvement in the republican governments of the 1650s for Restoration audiences.[56] In 1656–7 he was a useful figure to promote Vaughan's interests in London. Although they may not have been political or religious bedfellows, their backgrounds in the law gave them a common language, and it may well be that Vaughan suggested the possibility of inheriting his estates as an incentive to get Whitelocke's assistance without having any real intention of doing so.[57] Whitelocke would certainly not be the only devious Machiavel in this relationship.

Edward Vaughan was able to reintegrate himself much more fully into public life by the end of the Protectorate. He was, for example, appointed as Denbighshire sheriff in 1658. An even more emphatic illustration of his political rehabilitation can be seen in his election as knight of the shire to Richard Cromwell's parliament in 1659, held according to the franchise and distribution of seats which had obtained in 1640. He was returned alongside the member for Montgomery, his friend and kinsman, Charles Lloyd of London and Moel-y-Garth.[58] One witness later recalled that for around three months in early 1659 the two men would visit one another regularly in London and would 'both ride in the coach together to Parliament', or would share a boat to the House of Commons.[59] This picture of collegiate amity would collapse when Lloyd, who believed that his sons had been promised the Llwydiarth inheritance, was disappointed on Vaughan's death in 1661.[60] Although there is little evidence surrounding Vaughan's election, and none regarding his activities in the House, his return as knight must have been a sweet moment for him. His last election in 1647 was an unsettled and contested affair and he had not considered standing in the decade since. Despite the trials and tribulations over Llwydiarth, his return in 1659 showed that he had managed to climb back to the top of the tree in local politics. The troubled final months of the republic, however, would not leave him entirely unscathed.

Negotiating the Restoration, 1659–61

Following Oliver Cromwell's death in September 1658, the political situation became increasingly unstable. Cromwell's son, Protector Richard, did not manage the disparate and competing interests of the combustible republic as well as his father had. The army in particular was antipathetic to the growing influence of moderates (men like Vaughan, in fact), and in the face of this opposition Richard stood down, the Protectorate was dissolved and the old Rump Parliament recalled in May 1659. As the brief political experiment of the restored Commonwealth itself fell apart, many concluded that a return to monarchical government was the best way to restore stability and avoid a new civil war. In north Wales and Cheshire, the most explosive response to the confusion of these times was the so-called 'Booth Rebellion' of August 1659: an attempt by political Presbyterians and ex-royalists to restore Charles II to the throne. The leading north Walian in this unsuccessful insurrection was Vaughan's old adversary Sir Thomas Myddelton, who appeared at the head of a party of cavaliers at Wrexham where he proclaimed Charles as king.[61]

As the centre of the disaffection in north Wales emerged in Denbighshire, the regime inevitably questioned the loyalty of the county's sheriff, Edward Vaughan. On 3 August 1659, probably while he was at his Denbighshire home of Llangedwyn, Vaughan was 'seized by a company of soldiers' under the command of Captains Roger Sontley and John Manley, 'rudely handled' and carried as a prisoner to Shrewsbury.[62] Soldiers also raided Llwydiarth, battering down two doors and taking away Vaughan's horses and arms.[63] Petitioning the Council of State at the end of August, Vaughan unsurprisingly declared himself to be 'utterly ignorant of the late insurrection', adding that he had 'always submitted to the present government'. There is no independent evidence that Vaughan contemplated joining with the conspirators; his breach with Sir Thomas Myddelton may have been sufficient to dissuade him, or he may have considered it a doomed venture.[64] It is revealing, however, that the authorities sought quickly to secure him as a potential threat to republican and army interests, a reading that was apparently based on contemporary reports, but which would also be understandable when examining his troubled relationship with the republic. The Council of State ordered that Vaughan be brought to London for cross-examination and he appeared in the capital in early October.[65] He apparently asked for Bulstrode Whitelocke to assist him in his predicament, but the enquiry against him seems to have fallen victim to the political turmoil of the period and no further proceedings are recorded.[66]

As the tide moved against the 'Good Old Cause', so the Long Parliament was recalled in February 1660, complete with those members who had been secluded. Vaughan was among their number, and was listed in contemporary publications alongside other surviving local Presbyterians who returned to the Commons such as Sir Thomas Myddelton, Edward Harley and Thomas Hunt.[67] When that body was dissolved in March 1660, Vaughan had achieved new heights of local authority by being named as *custos rotulorum*, or principal justice, on the Montgomeryshire county bench, a body from which he had been absent for more than a decade.[68] He was also appointed a militia commissioner for north Wales, a prestigious post, and was named for the first time to the commissions of the peace for Denbighshire and Merioneth.[69] Alongside him on the Montgomeryshire bench were old friends and associates including George Devereux, Matthew Morgan and Robert Griffith.[70] As the republic's star waned, so that of Vaughan and his allies rose.

There can be no question but that Vaughan welcomed the Restoration of Charles II in May 1660, although he must have been concerned about what this development might mean for a return to favour of the royalist Herbert interest and, consequently, for his peaceful occupation of Llwydiarth. Vaughan was always a moderate parliamentarian and was dismayed by regicide and the breakdown of religious uniformity ushered in by the civil wars. As a secluded member he was well placed for a seat in the Convention Parliament and seems to have considered standing for Merioneth, but was 'put by' because of an agreement there that the next MP for the place would be 'an inhabitant in the county'.[71] He was also in the frame for the Montgomeryshire seat, but his ties to Charles Lloyd of Moel-y-Garth were said to have put paid to his hopes in that direction. His old friend and colleague George Devereux would later testify that Vaughan and Lloyd stood for election for the shire and borough seats, respectively, and that:

> most of the gentry of that county would have allowed of … Mr Vaughan
> for knight of the shire soe that they might have liberty to have nominated
> a burgesse, but … Mr Vaughan did then declare that hee would not then

> bee drawne to declyne … Charles [Lloyd] notwithstanding he was very
> much pressed therunto, and soe [they] lost both.[72]

It also seems that Vaughan's local enemies were moving against him, however, as in April 1660 he was arrested as being 'dangerous to the peace of the nation'.[73] There appear to be two possibilities behind this arrest. First, his enemies, such as the Herbert family, may have been concocting stories about his political credentials to exclude him from standing in the Montgomeryshire election. A second possibility, however, is that the man who was arrested was not our Edward Vaughan at all, but was in fact the sequestration agent of Tirymynach who had close ties with local Vavasorians. Whatever the truth of the matter, the individual who was returned to the Convention for the county, John Purcell of Nantcribba, was probably acceptable to Vaughan: he was his niece's husband.[74] Not only that, but Edward Vaughan was also said to be involved in arranging a match for Purcell's daughter with another of his nephews.[75] In the borough seat, however, Charles Lloyd lost to Thomas Myddelton, son of the parliamentarian general and Vaughan's old adversary, against whose return Lloyd petitioned unsuccessfully.[76]

Lending some weight to the theory that elements in the county were 'briefing' against Vaughan soon after the Restoration was achieved, around November 1660 one John Griffith petitioned Charles II about the disbanding monies that Vaughan had received in 1648.[77] Griffith maintained that £600 of the £1,600 levied on this occasion remained in Vaughan's hands and requested a warrant to help recover the money. This may simply have been a fishing trip based on rumours of the uncollected revenue, for Griffith would have been given a percentage of any monies recovered for the Crown. However, there is also the distinct possibility that Griffith was encouraged to step forward with these allegations by means of the Herbert affinity, or even by ex-republicans such as Rice Vaughan who wished to see Vaughan finally brought to book. Rather more serious were attempts to question Vaughan's political reliability in the spring of 1661. On 7 May 1661, a man named 'David' deposed that the previous February he had been present when Vaughan was told of proceedings for valuing estates in the county, and of accusations by Montgomeryshire's deputy lieutenants that Vaughan's lands had been under-valued by a local constable. Vaughan had then asked the constable not to give evidence on oath about the valuation process.[78] When the constable replied that he could not avoid providing testimony when ordered, Vaughan had responded that 'there would be a parliament shortly, and that he [the constable] would then know what power the deputy lieutenants had to rayse men without the consent of the parliament, in whom the power of rayseing men and arms was and is'. Vaughan had then supposedly concluded that the king could not raise men without a parliament. This, of course, was affirming the basic lineaments of the militia debates of 1642 which had helped give rise to the civil war by placing the sword in parliament's hand. Vaughan's statement was confirmed on 21 May by affidavits from John Herbert and John Lloyd, who testified that they had heard reports that Edward Vaughan 'was and still is in his discourse cleerely of the opinion of the Long Parliament was of ... which Edward Vaughan hath in very great esteeme'.[79] These depositions look decidedly suspect, however, and seem to be attempts, based on rather scant evidence, to discredit the Llwydiarth squire.

It is worth noting that Edward and John Herbert were the examining justices and that the examinations were taken around the time the Cavalier Parliament met, a body to which Vaughan had just been elected as Montgomeryshire knight. Following the Restoration, the Herberts of Cherbury had taken over the primacy from their Powis Castle namesakes in county politics, and doubtless had sought the shire seat for themselves. We know, in fact, that the county election was contested and that Vaughan had promised to provide freeholders who would vote for him with free lodging, meals and drink in several Montgomery hostelries.[80] The election, which began on 15 March 1661, was held over several days which suggests a bitter struggle, and, although we do not know his opponent's name, a representative of the Herbert interest must surely be suspected. In the context of this new rivalry, it is worth noting that Vaughan lost his place as *custos* of the Montgomeryshire bench after only five months to Lord Herbert of Cherbury.[81] It thus seems likely that the Herbert interest, frustrated with Vaughan's taking the county seat, sought to manufacture allegations that would at worst cast suspicion on his political reliability, and at best see him disabled from sitting.

Edward Vaughan's election as the Montgomeryshire knight for the Cavalier Parliament represents the culmination of his efforts to recover his place back among the local political elite after his bruising experiences under the Commonwealth. Throughout his period in the wilderness, however, Vaughan was never entirely without influence, as was demonstrated by his proxy defeat of Rice Vaughan in the Merioneth election of 1654. The rumours being cultivated by his enemies in the spring of 1661 probably told a truth about Vaughan's moderate parliamentarianism: that he did reverence parliament and supported a balanced constitution of the kind envisaged by the projected settlements of 1641. Ultimately, it is quite possible that, as in 1626 and 1647, he sought a seat in the Commons to frustrate any efforts by his enemies, now the Herberts of Cherbury, to question his title to Llwydiarth. Although no such challenges materialised, Vaughan would only enjoy the knightship for a few months as he died in September 1661. His portentous prediction that 'hee should not live longe' after emerging from his troubles did indeed come to pass, and his heirless status meant enormous uncertainty about the future and integrity of the estate he had defended so tenaciously during the 1640s and 1650s. It is to Vaughan's death and the mushrooming lawsuits around his inheritance that we turn in the book's final chapter.

CHAPTER 10

Death and Dynasty, 1661-1672

The history of Llwydiarth and the Vaughans in the seventeenth century is one of contest and discord. Such disruption was caused in no small measure by an inability, or a reluctance, to fashion a clear line of inheritance and ensure stability of title. The effect of such omissions was amplified enormously, of course, by the intense factional conflict which surrounded the estate. Given the bitter inheritance disputes which followed the death of Sir Robert Vaughan in 1624, then, it is surprising that Edward Vaughan, who was childless, did not leave clear instructions for the transmission of his hard-won estate. As a result, he effectively replicated the uncertainty and confusion which had attended his brother's demise. His unwillingness definitively to name an heir or make unambiguous provision for his inheritance meant that after his death a slew of interested parties jockeyed to claim the power and influence which Llwydiarth bestowed. And this situation, as was the way of early modern gentry society, engendered a deluge of lawsuits. In their efforts to win Llwydiarth (or at least to secure a part of it), the protagonists in these suits told partisan histories of Edward Vaughan's life and, in so doing they revealed something about his attitudes towards family, dynasty and lineage. One of the more startling elements to emerge from these disputes was that Edward Vaughan had a wife, albeit one whom he later refused to acknowledge. This episode is examined in this chapter, which reviews the evidence surrounding Vaughan's marriage in 1636 and his wife's subsequent efforts to secure alimony payments from a husband who denied that they had ever been betrothed. The chapter concludes by demonstrating the significance of the estate for the successful claimant, another Edward Vaughan, who established a dominant Tory political dynasty in Montgomeryshire in the later seventeenth and early eighteenth centuries. This thread of inheritance, and the power inherent in this enormous estate, can be traced down to the emergence of the political Leviathan Sir Watkin Williams-Wynn, the successor to the Vaughan landed legacy in the early eighteenth century who dominated north Wales politics under the first Hanoverians. These lawsuits, then, tell a parochial story about Edward Vaughan's life, family and connections; but they also help trace the foundations of one of the most powerful political dynasties in early modern north Wales.

Death in chambers, September 1661

We begin with a discussion of Edward Vaughan's death and the struggle to prove his will and the validity of two leases he was said to have made; circumstances which are eerily reminiscent of the disputes that followed his brother's death in 1624. Edward Vaughan was in London in the autumn of 1661, sitting in the Cavalier Parliament as member for Montgomeryshire. He had come down to the capital with his younger brother Rowland, whom he had installed in a house at Henley. Rowland was now his only surviving male sibling; his elder brother, Charles, had died around 1657.[1] As was usual when he was in town, Vaughan resided in his modest apartments at the Inner Temple. His servant at the time was Morgan Evans of Llanfihangel-yng-Ngwynfa (probably one of the Llwydiarth House retinue) who was only around twenty years old; Vaughan's usual servant, Vincent Edwards, had attended him up until August 1661, the date when, importantly, he had witnessed a document that would later be promulgated as Edward Vaughan's last will and testament.[2] Given the fact that Vaughan had drafted a will, it seems likely that he was unwell in August, and by mid-September he 'lay very sick in his bedd'. On the morning of 15 September he was found 'speechles' in his Inner Temple bedchamber, and he died around midday the same day.[3] As had happened upon his brother Sir Robert's death, there now ensued a scramble to secure the deeds and documents that were to be found in his rooms, and which, many believed, would prove title to estates that were generally agreed to be worth an enormous £3,000 per annum.

A critical figure in the next moves over the estate was Sir Charles Lloyd. We have encountered Lloyd (as merely 'Charles Lloyd') as a cousin and personal and political ally of Edward Vaughan from the 1620s onwards.[4] Although a parliamentary sympathiser who had sat in the first and second Protectorate parliaments for Montgomeryshire, and in 1659 alongside Vaughan in the borough seat, Lloyd had weathered the change of regime at the Restoration with some deft political footwork and deep pockets, purchasing a baronetcy in May 1661.[5] This, then, was an individual with close ties to Vaughan who evidently expected some return from his support for the Llwydiarth squire during the difficult period when he had been ejected from his patrimony. After being informed of Vaughan's demise, Lloyd hurried to the Inner Temple.[6] The interest in Edward Vaughan's health and the disposition of his estates was demonstrated by the press of individuals which greeted him in the Temple's chambers. In a scene that could almost be lifted from a Victorian novel in which the family gathers to hear the reading of the will, at his arrival Lloyd found 'many other persons in the roome and chamber', and, when he asked them their business, they replied that they:

> were come thither upon severall accompts or interests, some of them on the behalfe of themselves and others of them on the behalfe of others, to knowe howe ... Edward Vaughan had disposed of his estate and whether hee had made a will, and to knowe the contents thereof.[7]

The individuals present were Lewis Lewis, an agent of Howell Vaughan of Glanllyn in Merioneth; Katherine and Magdalen Vaughan, Edward's nieces by his brother John; Ralph Kynaston of Trewylan, Montgomeryshire; Edward Trevor, nephew of the royalist Welsh judge and Inner Templar Arthur Trevor; and Lumley Thelwall, brother of the Long Parliament MP Simon Thelwall, who, as we shall see, was present on behalf of Edward Vaughan's estranged wife, Frances. All of these individuals represented interests with a claim on the Vaughan estate.

After a search of Vaughan's chambers, a paper was found 'in the form of a will without a date'.[8] Sir Charles Lloyd read this document at least twice to the assembled throng, and, according to one hostile witness, when he read the disposition of the estates, Sir Charles 'began to tremble'.[9] We will see in a moment why this was so. Sir Charles took custody of the 'will' as the only individual identified as overseer who was then in London: the other two men it named as administrators of its provisions were in Wales. Lloyd then sealed up the chamber with a padlock and placed a guard over Vaughan's rooms. Ralph Kynaston rode to Wales to inform the executor and the other overseer named in the will of Vaughan's death and of their new roles.[10]

Sir Charles Lloyd, critically, then, had control of a paper which took the form of a will, and he had also taken some other papers out of the chamber with him. I say the 'form of a will' as the original has survived among the legal papers surrounding Vaughan's demise, and is covered with attestations of having been produced as evidence for witnesses to examine in the various suits which followed over the following decade.[11] It was clearly a draft document rather than a scribally finished piece, being written in Vaughan's own hand and possessing a number of ink blots, deletions and insertions. Unlike most wills, the document was undated, and it contained no religious preamble or directions for Vaughan's funeral or internment. The document was witnessed and signed, however, by Vaughan himself, along with his servant Vincent Edwards, Eubule Lloyd of London, an agent of the Salesbury family of Denbighshire,[12] and one Richard Roberts. Despite its draft appearance, the document was clearly a will, and one can see why Sir Charles, who was hoping to receive at least part of the estate as a bequest, would have been bitterly disappointed and 'trembling' when he read it. The will bequeathed Vaughan's estate in trust to his nephew, Charles Salesbury of Bachymbyd, Denbighshire (at that moment the county's sheriff), to manage on behalf of any sons which Edward's brother Rowland Vaughan might have. To this end, Vaughan asked that Rowland, who was then around sixty years of age, 'be married to a kinswoman of his owne with all convenient speed that may be'. In the (very likely) event that Rowland had no male heirs, then the estate was to pass to the male heirs of Vaughan's cousin, Howell Vaughan of Glanllyn in Merioneth, and in the event that he failed to have living male heirs then the sons of Charles Salesbury himself would inherit, as long as they 'tak[e] on them the names of Vaughans'. Vaughan provided £1,000 to his nieces Magdalen and Katherine Vaughan, daughters of his brother John, and confirmed a £500 annuity to Lady Katherine Palmer which he had agreed in the 1650s following litigation with her. He also directed that his lands in Machynlleth be sold and the proceeds given to the daughters of Bridget Powell (née Lloyd) of Pen y Pynt, Montgomeryshire: these were his illegitimate half-sisters fathered by Owen Vaughan of Llwydiarth, and upon whom a trust had been settled by Sir Robert Vaughan in 1622.[13] In addition to some other minor bequests, Vaughan then appointed 'my trustie and wellbeloved nephew' Charles Salesbury as his executor (giving him £100 per annum to discharge the trust), and constituted his cousins Sir Charles Lloyd and Howell Vaughan of Glanllyn as the will's overseers.

This was a confounding document. The enormous Llwydiarth estate was placed in trust and thus held in suspension until some future heir of Edward Vaughan's mentally compromised sexagenarian brother Rowland came of age. Rowland Vaughan now became an important bargaining chip in the scramble to control Llwydiarth, and his cognitive deficits almost certainly meant that many prospective claimants viewed him as eminently manipulable. Sir Charles Lloyd, meanwhile, was given a mere £50 by the will and the position of overseeing its implementation. In devising the will, Edward Vaughan had brought Lloyd, Salesbury and Howell Vaughan 'inside the tent', making them responsible for discharging its provisions, possibly in the hope that this would inhibit them from challenging its provisions in the courts.

Trustees, legatees and controlling Rowland Vaughan

The most critical individual in the whole business was now the will's executor and trustee Charles Salesbury of Bachymbyd. He was Edward Vaughan's nephew: Charles's father, William, had married Edward's sister Dorothy in 1612.[14] Taking on the role of trustee for this estate would be a daunting and thankless task. The 'settlement' of Llwydiarth without a clear line of succession would almost certainly invite a tsunami of litigation from interested parties. Indeed, we know that Salesbury took pause when presented with the prospect of taking on the role, 'making great difficulty to accept of the trust, hee being a man of an estate and not being willinge ... to incumber it in intermedling with [Edward Vaughan's] estate'.[15] Sir Charles Lloyd wrote to Salesbury on 24 September 1661 as a response to his request for advice about executing the trust, confirming that it was 'a thing of no small weight', and advising that Salesbury come to London 'with all ye convenient speed you can, whereby you may fully and thorowly understand your case and bee advized upon it'.[16]

Salesbury resolved to follow Lloyd's advice and journeyed from north Wales to the capital, arriving on 1 October 1661. His responsibilities including planning Vaughan's burial, and a good deal of time and money was spent 'buying and providing things necessary and fitting for the funerall and interment'. Vaughan was laid to rest in the Temple church on 8 October 1661 near the grave of the great lawyer, scholar and MP John Selden.[17] A month later a contract was signed with Joshua Marshall, a London 'tombemaker', to produce a monument for Vaughan in black and white marble 'after the same manner as a monument sett upp in the Temple Church for John Selden', only that there should be added an escutcheon of Vaughan's arms with mantling helmet and crest 'in propper collours'.[18] The work would cost £70. Selden was an interesting role model for Vaughan to emulate. A lawyer and historian, he was a moderate parliamentarian during the civil wars and an advocate of measured church reform which respected the supremacy of parliament in the constitutional balance. Like Vaughan, Selden was excluded at Pride's Purge. The two men must have known one another and seem to have held similar political views, but Vaughan was no scholar and it is doubtful that his admiration for Selden was reciprocated. As Vaughan finally found refuge from his earthly tribulations, however, so the troubles which he bequeathed to the world in his quixotic will had already begun to gather momentum.

As was mentioned above, Edward Vaughan's will thrust into the spotlight his only surviving sibling, Rowland. Edward Vaughan had lodged his younger brother with him at Llwydiarth and several deponents attested to the affection that existed between the two men.[19] However,

Rowland was, in the words of one Vaughan servant who lived in the house, 'weake in [his] … understanding', and would sometimes 'betake himselfe to his chamber and would not speake but few words sometymes or a moneth together … and at other tymes would growe outragious untill phisicke was given him and blooded'.[20] Despite these issues, his brother's will had charted a course that settled the estate on Rowland's children, so anyone who could make a match with him would have been able to sustain a strong claim to capturing Llwydiarth. This would probably be the case even if the union produced no children, as there was the prospect of manipulating Rowland into helping grant the property elsewhere. Securing Rowland's person thus became a matter of urgency for some interested figures.

Following his brother's death, and as the claimants began to circle around the Inner Temple chambers, Rowland Vaughan made his way back towards Llwydiarth in the company of Ralph Kynaston. Kynaston was a royalist plotter during the Protectorate who lived at Trewylan in Llansantffraid, Montgomeryshire.[21] He had married Catherine Vaughan of Glanllyn, and, in securing Rowland Vaughan's person and taking him back to Wales, he was almost certainly acting as a representative of Howell Vaughan of Glanllyn, the man whose family was slated to succeed to Llwydiarth if Rowland produced no sons.[22] Strengthening this connection even further is the fact that Howell Vaughan's mother was Mary Kynaston of Hordley, close kinsmen of the Montgomeryshire Kynastons.[23] On 21 September 1661, shortly after Kynaston and Rowland Vaughan had left (or, perhaps in the light of later testimony, fled) the house at Henley where Rowland had been ensconced by his brother, a messenger from King Charles II arrived looking for Rowland. The messenger had a warrant from the king, which had been secured by the duke of York to secure Vaughan and so 'preserve him and his estate'.[24] Surprisingly, there was a strong rumour circulating that before his death Edward had promised Llwydiarth to the king's brother, and the duke evidently believed that there was some substance to these reports. We do not know more about the background to such claims, but clearly in his lifetime Edward Vaughan had made some connection with York which does not appear in our records. Frustrated at finding Vaughan already on the road and in another's care, the king's messenger sent Kynaston a letter communicating Charles II's intentions and adding, 'I find that you have carried him [Rowland] away, tis beleeved out of a designe to destroy him for love of his estate'. As a result, the messenger had sent the duke of York's servant, the Flintshire Catholic John Conway, in pursuit of his quarry, demanding that Kynaston return Vaughan to Henley, 'least yt any prejudice befall him yow be caled to a strickt accompt for him, [so] yow may receave more advantage this way then by any other designe yow have'. Remarkably, then, the Crown had become directly involved in the brewing storm over Llwydiarth, and the pursuit of an aged and probably confused Rowland Vaughan as a pawn in the manoeuvres to capture the estate forms a striking if unedifying picture.

But matters were to get still more bizarre. On 25 September 1661, Vaughan and Kynaston had made it as far as Knockin near Oswestry and were resting at an inn. Before dawn, a group of around fifteen armed men surrounded the property.[25] Roused from his slumber and alert to the threat, Kynaston barricaded the property's entrance telling the men that 'their plott was discovered', but three of the assailants shot their pistols into the door, wounding Kynaston in the thigh. At this point, those within the house 'cryed "murther, murther", & some of them without cryed "fire the house, breake the door to pieeces"'. The raiding party did indeed break down the rear door and entered the property carrying swords and pistols. They 'ceised upon' Rowland Vaughan and forced him to ride with them. A witness testified that the 'ring leader of theese horsemen was one Henry Pursell', who had taken possession of Rowland Vaughan and was keeping him under armed guard at the family's property at Nantcribba in Montgomeryshire.

Henry Purcell was the younger brother of the family's head, John, the man who sat as MP for Montgomery Boroughs in the Cavalier Parliament, and Henry was doubtless operating on directions from his elder sibling. John Purcell had married into the Vaughan family in 1647/8, taking as his bride Eleanor, Sir Robert Vaughan's daughter. This was the young woman who had prosecuted Edward Vaughan in the Court of Wards in the 1630s in an effort to recover a £500 legacy from her father's estate.[26] Although Eleanor was now dead, the Purcells were aggrieved that Edward had still not paid her money, and a severely indebted John Purcell argued that a 'treatye' had been made with Edward Vaughan whereby he and his three daughters would receive £3,000 to discharge all their claims on the estate, but they had, as yet, received nothing.[27] Purcell's violent seizure of Rowland Vaughan, then, was almost certainly related to his effort to secure these monies, but he probably also had larger ambitions in mind, for Edward Vaughan had also apparently mooted his intention to settle his estate on a union between one of Purcell's daughters and the son of Howell Vaughan of Glanllyn.[28] This would, in fact, constitute the ultimate descent of the Llwydiarth properties, something discussed more fully below.

The dramatic pursuit of Rowland Vaughan gives an indication of what was at stake after Edward Vaughan's death. Enormous wealth and influence would accompany a settled conveyance of the estate, but a vicious battle in the courts would attend any candidate who claimed possession. It is not clear precisely what happened to Rowland immediately after he was taken by the Purcells. Around October 1661, Eubule Lloyd, Charles Salesbury's agent, described how, when Salesbury had arrived in London, much of his talk was that 'assoone as hee could get ... Rowland Vaughan out of the hands and posession of ... Mr Purcell ... he [Rowland] should be tendred in the first place' to marry a daughter of Sir Charles Lloyd.[29] By the end of December 1661, Rowland was finally 'enlarged and att his one [own] liberty'; he was then living with Salesbury at Llwydiarth and further discussions were being had regarding his 'disposall' in marriage.[30] A letter of 4 January 1662 to Sir Charles Lloyd from a correspondent at Llwydiarth mentioned negotiations between interested parties to settle the estate, but also noted, 'what disposall there wilbe of Mr Rowland's person I heare not soe much as whispered; he seems well contented with his present condicion but well inclyned to be perswaded in all things by [the trustee] Mr [Charles] Salesbury'.[31] Sir Charles Lloyd was desperate to know Rowland's disposition because, as was mentioned in some of these letters, he himself was negotiating, although how honestly it is impossible to know, to match Rowland with one of his own daughters and thus to claim the estate which had slipped through his fingers via the will.

Charles Salesbury and Sir Charles Lloyd

Charles Salesbury arrived in London in early October 1661 and grudgingly agreed to become the estate's trustee.[32] One of his first actions was to get the paper found in Edward Vaughan's study proved in the Prerogative Court of Canterbury as the dead man's will. This was done on 10 December 1661.[33] At this point, Sir Charles Lloyd was apparently in favour of having the will proved because he was exploring the possibility of matching a daughter with Rowland Vaughan.[34] Lloyd communicated through intermediaries to try and get a sense of Salesbury's attitude towards a match with his daughter, and was encouraged by what he heard.[35] However, in early 1662 Sir Charles met Salesbury and his brother-in-law, the lawyer Eubule Thelwall, in the latter's chambers in Gray's Inn for a 'long discourse' about the estate. Sir Charles left this summit 'verie discontented and angrie' because, despite Lloyd's promptings, Salesbury had 'not spoken one word to him of the intended match'.[36] In fact, it emerged that Charles Salesbury had been feeding the London merchant disinformation in an effort to prise out of his hands a deed which he considered crucial for settling the estate instead on Howell Vaughan's children. At this point, then, Sir Charles Lloyd 'despaired' of his initial plan and rejected the possibility of a match, now asserting that Rowland was 'a person that was neere three tymes her [his daughter's] age and decrepit and [he] appeared to bee of a distempered brayne and to bee weake in his intellects, and was soe reputed to bee by his brother … Edward Vaughan'.[37] This rejection stemmed from Lloyd's resolution to pursue an alternative course to gain Vaughan's estate: he would allege that the will was a forgery; open the floodgates of litigation against Salesbury and other claimants; and would promote his own sons' title to the estate through a contentious deed.[38]

A good deal of the controversy as it developed over the next few years was thus eerily reminiscent of the disputes in which Edward Vaughan had been involved after his elder brother's death in 1624. There was a will whose provenance and authenticity were disputed, and there were critical deeds of conveyance whose veracity and credibility also came under close scrutiny. On one side, Howell Vaughan's interests were bolstered by a deed which, he and his supporters claimed, echoed and thus strengthened the provisions of Edward Vaughan's will. Dated 1 November 1655, this deed demised the estate to Howell Vaughan and John Lloyd of Maesypandy for 500 years, provided that the two men supported Edward Vaughan's surviving sibling(s).[39] For his part, however, Sir Charles Lloyd claimed to have uncovered another document among Vaughan's papers, crucially one that post-dated the Howell Vaughan conveyance, which provided for a quite different settlement. Lloyd asserted that this deed was executed on 4 May 1656, and that it turned over the entire estate to John Lloyd, Sir Charles's heir, as long he and his heirs provided £200 per annum for Edward's brothers and were willing to 'take [...] on them the name of Vaughan'. The latter conveyance, was suspicious, however, because it was 'discovered' among a bundle of papers that Sir Charles had taken clandestinely from Edward Vaughan's chambers in November 1661 under cover of night and 'without any light'.[40] Moreover, one of the supposed witnesses to the deed later asserted that his name had been forged and that he had been in Ireland when the deed was supposedly witnessed.[41] Lloyd claimed only to have found the deed among this haul of documents in mid-December 1661, and only to have informed his counsel about its existence in early 1662, after the negotiations for his daughter's marriage to Rowland Vaughan had collapsed. It was also the case that the 1655 conveyance favouring the Glanllyn squire had been scooped up by Lloyd and remained in his custody. In mid-November 1661 Howell Vaughan had initiated a Chancery suit against Sir Charles for taking this material out of Edward's chambers, maintaining he had done so upon 'mere pretences lined with some sinister ends of his owne and for his owne private profitt'.[42] Some commentators even alleged that Charles Salesbury had allowed marriage negotiations with Lloyd to progress simply as a ruse to prise the 1655 deed out of his hands and thus advance Howell Vaughan's title. There seems no question that Salesbury supported Howell Vaughan's claim, and the latter wrote to the former in October 1663 describing Sir Charles as 'le grand enemy'.[43]

In early 1662, then, the tense truce over the Vaughan legacy was broken and a flood of litigation, centred on the High Court of Chancery, engulfed all parties. In fact, the starting gun to a deluge of bills, answers, replications, interrogatories and depositions had been fired by Edward Vaughan's nieces, Magdalen and Katherine, who placed a bill against Charles Salesbury in early November 1661, challenging his trusteeship of the estate and demanding their much-delayed settlement out of their grandfather Owen Vaughan's estate.[44] The most significant of these early suits, however, was that launched in April 1662 by Sir Charles Lloyd in the name of his three sons Charles, John and Edward. These submitted a bill in Chancery with all three now appearing under the surname of 'Vaughan'.[45] They prosecuted Charles Salesbury, the trustee, Rowland Vaughan, Howell Vaughan, John Lloyd, Katherine and Magdalen Vaughan in an effort to prove their title to the estate on the strength of the 1 November 1655 conveyance. This became a monstrous and all-consuming lawsuit and it would run for more than two years. It pulled other actions and disputes into its gravitational maw and proliferated in a mountain of paper and parchment. Ancillary actions were brought in the Exchequer, the Council in the Marches of Wales and the Prerogative Court of Canterbury which were offshoots of or related to the core actions for gaining possession of Llwydiarth. In essence, however, this was a clash between two parties: Sir Charles Lloyd and his sons on the one hand, and Howell Vaughan and his associates on the other, although Charles Salesbury's role as 'trustee-in-the-middle' saw him battling his own corner and bringing his own actions too. As one commentator after Salesbury's death plaintively reflected, Salesbury, 'haveinge very worthily undertaken the trust', had found 'very greate opposition ... by divers persons of ... Edward Vaughans kindred and relation and others who opposed the will and sett on foote many pretences to the ... estate', so that the trustee 'soone found himselfe greatly involved in law suites'.[46] It is doubtful that Salesbury would have undertaken the trust had he known how difficult and expensive the process would become. One report asserted that he had spent some £2,000 of his own money in discharging the role.[47]

It would be easy to become consumed by the voluminous evidence these suits produced as they played out over the next years, and as they were revived in 1667, but that is not this chapter's purpose or design. Although I will sketch out the denouement of this mammoth struggle below, I wish to use the evidence produced by these and other actions to reflect upon the book's principal subject, Edward Vaughan, in two main areas. These are, first, his attitudes towards family and lineage, threads which have already been important in our discussions in chapters 1 and 2; and, secondly, to discuss his clandestine marriage which has been largely unknown to historians, but which helps us understand how Edward Vaughan came to the pass of dying childless and casting about for kin and relatives to take over his estate. It seems deeply ironic that this individual, who laid such store on blood and lineage, should have ended up with a will in which one provision was that prospective heirs needed to change their name to 'Vaughan' to conceal an interruption to his bloodline.

Edward Vaughan: kinship, name and lineage

We turn first to the question of family and lineage. In their jostling to prove title and make good their claims on the Llwydiarth estate, the litigants and deponents of the early 1660s frequently recalled conversations with Edward Vaughan concerning his intentions as to the disposal of his patrimony. Although we must treat these recollections with some caution as, of course, those describing the discussions had agendas which they wished to press and candidates they wished to support, they nevertheless constitute important evidence concerning Vaughan's ideas about family and kin. A striking element to emerge from this material is that Edward Vaughan held an attitude towards family which many scholars would associate with sixteenth century or even late medieval concepts of bloodlines, lineage and honour, rather than the more 'modern' mindset usually associated with the later seventeenth century.[48] Vaughan also emerges as a misogynist who focused on male descent and disparaged heiresses.

Edward Vaughan was born into a family that was deeply concerned with its heritage and descent. As we saw in chapter 1, the church at Llanfihangel-yng-Ngwynfa was dominated by the Vaughan heraldic pew covered in armorial panels tracing the family's elevated bloodlines. The Vaughan dispute with the Herberts in the Elizabethan and early Stuart eras was conceptualised by some as a clash of 'names', or lineages. Although we have discussed in detail Vaughan's involvement in the ideological ferment of the 1640s and 1650s, which takes us into a very different world of gentry politics, he nevertheless possessed an abiding concern with older forms of lineage and kinship. An illuminating illustration of such attitudes comes from a deposition made by Edward Wynne of Llangower, Merioneth, at *The Black Raven* inn, Shrewsbury, in August 1663.[49] Wynne had lived at Llwydiarth for several years in the 1650s, possibly as Vaughan's steward, and he recalled a conversation with Edward from around 1658 concerning the latter's connections with his cousin and godson Howell Vaughan. Vaughan described how 'my cousin Howell Vaughan and my selfe are many wayes a kinne', concluding 'I thinke there are soe many degrees of kindred betweene mee and my cosen … that there is scarce a herald that cann derive the pedigree'. One can hear the pride in this statement, but also the sense of affinity which brought Howell Vaughan within Edward's ambit of potentially worthy heirs. Howell sought to trade on this, of course, and in one Chancery action he described how Edward had said he would support the children of Glanllyn as 'there had beene soe many matches and soe neere kindred between his family of Lloydiarth and the Vaughans of Glan y Llyn … that he did owne … Howell to be as nigh to him as any kinsman he had'.[50] Another of Edward Vaughan's servants, David Jones of Newtown, deposed in 1663 that around four years previously there was a rumour that Vaughan would make William Whitelocke his heir. When asked about this, Edward replied that Whitelocke would not inherit and that if he had no son of his own 'hee had a kinsman and a godsonne of his owne name', meaning Edward, Howell Vaughan's eldest son, who was then only around ten years of age.[51]

The emphasis on 'name' in Edward Vaughan's conversations is suggestive of an animating force in his social relations based on blood rather than on religion or politics. It is interesting, for example, that Simon Oliver recalled Vaughan's response to a question about whether he would make his sister's family, the Salesburys, his heirs, answering, 'hee must have a Vaughan to be heire to his estate'.[52] Similarly, Ralph Kynaston, the man who accompanied Rowland on his eventful journey towards Wales in September 1661, averred that Edward Vaughan had said he would 'settle his lands upon one person who was a Vaughan of his owne name and kindred, and that hee would not devide a foote of the lands'.[53] Such attitudes account for the provision in Edward Vaughan's will which required that Sir Charles Lloyd's children could inherit only if they assumed the name of 'Vaughan'. These children, in an answer to one of Howell Vaughan's Chancery actions, declared that Edward Vaughan had a special affection for them and had wished 'to continue his estate or some considerable parte thereof … not only in his blood but in his name alsoe by changing of these defendants names of Lloyd to Vaughan'.[54] They did not dilate on the fact that this was their own idea (or their father's) and others were less convinced, describing them disparagingly as 'the new created Vaughans'.[55] The sense of something distasteful about the Lloyd children attempting to conceal their inferior lineage in the illustrious Vaughan name was also articulated by Edward's brother Rowland, who claimed that Edward 'had a very speciall and constant disaffection to the plaintiffs [Sir Charles Lloyd's children] and their father's blood', adding his belief that 'he had hardly any kinsman he could have bene more unwilling should have taken and worne his name then the plaintiffs'.[56]

These comments on lineage and name hearken back to a world of familial, factional politics, and the kinds of dynastic clashes which were discussed in chapter 1. Indeed, in his attitude towards inheritance Edward was rehearsing positions held by his own father, Owen, who wished that his estates 'might contynewe in his name stocke and bludd', and who, when confronted with the prospect of no male heirs, insisted that he would assure his lands 'uppon a kinsman of his name and bludd', rather than see them descend through a female line.[57] It is interesting, therefore, to see signs that ideas about service to a house, retainership and attachment to a name through public display of livery also surface in some of these depositions, even as late as the Restoration period. When Edward Vaughan was sheriff of Denbighshire in 1658, for example, Charles Bowdler described how he 'did at Mr Vaughan's request weare his liverye cloake' to display his attachment to Llwydiarth.[58] Simon Oliver described himself as a 'retayner belonging to [Edward Vaughan] for the space of thirty years', while one Richard Edwards identified as 'a retainer to the house of Lloydiarth'.[59] Edwards also mentioned an intriguing episode when Charles Salesbury had been made Denbighshire's sheriff in 1660. On this occasion he was one of '12 men in liveryes' who Vaughan sent to attend Salesbury in a display of support, but also as a declaration of familial power to '[as] honest a man as any of his kindred or name'.[60] The display of livery cloaks and the language of retainership was somewhat unusual in Restoration England and Wales. These were elements which historians generally connect with Elizabethan dynastic politics. Given Vaughan's interest in and emphasis upon blood and name, however, such aspects of his personal authority are perhaps understandable. Retainers and livery badges were a material extension of the Vaughan lineage, a physical manifestation of the dynasty's authority, but also of its noble heritage and the social and political ties which emerged from the bloodlines of north Wales.

In addition to the critical role of name and blood in Edward's worldview, he also evinced a particular sense of patriotism and place in some of his discussions about potential heirs. As several scholars have noted, 'lineage' was a concept that encompassed place as well as bloodlines, and the continuity in tenure of ancestral manors within a family remained very important.[61] Moreover, the traditional gentry culture of north Wales placed special emphasis on the connection between ancestry and estate in its construction of a particularist species of gentility.[62] For an estate such as Llwydiarth, which reached across several counties, the Vaughan lineage was essentially constructed as a north Walian kinship group, and we see some striking demonstrations of a patriotic sense of family and lineage in some of Edward Vaughan's comments about his inheritance. For example, John Thomas, Vaughan's cook, butler and chamberlain, recalled how in 1656 he was mending one of Edward's shirts in the study at Llwydiarth and jokingly said he would cripple himself in his service and would have no lodging if his master died. Vaughan asked him why he said this, and Thomas replied that it was reported that he might leave his estate to William Whitelocke. Vaughan responded:

> English men will not come to our country but for their advantage, thou maist assure thy selfe but I shall leave my estate to a Welshman borne & of my name; does not thou know that I have a god sonne in Glan y Llyn of my owne name[?] I have kindred enough in Wales besides going to England for an heyre.[63]

This was a striking kind of cultural patriotism at a time when a considerable number of Welsh gentry sons were matching with English brides, which generally proved more lucrative unions. We need not take Vaughan entirely at his word here, because there were discussions in the 1650s about settling his estate on a marriage between Rowland Vaughan and a daughter of Roger Kynaston of Hordley in Shropshire. It is nevertheless suggestive of the kinds of connections between lineage ('name') and Welshness which we can see replicated in some of the genealogical interests of the gentry of north Wales in this era.

Another interesting reflection on ancestry, inheritance and Welshness was described by Thomas Maurice of Trefedrid in Montgomeryshire in September 1663.[64] He recalled visiting Llwydiarth around a decade before, and staying up with Edward Vaughan late into the night. Edward lapsed into a melancholy silence because he was troubled about who would succeed him. Maurice suggested to him that Queen Elizabeth was a model to follow because she considered hers to be a throne of princes and that none but princes should succeed her. When Vaughan asked how this applied to his situation, Maurice responded, 'Mr Vaughan, you are descended from some of the Welsh Princes, and none but the best of your family must inheritt'. Maurice here seemed to be playing to Vaughan's prejudices about the elevation and superiority of his bloodline, but he was also communicating within a common language about native ancestry and the strong cultural dimensions of Welsh lineage.

As these conversations stressed ideas of continuity and lineage, so other reports demonstrated how Vaughan disparaged undistinguished or broken bloodlines, and also how he stressed the importance of male succession. Although the depositions against Sir Charles Lloyd found among the voluminous court papers are polemical, there are enough that broadly agree to substantiate the claim that Vaughan was sceptical about his family succeeding to Llwydiarth, despite Lloyd's substantial wealth, because of his problematic heritage. Sir Charles's father was a fourth son of the main Lloyd line at Leighton in Montgomeryshire and a member of the Shrewsbury Drapers' Company, but there was a question mark over his legitimacy which caused Edward Vaughan some discomfort. John Ellis of Trefeglwys, for example, described how, when someone suggested Sir Charles should become his heir, Vaughan 'grewe very angry, saying "What? Shall a bastard of the howse of Llay [Leighton] be heir of Lloydyarth? Noe"'.[65] The cook John Thomas also recalled him saying that 'no bastard of the house of Llai [Leighton] would have a foot of his land'.[66] Although this was a grotesque double standard (we should remember that Vaughan's will bequeathed money to his father's illegitimate offspring), it is suggestive of the manner in which gentlemen such as himself framed ideas of inheritance in terms of patriarchal blood continuity. And Vaughan prized a particularly masculine transmission of lineage, as seen through the strict male entail provisions of his will. Ellis further deposed that when he had suggested that one of the Purcell daughters might inherit, Vaughan had angrily replied that he 'would have noe females to be his heire but one that could pisse against the wall'.[67] When Thomas Maurice also suggested one of the Purcell heiresses as future inheritors, Vaughan was again very displeased, saying 'Noe wooman cosen Maurice! Fie! Fie! Noe wooman'.[68] Inheritance through an heiress would constitute a breach of the Vaughan bloodline which was understood to run principally, though not exclusively, through male members of the family. There was perhaps also, however, an element in Vaughan's misogyny of his failed marriage, an episode that has remained shadowy but which resurfaced in the 1660s as his wife pressed her own claim to a share of Edward Vaughan's legacy. This aspect of his life is examined in the next section.

Edward Vaughan's secret wife: Frances Vaughan and the struggle for alimony

In an action brought in 1663 by Llwydiarth's trustee, Charles Salesbury, against Howell Vaughan and John Lloyd, deponents were asked about a settlement which Salesbury had made at Welshpool shortly after Edward Vaughan's death. This was a substantial annuity which was to be paid out of the estate to one Frances Vaughan, who claimed to be Edward's wife. This tantalising glimpse of Vaughan's spouse leads us to a separate lawsuit from around six years before, records of which are preserved among the papers of the Hanmer family of Pentrepant in the Shropshire

Archives. These documents relate a remarkable tale of Edward Vaughan's surreptitious marriage in the 1630s. In a biography of an early modern gentleman, his marriage and relationship with his wife would usually form an important part of the discussion. Such an analysis is not possible in this case due to the nature of our evidence, but part of the interest in finally fitting this piece into its rightful place in the jigsaw of Edward Vaughan's life is that it has remained hidden for so long.[69]

The material in the Pentrepant archive relates to a suit brought in Chancery (or, more properly, before the Commissioners of the Great Seal) in November 1655 by which Frances Vaughan of Pentrepant sought alimony payments from Edward Vaughan. Following the collapse of the ecclesiastical courts, the Rump Parliament established Chancery as the principal jurisdiction for wives to sue their husbands for payment of alimony: a sum which was paid out of the property that the woman had brought to the marriage.[70] Divorce for married couples was not an option in early modern England and Wales, and so separations were often the only path in dysfunctional unions, but these were often informal, messy and difficult, particularly as marriages between elites involved transfers of significant amounts of money and land. The wife was often in a subordinate position when seeking to recover reasonable maintenance from an estate to which she had contributed at her marriage but from which she was often excluded following a separation. Although we do not possess a copy of Frances's 1655 supplication to the court, we know that Edward Vaughan delayed for a year before answering it, and that 'when he was forced to answer, he denyed her to be his wife'.[71] As this case unfolded, depositions were taken on both sides, and these tell something of the story behind this obscure episode and they help reveal the identity of this mysterious bride.

Vaughan's wife was born Frances Meredith, and she was the daughter of Andrew Meredith of Glantanat in Denbighshire and his wife Dorothy Vaughan, who was Edward Vaughan's aunt (his father's sister). In another illustration of the dense kin and familial networks in which Edward moved, and which he seemed to cherish, following Andrew Meredith's death, his widow Dorothy married Simon Thelwall the elder, grandfather of his namesake who was Vaughan's close political ally during the civil war years.[72] Simon Thelwall the younger was also Andrew Meredith's grandson. Frances Meredith had been married before her union with Edward Vaughan, being matched in 1614 with James Phillips of Llanddewi Hall in Radnorshire.[73] He was the heir of another James Phillips and the family were an important fixture in a county which was poorly stocked with major gentry.[74] Frances bore her husband three sons including the heir who succeeded to the estate in 1633, Andrew Phillips, named no doubt after his Denbighshire grandfather. Frances's husband had an interest in Montgomeryshire through his father's settlement of the manor of Celynog on the couple, and in 1626 he described himself as 'of Celynog', and he served as the county's sheriff in 1632.[75] Edward Vaughan and his allies would later attest that Frances was unfaithful to her first husband, with one witness testifying that they 'lived assunder', while another claimed that James Phillips lamented that his daughter (Dorothy) was not his own but that of Edward Maurice of Penybont, Frances's brother-in-law.[76] Part of the defence in an alimony case such as this was to prove the moral bad character of one's (alleged) wife, and so these were statements made with explicit polemical purposes and we should be very careful about accepting them at face value.

James Phillips of Llanddewi and Celynog died in June 1633 leaving a widow and an heir who was then only eleven years of age.[77] The depositions suggest that Phillips had bequeathed some debt problems to his widow and that Simon Thelwall the elder, her stepfather, and Edward Vaughan, her first cousin, had journeyed to London to assist her with these. Some letters, one dated October 1638, survive among the Hanmer papers in which Edward Vaughan writes to Frances (as 'Frances Phillips'), and addresses her as 'loving cosen'.[78] He refers in one of these to her 'suites', but also describes his efforts to secure a lucrative match for her young son. These are letters from an interested and supportive kinsman as much as anything, but it appears that by this time the two had already contracted a secret marriage in Herefordshire. A marriage certificate dated 19 October 1636 was submitted as evidence in the 1655 action. This was written by Richard Vale, a clergyman who officiated in the parish of Aymestrey in Herefordshire, along with Humphrey Vale, the parish's curate and possibly Richard's father.[79] Edward Vaughan had summoned Humphrey Vale to perform the service, and the curate later deposed that he 'did marry them lawfully and effectually'.[80] However, Richard Vale informed the court that, when he was drawing up the certificate, Edward Vaughan gave him directions to 'alter their names least their friends should know of it suddenly'. Thomas Powell, an alehouse keeper in Llanfyllin, was an important witness for Frances on this point; he had supposedly given her away at the wedding. Powell deposed that the couple adopted the Welsh patronymic naming system to help conceal their identities. The groom was recorded as 'Edward Owen of Keven Coch': Edward's father was Owen Vaughan, of course, and Cefn-Coch was the township in which Celynog sat and was where Vaughan resided at the time, having leased the property from the Phillipses in 1631.[81] His bride, meanwhile, named herself as 'Frances Andrew of Trevilo' in Denbighshire: her father was Andrew Meredith and 'Trevilo' was Trefeiliw, a property settled by Owen Vaughan on his sister Dorothy and her husband Andrew Meredith, and which lay only a short distance from the Meredith home of Glantanat.[82] Unfortunately, although witnesses asserted that the marriage was recorded, Aymestrey's surviving parish register only begins with the Restoration and so we have no formal record of this.

It is unclear why Vaughan went to these lengths to conceal his identity and that of his new wife. It could be that he was anxious lest his holding of an estate through marriage leave him open for legal costs and attacks on the part of the Powis Castle interest. This was the period in which he was ejected from Llwydiarth and was in dire need of funds. There seems to be some substance to this conjecture for, in a later suit, Frances averred that:

> she did not long cohabit with ... Edward Vaughan after the marriage, he being then busied and intangled in many suits and in much trouble concerning his estate, ... [and he] perswaded [her] that it would be of some disadvantage to him in his affayrs to publish to the world the mariage.[83]

As we shall see in a moment, he secured some property from the union, but the couple apparently also had a child. Deponents testified that Frances Vaughan gave birth to Edward Vaughan's (unnamed) daughter in Griffith Thomas's house on Fetter Lane, London, around August 1637.[84] However, there is no record of a christening in the registers of St Dunstan-in-the-West or St Andrew Holborn, the churches closest to Fetter Lane, while the census of London inhabitants taken in 1638 shows no sign of a Griffith Thomas on Fetter Lane either.[85] It is a problem that the deponents were giving evidence so long after the fact with some providing demonstrably incorrect information and others were vague on details. Nevertheless, at least three deponents agreed that a daughter was born in Thomas's house in London, and it would seem safe to assume that Vaughan did, in fact, once have an heiress, but that she did not survive into adulthood.

It seems that Edward's marriage to Frances was predicated partly upon securing resources at a time when he desperately needed money.[86] Frances's daughter from her first marriage, Dorothy Hanmer, testified to her mother's union with Edward Vaughan, but also described how he had exploited her financially.[87] Frances was an attractive prospect because her son was a minor in 1636 and so Edward may have thought to control the Phillips' lands and estates to support his legal campaigns. He certainly had possession of Frances's jointure lands, and Dorothy Hanmer later alleged that her mother was worth some £400 per annum, but that she had lost an enormous £4,000 through Edward's ruthless exploitation of their estate. Frances herself later testified that 'much of [her] fortune was expended' in Edward's suits during the 1630s.[88] Interestingly, witnesses also deposed that, around 1640, Vaughan had demised away Frances's jointure properties to cover a bond of £1,000 which was due to none other than Lloyd Pierce, Vaughan's nemesis during the 1640s and early 1650s. Might it be that part of the animus between the two men in this period arose from some unhappy financial entanglements?

So in 1655 Frances and her witnesses alleged that Edward Vaughan had cast her aside, refused to acknowledge their marriage, ruinously exploited her estates, sold her jointure lands and refused to provide any recompense by way of alimony.[89] As Vaughan had managed to acquire a degree of settled title to the Llwydiarth lands by 1655, so this represented an opportunity for Frances to recover some money from her exploitative husband. For his part, Vaughan attacked Frances's character and that of her witnesses. She was portrayed as an adulteress to her first husband and a woman of loose morals. Thomas Powell's testimony came under particular attack, and he was described as a drunk and a 'doteing old man' who had run into debt. His poverty allegedly made him susceptible to suborning by the plaintiff, and some suggested that he had received gifts to depose on Frances's behalf. Several witnesses testified that he suffered from hallucinations, with one Llanfyllin blacksmith reporting that he 'did often see several fancies, as monkies, baboones and women and did see the said beasts copulate with the women'. Among those who testified on Edward Vaughan's behalf were individuals who we have encountered as part of his orbit before; these included his future trustee, Charles Salesbury of Bachymbyd, Robert Lloyd of Castellmoch, Charles Kyffin of Cae Coch and John Kyffin of Bodfach. Charles Kyffin alleged that Vaughan's sister, Mary Price, had spoken with Frances Vaughan around 1643 and asked her 'whether she were married' to her brother, to which Frances had replied that they were not. Although this might have seemed like evidence supporting Edward Vaughan, having one's own sister enquire about one's marital status indicates that Edward was far from open about his personal life, and it also shows that there was a good deal of speculation about the topic.

The alimony case made its slow way through the courts and was ultimately referred for a hearing before the Shropshire assizes in August 1659.[90] Following Edward Vaughan's death, several witnesses testified to having been present at the trial and some had even acted as commissioners. The verdict passed for Frances, who was declared to be Edward Vaughan's lawful spouse. John Price of Derwen in Denbighshire later testified that he considered the marriage to have been sufficiently established, 'for that the minister that married them and his sonne did punctually prove that they were present at the marriadge and that they saw them married'.[91] He also reported that the trial had demonstrated how Vaughan had wished for the marriage to be 'kept private and that therefore they went to a strange place to be married' under different names. So in the final years of his life Edward Vaughan had to pay alimony to the woman he had put aside for more than a decade. He appears to only have seen his spouse as a financial resource in his legal struggles, and his misogyny with regards to his future heirs was also directed at his wife: one deponent reported that Edward Vaughan 'doth scandall women in their reputacion and say that non of that sex are honest'.[92]

Edward Vaughan's death, with no provision for or acknowledgement of Frances in his will threatened her hard-won settlement of 1659. Indeed, we know that she challenged Edward's will, doubtless because it did not recognise her as his wife, and Charles Salesbury brought the matter before the Prerogative Court of Canterbury to have the document's authenticity confirmed and to oppose the claims of Edward's 'alleged relict'.[93] Frances was close to William Owen of Brogyntyn, Shropshire, and used him as an intermediary to negotiate with Charles Salesbury in an effort to secure her dowry payments. After negotiations broke down, she brought a writ of dower before Montgomeryshire's great sessions in 1661, and Salesbury quickly agreed that she should receive £500 per annum out of the estate. This money was paid while Charles Salesbury was alive, but Frances experienced problems after his death in April 1666. In 1669 she stated that she was in arrears to the tune of £533, and in 1671 opened up a new legal front against the estate's administrators to try and obtain her money, claiming that she had not received a penny of her settlement for two years.[94] This was a battle that remained unresolved at her death: she was buried at Selattyn near Oswestry on 26 January 1672.[95] Frances made her will in September 1669 as 'Frances Vaughan now of Pentrepant', and bequeathed 'all my rents and arrerages ... for my dower and joynture and in recompence thereof out of the lands of ... Edward Vaughan late of Llydarth ... and alsoe out of the lands of ... James Philipps late of Llandewy' to her 'beloved daughter', Dorothy Hanmer.[96] And so the memory of Edward Vaughan's neglected and exploited wife largely disappeared from history as her line continued through her daughters and through names other than her own.

Conclusion. *Llwydiarth and the making of political leviathans: Edward Vaughan of Glanllyn and Sir Watkin William-Wynn*

By way of conclusion, we may now return to trace briefly the course of the legal efforts to secure the Llwydiarth estates in the 1660s and 1670s. Suits in Chancery between the interested parties proliferated like weeds in the early 1660s. Depositions were taken over a period of two years in a variety of venues, and a contemporary census of the evidence in a single case enumerated over 1,000 folios of depositional evidence to be digested.[97] An important moment in these proceedings was a trial of the issue at the Exchequer Bar on 16 November 1664, when evidence was given 'upon both sides for about fourteene houres'.[98] This hearing ruled that the deed of May 1656 by which Sir Charles Lloyd's children claimed the estate was insufficient, and it determined that Edward Vaughan's will should continue to be the basis upon which the estate was administered. However, there was a series of deaths among major figures in these actions which shifted the ground upon which the settlement had rested. The trustee Charles Salesbury died on 1 April 1666, and he constituted his nephews William and Gabriel Salesbury of Rûg to discharge the trust in his place, although the running of the estate was left largely to the lawyer, Gabriel.[99] Another important development was Rowland Vaughan's death, unmarried and childless, in April 1667.[100] This removed a critical piece from the line of succession, although it was always unlikely that Rowland would have produced the required offspring to claim the estate. Nevertheless, following his demise attention focused firmly on the next individual in the sequence of reversions outlined by Vaughan's will: Edward Vaughan, eldest son of Howell Vaughan of Glanllyn, who was then still a minor of eighteen.[101] An attempt was made by Howell Vaughan forcibly to enter into Llwydiarth at the head of 100 men in October 1667, but after some shooting and a brief period of occupation, he was turned out by a local justice who convicted fifty-seven of his followers.[102] A further destabilising factor, however, was Howell Vaughan's own death in mid-1669.[103] Howell described mournfully in his will how he had:

> been att greate trouble and expences in diverse law suites touching
> Lloydiarth estate and principally in order to performe the inheritance
> thereof in my eldest sonn ... which proved chargeable unto me ...
> whereof I have contracted neare all the debts that I am indebted unto.[104]

He constituted a set of trustees to look after Edward's interests, the
most prominent of whom were Roger Kynaston of Hordley and Edward
Kynaston of Albrightlee in Shropshire, his mother's close kinsmen.

These deaths and the shift of 'management' in the estate's
administration initiated a whole new series of suits from parties such as Sir
Charles Lloyd's two surviving children, who sought to revive their claims
and exploit potential weaknesses in the estate's legal foundations. These
suits questioned the robustness of the settlement under the 1661 will and
Chancery's earlier orders, and so, in November 1668, 'considering how
greate the value of the estate in question', the court ordered that a second
trial should be held.[105] Moreover, it determined that the hearing should
be held in Shropshire, a provision which was strenuously resisted by Sir
Charles Lloyd's children. They probably felt that the Vaughan of Glanllyn
interest was too strong in the county as the family was closely connected
to the influential Kynastons.[106] Nevertheless, the court's orders stood, and
the Lloyd interest ultimately decided not to contest the case. As a result, in
1670 a determination was made for the continuation of the arrangements
set down in the will, a settlement that was enrolled in Chancery in early
1671.[107] Edward Vaughan of Glanllyn attained his majority soon thereafter
and thus succeeded to the estate of his 'uncle' and namesake. In May
1676 it was reported that he had 'non-suited the old heirs-at-law for [the]
Llwydiarth estate'; his tenure was secure.[108]

Edward Vaughan of Glanllyn's succession united his estates in
Merioneth with the Llwydiarth holdings across north Wales to produce
an imposing property portfolio, but more was to come. In the summer
of 1672, the same year that he attained his majority, Edward Vaughan
married Mary, daughter and co-heiress of John Purcell of Nantcribba
(and his late wife Eleanor Vaughan), forging a truly formidable landed
interest across north Wales, but particularly in Montgomeryshire.[109]
The Powis Castle Herberts were largely excluded from public politics

by dint of their Catholicism while the Herbert line at Montgomery Castle failed in 1691. With the field clear of meaningful rivals in the area, Edward Vaughan became a leviathan in county politics, and was Montgomeryshire's Tory MP from 1679 down to his death in 1718, being returned in some sixteen consecutive elections.[110] His memorial tablet in Llangedwyn church, set up by his two daughters, records him as 'ye adopted heir of Edward Vaughan of Llwydiarth', who 'by the addition of so plentifull an estate and his own endowments ... was soon pitched upon [by] ye county of Mountgomery & continued to be their representative in several parliaments'.[111] The text continued that by his marriage with Mary Purcell, 'was happily united not only these two excellent persons, but all the title to ye antient and great estate of Llwydiarth'. The tumultuous and protracted struggle over Llwydiarth was thus settled by Edward's accession. However, he himself possessed no male heirs who survived into adulthood and, as a consequence, part of the estate passed down through the line of his daughter Anne, who married Watkin Williams, the son of James II's solicitor-general in 1715.[112] Williams acquired much of the remainder of the estate after his sister-in-law's death in 1725, but by this point he had already inherited extensive properties elsewhere in north Wales, a requirement of which was that he had to change his name to 'Wynn'. Thus emerged the 'Prince of Wales' of a 'vast estate', Sir Watkin Williams-Wynn, the Tory grandee who dominated north Wales politics down to the mid-eighteenth century.[113]

The Edward Vaughan who is the subject of this book would have been simultaneously horrified and delighted at this turn of events. Horrified that the name of 'Vaughan' had been lost in the caprice of dynastic inheritance, and through heiresses at that! But he would have been delighted that his ancestral estate lay at the heart of such a commanding political empire in north Wales. The wilful, proud and indefatigable Edward Vaughan would doubtless argue that his family had triumphed from beyond the grave.

Conclusion

This book has argued that Edward Vaughan's life and career deserve to be better known, and also that he was a more significant individual in the history of north Wales during the mid-seventeenth century than scholars have previously recognised. Part of the reason why Vaughan's turbulent life has remained relatively unexplored is because the family's direct line died with him, although this fact was concealed by the apparent continuity of an 'Edward Vaughan' succeeding to the Llwydiarth estate in the 1670s. Our Edward Vaughan did not have children to valorise him, while his parliamentarianism, the unscrupulous means by which he first obtained and then managed to hold on to Llwydiarth, as well as his shameful treatment of his wife, made him a difficult figure for subsequent generations of the Vaughan dynasty to eulogise. It was easier to pass over Edward Vaughan's troubled and tumultuous tenure as Llwydiarth's owner (it was even problematic to call him the 'head of the family' given the presence of his elder brothers) and contemporaries as well as later historians tended to do just that. In his discussion of the Vaughan family, William Lloyd, the diligent Victorian chronicler of Montgomeryshire's early modern gentry order, recorded only that Edward Vaughan became a member of the Inner Temple in 1618. His neglect doubtless accounts for the fact that *The Dictionary of Welsh Biography* entry on the dynasty, which was based largely on Lloyd's work, neglected to mention Edward Vaughan entirely.[1] It has only been in the twenty-first century that Vaughan has begun to receive some belated scholarly attention, although this has often been partial, has sometimes been confused, and has generally failed adequately to draw together the diverse strands of his personal and political life.[2]

Another reason for the relative neglect of Edward Vaughan's life and travails has been the nature of the evidence upon which the analysis found in this book is founded. For a start, this material is almost exclusively to be found in the form of manuscript evidence, and the lack of readily accessible printed sources relating to his life makes Vaughan something of a forbidding subject for prospective researchers. It is also the case that Vaughan is not, at first glance, particularly visible in the major collections of manuscript evidence which relate to him. The key part of the Wynnstay muniments, which constitutes the single greatest archive of Vaughan material, was only deposited at the National Library of Wales in 1952 (and only purchased in 2001), and historians had no opportunity readily to examine the material before this time.[3] Moreover, the archive's cataloguing tended to obscure the nature of the Vaughan material within, with much of the collection relating to Vaughan's civil war activities being recorded confusingly (and largely incorrectly) as 'Sequestration papers'. Moreover, until a recent re-cataloguing by the library, the Wynnstay estate and family papers were listed somewhat cursorily and arranged rather haphazardly, a fact that militated against bringing together related materials from different parts of the collection. It is also the case that the rich collection of Vaughan material which is to be found in the National Archives is similarly hidden behind rather blank and unpromising catalogue entries. The accounts sub-committee correspondence in which the Vaughan-Pierce dispute features prominently, for example, is simply listed as part of the Accounts Committee archive among the Commonwealth Exchequer Papers; the volumes are arranged by year but have no item information which might suggest the extent of their coverage of the Montgomeryshire feud. The same is true for the material among the papers of the Committees for the Advance of Money and for Compounding with Delinquents: there are glimpses of the archive relating to Vaughan and his antagonists in the committee's Victorian calendars, but one must consult the original volumes to gain a true understanding of their nature, extent and importance.[4] These problems of visibility in the archive are compounded by the fact that Vaughan's extensive entanglements with the law have to be recovered from the extensive, obscure and sometimes forbidding collections of courts such as Chancery and Wards.

This book argues that bringing these materials into the light and making connections across these archives affords real dividends for our understanding not only of Vaughan himself, but also of his political and cultural milieux. The discussion elaborated above has revealed how Vaughan's confrontation with the Herberts of Powis Castle was the continuation of a factional dispute which had been rumbling on for decades. The analysis has also demonstrated how this intergenerational dispute was the central feature of political life in late Elizabethan and early Stuart Montgomeryshire. Examining the feud's dynamics and the personalities it involved also foregrounds the importance of family, kinship and lineage in the region's gentry politics. The 'ancient and inveterat hatred to … the whole name and family of the Herberts' was characteristic not only of earlier generations of the Llwydiarth clan, but was also something of a mantra for Edward Vaughan himself.[5] Indeed, it is part of the argument at the core of this volume that pre-war factional loyalties remained important considerations in the patterns of allegiance that emerged in civil war Montgomeryshire.

The struggle over possession of the Llwydiarth estate in the 1620s and 1630s became the central focus of Edward Vaughan's life, and his ejection from his family's patrimony added fuel to the fires of his animosity towards Sir William Herbert and his kin. As we have seen, although Vaughan was a minor figure before his brother's untimely demise in 1624, when he did emerge from the shadows he revealed himself to be an indefatigable adversary possessed of deep reserves of resolve, guile and duplicity. The tenacity and determination with which this minor lawyer confronted the powerful Herbert interest is impressive, although the tactics and strategies he adopted in his struggle are much harder to admire. The complex narrative of his campaign to secure Llwydiarth presents us with the 'litigious subject' of Edward Vaughan, an historical personality refracted through legal texts of bill and answer, deposition and counter-deposition. Although the nature of such evidence means that Vaughan's interior life remains elusive to us, we can nevertheless reconstitute a remarkably dogged and single-minded individual who, despite his reduced circumstances and reliance on the charity of kinsmen, deployed his creative (and often unscrupulous) legal energies to maintaining a foothold in the Llwydiarth cause, often through questioning the legitimacy of his nephew who was now in nominal possession.

Edward Vaughan's travails at the hands of Star Chamber, the Court of Wards and the Council in the Marches of Wales allowed him to embrace the role of martyr in the new political world ushered in by the collapse of Charles I's 'Personal Rule' and the calling of the Long Parliament. The shift in Vaughan's political fortunes in the early 1640s was profound and dramatic as the dispossessed underdog now became something of a proxy champion in parliament's campaigns against 'arbitrary' justice. Although the Long Parliament's support for Vaughan's case enormously strengthened and advanced his cause, the political breakdown of the civil wars and Montgomeryshire's prevailing royalism saw the Herberts' local power enhanced and Vaughan exiled to London. His reappearance in Montgomeryshire in parliamentary colours during 1645 was clearly a result of the royalist collapse in the area, a development that allowed Vaughan finally to make good on his claims to the ancestral estate. However, another thread which runs through this volume is that we should not rush to read his political allegiance as merely instrumental and emptied of genuine commitment. There is no question but that supporting parliament allowed Vaughan to get his hands on Llwydiarth's riches. However, it seems evident that his political Presbyterianism in the 1640s and 1650s was genuine: he was a moderate parliamentarian by conviction, even if that resolve was stiffened by Llwydiarth's rent roll. The personal and the political are so intermingled and inextricable in Vaughan's motivations and actions during this period that it is unproductive, and possibly even artificial, to attempt to prioritise one over the other.

Perhaps this book's central scholarly contribution is in its analysis of Vaughan's role as chairman of Montgomeryshire's sub-committee of accounts and in his emergence as one of the leading figures in the Presbyterian politics of north Wales during the second half of the 1640s. Historians have long known of Vaughan's antagonism with Lloyd Pierce, but previous accounts have failed fully to understand the ideological and institutional nature of their differences. As the central chapters of this book have shown, Pierce's position as the chair of Montgomeryshire's sequestration committee, his close ties with the army and his connections with the emergent Independent politics of the post-war period underpinned his spectacular and protracted feud with Vaughan in the later 1640s and early 1650s. There is no doubt that the two men despised one another personally, but, although their animosity might have had its roots in disputes over the marriage of Pierce's daughter, it is clear that their quarrel represented a vicious and protracted clash between the two major ideological threads of parliamentarian politics. The discussion offered above traced how Edward Vaughan and his allies, such as George Devereux and Samuel More, weaponised the Montgomeryshire sub-committee of accounts to attack and undermine Pierce and his Independent allies. Their efforts were not limited only to the few active members of Montgomeryshire's sequestration committee, however, but encompassed a broader assault on the military establishment and the nascent Independent interest in north Wales. Vaughan's attacks on Sir Thomas Myddelton and Thomas Mytton offer revealing evidence of the deep fissures that had developed within the parliamentarian coalition in the region by 1645–6, and the analysis offered here helps us make better sense of the political and military narrative in this area during the post-war years.

This discussion of Vaughan's Presbyterian politics has helped illuminate the dynamics of parliamentary factionalism across north Wales and the Marches, but has also shown its intimate connections with London and Westminster. Vaughan had his allies in places such as Shropshire and Denbighshire, but the circuitry of his authority ran through Westminster and drew on the influence of national Presbyterian figures such as William Prynne. Indeed, it is hoped that this book, while focused on an individual, has contributed to a developing thread in the historiography concerning the complex nature of centre-locality relations and political communication in the seventeenth century.[6] The ambition has been to anatomise and understand Montgomeryshire's political dynamics during the civil wars and republic, while exploring how such dynamics were shaped by intensive and sustained interactions with the political centre. The attempt to integrate the personal, local, regional and national dimensions of Edward Vaughan's worlds is one way in which this volume seeks to contribute to scholarship that examines the mutually constitutive character of local and national politics in the seventeenth century.

Exploring Vaughan's political manoeuvrings in 1645–7, examples of which include his 'Propositions' for military reorganisation; his involvement with initiatives such as the draft 'ordinance' for reforming local bureaucracy in north Wales, Montgomeryshire's 'county petition' of January 1646 and the tax strikes of 1646–7; his return as member for Montgomeryshire in the recruiter election of February 1647; and his activities in parliament in 1647–8, casts much new light on the region's politics during this period. These initiatives, alongside Vaughan's protracted struggles with Pierce, Myddelton and Mytton, reveal that he was a more significant political player than has been recognised hitherto. The Independents' triumph over their Presbyterian adversaries at Westminster in mid-1647, however, meant that Vaughan was now on insecure political ground. Although he stood firm to parliament's cause during the Second Civil War, his seclusion at Pride's Purge in December 1648 was a critical moment and, following this intervention, Vaughan was cast into the political outer darkness for the better part of a decade.

The book's later chapters examined how Vaughan's fall from grace was accompanied by a renewed threat to his possession of Llwydiarth, only this time the danger came not from the Herbert clan, but rather from his Independent adversaries Lloyd Pierce and, latterly, Rice Vaughan. In Edward Vaughan's struggle to retain control over his estates during the early years of the republic, he once more demonstrated the qualities of obduracy and pugnacious legal cunning which had sustained his cause in the 1620s and 1630s. His interactions with and manipulation of the various parliamentary committees which, between 1649 and 1655, investigated both his title to Llwydiarth and the monies owed to the state from his involvement with the disbandment process, produced a complex, convoluted and sometimes confounding narrative. But such confusion was precisely Vaughan's intention as he sought to exasperate and ultimately to stymie the investigations against him. Tracing Vaughan's activities during the 1650s is instructive but also historiographically innovative: it is unusual for us to be able to trace the activities of a parliamentary moderate in Wales during the republic. This is an era when we are generally drawn to discuss the radicals who seized the reins of government under the auspices of the Commission for the Propagation of the Gospel in Wales. So Vaughan provides something of a novel alternative to the Vavasorian radicals who usually provide the *dramatis personae* through which we understand this period. His political trajectory during the republic is from pariah to parliament man. The Protectorate saw a general drift back to the politics of the parliamentarian moderates, and Vaughan's successful challenge to Rice Vaughan at the Merioneth election of 1654 demonstrates that he remained a force to be reckoned with in north Wales, even as the threat of sequestration continued to hang over him.

Vaughan's patronage of ejected Anglican ministers and his election as knight of the shire to the Cavalier Parliament demonstrate his conservative credentials and deft political footwork. Yet he remained sufficiently tied to the parliamentarian cause for rumours about his reliability at the Restoration to be taken seriously. This once again suggests that his civil war politics were more than simply about challenging the Herberts and seizing his ancestral patrimony. Vaughan did not enjoy his success for long, however, and the protracted struggle for control of his legacy argues for the significance and consequence to social and political life in the region of the estate that he had struggled for so long to secure.

* * *

The Flintshire minister Philip Henry wrote in his diary on 2 October 1661, 'I went to Wrexham, [and] heard of ye death of Mr [Edward] Vaughan of Cludyatt [Llwydiarth], a great & rich man, but a leper & his name will rott'.[7] As a fellow moderate parliamentarian, Presbyterian and 'hearty well-wisher to the return of the king', we might have expected Henry to have been a supporter of Edward Vaughan.[8] Yet Vaughan was an unscrupulous schemer whose single-minded pursuit of the family estate left much wreckage in its wake, not least in the shape of his abandoned wife and his defamed and ousted nephew. Vaughan considered his 'name' to be one of the most precious things that he possessed, but in seeking to ensure that the Vaughans retained control of Llwydiarth by any means, fair or foul, in the eyes of some contemporaries at least, he had tainted his legacy and sullied his lineage. The biblical verse from which Henry drew his diary entry about Vaughan continued that the memory of wicked men would 'be turned to dust'. Although not an individual who can readily be admired, it is nevertheless this book's argument that Edward Vaughan's life and career is worth rescuing from the dust of memory, both for its insights into the dynamics of gentry faction and the law, and for the light that it throws onto the turbulent and absorbing politics of his age.

Notes

Introduction

1   Lloyd, *Sheriffs*; Lloyd, 'Sheriffs'.
2   These are, respectively, HPO (1660–90): 'Vaughan, Edward I'; HPO (1604–29): 'Vaughan, Edward'; *HoC, 1640–1660*, IX, pp. 339–44.
3   E. R. Morris, 'The Vaughans of Llwydiarth in Early-Seventeenth-Century Politics in Montgomeryshire', *MC*, 107 (2019), 57–76. The piece was carefully edited by Murray Ll. Chapman.
4   For an excellent example of one of Vaughan's contemporaries who did leave such material, see Christine Jackson, *Courtier, Scholar, & Man of the Sword: Lord Herbert of Cherbury and his World* (Oxford, 2021).
5   Something of a cognate undertaking can be found in L. R. Poos, *Love, Hate, and the Law in Tudor England: The Three Wives of Ralph Rishton* (Oxford, 2022).
6   For Brooks and his scholarship, see the essays by Michael Braddick and David Sugarman in Michael Lobbam, Joanne Begiato and Adrian Green (eds), *Law, Lawyers and Litigants in Early Modern England* (Cambridge, 2019), pp. 11–57.
7   Jason Peacey, *The Madman and the Churchrobber: Law and Conflict in Early Modern England* (Oxford, 2022).
8   For a more developed discussion of this point, see Lloyd Bowen, 'Faction, Connection and Politics in the Civil Wars: Pembrokeshire, 1640–1649', *English Historical Review* (2023), 92–131.
9   For more on this literature, see Jacqueline Eales and Andrew Hopper (eds), *The County Community in Seventeenth-Century England and Wales* (Leicester, 2012); Jason Peacey and Chris Kyle (eds), *Connecting Centre and Locality: Political Communication in Early Modern England* (Manchester, 2020).
10 Richard Cust and Peter Lake, *Gentry Culture and the Politics of Religion: Cheshire on the Eve of Civil War* (Manchester, 2020).
11 NLW, MS 6449B, p. 621.
12 Norman Tucker, *North Wales in the Civil War* (Denbigh, 1958); *idem*, *North Wales and Chester in the Civil War* (Derbyshire, 2003); R. N. Dore, 'Sir Thomas Myddelton's Attempted Conquest of Powys, 1644–5', *MC*, 62 (1961–2), 91–118; Jonathan Worton, *The Battle of Montgomery, 1644* (Solihull, 2016); *idem*, '"A Voyage into Wales": Revisiting Sir Thomas Myddelton's 1644–1645 Campaign', *Cromwelliana*, 3rd series, 8 (2019), 58–79.
13 Dodd, *Studies*, pp. 110–76.

14 Stephen K. Roberts, 'State and Society in the English Revolution', in Michael J. Braddick (ed.), *The Oxford Handbook of the English Revolution* (Oxford, 2015), p. 298.

15 Sarah Ward Clavier, *Royalism, Religion and Revolution: Wales, 1640–1688* (Woodbridge, 2021); *idem*, '"Horrid Rebellion" and "Holie Cheate": Royalist Gentry Responses to Interregnum Government in North-East Wales, 1646–1660', *Welsh History Review*, 29 (2018), 51–72.

16 See the discussion in Lloyd Bowen, 'Wales, 1587–1689', in John Coffey (ed.), *The Oxford History of Protestant Dissenting Traditions, Volume I: The Post-Reformation Era, 1559–1689* (Oxford, 2020), pp. 224–43.

17 Stephen K. Roberts, '"One of the Least Things in Religion": The Welsh Experience of Church Polity, 1640–60', in Elliot Vernon and Hunter Powel (eds), *Church Polity and Politics in the British Atlantic World, c.1635–66* (Manchester, 2020), pp. 60–79.

18 On this, see Mark Stoyle, *Soldiers and Strangers: An Ethnic History of the English Civil War* (New Haven and London, 2005).

19 BL, Egerton MS 1048, fo. 188.

20 Although see Clavier, '"Horrid Rebellion" and "Holie Cheate"', and Lloyd Bowen, '"This Murmering and Unthankful Peevish Land": Wales and the Protectorate', in Patrick Little (ed.), *The Cromwellian Protectorate* (Woodbridge, 2007), pp. 144–64.

PART ONE: FAMILY, FACTION AND THE LAW

Chapter 1: Families and Faction in Elizabethan and Early Stuart Montgomeryshire

1 Lloyd, *Sheriffs*, p. 215; Dwnn, *Visitations*, I, pp. 291, 294; BL, Harleian MS 1973, fos 141–42v; Bodl., Add. MS c.177, fo. 73.

2 Phillips, *Justices*, pp. 37, 125. It seems that this individual's father, John ap Howell Vaughan, may also have been a justice, but his name does not appear in Phillips's text: Lloyd, *Sheriffs*, pp. 218–19.

3 Dwnn, *Visitations*, I, p. 291; Lloyd, *Sheriffs*, pp. 219–20; NLW, MS 6499B, pp. 620–3.

4 David N. Klausner (ed.), *Records of Early English Drama: Wales* (Toronto, 1990), p. 170.

5 NLW, SA/1569/R2, fos 35, 71v; WSTY YA5/1: lease of Llwydiarth, 1569; BL, Harleian MS 1973, fo. 142v; TNA, STAC 5/L40/32, m. 20.

6 Lloyd, *Sheriffs*, p. 221; Phillips, *Justices*, p. 128.

7 W. R. B. Robinson, 'Sir Richard Herbert, kt. (d.1539) of Montgomery', *MC*, 87 (1999), 91–110 and 88 (2000), 1–24; Murray Ll. Chapman, 'The Creation of the County of Montgomery', *MC*, 100 (2012), 127–48; Sidney Lee (ed.), *The Autobiography of Edward, Lord Herbert of Cherbury* (London, 1886), pp. 10–11.

8 HPO (1509–1558) and (1558–1603): 'Herbert, Edward'.

9 HPO (1509–1558) and (1558–1603): 'Montgomeryshire'; 'Montgomery Boroughs'.

10 Lloyd, *Sheriffs*, pp. 221–2.

11 TNA, STAC 5/G4/39; 5/G37/19; 5/G11/19; 5/G46/20; E. G. Jones (ed.), *Exchequer Proceedings (Equity) Concerning Wales, Henry VIII–Elizabeth* (Cardiff, 1939), p. 273.

12 NLW, Powis Castle MS 10250; NEWA (F), D/GW/2084; Melvin Humphreys, *Plas Newydd and the Manor of Talerddig* (Welshpool, 2022), pp. 51–61, 94–5. I am most grateful to Dr Humphreys for generously providing me with a copy of his book.

13 Quoted in Lloyd, *Sheriffs*, p. 205.

14 For disputes between John Owen Vaughan and a Leicester servant, see TNA, STAC 5/L40/32.

15 Quoted in Lloyd, *Sheriffs*, p. 208.

16 On retaining and kin animosity among the Welsh gentry, see Sadie Jarrett, *Gentility in Early Modern Wales: The Salesbury Family, 1450–1720* (Cardiff, 2024).

17 TNA, STAC 5/V9/8; NLW, Great Sessions 4/133/3/14–22; 4/133/5/14–15, 20–22, 166–7; 4/134/1/8, 63.

18 NLW, Great Sessions 4/133/3/25; 4/133/5/22–32, 174; TNA, STAC 5/V9/8.

19 W. A. Leighton (ed.), *Early Chronicles of Shrewsbury, 1372–1603* (n.p., 1880), p. 74.

20 NLW, Great Sessions 4/134/1/9.

21 J. E. Neale, 'Three Elizabethan Elections', *English Historical Review*, 46 (1931), 227–38, esp. 230. For Edward Vaughan doing something similar in Merioneth in 1654, see below, p. 249.

22 TNA, STAC 5/H53/8.

23 Morris Charles Jones, *The Feudal Barons of Powys* (London, 1868), pp. 90–4.

24 TNA, SP46/18, fo. 40.

25 NLW, Powis Castle MS 10250; WSTY L.1297. An exemplary study can now be found in Humphreys, *Plas Newydd*.

26 Jones, *Exchequer Proceedings*, p. 278; TNA, E134/33Eliz/Hil16.

27 *APC, 1588–9*, pp. 97, 178–9, 266–8, 291–3.

28 Leighton (ed.), *Chronicles of Shrewsbury*, p. 76; TNA, STAC 7/8/5; HPO (1558–1603): 'Herbert, Richard I'.

29 Lee (ed.), *Autobiography*, pp. 2–3. For a contemporary assessment by the surgeon who treated Richard which confirms the seriousness of the injury, see TNA, STAC 5/H6/39. See also NLW, Great Sessions 4/134/1/6–7, 9.

30 The complex and intertwining suits can be followed in TNA, STAC 5/H6/39; H53/8; V2/11; V6/11; V7/36; V9/8, 13, 30; 7/16/3.

31 In December 1588 the Privy Council spoke of Richard Herbert's intention to 'molest and undoe' Howell Vaughan (John Owen's brother) by 'under hande' means at the coming quarter sessions, relying on his 'greate alliaunce to moste of the chiefe gentlemen which are of creditt and aucthority in that shire wher he is perswaded to procure all favor possible': *APC, 1588*, pp. 419–20.

32 TNA, STAC 5/V9/30.

33 TNA, STAC 5/H35/37.

34 W. V. Lloyd, *Description of the Armorial Insignia of the Vaughans of Llwydiarth* (London, 1881).

35 Lloyd, *Description*, p. 5.

36 Richard Cust, 'The Material Culture of Lineage in Late Tudor and Early Stuart England', in Catherine Richardson, Tara Hamling and David Gaimster (eds), *The Routledge Handbook of Material Culture in Early Modern Europe* (London, 2017), pp. 247–74; Jan Broadway, *'No Historie so Meete': Gentry Culture and the Development of Local History in Elizabethan and Early Stuart England* (Manchester, 2006).

37 For explorations of these themes in a Welsh context, see J. Gwynfor Jones, *Concepts of Order and Gentility in Wales, 1540–1640* (Llandysul, 1992); *idem, The Welsh Gentry, 1536–1640: Images of Status, Honour and Authority* (Cardiff, 1998); Michael P. Siddons, 'Welsh Heraldry', *Transactions of the Honourable Society of Cymmrodorion* (1993), 27–46; Shaun Evans, '"To Contynue in my Bloud and Name": Reproducing the Mostyn Dynasty, *c.*1540–1692' (unpublished PhD thesis, Aberystwyth University, 2013); Jarrett, *Gentility in Early Modern Wales.*

38 TNA, PROB 11/94, fo. 336v; C142/260/144.

39 WSTY PA3/1, bundle 2. The marriage articles were concluded as early as December 1573: NEWA (D), DD/WY/6506–7; TNA, C6/138/206.

40 WSTY PA3/1, bundle 1: extent of Owen Vaughan's lands, November 1620; NLW, SA/1584/23; WSTY YB2/1: copy will of Moris ap Robert ap Moris, 1584.

41 TNA, C142/260/144; NEWA (D), DD/WY 5413–14; WSTY PA3/1, bundle 1: extent of Vaughan estates, 1620.

42 T. C. Mendenhall, *Shrewsbury Drapers and the Welsh Wool Trade in the XVI and XVII Centuries* (Oxford, 1953).

43 Quoted in Melvin Humphreys, *The Crisis of Community: Montgomeryshire, 1680–1815* (Cardiff, 1996), p. 8.

44 E. W. Williams, 'The Wynns of Wynnstay and their Llwydiarth Inheritance: Part 1', *MC*, 108 (2020), 100–1.

45 Phillips, *Justices*, p. 132.

46 TNA, STAC 5/H35/37.

47 NEWA (F), D/GW/2084.

48 TNA, STAC 8/9/3. The 'riot' at Llanfyllin was also part of the suit in STAC 5/H35/37.

49 Lloyd Bowen, *Early Modern Wales, c.1536–c.1689: Ambiguous Nationhood* (Cardiff, 2022), pp. 151–2 and sources cited.

50 See below, pp. 273–4.

51 HPO (1604–29): 'Herbert, Sir Edward'; Christine Jackson, *Courtier, Scholar, and Man of the Sword: Lord Herbert of Cherbury and his World* (Oxford, 2021).

52 HPO (1604–29): 'Montgomeryshire'; 'Montgomery Boroughs'.

53 'Miscellanea Historica', *MC*, 4 (1871), 24–5; HPO (1558–1603): 'Herbert, Edward II'; Penry Williams, *The Council in the Marches of Wales under Elizabeth I* (Cardiff, 1958), pp. 86, 91.

54 Hatfield House, Cecil MS CP 2068. Cf. Hatfield House, Cecil MS 92/87.

55 Powys Archives, M/EP/43/R/A/1, fo. 15; NEWA (D), DD/WY/6509; WSTY PA3/1, bundle 2: survey of Owen Vaughan's lands, 16 November 1616. John's mother, Catherine, died only a week after the union. Our evidence is silent as to whether the match contributed to her decline!

56 Lee (ed.), *Autobiography*, p. 14. Cf. WSTY PA1/3: articles of agreement between Sir William Herbert and Owen and John Vaughan, 1608.

57 Lee (ed.), *Autobiography*, p. 14, n. 8; WSTY PA6/2: Exchequer suit, 1676; NEWA (D), DD/WY/6881.

58 This can be followed in WSTY PA3/1; TNA, WARD 13/119; NEWA (D), DD/WY/6880–1.

59 WSTY PA3/3, bundle 1: 'A briefe of the cause between Herbert Vaughan … and Edward Vaughan'.

60 NLW, Great Sessions 4/144/2/43, 49–85, 196; Lloyd, *Sheriffs*, pp. 403–5.

61 See below, pp. 60–3.

62 NLW, Powis Castle MS N.19898.

63 WSTY PA3/3, bundle 1: 'A briefe of the cause'. This claim of Owen Vaughan's suicide is also repeated in another brief found in WSTY PA3/3, bundle 2.

64 WSTY PA4/6, bundle 7: dep. Charles Kyffin, 23 April 1662.

65 NLW, Great Sessions 4/144/2/356.

66 W. J. Smith (ed.), *Calendar of the Salusbury Correspondence, 1553–circa 1700* (Cardiff, 1954), pp. 145–6.

67 WSTY PA3/3: breviat of cause between Herbert Vaughan and Edward Vaughan; draft petition, Lord Powis *versus* Edward Vaughan, *c*.1630; Bodl., Add. MS c.303, fo. 25.

68 WSTY PA3/3: Lord Powis's petition to the Lords, *c*.March 1641.

69 *CSPD, 1611–18*, p. 443.

70 W. A. Shaw, *The Knights of England*, 2 vols (London, 1906), II, p. 172.

71 Lee (ed.), *Autobiography*, p. 100.

72 WSTY PA3/1.

73 Lee (ed.), *Autobiography*, p. 101.

74 There were also two daughters, Dorothy who married William Salesbury of Rûg and Mary who married Arthur Price of Vaynor.

75 NEWA (D), DD/WY/6512; WSTY PA6/2, bundles 3–4: abstract of inquisitions and pedigree of Vaughan family, *c*.1676; WSTY PA4/6, bundle 7: deps. David Price, Roger Griffith, Elizabeth Bynner, 23 April 1663; Dwnn, *Visitations*, I, pp. 291–2, 294.

76 Roger appears to have died before his father's inquisition post-mortem of 1620.

77 TNA, C3/417/12; C2/ChasI/U14/18; NLW, Chirk Castle MS E.3314; NEWA (D), DD/WY/6524.

78 Several deponents stated that Vaughan was aged 60 in 1656: WSTY PA4/6, bundle 7: deps David Price, Roger Griffiths, Humphrey Lloyd, 1662–3. This is different to his birth date of '*c*.1600' given in standard reference works.

79 E. Calvert (ed.), *Shrewsbury School Regestum Scholarium, 1565–1635* (Shrewsbury, 1892), p. 72; WSTY PA4/6, bundle 7: dep. Charles Kyffin, 23 April 1662.

80 TNA, STAC 5/V6/25.

81 F. C. Inderwick and R. A. Rogers (eds), *A Calendar of the Inner Temple Records*, 5 vols (London, 1896–1936), II, p. 226.

82 WSTY PA3/3: breviat, Herbert Vaughan *versus* Edward Vaughan, *c*.1639.

83 WSTY PA3/3: digest of Court of Wards proceedings, 1626.

84 TNA, C3/387/43.

85 WSTY PA3/3: breviat of Edward Vaughan's proofs for his title.

86 One deponent noted that Sir Robert had suffered from scrofula since *c*.1621/2: NEWA (D), DD/WY/6895.

87 TNA, C3/387/43; WSTY PA3/3, bundle 1: 'A brief of the cause', *c*.1639; NEWA (D), DD/WY/6896. Another account in Star Chamber had it that he kept the mansion with thirty men of Sir Robert's household: TNA, SP16/167, fos 91v, 118v.

88 WSTY PA3/3: Lord Powis petition to the Lords, *c*. March 1641; TNA, WARD 13/119.

89 *APC, 1623–5*, p. 270.

90 TNA, C231/4, p. 341.

91 WSTY L.109.

92 TNA, WARD 13/119.

93 Lloyd, *Armorial Insignia of the Vaughans of Llwydiarth*, pp. 36–7.

94 NLW, Great Sessions 4/146/1/20.

95 NLW, Great Sessions 4/146/1/21.

96 NLW, Great Sessions 4/146/2/8. In a partisan paper he or his supporters later produced, Vaughan claimed his servants were held in gaol for six years without trial and were then acquitted: WSTY L.109.

97 The entail can be found at NEWA (D), DD/WY/6515.

98 WSTY PA3/3: copy will of Sir Robert Vaughan, 3 February 1622.

99 For the date of his birth, see WSTY PA3/3: Lord Powis's petition to the Lords, *c*.March 1641.

Chapter 2: A Labyrinth of Lawsuits: Contesting the Llwydiarth Inheritance, 1622–1631

1 For other important recent examples along these lines, see L. R. Poos, *Love, Hate and the Law in Tudor England* (Oxford, 2022); Jason Peacey, *The Madman and the Churchrobber: Law and Conflict in Early Modern England* (Oxford, 2022).

2 Richard Cust, 'Honour and Politics in Early Stuart England: The Case of Beaumont *v* Hastings', *Past & Present*, 149 (1995), 76–7.

3 Although important recent contributions to this literature include K. J. Kesselring and Natalie Mears (eds), *Star Chamber Matters: An Early Modern Court and its Records* (London, 2021); Mark Jervis, 'The Caroline Court of Wards and Liveries, 1625–41' (unpublished DPhil thesis, University of York, 2011); Diane Strange, '"The Contempt and Reproach of Our Nation"? Wardship in England and Wales, 1617–1624 (unpublished PhD thesis, University of Leicester, 2023).

4 Poos, *Love, Hate and the Law*; Lloyd Bowen, *Anatomy of a Duel in Jacobean England* (Woodbridge, 2020), pp. 33–49.

5   Henry Mares, 'Fraud and Dishonesty in King's Bench and Star Chamber', *American Journal of Legal History*, 59 (2019), 210–31; Sadie Jarrett, 'Credibility in the Court of Chancery: Salesbury v. Bagot, 1671–1677', *The Seventeenth Century*, 36 (2021), 55–79.

6   TNA, C3/387/43. For the date of the information in the Council in the Marches, see WSTY PA3/3, bundle 1: 'The tymes materially to bee observed', *c*.1630.

7   TNA, C3/387/43.

8   TNA, E112/273/1, m. 3; WARD 13/119.

9   Peacey, *Madman.*

10   TNA, SP16/474, fo. 166.

11   HPO (1604–29): 'Herbert, Sir William'.

12   HPO (1604–29): 'Vaughan, Edward'.

13   HPO (1604–29): 'Vaughan, Edward'; 'Montgomeryshire'; 'Merioneth'.

14   HPO (1604–29): 'Merioneth'.

15   NLW, MSS 9063E/1371, 1380.

16   NLW, MS 9063E/1389.

17   HPO (1604–29): 'Merioneth'; 'Wynn, Henry'; 'Vaughan, Edward'; TNA, C219/40/19.

18   Phillips, *Justices*, pp. 138–9.

19   Maija Jansson and William B. Bidwell (eds), *Proceedings in Parliament, 1626: The House of Commons*, 4 vols (London and New Haven, 1991), III, p. 146.

20   HPO (1604–29): 'Palmer, James'.

21   TNA, C115/107/8538.

22   Thomas Cogswell, 'The Canterbury Election of 1626 and *Parliamentary Selection* Revisited', *Historical Journal*, 63 (2020), 291–315.

23   TNA, SP16/167, fo. 96v.

24   HPO (1604–29): 'Vaughan, Edward'; 'Herbert, Sir William'; 'Montgomeryshire'.

25   *CSPD, 1628–9*, pp. 503, 506, 524.

26   Harvard University, Houghton Library, Law School MS 1101, fo. 34.

27   WSTY PA3/3, bundle 2: 'Plea and demurrer of Edward Vaughan', July 1628.

28   TNA, C3/387/43, m. 4.

29   WSTY PA3/3, bundle 2: 'Plea and demurrer of Edward Vaughan', July 1628; bundle 1: 'The tymes materially to be observed', *c*.1630.

30   WSTY PA3/3, bundle 2: 'Information of Sir William Herbert *versus* Edward Vaughan', 17 June 1628, and 'The plea and demurrer of Edward Vaughan', July 1628.

31   Harvard University, Houghton Library, Law School MS 1101, fo. 34.

32   TNA, SP16/167, fo. 128v.

33   TNA, SP16/167, fo. 129.

34   In one Herbert version of the tale, Lewis copied out John Owen Vaughan's old deed in the buttery and it was Sir Robert who pointed out the omission of male heirs: WSTY PA3/3, bundle 1: 'A briefe of the cause'.

35   TNA, SP16/531, fo. 52; WSTY PA3/3: 'Proofs and reasons in the Star Chamber on behalf of Herbert Vaughan', 1630.

36 The Herbert case had it that Lewis produced two copies of the deed, one in the 'Gallery' at Llwydiarth shortly after Sir Robert died in July 1624, and another on 29 August 1624 written in 'The White Chamber' at the house, and which was copied from the first document: WSTY PA3/3: 'A brief colleccion of the obiections'.

37 TNA, SP16/167, fos 88v–90.

38 WSTY PA3/3: 'Proofs and reasons in the Star Chamber on behalf of Herbert Vaughan', 1630; TNA, SP16/531, fo. 52.

39 TNA, SP16/167, fo. 180.

40 WSTY PA3/3, bundle 1: 'A brief colleccion of the obiections', p. 5. Cf. WSTY PA3/3, bundle 1: 'A breife of the cause': 'certeynelie it had byn farr more to Edward Vaughans advauntaige to have made that deede ... knowne to Sir Walter Pye if it had byn a true deede then to leave Edward Vaughan in remainder only after the heires males of Sir Robert'.

41 WSTY PA3/3: 'Proofs and reasons in the Star Chamber on behalf of Herbert Vaughan', 1630; TNA, SP16/531, fos 51v–52; SP16/167, fo. 108.

42 WSTY PA3/3, bundle 2: plea and demurrer of Edward Vaughan, July 1628.

43 Bodl., Add. MS c.303, fo. 27.

44 Bodl., Add. MS c.303, fo. 27.

45 For the following, see TNA, SP16/167, fos 94–96v.

46 NEWA (D), DD/WY/6895.

47 Two deponents, Anne Lloyd and Margaret Kenniston (Kynerton?), indicated that the 'jealosie' between Sir Robert and Lady Katherine arose from a letter Sir William Herbert had written, almost certainly to Sir James Palmer, promising the heiress in marriage should Vaughan die: TNA, SP16/167, fo. 116v.

48 For the following, see WSTY PA3/3, bundle 1: 'A briefe colleccion of the obiections made by the defendants counsell', 1630; WSTY L.108.

49 On this, see Katharine W. Swett, 'Widowhood, Custom and Property in Early Modern Wales', *Welsh History Review*, 18 (1996), 189–227.

50 See, for example, WSTY L.109.

51 TNA, SP16/167, fo. 103.

52 WSTY PA3/3, bundle 2: 'Information in Star Chamber', 17 June 1628.

53 TNA, SP16/167, fo. 103v.

54 WSTY PA3/3, bundle 2: 'Answer of Eleanor Gilbert', c.1628.

55 On this, see Hillary Taylor, 'The Price of the Poor's Words: Social Relations and the Economics of Deposing for One's "Betters" in Early Modern England', *Economic History Review*, 72 (2019), 828–47. Herbert's later account describes her as a 'poore wooman that was newly delivered of a daughter' and claimed that she had 'confest upon her oath in ... Starchamber': WSTY PA3/3, bundle 1: 'A briefe of the cause', c.1639.

56 TNA, SP16/167, fo. 106.

57 Bodl., Add. MS c.303, fo. 25v.

58 TNA, SP16/167, fo. 104r–v.

59 WSTY PA3/3: plea and demurrer of Edward Vaughan, July 1628.

60 TNA, SP16/167, fo. 106.

61 WSTY PA3/3, bundle 2: answers of John Lloyd and William Salesbury, *c*. September 1628.
62 WSTY PA3/3, bundle 2: examination of Edward Vaughan, 14 October 1628.
63 TNA, SP16/167, fo. 106.
64 TNA, SP16/167, fo. 103. This may be a paraphrasing of a Herbert attorney's argument in the court: 'He yt owt of light peoples mouths would deliver an opinion uppon oath yt it is a changling childe would straine a point in conscience about a changling deede': TNA, SP16/167, fo. 107.
65 Bodl., Add. MS c.303, fo. 25v.
66 Folger Shakespeare Library, V.a. 278, fo. 28v.
67 Quoted in Thomas G. Barnes, 'Due Process and Slow Process in the Late Elizabethan-Early Stuart Star Chamber', *The American Journal of Legal History*, 6 (1962), 236.
68 TNA, SP16/474, fo. 166.
69 WSTY PA3/3, bundle 1: petition of Lord Powis to the Lords, *c*.March 1641.
70 TNA, SP16/167, fo. 123r–v.
71 Bodl., Add. MS c.303, fo. 26.
72 John Rushworth, *Historical Collections of Private Passages of State*, 7 vols (London, 1721), III, Appendix, p. 28.
73 TNA, SP16/167, fo. 123v.
74 TNA, SP16/167, fo. 123v; Bodl., Add. MS c.303, fo. 26r–v.
75 Bodl., Add. MS c.303, fo. 26v.
76 WSTY PA3/3, bundle 1: petition of Lord Powis to the Lords, *c*.March 1641.
77 TNA, WARD 13/119.
78 TNA, WARD 13/122.
79 WSTY PA3/3, bundle 1: answer of Edward Vaughan, 6 May 1628.
80 TNA, WARD 2/55B/186.
81 WSTY K2/3, bundle 2: 'Mr Edward Vaughans Case', *c*.1641; WSTY L.109.
82 TNA, C142/472/97; WSTY PA2/4: copy of Sir Robert Vaughan's inquisition post-mortem, 1631; WSTY PA3/3, bundle 1: 'A briefe of the cause', *c*.1639; NEWA (D), DD/WY 5413–14.
83 WSTY K2/3, bundle 2: 'Mr Edward Vaughans Case', *c*.1641; WSTY L.109; TNA, SP16/167, fo. 132.
84 WSTY PA3/6.
85 WSTY K2/3, bundle 1: *Master Edward Vaughans Case* (1641); WSTY PA3/6.
86 WSTY PA3/6.
87 WSTY K2/3, bundle 2: 'Mr Edward Vaughans Case', *c*.1641.
88 TNA, C2/ChasI/P44/36.
89 TNA, SP16/167, fo. 132.
90 TNA, WARD 9/208, fo. 104v; SP16/429, fo. 154.
91 TNA, SP16/167, fo. 131.
92 TNA, C142/472/97.
93 HL, Ellesmere MS 7515; WSTY PA4/6, bundle 7: dep. Charles Rees, 23 April 1662; WSTY DH/10/15: Edward Vaughan lease of Celynog, 1631.
94 WSTY PA6/4, bundle 7, dep. Sir Charles Lloyd, 26 October 1663.

95 WSTY K2/3, bundle 2: 'Mr Vaughans Case', *c*.1641.
96 F. A. Inderwick and R. A. Roberts (eds), *A Calendar of Inner Temple Records*, 5 vols (1896–1937), II, p. 226.

Chapter 3: Powis *versus* Vaughan and the Downfall of Prerogative Justice, 1631–1642

1   For Vaughan and Selden, see below p. 264.
2   Lloyd, *Sheriffs*, pp. 510–16.
3   HL, Ellesmere MS 7326.
4   George Grazebrook and John Paul Rylands (eds), *The Visitation of Shropshire ... in 1623 ... [Part I]* (London, 1889), p. 272; Dwnn, *Visitations*, I, p. 285.
5   HL, Ellesmere MS 7515.
6   For the date of the action, see HL, Ellesmere MS 7516.
7   HL, Ellesmere MS 7516.
8   Caroline A. J. Skeel, 'The St Asaph Cathedral Library MS of Instructions to the Earl of Bridgewater, 1633', *Archaeologia Cambrensis*, 6th series, 17 (1900), 204–5, 208–9.
9   Longleat House, Whitelocke MS II, fos 132–35v.
10 Skeel, 'Instructions', 208.
11 Penry Williams, 'The Attack on the Council in the Marches, 1603–1642', *Transactions of the Honourable Cymmrodorion Society* (1961), 16.
12 HL, Ellesmere MS 7508.
13 William Bliss et al. (eds), *The Works of ... William Laud*, 8 vols (London, 1847–60), V, p. 345.
14 Bliss, *Works of ... William Laud*, VI, pp. 490–1.
15 HL, Ellesmere MS 7508.
16 Bodl., Add. MS c.303, fos 25–27, 84–93v.
17 TNA, SP16/167, fo. 123v.
18 Kenneth Fincham and Nicholas Tyacke, *Altars Restored: The Changing Face of English Religious Worship, 1547–c.1700* (Oxford, 2007), pp. 126–273; Peter Lake, *On Laudianism: Piety, Polemic and Politics during the Personal Rule of Charles I* (Cambridge, 2023).
19 HPO (1604–29): 'Jones, Charles'; 'Henden, Edward'; *HoC, 1640–60*, V, pp. 328–9.
20 HL, Ellesmere MS 7520.
21 This mirrors the argument in Longleat House, Whitelocke MS II, fo. 133r–v.
22 HL, Ellesmere MS 7520; TNA, SP16/372 fos 33–34.
23 HL, Ellesmere MS 7518.
24 TNA, SP16/372, fo. 18. Cf. HL, Ellesmere MS 7522: 'my Lo[rd] of Canterburye doth tickle in the [Edward Vaughan] busines'.
25 HL, Ellesmere MS 7521.
26 For this, see Williams, 'Attack'; R. E. Ham, 'The Four Shire Controversy', *Welsh History Review*, 8 (1977), 381–400.
27 HL, Ellesmere MS 7376. Cf. Ellesmere MS 7379.
28 HL, Ellesmere MS 7527.
29 HL, Ellesmere MS 7523.

30 HL, Ellesmere MS 7527. For Sir John Bridgeman's mobilisation of attorneys and clerks to search out precedents concerning legacies, see Ellesmere MSS 7528–29.

31 Williams, 'Attack', 16.

32 HL, Ellesmere MSS 7530–31.

33 TNA, SP16/474, fo. 166.

34 Several of the jurors did leave their marks rather than subscribe the document, which may indicate that Vaughan was not being as defamatory as he might first appear: TNA, C142/472/97.

35 TNA, SP16/474, fo. 167. Another copy can be found at SP16/167, fo. 132.

36 For a fuller discussion see Richard Cust and Andrew Hopper (eds), 'Introduction', in *Cases in the High Court of Chivalry, 1634–1640*, Harleian Society, new series 18 (London, 2006), pp. xi–xxxi; Richard Cust, *Charles I and the Aristocracy, 1625–1642* (Cambridge, 2013), pp. 140–211.

37 Cust, *Charles I and the Aristocracy*, p. 149.

38 Details of these proceedings can be found in Richard Cust and Andrew Hopper (eds), 'The Court of Chivalry, no. 539: Powis *v* Vaughan', *British History Online*, *www.british-history.ac.uk/no-series/court-of-chivalry/539-powis-vaughan* (accessed 22 May 2023).

39 For a copy of his submission in Law French, see TNA, SP16/439, fos 75–76v.

40 'An Acte for Lymytacion of Accions', *Statutes of the Realm, Volume IV* (London, 1819), p. 1221.

41 He was also an intimate of Vaughan's counsel in his case before the Court of the Marches, Charles Jones.

42 TNA, C115/109/8854.

43 TNA, C2/ChasI/P44/36.

44 *HoC, 1640–60*, II, p. 718; V, pp. 738–9; VII, p. 803; Edward Powell, 'Pryce (Newton Hall) Correspondence', *MC*, 31 (1900), 66–7, 302–3; BL, Harleian MS 1973, fo. 11v.

45 Powell, 'Pryce Correspondence', 289–90, 292, 294, 298; E. G. Jones (ed.), *Exchequer Proceedings Concerning Wales in Tempore James I* (Cardiff, 1955), p. 271; NLW, Powis Castle MS C.12507; Phillips, *Justices*, p. 140.

46 NLW, Powis Castle MS C.11203.

47 TNA, C219/43, pt. 3, fo. 202.

48 Phillips, *Justices*, p. 143; TNA, C231/5, p. 14.

49 Shropshire Archives, 212/364/36.

50 *LJ*, IV, p. 98; James S. Hart, *Justice upon Petition: The House of Lords and the Reformation of Justice, 1621–1675* (London, 1991), pp. 46–7.

51 NEWA (D), DD/WY/6896.

52 It is possible that this is a mistake for a report of the case on 19 March which is discussed below. However, the reports appear rather distinct, with Verney not mentioning the 'suppositious child', while D'Ewes does not discuss the Herbert force which seized Llwydiarth, arresting details one might expect to see in such sources.

53 John Bruce (ed.), *Notes of Proceedings in the Long Parliament … [by] Sir Ralph Verney*, Camden Society, 31 (1845), p. 28.

54 WSTY PA3/3, bundle 1: petition of Lord Powis to the Lords, *c*.March 1641. Although this document is a working draft, a later legal brief indicates that such a petition was submitted: NEWA (D), DD/WY/6896.

55 TNA, SP23/126, p. 103.

56 Wallace Notestein (ed.), *Journal of Sir Simonds D'Ewes* (New Haven, 1923), p. 512.

57 TNA, SP23/126, pp. 103–4: WSTY K2/3, bundle 1: *Master Edward Vaughans Case* (1641).

58 NEWA (D), DD/WY/6896.

59 WSTY K2/3, bundle 1: *Master Edward Vaughans Case* (1641). A manuscript version can also be found at WSTY K2/3, bundle 2. For a discussion of such ephemeral parliamentary 'lobbying' material such as this, see Jason Peacey, *Print and Public Politics in the English Revolution* (Cambridge, 2013).

60 For an indication of this, see the petition of Vaughan's tenants in Denbighshire and Merioneth from 1642/3: WSTY K2/3, bundle 1.

61 Maija Jansson (ed.), *Proceedings in the Opening Session of the Long Parliament, Volume 2* (New Haven and London, 2000), pp. 306, 310, 312. See also NLW, Clenennau Letters and Papers, no. 522.

62 NLW, Lleweni MS (Correspondence), no. 181; David Laing (ed.), *The Letters and Journals of Robert Baillie*, 3 vols (Edinburgh, 1841), I, p. 310; Bodl., Rawlinson MS. D.1099, fo. 41; TNA, PRO 30/53/7/26.

63 *LJ*, IV, p. 386.

64 W. H. Coates (ed.), *The Journal of Sir Simonds D'Ewes* (New Haven, 1942), p. 154; BL, Harleian MS 255, fo. 25v.

65 BL, Add. MS 70,002, fo. 316v.

66 NEWA (D), DD/WY/6896.

67 WSTY K2/3, bundle 2: a set of 'Accusations'; bundle 1: 'Mr Vaughan's petition'; petition from the farmers of Sir Robert Vaughan's lands in Denbigh and Merioneth, 1643.

68 WSTY K2/3, bundle 1: 'Mr Vaughan's petition'.

69 NLW, Add. MS 467E/1700.

70 NEWA (D), DD/WY/6896.

PART TWO: POLITICS AND PATRIMONY DURING THE BRITISH CIVIL WARS

Chapter 4: Civil War, Conquest and Committees, 1642–1645

1 John Morrill, *Revolt in the Provinces* (Basingstoke, 1999), p. 114.

2 For some splendid reflections on how to take the county study forward, see Richard Cust and Peter Lake, *Gentry Culture and the Politics of Religion: Cheshire on the Eve of Civil War* (Manchester, 2020), pp. 1–18.

3 Ann Hughes, 'Diligent Enquiries and Perfect Accounts: Central Initiatives and Local Agency in the English Civil War', in Jason Peacey and Chris R. Kyle (eds), *Connecting Centre and Locality: Political Communication in Early Modern England* (Manchester, 2020), pp. 116–32; *idem*, '"The Accounts of the Kingdom": Memory,

Community and the Civil War', *Past & Present*, 230, supplement 11 (2016), 311–29; Jason Peacey, 'Politics, Accounts and Propaganda in the Long Parliament', in *idem* and Chris R. Kyle (eds), *Parliament at Work: Parliamentary Committees, Political Power and Public Access in Early Modern England* (Woodbridge, 2002), pp. 59–78.

4   Although see now Sarah Ward Clavier, *Royalism, Religion and Revolution: Wales, 1640–1688* (Woodbridge, 2021); Lloyd Bowen, *John Poyer, the Civil Wars in Pembrokeshire and the British Revolutions* (Cardiff, 2020); Stephen K. Roberts, 'How the West was Won: Parliamentary Politics, Religion and the Military in South Wales, 1642–9', *Welsh History Review*, 21 (2003), 646–74.

5   Lloyd Bowen, 'Wales in British Politics, *c*.1603–42' (unpublished PhD thesis, University of Wales, Cardiff, 2000), 489–92.

6   NLW, MS 9063E/1711; TNA, SP19/21/231.

7   *The True Informer* (Oxford, 1643), p. 40.

8   Northamptonshire Archives, Finch-Hatton MS 133; NLW, Powis Castle MS D24/1/15.

9   Dodd, *Studies*, p. 113.

10 WSTY K2/3, bundle 1: 'Accusations' and 'answere', *c*.1643.

11 TNA, C6/158/164.

12 WSTY K2/3, bundle 1: 'Accusations' and 'answere', *c*.1643.

13 WSTY K2/3, bundle 3: articles against Sir Thomas Myddelton, 1646.

14 For this meeting, see NLW, MS 9063E/1711; Shropshire Archives, 212/364/77. Activity was already advanced in the county to send a petition of support to the king: NLW, Lleweni MS (Correspondence), no. 194; MS 1595E, fo. 228.

15 WSTY PA3/8: Edward Vaughan's narrative, *c*.February 1646.

16 WSTY K2/3, bundle 1: deps. Owen Andrewes and others, 24 February 1646. Other copies can be found at TNA, SP28/251, unfol.

17 WSTY K2/3, bundle 1: 'A copy of a warrant'.

18 WSTY K2/3, bundle 1: 'Accusations' and 'answere', *c*.1643. These men were secured by the Anglesey royalist Sir Thomas Cheadle: Dodd, *Studies*, p. 114.

19 On the region's royalism, see Clavier, *Royalism, Religion and Revolution*, pp. 179–86.

20 Myddelton had been asked by the Commons in June 1642 to implement the militia ordinance in Denbighshire: *CJ*, II, p. 623.

21 WSTY PA3/8: Edward Vaughan's narrative, *c*.February 1646.

22 WSTY K2/3, bundle 1: 'Accusations' and 'answere', *c*.1643.

23 Robert Williams (ed.), 'An Account of the Civil War in North Wales', *Archaeologia Cambrensis*, 1 (1846), 33.

24 *HoC, 1640–1660*, V, p. 266.

25 *The Pedigree of the Ancient Family of the Palmers of Sussex, 1672* (privately printed, 1867), p. 7.

26 WSTY K2/3, bundle 1: 'Cop[y] of the Kings Warr[an]t', 1643; TNA, SP16/539/2, fo. 48; Shropshire Archives, 894/221.

27 WSTY K2/3, bundle 1: 'Cop[y] of the Kings Warr[an]t', 1643, and 'A copie of a warrant', *c*.1643.

28 WSTY PA3/8: Edward Vaughan's narrative, *c*.February 1646.

29 WSTY K2/3, bundle 1: 'Accusations' and 'answere', *c*.1643.

30 WSTY K2/3, bundle 2: Montgomeryshire sub-committee of accounts to central Committee of Accounts, 4 December 1646; WSTY PA3/8: deps. before central Committee of Accounts, 24 February 1646; TNA, SP28/253B, pt. 1; SP28/251, unfol.

31 See particularly WSTY K2/3, bundle 2: articles against Edward Vaughan, 3 November 1646.

32 WSTY PA3/8: Owen Andrewes before central Committee of Accounts, 24 February 1646; TNA, SP28/251, unfol.

33 TNA, SP28/251, unfol.

34 TNA, SP16/539/2, fo. 48r–v. These accusations closely tracked the 5 February 1643 warrant that Sir James Palmer had procured against Vaughan: WSTY K2/3, bundle 1: 'A copy of a warrant'.

35 WSTY K2/3, bundle 2: Montgomeryshire sub-committee of accounts to central Committee of Accounts, 4 December 1646.

36 WSTY PA3/8: Owen Andrewes before central Committee of Accounts, 24 February 1646.

37 B. E. Howells (ed.), *A Calendar of Letters Relating to North Wales* (Cardiff, 1967), p. 57.

38 WSTY PA3/8; K2/3, bundle 3: Edward Vaughan's case, 1647.

39 NLW, MS 468E/1932; Brogyntyn Estate MSS PEC1/3; TNA, SP23/16, p. 665; SP23/63, p. 867.

40 Vaughan had married Simon's aunt in 1636, while Simon's grandfather, who was still alive, had married Vaughan's aunt.

41 WSTY PA3/8: Edward Vaughan's narrative, *c*.February 1646.

42 Although this is noted briefly in Dodd, *Studies*, pp. 115, 117.

43 *A&O*, I, pp. 378–81. Cf. *A&O*, I, pp. 179–80.

44 WSTY K2/3, bundle 3: articles against Sir Thomas Myddelton, *c*.1647.

45 WSTY K2/3, bundle 2: certificate for George Devereux, 4 December 1646; NLW, Powis Castle 1990 Deposit, large box 11, bundle no. 12. I am most grateful to Melvin Humphries and Murray Chapman for providing me with details of these documents while they were being catalogued. The committee's treasurer later submitted accounts for his work which commenced in October 1644: TNA, SP28/252, fo. 318v.

46 The committee in Pembrokeshire was established in June 1644.

47 Jones's recent History of Parliament biography does not mention his work on this committee: *HoC, 1640–60*, VI, pp. 334–5.

48 TNA, SP28/189, pt. 2. Radnorshire acquired its own sequestration committee by February 1646.

49 WSTY K2/3, bundle 3: paper against committees, *c*.April 1646.

50 Edward Powell, 'Pryce (Newton Hall) Correspondence', *MC*, 31 (1900), 111.

51 *HoC, 1640–1660*, VII, pp. 800–1.

52 *CJ*, II, p. 594; *LJ*, V, pp. 92, 95.

53 Phillips, *Justices*, p. 139; Lloyd, *Sheriffs*, pp. 521–7.

54 TNA, E113/3.
55 TNA, PROB 11/291, fo. 312.
56 Lloyd, 'Sheriffs', 192–214; *HoC, 1640–1660*, IV, pp. 667–9; NLW, Vaynor Park Estate Records 599.
57 WSTY PA4/6, bundle 7: dep. of George Devereux, 28 September 1663.
58 WSTY K2/3: certificate for George Devereux, 4 December 1646.
59 *CJ*, IV, p. 56; *LJ*, VII, pp. 216–17, 291; WSTY K2/3: copy of Devereux's commission, 20 February 1645. Devereux's nomination as deputy lieutenant came from the Lords, suggesting Essex's intervention.
60 WSTY K2/3, bundle 1: 'Mr Vaughan's petition'; bundle 3, 'Edward Vaughan's case', *c*.April 1647; TNA, SP23/164, pp. 486–7; Williams (ed.), 'Civil War in North Wales', 40.
61 Powell, 'Pryce Correspondence', 309.
62 WSTY PA3/8: Edward Vaughan's narrative, *c*.February 1646; WSTY K2/3, bundle 1: account of Edward Vaughan's troop, *c*.1646. Another copy of this document, with some variations, can be found at WSTY PA3/8.
63 *The True Informer*, 40 (24–31 January 1646), p. 318.
64 TNA, SP23/164, pp. 457, 462–3, 501, 503, 505; WSTY K2/3, bundle 1: account of Llwydiarth rents, 27 September 1645. This account of rents due to the state begins on 19 April 1645; Herbert Vaughan, Sir James Palmer and Katherine Palmer were only formally sequestered in February and April 1646: TNA, SP20/2, fos 95v, 119, 240. A much later rental contentiously dates Vaughan's possession to March 1644: NEWA (D), DD/WY/5378.
65 WSTY K2/3, bundle 1: report of John Bradshaw, 3 August 1645.
66 WSTY K2/3, bundle 1: warrant regarding Llwydiarth, 3 August 1645.
67 NLW, Herbert of Cherbury MS P1/4.
68 WSTY K2/3, bundle 1: copy order Montgomeryshire committee, 25 September 1645; TNA, SP20/1, p. 1036. Another copy dates this to 24 September: TNA, SP23/164, p. 465.
69 NLW, Herbert of Cherbury MS P1/4.
70 TNA, SP20/1, pp. 987, 1036; SP23/126, pp. 129, 131, 165, 191.
71 NLW, Herbert of Cherbury MS P1/4.
72 *LJ*, VII, pp. 364, 367; *CJ*, IV, p. 139.
73 TNA, SP28/252, fo. 209: certificate of Sir Thomas Myddelton's accounts, 6 April 1646.
74 It may also be relevant to note that Vaughan brought a suit against Myddelton in April 1640 over possession of a small estate in Montgomeryshire: TNA, C2/ChasI/U12/42.
75 TNA, SP20/1, p. 987; SP20/2, fo. 124v.
76 TNA, SP21/5, pp. 55, 57, 63; SP21/22, p. 74.
77 WSTY K2/3, bundle 1: 'Reasons Whereupon the … Propositions are Grounded', *c*.November 1645.
78 WSTY K2/3, bundle 1.

79 J. E. Auden, '"My Case with the Committee of Salop": Colonel Mytton *versus* the Parliamentarian Committee', *Transactions of the Shropshire Archaeological Society*, 47 (1934–5), 49–60; *HoC, 1640–1660*, VII, pp. 278–80.

80 *LJ*, VII, p. 364; *CJ*, IV, p. 139.

81 WSTY, K2/3, bundle 1: draft of ordinance for associating north Wales; bundle 2: draft of ordinance for associating north Wales.

82 WSTY K2/3, bundle 2: articles against Sir Thomas Myddelton.

83 Lloyd Bowen, 'Wales and Religious Reform in the Long Parliament, 1640–42', *Transactions of the Cymmrodorion Society*, new series, 12 (2005), 36–59; Stephen K. Roberts, '"One of the Least Things in Religion": The Welsh Experience of Church Polity, 1640–60', in Elliot Vernon and Hunter Powell (eds), *Church Polity and Politics in the British Atlantic World, c.1635–66* (Manchester, 2020), pp. 60–79.

84 John Lewis, *The Parliament Explained to Wales* (1646), sig. A3.

85 On this, see Roberts, 'Welsh Experience of Church Polity'.

86 TNA, SP21/5, p. 79; *BLB*, II, p. 221. The calendar changes the Committee of Both Kingdoms' reference to the 'Committee of North Wales' in the manuscript to 'Committees of North Wales': *CSPD, 1645–7*, p. 245.

87 Dodd, *Studies*, pp. 115, 117, 123; Sarah Ward Clavier, '"Round-headed Knaves": the Ballad of Wrexham and the Subversive Political Culture of Interregnum North-East Wales', *Historical Research*, 91 (2018), 39, 46–7. This article, like some contemporaries, is rather confused about nomenclature. Its subject is not a Denbighshire 'county committee' but rather the peripatetic Committee for North Wales which, ultimately, came to reside in Denbighshire. This body was superseded by an ordinance for associating north Wales in August 1648: *A&O*, I, pp. 1183–5. Cf. Bodl., Tanner MS 60, fo. 453; NLW, Clenennau Letters and Papers, no. 605 (which mentions an order made 'by the committee att theyr meetinge at Conwey in November last [i.e. 1645]'); Clenennau Letters and Papers, Appendix II/14; MS 467E/1773; Chirk Castle MS F.10387; TNA, PRO 30/51/11, fo. 35v; SP21/23, p. 104; 'Royalist Composition Papers', *MC*, 18 (1885), 265; NEWA (F), MS D/G/3275/85; HMC, *Egmont MSS*, I, p. 361.

88 *HoC, 1640–1660*, VI, pp. 334–5.

89 TNA, WARD 9/208, fo. 215; C66/2764/5; Shropshire Archives, 2922/11/81–2: Stanley Leighton, 'The Mytton Letters', *MC*, 7 (1874), 362.

90 *BLB*, II, p. 279; *CJ*, IV, p. 337; *LJ*, VII, p. 687; TNA, SP28/251, pt. 1.

91 WSTY K2/3, bundle 3: paper against committees, *c*.April 1646. Cf. the contemporary grand jury petition of Staffordshire which lamented that 'almost all the committees [of the county] are commanders and captains, which is both an hindrance to the duties of their places and to the redresse of complaints made by the countrey against the abuses of their souldiers': D. H. Pennington and I. Roots (eds), *The Committee at Stafford, 1643–1645* (Manchester, 1957), p. 343.

92 For the date of this commission, see TNA, SP28/260, fo. 252v. There is a dispatch from the 'Committee at Montgomery Castle' to one at Red Castle in October 1645, but it seems that this was likely an offshoot of the sequestration committee rather than the accounts sub-committee itself: *BLB*, II, p. 135.

93 Peacey, 'Politics, Accounts and Propaganda'.

94 We know that the accounts sub-committee sent a warrant requesting the sequestrators' books and papers on 26 January 1646: TNA, SP28/256, pt. 1.

95 WSTY K2/3, bundle 1: 'Directions to Mr Lloyd Pierce'. Although undated, the demand refers to the parliamentary assessments placed upon the county for fifteenth months. This would suggest a date of January or February 1646.

Chapter 5: Edward Vaughan, the Governance of North Wales and the Struggle over Accounts, January–October 1646

1 TNA, SP23/164, p. 439.

2 *CSPD, 1648–9*, p. 14; BL, Harleian MS 255, fo. 26.

3 HPO (1604–29): 'More, Samuel'; *HoC, 1640–1660*, VII, pp. 193–200.

4 Samuel Leighton, 'Records of the Corporation of Oswestry', *Transactions of the Shropshire Archaeological and Natural History Society*, 3 (1880), 145.

5 NLW, Powis Castle MS E6/1/3.

6 TNA, SP28/251, unfol.; SP23/126, pp. 83, 101, 199; SP23/164, pp. 447, 485–6; WSTY PA4/6, bundle 7: dep. Robert Lloyd, 26 October 1663; TNA, PROB 11/348, fo. 261v; NEWA (D), DD/WY/6896.

7 Professor Morrill was thus incorrect to suggest that the accounts sub-committee in Montgomeryshire was 'allied to county radicals'; it was quite the opposite: John Morrill, *Revolt in the Provinces* (London, 1999), pp. 98–9.

8 David Underdown, *Somerset in the Civil War and Interregnum* (Newton Abbott, 1973), pp. 141–3; Clive Holmes, 'Colonel King and Lincolnshire Politics, 1642–1646', *Historical Journal*, 16 (1973), 474–84; Ann Hughes, *Politics, Society and Civil War in Warwickshire, 1620–1660* (Cambridge, 1987), chs 5 and 6.

9 WSTY K3/2: Montgomeryshire petition to the Commons, January 1646.

10 NLW, Great Sessions 4/153/2; Great Sessions 24/182; Phillips, *Justices*, p. 143. A commission of the peace for the county was issued in November 1645 (which included Vaughan), but it does not appear to have sat: WSTY JA1/3: Montgomeryshire commission of the peace, November 1645.

11 Clement Walker, 'The Mystery of the Two Juntoes', in Francis Maseres (ed.), *Select Tracts Relating to the Civil War in England*, 2 vols (London, 1815), II, p. 339.

12 *CJ*, II, p. 762; IV, p. 316; BL, Harleian MS 255, fos 25v–26.

13 David Underdown, 'Party Management in the Recruiter Elections, 1645–1648', *English Historical Review*, 82 (1968), 235–64.

14 *BLB*, II, p. 119.

15 For complaints about the lack of sheriffs elsewhere in north Wales in 1646, see NEWA (F), D/G/3275/82, 85.

16 For some discussion of this rhetoric, see Morrill, *Revolt in the Provinces*, pp. 104–11; Clive Holmes, 'Centre and Locality in Civil War England', in John Adamson (ed.), *The English Civil War, 1640–49* (Basingstoke, 2009), pp. 153–74.

17 See above, pp. 109–10.

18 TNA, SP28/256, pt. 1.

19 See below, pp. 246–50.

20 NEWA (D), DD/WY/6896.

21 TNA, SP23/126, pp. 53, 55, 185–8, 201; SP23/164, pp. 467, 483–4.

22 WSTY K2/3, bundle 2: deps. Owen and Evan Vaughan, 10 and 21 July 1646; TNA, SP16/514, fo. 92. Owen Vaughan would also go on to endorse Edward Vaughan's 1647 election indenture: TNA, C219/43, pt. 3, fo. 204.

23 TNA, SP23/126, pp. 81, 178; SP23/164, pp. 445–6; WSTY K2/3, bundle 2: warrants for sequestration, 24 November 1646. Robert Vaughan also endorsed Edward Vaughan's election indenture: TNA, C219/43, pt. 3, fo. 204.

24 TNA, SP28/260, fo. 252v.

25 TNA, SP28/260, fos 252v–54.

26 For Thomas, see *HoC, 1640–1660*, IX, pp. 5–8.

27 See also Mytton's letter to parliament of 29 January complaining of his soldiers' lack of pay: HMC, *Portland MSS*, I, p. 346; *CJ*, IV, p. 429. Cf. TNA, SP21/23, p. 76.

28 Bodl., Tanner MS 60, fo. 453.

29 A tax strike was also a tactic employed by another Presbyterian in dispute with the local committee, Edward King of Lincolnshire: Holmes, 'Colonel King', 472.

30 WSTY K2/3, bundle 2: 'Vaughan's reasons against delinquency', *c*.March 1646.

31 TNA, SP28/252, fo. 71. The 'exceptions' are to be found at TNA, SP28/260, fo. 349. The document can be dated to mid-February as a series of depositions in response was given on 24 February 1646: WSTY PA3/8.

32 NLW, MS 9063E/1823.

33 HMC, *Portland MSS*, I, p. 346; *CJ*, IV, p. 429; *A Perfect Diurnall*, 132 (2–9 February 1646), pp. 1058–9.

34 TNA, SP28/260, fo. 349.

35 On the problem of plundering in north Wales in 1644, see *BLB*, I, *passim*.

36 TNA, SP28/251, pt. 1; WSTY PA3/8: dep. Henry Thomas, 24 February 1646. Cf. NEWA (D), DD/WY/6896.

37 WSTY PA3/8: deps. before central Committee of Accounts, 24 February 1646; TNA, SP28/251, pt. 1. For the interrogatories to which these deps. are responses, see TNA, SP28/253B, pt. 1.

38 TNA, SP28/253B, pt. 1. Cf. WSTY MS PA3/8: deps. before the central Committee of Accounts, 24 February 1646.

39 TNA, SP28/252, fo. 71. A copy can be found at WSTY K2/3, bundle 2.

40 Prynne's annotations to the original missive, which formed the basis of his committee's March letter, can be seen on TNA, SP28/260, fos 252v–3.

41 TNA, SP28/256, pt. 1.

42 TNA, SP20/2, fo. 119; SP23/126, p. 117.

43 WSTY K2/3, bundle 3: 'Reasons why the examination …': March 1646.

44 See the signatories to the committee's letters in TNA, SP28/256, and its orders in 'Royalist Composition Papers', *MC*, 18 (1885), 71–92; NLW, Powis Castle 1990 deposit, large box 11, bundle 12.

45 Clement Walker, *Relations and Observations* (London, 1648), p. 67.

46 There are echoes of his arguments in his petition to the sequestration committee later that month: TNA, SP23/126, p. 119.

47 TNA, SP23/126, p. 209.

48 TNA, SP20/2, fo. 146.

49 TNA, SP23/126, p. 119.

50 WSTY K2/3, bundle 1: 'Mr Vaughan's Petition', April 1646.

51 A similar argument is rehearsed in WSTY K2/3, bundle 2: 'Edward Vaughan ... his case at present', 18 May 1646.

52 TNA, SP28/251, unfol.

53 TNA, SP28/256, pt. 1.

54 WSTY K2/3, bundle 3: 'A copie of the paper found the 1 of May in Lloyd Pierces hous'.

55 J. B. Williams, 'The Biggs Family of Churchstoke', *MC*, 43 (1934), 66–8.

56 Shropshire Archives, 1037/10/17.

57 For his appointment, see TNA, SP28/253A, fo. 49. As a 'cittizen and scrivener of London', see SP23/126, p. 167. Barbour appeared to have a connection to Lord Herbert of Cherbury: TNA, PRO 30/53/11, fo. 30.

58 *HoC, 1640–1660*, VII, pp. 327, 878.

59 WSTY PA4/6, bundle 7: dep. William Barbour, 23 October 1663.

60 'Some Remarkable Passages out of ... Southwales', in Charles H. Firth (ed.), *The Clarke Papers, Vol. 2*, Camden Society, new series, 59 (1894), pp. 157–60; HMC, *Egmont MSS*, I, p. 363; M. A. E. Green (ed.), *Calendar of the Proceedings of the Committee for Compounding with Delinquents*, 5 vols (London, 1889–92), I, p. 578.

61 For what follows, see TNA, SP28/256, pt. 1.

62 Price later countered that he sent the troops 'upon notice that the said Mr Pierce his howse was besett by armed men and not knowing who they were, the enemie about that time being passing through this countie in troopes and companies': TNA, SP28/256, pt. 1.

63 *LJ*, VIII, p. 352.

64 TNA, SP28/256, pt. 1; SP16/514, fo. 36.

65 TNA, SP23/126, p. 117.

66 TNA, SP23/164, p. 473; SP16/506, fo. 158.

67 For Pembroke, see S. K. Roberts, 'How the West was Won: Parliamentary Politics, Religion and the Military in South Wales', *Welsh History Review*, 21 (2003), 646–74.

68 TNA, SP28/256, pt. 1.

69 Dodd is incorrect in stating that Price 'served on the local committee of accounts at the end of the war': Dodd, *Studies*, p. 129.

70 WSTY K2/3, bundle 2.

71 Hertfordshire Archives and Local Studies, DE/Lw/58.

72 TNA, SP28/346, pt. 2; *HoC, 1640–1660*, V, pp. 805–8.

73 *A Letter to ... William Lenthall ... Concerning the Surrender of Ruthin-Castle* (London, 1646), p. 3; *An Exact Relation of ... Gallant Col. Mitton in North-Wales* (London, 1646), p. 7.

74 S. C. Lomas (ed.), *Letters and Speeches of Oliver Cromwell*, 3 vols (London, 1904), III, p. 408.

75 W. M. Myddelton (ed.), *Chirk Castle Accounts, A.D. 1605–1666* (St Albans, 1908), p. 36.

76 *Perfect Occurrences*, 23 (30 May–5 June 1646), sig. Z2.

77 Bodl., Tanner MS 59, fo. 368.
78 TNA, SP28/256, pt. 1.
79 TNA, SP28/256, pt. 1.
80 TNA, SP16/514, fo. 36.
81 *LJ*, VIII, p. 386; TNA, SP28/252, fo. 301; TNA, SP28/251, unfol.
82 TNA, SP28/256, pt. 2.
83 TNA, SP28/253A, fo. 8.
84 TNA, SP28/256, pts 2 and 3; TNA, SP28/253A, fo. 10v.
85 TNA, SP16/514, fo. 101; SP28/256, pt. 3.
86 TNA, SP16/514, fo. 101.
87 TNA, C8/96/122.
88 TNA, SP28/253A, fo. 12v.
89 TNA, SP28/256, pt. 1.
90 TNA, SP23/253A, fo. 13.
91 TNA, SP28/256, pt. 2.
92 TNA, SP28/256, pt. 1.
93 TNA, SP28/253A, fo. 15.
94 TNA, SP28/256, pt. 3.
95 For this kind of print in Pembrokeshire, see Lloyd Bowen, 'History, Politics and Power: Shaping the Recent Past in Civil War Pembrokeshire', in *idem* and Mark Stoyle (eds), *Remembering the English Civil Wars* (Abingdon, 2022), pp. 60–80.
96 TNA, SP28/256, pt. 1; SP28/252, fo. 315v; SP28/253A, fo. 17.
97 TNA, SP28/252, fos 318v, 320v.
98 TNA, SP28/253A, fo. 19v.
99 *CJ*, IV, p. 622. For Glynne, see *HoC, 1640–1660*, V, pp. 251–90.
100 *Perfect Diurnall*, 156 (20–7 July 1646), p. 1251.
101 WSTY K2/3, bundle 2: Thomas Mytton to Montgomeryshire accounts sub-committee, 5 September 1646.
102 See above, pp. 134–41.
103 WSTY K2/3, bundle 2: Montgomeryshire accounts sub-committee to Thomas Mytton, September 1646.
104 TNA, SP28/256, pt. 3.

Chapter 6: The Army, Civilians and Parliamentary Elections, October 1646–April 1647

1 *CJ*, IV, pp. 703, 705; *LJ*, VIII, p. 548.
2 *HoC, 1640–1660*, VI, pp. 123–7.
3 Lloyd, 'Sheriffs', 165–9. For later indications of a connection between the Hunts and Edward Vaughan, see WSTY PA5/8: Rowland and Elizabeth Hunt *versus* William and Gabriel Salesbury, 1675.
4 WSTY K2/3, bundle 2: dep. Evan Vaughan, 21 July 1646; warrants for sequestration, 24 November 1646; TNA, SP23/126, p. 83.
5 TNA, SP28/256, pt. 1.
6 See, for example, Bodleian Library, Tanner MS 59, fos 298, 368, 568. For more information on these figures, see *HoC, 1640–1660*, VI, pp. 334–43; VII, pp. 744–5.

7   WSTY K2/3, bundle 2: charges against Edward Vaughan and George Devereux, 3 November 1646.

8   TNA, E113/3; Lloyd, 'Sheriffs', 186–8.

9   WSTY K2/3, bundle 3, 'Edward Vaughan's case', April 1647.

10 WSTY K2/3, bundle 1: petition of Lewis Price to central sequestration committee, 10 September 1646.

11 Lewis Price had also sought the central sequestration committee's guidance on possession of Llwydiarth, and was told that the local committee should pursue their former order for securing the property for the state and obtain the earl of Pembroke's permission to proceed 'by faire meanes if they can, or by power if it be needfull': WSTY K2/3, bundle 1: central committee of sequestrations, answer to Lewis Price, September 1646.

12 *LJ*, VIII, p. 547.

13 *CJ*, V, pp. 143–4; WSTY K2/3, bundle 3: 'The true state of Mr George Devereux his case', *c*.April 1647.

14 TNA, SP28/256, pt. 1.

15 TNA, SP28/251, unfol.; SP28/256, pt. 1.

16 TNA, SP28/256, pt. 1.

17 *CJ*, IV, p. 719; WSTY K2/3, bundle 2: copy order for Montgomeryshire election, 11 November 1646.

18 HPO (1604–29): 'Palmer, James'.

19 HPO (1604–29): 'Buller, Francis'; *HoC, 1640–1660*, III, pp. 857–62: R. N. Worth (ed.), *The Buller Papers* (Plymouth, 1895), pp. 94–7; NLW, Powis Castle Estate MSS N.17187–8; Kresen Kernow, BU206; TNA, C9/18/30.

20 Worth, *Buller Papers*, pp. 98–9.

21 WSTY K2/3, bundle 3: 'The True State of Mr George Devereux his Case'.

22 WSTY K2/3, bundle 2: order to sequester George Devereux, 16 November 1646.

23 Bodl., Tanner MS 59, fo. 575.

24 For Vaughan as a member of a new Montgomeryshire commission of the peace appointed in November 1645, see WSTY JA1/3. This commission is not recorded in Phillips, *Justices*.

25 WSTY K2/3, bundle 2: examination of John Mottershed, 20 November 1646.

26 TNA, SP28/256, pt. 2.

27 For the sub-committee's efforts to examine Lovingham, see TNA, SP28/256, pt. 3; SP28/253A, fo. 21, and see above, p. 157.

28 Cf. similar complaints about Vaughan voiced by the Committee for North Wales in June: Bodl., Tanner MS 59, fo. 368.

29 *CJ*, IV, p. 726.

30 *HoC, 1640–1660*, III, pp. 439, 446; VII, p. 346. These volumes attribute both Bences as the teller; unfortunately, the last entry for Nicoll badly mangles this episode.

31 WSTY K2/3, bundle 2: warrant for sequestration, 24 November 1646. The others were Robert Vaughan, Evan Vaughan and Robert Lloyd. A letter of 24 November 1646 showed that the sequestration committee had been augmented not just by Mytton, Jones and Pope, but also by two of Mytton's senior officers, George Twistleton and Thomas Mason: TNA, SP28/256, pt. 1.

32 One of the sequestration committee's collectors divulged on 23 November that there was a 'designe or purpose' to 'make Mr Vaughan a delinquent [so] that then they [himself and other sequestration officers] should not have soe many journys' to Montgomery Castle: TNA, SP28/253B, pt. 1.

33 TNA, SP28/256, pt. 3.

34 WSTY K2/3, bundle 2: copy warrant for arrest of Edward Vaughan, 25 November 1646.

35 TNA, SP28/256, pt. 3.

36 WSTY K2/3, bundle 2: warrant for Devereux's commitment, 26 November 1646.

37 WSTY K2/3, bundle 3: 'The True State of Mr George Devereux his Case', *c*.April 1647.

38 WSTY K2/3, bundle 2: Montgomeryshire accounts sub-committee to Montgomeryshire sequestration committee: 4 December 1646.

39 TNA, C231/6, p. 32; WSTY JA1/3: commission of the peace, 28 November 1645.

40 The other (non-honorific) JPs were Vaughan allies Charles Lloyd, Samuel More, Matthew Morgan and William Kyffin, as well as his opponents Lloyd Pierce and John Price. Given this balance of power, it seems clear why the commission's authority was a dead letter as the sequestration committee would have been overruled in any decisions, and probably sought to hinder any formal business under its aegis.

41 WSTY K2/3, bundle 2: Montgomeryshire sub-committee of accounts to central Committee of Accounts, 4 December 1646.

42 WSTY K2/3, bundle 2: Montgomeryshire sub-committee of accounts to central Committee of Accounts, 4 December 1646; WSTY K2/3, bundle 2: John Jones to Edward Thelwall, 6 December 1646.

43 WSTY K2/3, bundle 2: order for release of George Devereux, 8 December 1646.

44 TNA, C33/188, fo. 109.

45 TNA, C33/188, fo. 178; WSTY K2/3, bundle 3: copy of Chancery decree, 26 December 1646.

46 WSTY K2/3, bundle 3: 'The habeas corpus', 2 January 1647.

47 TNA, SP28/257, pt. 1.

48 TNA, SP28/252, fos 340–1.

49 TNA, C33/188, fo. 210v; WSTY K2/3, bundle 3: petition of Edward Vaughan and George Devereux, 14 January 1647; WSTY K2/3, bundle 3: 'The True State of Mr George Devereux his Case', *c*.April 1647.

50 WSTY K2/3, bundle 3: 'A coppie of Mr Vaughan & Mr Devereux their recognizances', 20 January 1647.

51 TNA, SP28/252, fo. 345v; WSTY K2/3, bundle 3: order of the Committee for Taking the Accounts of the Kingdom, 22 January 1647.

52 WSTY K2/3, bundle 2: warrant of sequestration committee, 22 January 1647.

53 These were Robert Lloyd, one Lieutenant Price and Devereux's servant, Edward Lloyd.

54 WSTY K2/3, bundle 3: 'The True State of Mr George Devereux his Case', *c*.April 1647.

55 WSTY K2/3, bundle 3: Edward Vaughan and Samuel More to constables of Deuddwr, 30 January 1647.
56 WSTY K2/3, bundle 3: Edward Vaughan's Case, *c*.February 1647.
57 TNA, C219/43, pt. 3, fo. 204.
58 TNA, SP28/257, pt. 1.
59 TNA, SP23/126, p. 210.
60 TNA, SP23/126, p. 210.
61 TNA, SP16/539, pt. 4, fo. 20.
62 TNA, SP28/257, pt. 1; SP28/253A, fo. 49v.
63 WSTY K2/3, bundle 3: Chancery order for writ of habeas corpus, 6 April 1647.
64 TNA, SP28/257, pt. 1.
65 *A Perfect Diurnall of Some Passages in Parliament*, 186 (15–22 February 1647), p. 1488; *Perfect Occurrences of Every Daie Iournall in Parliament*, 7 (12–19 February 1647), p. 53.
66 *CJ*, V, p. 90.
67 These can be found in WSTY K2/3, bundle 1.
68 *HoC, 1640–1660*, IX, pp. 841–5.
69 NLW, Peniarth Estate MS NA73; Coleman Deeds MSS D.D. 111, 113, 505; Chirk Castle MS F.7208.
70 Melvin Humphreys, *Plas Newydd and the Manor of Talerddig* (Welshpool, 2022), pp. 103–7; Hertfordshire Archives, DE/Lw/Z21, p. 8.
71 Two copies of his articles can be found at WSTY K2/3, bundle 3.
72 For confirmation of Myddelton's relatively small forces, see his own dispatches to the Committee of Both Kingdoms in the autumn of 1644: TNA, SP21/17, fos 1–2, 15–16, 47–8.
73 For this, see *BLB*, I, pp. 239, 272, 294–5, 312, 313–15, 318–20.
74 NLW, Sweeney Hall MS A1, no. 35.
75 *CJ*, V, p. 135.
76 *Two Petitions to the Generals Excellency* (London, 1647), p. 3. This text reproduces a letter from Fairfax to the gentry of north Wales of November 1647, which describes how 'there hath beene levied great summes of monies upon your counties without any authority of parliament, which hath much impoverished the inhabitants', and allowed them to resist any levies that were not authorised by ordinance.
77 Bodl., Tanner MS 58, fo. 520.
78 Bodl., Tanner MS 59, fo. 675.
79 NEWA (F), D/G/3275/78 (misdated); *A Perfect Diurnall*, 192 (29 March–5 April 1647), p. 1540. Cf. *The Kingdomes Weekly Intelligencer*, 205 (13–20 April 1647), p. 495.
80 *CJ*, V, p. 125; W. J. Smith (ed.), *Herbert Correspondence* (Cardiff, 1963), pp. 125–30.
81 AJK, 'Some Original Inedited Documents relative to Montgomery Castle ... during the Great Rebellion', *The Gentleman's Magazine*, 173/4 (1843), 152.
82 AJK, 'Some Inedited Documents', 152.
83 Lewis Price reported that Llwyd was paid £53 in this capacity between 1645 and early 1647: TNA, E113/3.

84 For Powell and Mostyn, see AJK, 'Some Inedited Documents', 153.

85 John Morrill, *Cheshire, 1630–60* (Oxford, 1974), pp. 81, 96, 101, 185, 187, 224; *BLB*, I, p. 331; NEWA (F), D/HE/875.

86 WSTY K2/3, bundle 3: Thomas Mytton to 'Mrs Pryce', 3 and 5 April 1647.

87 *HoC, 1640–1660*, II, p. 429.

88 AJK, 'Some Inedited Documents', 153.

89 For Edward, see TNA, PROB 11/205, fo. 257v.

90 HPO (1604–29): 'Montgomery Boroughs'; *HoC, 1640–1660*, II, pp. 719–20; HPO (1660–90): 'Montgomery Boroughs'.

91 HPO (1690–1715): 'Montgomery Boroughs'.

92 TNA, C219/43, pt. 3, fo. 207. A comparison with the list of Montgomery burgesses from 1633 suggests these continuities: Powys Archives, M/B/MO/1.

93 Stanley Leighton, 'Mytton Manuscripts', *MC*, 8 (1875), 157.

94 *CJ*, V, p. 143; *Kingdomes Weekly Intelligencer*, 205 (13–20 April 1647), p. 497; *A Perfect Diurnall*, 194 (12–19 April 1647), p. 1557.

95 *CJ*, V, p. 143.

96 WSTY K2/3, bundle 3: 'The True State of Mr George Devereux his Case', *c*.April 1647.

97 *CJ*, V, pp. 143–4.

98 *CJ*, V, p. 237; WSTY K2/3, bundle 3: 'The True State of Mr George Devereux his Case', *c*.April 1647; 'The suspension from ye House', 15 April 1647.

99 WSTY K2/3, bundle 3; 'The True State of Mr George Devereux his Case', *c*.April 1647.

Chapter 7: Parliament Man? Edward Vaughan, Parliamentary Presbyterians and Pride's Purge, April 1647–February 1649

1 For discussion of this 'Presbyterian mobilisation', see Ann Hughes, *Gangraena and the Struggle for the English Revolution* (Oxford, 2004), pp. 318–415; Elliot Vernon, *London Presbyterians and the British Revolutions, 1638–64* (Manchester, 2021), pp. 138–67.

2 David Underdown, 'Party Management in the Recruiter Elections, 1645–1648', *English Historical Review*, 83 (1968), 256–64.

3 David Scott, *Politics and War in the Three Kingdoms, 1637–49* (Basingstoke, 2004), pp. 132–3.

4 Worcester College, Oxford, Clarke MS 110, fo. 16, quoted in *HoC, 1640–1660*, IV, p. 668.

5 *A Perfect Diurnall*, 194 (12–19 April 1647), p. 1557.

6 *Perfect Occurrences*, 25 (18–25 June 1647), p. 167.

7 C. H. Firth (ed.), *The Clarke Papers, Volume II*, Camden Society, new series, 54 (London, 1894), p. 157. See also *A Particular Charge or Impeachment …* (London, 1647), pp. 22–4.

8 See the relevant entries for constituency articles in *HoC, 1640–1660*, II, pp. 682–731.

9 NEWA (F), D/G/3275/79, 81, 84, 87–9.

10 *HoC, 1640–1660*, VII, p. 745.

11   *CJ*, V, p. 133.
12   *CJ*, III, p. 661; IV, pp. 243, 461, 572, 593, 671, 678; NLW, Kyrle Fletcher (Second Group) A/27.
13   *CJ*, IV, pp. 572, 593.
14   Although one contemporary described it as 'the North Wales Comittee': Stanley Leighton, 'Mytton Manuscripts', *MC*, 8 (1875), 157.
15   WSTY K2/3, bundle 3: Note of 'Proceedings at the Committee of Wales', 3 April 1647. Also present were Sir John Meyrick (who came from Pembroke); Sir Richard Pryse* (MP for Cardiganshire); Sir Robert Pye (who came from Herefordshire); Sir Robert Harley (MP for Herefordshire); Arthur Owen* (MP for Pembrokeshire); Col. William Davies* (MP for Carmarthen); and the committee was chaired by Col. John Lloyd* (MP for Carmarthenshire) (*indicates recruiter MP).
16   WSTY K2/3, bundle 3: note of 'Proceedings at the Committee of Wales', 3 April 1647.
17   For a copy of the committee's order, see Herefordshire Archives and Local Studies, AD30/216. See also John Bodvel's letter of 30 April 1647 in which he mentioned a letter sent from John Glynne which contained 'the order of a committee here to stay sequestrations': NLW, MS 9063E/1823.
18   Leighton, 'Mytton Manuscripts', 156.
19   NLW, MS 9063E/1823.
20   BL., Add. MS 46931A, fos 57r–v, 66, 79.
21   *CJ*, V, p. 119.
22   WSTY JA1/3: articles against Edmund Hall, 1647.
23   *CJ*, V, pp. 221–3; *A&O*, I, pp. 985–6; *An Additional Ordinance of the Lords and Commons ... Concerning Dayes of Recreation* (London, 1647).
24   *CJ*, V, p. 166.
25   John Morrill, 'Mutiny and Discontent in English Provincial Armies, 1645–47', *Past & Present*, 56 (1972), 49–75.
26   AJK, 'Some Original Inedited Documents relative to Montgomery Castle ... during the Great Rebellion', *The Gentleman's Magazine*, 173/4 (1843), 153.
27   TNA, PRO 30/51/11, fo. 35v.
28   *Perfect Occurrences*, 19 (7–14 May 1647), p. 148; *Kingdomes Weekly Intelligencer*, 209 (11–18 May 1647), p. 527; NLW, Powis Castle 1990 Deposit, large box 11, bundle 12.
29   Parliamentary Archives, HL/PO/JO/10/1/232; *LJ*, IX, p. 186. For Allen, see AJK, 'Some Inedited Documents', 151–2.
30   *CJ*, V, p. 169; W. V. Lloyd, 'Montgomery', *MC*, 23 (1889), 72.
31   Lloyd, 'Montgomery', 72–3. Although unattributed, this must be the letter Vaughan wrote at the Commons' direction.
32   *A Perfect Diurnall*, 200 (24–31 May 1647), p. 1606.
33   HMC, *Egmont MSS*, I, p. 451; TNA, PRO 30/53/11, fo. 37.
34   NLW, Powis Castle 1990 Deposit, large box 11, bundle 12. Although see W. J. Smith (ed.), *Herbert Correspondence* (Cardiff, 1963), p. 127 for committee business being conducted in this period.
35   TNA, PRO 30/53/11, fo. 37.

36 For some discussion of the composition of these committees in Wales, see Dodd, *Studies*, pp. 123–35.

37 *A&O*, I, p. 979.

38 See below, pp. 220–50.

39 WSTY PA3/11: Brochwell Griffiths *versus* Edward Vaughan, *c.*1653–7; WSTY Q4: Montgomeryshire quarter sessions papers, 1633. For his Myddelton associations, see Hertfordshire Archives and Local Studies, DE/Lw/72.

40 BL, Egerton MS 1048, fo. 188.

41 HMC, *Egmont MSS*, I, p. 451. See also the directive of the Montgomeryshire commissioners, which seems to have been their first effort to implement this levy, but was only dated 10 September 1647: Lloyd, 'Montgomery', 73. The order was signed by a mixture of the two 'sides' on the commission.

42 R. Bell (ed.), *Memorials of the Civil War*, 2 vols (London, 1849), II, p. 377.

43 Bell, *Memorials*, II, p. 378.

44 Bell, *Memorials*, II, pp. 378–80.

45 *A Full Vindication and Answer of the XI Accused Members* (London, 1647), p. 26.

46 *CJ*, V, p. 244.

47 *CJ*, V, p. 250.

48 *CJ*, V, p. 265.

49 *CJ*, V, pp. 400–1.

50 TNA, SP28/252, fos 361–2; WSTY K2/3, bundle 3: copy of central Accounts Committee order, 15 April 1647.

51 TNA, SP28/252, fo. 375v.

52 TNA, SP28/257, pt. 1. The signatories were Matthew Morgan, Edward Owen, Richard Griffith, Samuel Bigg and Robert Lloyd.

53 TNA, E113/3.

54 Lloyd Bowen, *John Poyer, the Civil Wars in Pembrokeshire and the British Revolutions* (Cardiff, 2020); Robert Ashton, *Counter Revolution: The Second Civil War and its Origins, 1646–8* (New Haven and London, 1994).

55 *A Narrative … Concerning the Late Successe … in Carnarvanshire in North Wales* (London, 1648), p. 9.

56 Norman Tucker, *North Wales in the Civil War* (Denbigh, 1958), pp. 131–55.

57 *A Perfect Diurnall*, 252 (22–9 May 1648), pp. 2029–30.

58 TNA, SP28/256, pt. 3; SP28/257, pt. 1; SP28/253A, fo. 34.

59 Leighton, 'Mytton Manuscripts', 160–1.

60 Leighton, 'Mytton Manuscripts', 165–6.

61 Lloyd, 'Montgomery', 76.

62 *CJ*, V, p. 581.

63 *CJ*, V, p. 599.

64 TNA, SP23/126, p. 57.

65 TNA, SP23/126, p. 210.

66 TNA, SP23/126, p. 199.

67 WSTY MS K2/3, bundle 3: Fairfax to officers and soldiers, 29 September 1648.

68 WSTY MS K2/3, bundle 3: certificate of Montgomeryshire sequestration committee, 25 October 1648. The directive was signed by Lloyd Pierce, Hugh and Richard Price and Evan Lloyd.

69 TNA, SP23/126, p. 465; Lloyd, 'Sheriffs', 172–3.

70 *A&O*, I, p. 1184; *LJ*, X, p. 448.

71 *A&O*, I, p. 1247.

72 *Mercurius Elencticus*, 55 (5–12 December 1648), p. 527. The classic study of this episode is David Underdown, *Pride's Purge: Politics in the Puritan Revolution* (Oxford, 1971).

73 [William Prynne], *A Vindication of the Imprisoned and Secluded Members of the House of Commons* (London, 1649), p. 24.

74 BL, Add. MS 70,006, fo. 62.

75 *The Humble Answer of the General Councel of Officers of the Army* (London, 1649), p. 5.

76 [Prynne], *A Vindication*, p. 7.

77 BL, Add. MS 70,006, fo. 67.

PART THREE: FROM REPUBLIC TO RESTORATION

Chapter 8: Republican Revenge, 1648–1655

1 Phillips, *Justices*, p. 144.

2 *A&O*, II, p. 47.

3 NEWA (F), D/G/3275/97; NLW, MS 9063E/1837.

4 *CJ*, V, pp. 400–1; TNA, SP28/50, fo. 279; SP23/126, pp. 149, 167; NLW, Carreglwyd MS I/1704.

5 NLW, MS 9063E/1848.

6 NLW, MSS 9063E/1848, 1861/1. The troops in Montgomeryshire were Captain Gerald Barbour's, Captain Farrer's, Captain Edward Price's, Captain George Edgeley's and Captain Taylor's: TNA, SP23/126, p. 197.

7 *A&O*, I, pp. 1053–4.

8 For a similar arrangement in Caernarvonshire, see NLW, MS 9063E/1849.

9 TNA, SP23/126, pp. 168–73, 197; NLW, MS 9063E/1861/1. For some of the accounts of the disbanding effort in Montgomeryshire, see NLW, Powis Castle MS L.109.

10 John Rushworth, *A True Relation of Disbanding the Supernumerary Forces* (London, 1648), pp. 6–7.

11 TNA, SP23/126, p. 135.

12 TNA, SP23/126, pp. 137–42.

13 *A Perfect Diurnall*, 298 (16–23 April 1649), p. 2445. Cf. *The Moderate Intelligencer*, 214 (19–26 April 1649), sig. 10G6.

14 *The Moderate*, 41 (17–24 April 1649), sig. Ssv.

15 TNA, SP23/126, pp. 149, 193.

16 TNA, SP23/126, p. 186.

17 This follows a search of extant newsbooks for April 1649 and consulting the English Short Title Catalogue.

18 Jason Peacey, *Print and Public Politics in the English Revolution* (Cambridge, 2013).
19 TNA, SP23/126, pp. 186, 193.
20 *CJ*, VI, p. 188; TNA, SP23/126, p. 189.
21 M. A. E. Green (ed.), *Calendar of the Proceedings of the Committee for Advance of Money*, 3 vols (London, 1888), II, p. 995.
22 TNA, SP23/126, p. 157.
23 A third witness was the unidentified John Egleston.
24 Green (ed.), *Committee for Advance of Money*, II, p. 996.
25 Green (ed.), *Committee for Advance of Money*, II, p. 996.
26 TNA, SP23/126, p. 173.
27 TNA, SP23/126, p. 197.
28 All these men were also signatories to a county petition to parliament in July/ August 1649 which sought some exemptions for the county from the general sequestration ordinance for north Wales: BL, Egerton MS 1048, fo. 188.
29 For some of these individuals, see particularly the essays on Montgomeryshire's sheriffs between 1640 and 1660 in Lloyd, 'Sheriffs'.
30 The figure for revenue was derived from £1,500 and £651 9s. 0d of assignation money from Staffordshire and Montgomeryshire, respectively, and £1,600 from two months' worth of contribution money from Montgomeryshire taxpayers 'who hee enforced the country to advance upon promise of restitution when the Staffordsheire money came in'.
31 TNA, SP23/126, p. 199.
32 TNA, SP23/126, p. 193.
33 TNA, SP23/126, p. 195.
34 TNA, SP23/126, p. 55.
35 See above, p. 168.
36 *A List of the Imprisoned and Secluded Members* (London, 1648).
37 TNA, SP23/126, p. 195.
38 TNA, SP23/126, pp. 213–15.
39 Green (ed.), *Committee for Advance of Money*, II, p. 996; TNA, SP23/126, pp. 45–6, 163.
40 TNA, SP23/126, p. 161.
41 TNA, SP20/1–5.
42 *A&O*, I, p. 443; II, p. 343.
43 TNA, SP23/126, p. 174.
44 TNA, SP23/126, p. 175.
45 TNA, SP23/126, pp. 58, 210.
46 *A&O*, II, pp. 207–12.
47 TNA, SP23/126, p. 57.
48 TNA, SP23/126, p. 53.
49 TNA, SP23/126, p. 57.
50 TNA, SP23/126, p. 57.
51 TNA, SP23/164, pp. 475, 479–80.
52 TNA, SP23/126, p. 178.
53 TNA, SP23/126, p. 185.

54 TNA, SP23/126, pp. 167–75.

55 TNA, SP23/126, p. 46.

56 Although a contemporary account of the disbandment monies has a note dated 23 March 1648 about borrowing £200 from Edward Vaughan 'which he had received from Capt[ain] Edw[ard] Price from the assignation appoynted by the Comittee of the Armye from the County of Stafford': NLW, Powis Castle MS L.109.

57 These depositions can be found at TNA, SP23/126, pp. 176–81.

58 TNA, SP23/126, p. 185.

59 TNA, SP23/126, p. 186.

60 TNA, SP23/126, p. 201.

61 Green (ed.), *Committee for Advance of Money*, II, p. 996.

62 TNA, SP23/126, pp. 205–6.

63 TNA, SP23/251, fo. 74.

64 TNA, SP23/249, fo. 122.

65 This is why the Committee for the Advance of Money proceedings appear in the Compounding Committee's papers.

66 TNA, SP23/126, p. 205.

67 M. A. E. Green (ed.), *Calendar of the Proceedings of the Committee for Compounding with Delinquents*, 5 vols (London, 1889–92), II, p. 1627.

68 WSTY PA3/12: documents relating to Katherine Vaughan's dower, 1653–61.

69 HPO (1604–29): 'Herbert, Sir William'.

70 TNA, SP23/126, pp. 209–12.

71 It seems that Rice Vaughan did indeed do this, for several committee orders copied by him are to be found in the Committee for Compounding papers. See, for example, TNA, SP23/126, p. 131.

72 TNA, SP23/126, p. 155.

73 TNA, SP25/10, p. 33; SP23/233, p. 188.

74 *CSPD, 1650*, pp. 523, 560.

75 TNA, SP25/120, p. 48.

76 Green (ed.), *Committee for Compounding*, II, p. 1627.

77 TNA, SP23/126, pp. 17–38.

78 TNA, SP23/126, pp. 123–4.

79 Green (ed.), *Committee for Compounding*, II, p. 1627.

80 TNA, SP23/164, pp. 467–506.

81 TNA, SP23/164, pp. 509, 512.

82 TNA, SP23/126, p. 15; SP23/164, p. 513.

83 TNA, SP23/164, p. 453.

84 TNA, SP23/164, pp. 461–3.

85 Green (ed.), *Committee for Compounding*, II, p. 1628; TNA, SP18/74, fo. 93.

86 Green (ed.), *Committee for Compounding*, II, p. 1628.

87 TNA, SP23/126, pp. 99, 101.

88 TNA, SP23/126, p. 97.

89 TNA, SP18/74, fo. 93.

90 TNA, SP23/126, p. 81.

91 TNA, SP23/126, pp. 17–38.

92   *CSPD, 1655–6*, p. 325.
93   It is not correct to say that 'the protectoral regime confirmed his rights to Llwydiarth in 1654': HPO (1604–29): 'Vaughan, Edward'.
94   Phillips, *Justices*, p. 144.
95   Phillips, *Justices*, p. 145; Dodd, *Studies*, p. 156; *A&O*, II, pp. 47, 483, 680.
96   Dodd, *Studies*, pp. 145–54.
97   *CSPD, 1651*, pp. 200, 204, 337.

Chapter 9: Religion, Politics and Rehabilitation, 1650–1661

1   *Severall Proceedings in Parliament*, 12 (14–21 December 1649), p. 149.
2   Dodd, *Studies*, p. 148.
3   Thomas Birch (ed.), *A Collection of the State Papers of Thomas Thurloe*, 7 vols (London, 1742), II, p. 124.
4   Thomas Richards, *Puritan Movement in Wales* (Liverpool, 1920), p. 236.
5   Phillips, *Justices*, p. 144.
6   Dodd, *Studies*, pp. 156, 162–3. This identification is followed in HPO (1604–29): 'Vaughan, Edward'.
7   NLW, MS 11,439D, fo. 2. He is misnamed in the MS as 'Will: Vaughan'.
8   TNA, SP23/251, fo. 74; Edward Allen, et al., *Vavsoris Examen & Purgamen* (London, 1654), sig. A3, p. 13; Shropshire Archives, 631/2651. For his identification, see TNA, SP23/252, fo. 128.
9   *The Petition of the Six Counties of South-Wales ... Presented to the Parliament of the Common-wealth of England* (London, 1652), pp. 15–16.
10   NLW, MSS 9064E/1987–8; MS 11,440D.
11   Richard Jones, *Testûn Testament Newydd* (London, 1653); Richards, *Puritan Movement in Wales*, p. 119.
12   On this, see Sarah Ward Clavier, 'God's Vigilant Watchmen: The Words of Episcopalian Clergy in Wales, 1646–1660', in Fiona McCall (ed.), *Church and People in Interregnum Britain* (London, 2021), pp. 217–41.
13   For what follows, see Robert Williams, 'A History of the Parish of Llanfyllin', *MC*, 3 (1870), 51–112.
14   TNA, SP20/13/1, fos 1–4; NLW, Herbert of Cherbury MS P1/3: *The State of the Cause of Sir Percy Herbert* (*c*.1651); Powis Castle Estate MS D/1/1/12; M. A. E. Green (ed.), *Calendar of the Proceedings of the Committee for Compounding with Delinquents*, 5 vols (London, 1889–92), III, p. 2195.
15   Frederick Arthur Crisp, *Visitation of England and Wales Notes, Vol. 13* (privately printed, 1913), pp. 6–11.
16   TNA, PRO 30/53/7, fo. 89; C8/99/32, 119. The property was settled by Sir Percy Herbert on his son and Elizabeth, daughter of the earl of Worcester, at their marriage in 1654: NLW, Powis Castle MSS 12837; D1/1/13–14.
17   TNA, STAC 5/H/35/37; STAC 8/9/3.
18   The following account is based on NLW, Powis Castle MSS 12508–12.
19   NLW, Powis Castle MS 12508.
20   Mytton signed one of the submissions against Vaughan over the disbandment monies in 1649, see above, p. 213.

21 WSTY K2/3, bundle 3, certificate to Howell Evans, 15 February 1647; PA4/6, bundle 7: dep. Charles Kyffin, 23 April 1662; TNA, SP28/251, unfol.; SP23/126, pp. 67, 155; SP16/514, fo. 36.

22 WSTY PA4/6, bundle 7: dep. Charles Kyffin, 23 April 1662; JA1/1: bond indemnifying Charles Kyffin as bailiff, 1652. Charles was brother of Sir Thomas Myddelton's agent Watkin Kyffin: NLW, Chirk Castle MS F.6731; WSTY FA5/4: Charles Kyffin to Watkin Kyffin, 1659.

23 TNA, SP23/126, pp. 61, 65; WSTY PA3/11: Brochwell Griffiths *versus* Edward Vaughan, 1657.

24 NLW, Powis Castle MS 11249.

25 The classic study is Austin Woolrych, *Commonwealth to Protectorate* (Oxford, 1982).

26 Joseph Mayer (ed.), 'Inedited Letters of Cromwell, Col. Jones, Bradshaw and other Regicides', *Transactions of the Historical Society of Lancashire and Cheshire*, new series, 1 (1861), 217; Woolrych, *Commonwealth to Protectorate*, pp. 209–10, 213–14.

27 *A True Catalogue* (London, 1659), p. 10.

28 David L. Smith and Patrick Little, *Parliaments and Politics during the Cromwellian Protectorate* (Cambridge, 2007), pp. 49–54, 57.

29 Peter Gaunt, 'Cromwell's Purge? Exclusions and the First Protectorate Parliament', *Parliamentary History*, 6 (1987), 13; TNA, SP18/75, fo. 121; SP18/77, fo. 72.

30 TNA, SP18/74, fo. 93.

31 *CSPD, 1653–4*, p. 94; *LJ*, VIII, p. 78; NEWA (F), D/G/3276/83.

32 TNA, SP18/74, fo. 93. Much of what follows is based on this petition.

33 HPO (1604–29): 'Salesbury, William'.

34 NLW, MS 9268E, p. 12. For the use of the term 'Presbyterians' to describe Vaughan and his ilk in this period, see Smith and Little, *Parliament and Politics*, pp. 114–20.

35 *HoC, 1640–1660*, IX, pp. 350–1.

36 WSTY K2/3, bundle 2: examination of Lewis Price, 13 November 1646.

37 Dwnn, *Visitations*, II, p. 230; 'Llyfr Silin', *Archaeologia Cambrensis*, 5th series, 8 (1891), 97.

38 NLW, SA/1671/145.

39 Vaughan had a presence in the town; we know he possessed a house here: PROB 5/2231, p. 10; NEWA (D), DD/WY/5419.

40 NLW, MS 9268E, p. 12; *HoC, 1640–60*, VII, pp. 808–10.

41 See below, p. 269.

42 TNA, E134/17Chas2/Mich11.

43 TNA, E134/17Chas2/Mich11.

44 *CSPD, 1654*, p. 300.

45 *A&O*, II, p. 1086.

46 *Mercurius Politicus*, 248 (8–15 March 1655), p. 5194.

47 For Berry, see Sir James Berry and Stephen G. Lee, *A Cromwellian Major-General: The Career of Col. James Berry* (London, 1938); *HoC, 1640–1660*, III, pp. 487–93.

48 Birch (ed.), *Thurloe State Papers*, V, p. 242.
49 NLW, MS 6449B, pp. 620–3.
50 TNA, E134/17Chas2/Mich11.
51 *HoC, 1640–1660*, IX, p. 343. I am most grateful to Stephen Roberts and to Vivienne Larminie for allowing me to see this biography prior to publication.
52 NLW, Coleman Deeds II. 116.
53 Ruth Spalding (ed.), *The Diary of Bulstrode Whitelocke, 1605–1675* (Oxford, 1990), pp. 452, 473, 475.
54 WSTY PA4/6, bundle 7: dep. Charles Kyffin, 23 April 1662.
55 WSTY PA4/6, bundle 7.
56 Jonathan Fitzgibbons, '"To Settle a Governement without Something of Monarchy in it": Bulstrode Whitelocke's Memoirs and the Reinvention of the Interregnum', *English Historical Review*, 137 (2022), 655–91.
57 Indeed, when a list of candidates including William Whitelocke was suggested around 1656 as possible inheritors, Edward Vaughan apparently replied that 'none of them should have a foote of his lands': WSTY PA4/6, bundle 7: dep. Ralph Kynaston, 23 April 1662.
58 *HoC, 1640–1660*, II, pp. 718, 721.
59 WSTY PA4/6, bundle 7: dep. David Price, 23 April 1662.
60 See below, pp. 261–71, 283–4.
61 C. H. Firth (ed.), *The Memoirs of Edmund Ludlow*, 2 vols (Oxford, 1894), II, pp. 108–9; Gwyn R. Thomas, 'Sir Thomas Myddelton II. 1586–1666' (unpublished MA thesis, University of Wales, 1967), pp. 143–203.
62 *CSPD, 1659–60*, p. 159; Dodd, *Studies*, p. 167.
63 WSTY PA4/6, bundle 7: deps. of David Jones, 23 April and 25 August 1663.
64 He does not appear in the comprehensive list of participants in Thomas, 'Sir Thomas Myddelton', pp. 465–9.
65 *CSPD, 1659–60*, pp. 190, 193, 241.
66 *HoC, 1640–1660*, IX, p. 343.
67 *The Grand Memorandum* (London, 1660); *A Full Declaration of the True State of the Secluded Members Case* (London, 1660), [p. 57].
68 *A Perfect List of all Such Persons as by Commission ... are now Confirmed to be Custos Rotulorum ...* (London, 1660), p. 76.
69 *A&O*, II, p. 1448.
70 Cf. the composition of the assessment commission named in January 1660: *A&O*, II, pp. 1383–4; Dodd, *Studies*, p. 168.
71 NLW, MS 9066E/2245.
72 WSTY PA4/6, bundle 7: dep. Sir George Devereux, 28 September 1663. See also in this bundle the dep. of Humphrey Lloyd, 23 April 1662.
73 HMC, *Portland MSS*, III, p. 221.
74 HPO (1660–90): 'Purcell, John'.
75 WSTY PA4/6, bundle 7: dep. Charles Kyffin, 13 October 1663.
76 HPO (1660–90): 'Montgomery Boroughs'; TNA, PRO 30/53/7, fo. 122.
77 TNA, SP29/22, fo. 55.
78 TNA, SP29/35, fo. 34.

79 TNA, SP29/35, fo. 35.

80 WSTY PA4/8: Montgomery publicans *versus* Charles Salesbury, 1664.

81 Phillips, *Justices*, p. 145.

Chapter 10: Death and Dynasty, 1661–1672

1   See case breviates in WSTY PA6/2, bundle 2.

2   WSTY PA4/6, bundle 7: dep. Morgan Evans, 25 August 1663; dep. Vincent Edwards and 23 July and 25 August 1663; WTSY PA4/6, bundle 1: original will of Edward Vaughan, *c*.August 1661.

3   WSTY PA4/6, bundle 7: dep. Lewis Lewis, 20 July 1663.

4   See above, pp. 69, 164–5, 171, 230.

5   William A. Shaw (ed.), *Calendar of Treasury Books, Volume 1: 1660–1667* (London, 1904), p. 247.

6   WSTY PA4/6, bundle 7: dep. Sir Charles Lloyd, 26 October 1663; TNA, C9/24/144.

7   WSTY PA4/6, bundle 7: dep. Sir Charles Lloyd, 26 October 1663; TNA, C9/94/99.

8   WSTY PA4/6, bundle 7: dep. Sir Charles Lloyd, 26 October 1663; dep. Ralph Kynaston, 22 April 1662.

9   WSTY PA4/6, bundle 7: dep. Ralph Kynaston, 22 April 1662; bundle 1: breviat of the case, *c*.1663.

10 TNA, C9/94/99.

11 WSTY PA4/6, bundle 1: original will of Edward Vaughan, *c*.August 1661.

12 WSTY PA5/5: affidavit of Eubule Lloyd, 1668; WSTY PA6/1: answer of Frances Vaughan, 1671.

13 WSTY DL7/3: trust settlement, 1622. On Owen Vaughan's adulteries, see also NEWA (F), D/GW 2084; NEWA (D), DD/WY/6524.

14 Sadie Jarrett, 'Credibility in the Court of Chancery: Salesbury *v.* Bagot, 1671–1677', *The Seventeenth Century*, 36 (2021), 55–79.

15 WSTY PA4/6, bundle 7: dep. Sir Charles Lloyd, 26 October 1663. This reluctance was confirmed by Salesbury himself: TNA, C6/158/163.

16 WSTY PA4/1: Sir Charles Lloyd to Charles Salesbury, 24 September 1661.

17 H. G. Woods (ed.), *Register of Burials at the Temple Church, 1628–1853* (London, 1905), p. 15.

18 WSTY PA4/1: articles of agreement, 15 November 1661.

19 The post-mortem inventory of Llwydiarth noted 'the chamber where Mr Rowland Vaughan formerly lay': TNA, PROB 5/2231, p. 5.

20 WSTY PA4/6, bundle 7: dep. David Price, 23 April 1662.

21 John Birch (ed.), *The State Papers of John Thurloe*, 7 vols (1742), III, pp. 209–11, 214, 259, 336–7.

22 Thomas Griffith Jones, 'A History of the Parish of Llansantffraid-yn-Mechain', *MC*, 4 (1871), 153–4.

23 E. R. M., 'A 17th Century Act for the Preservation of Game, etc.', *MC*, 61 (1969–70), 136.

24 WSTY PA4/1: S. Biggs to Ralph Kynaston, 21 September 1661.

25 WSTY PA4/7: affidavit of John Vaughan, 15 October 1661.

26 See above, pp. 72–3.

27 TNA, C5/412/168; copy in WSTY PA4/3.

28 WSTY PA4/6, bundle 7: dep. Charles Kyffin, 23 April 1662.

29 WSTY PA4/6, bundle 7: dep. Sir Charles Lloyd, 26 October 1663. For his status as a Salesbury agent, see WSTY PA5/5: affidavit of Eubule Lloyd, 1668; WSTY PA6/1: Chancery answer of Frances Vaughan, *c*.1671.

30 WSTY PA4/6, bundle 1: William Lloyd to Ellis Lloyd, 28 December 1661; WSTY PA4/6, bundle 7: dep. William Lloyd, 20 July 1663.

31 WSTY PA4/1: William Lloyd to Sir Charles Lloyd, 4 January 1662.

32 For some of his correspondence in this capacity, see NEWA (D), DD/WY/6546.

33 TNA, PROB 11/306, fo. 398r–v. Copies can also be found at NEWA (D), DD/WY/6528–30.

34 WSTY PA4/6, bundle 1: William Lloyd to Ellis Lloyd, 28 December 1661.

35 WSTY PA4/1: William Lloyd to Sir Charles Lloyd, 4 January 1662.

36 WSTY PA4/6, bundle 7: dep. William Lloyd, 20 July 1663.

37 WSTY PA4/6, bundle 7: dep. Sir Charles Lloyd, 26 October 1663.

38 TNA, C6/158/163.

39 WSTY PA4/6, bundle 7: deps. Ellis Lloyd, 18 July, 25 August and 13 October 1663; WSTY YA5/3: deed of 1 November 1655.

40 WSTY PA4/5, bundle 2: breviat of Howell Vaughan *versus* John Vaughan, 1664; TNA, C9/94/99.

41 WSTY PA4/6, bundle 1: memorandum of Evan Vaughan, *c*.1662.

42 TNA, C9/25/144. See copies of materials in WSTY PA4/5.

43 NEWA (D), DD/WY/6548.

44 TNA, C6/149/100; C9/24/155.

45 TNA, C6/158/162–4. The papers relating to this suit can be found in WSTY PA4/6.

46 WSTY PA6/1: bill of Edward Vaughan of Llwydiarth, *c*.1671.

47 WSTY PA5/4, bundle 1: breviat of Edward Vaughan *versus* William and Gabriel Salesbury, 1667.

48 Although such attitudes were found in other families too: Melvin Humphreys, *The Crisis of Community: Montgomeryshire, 1680–1815* (Cardiff, 1996), p. 101.

49 WSTY PA4/6, bundle 7: dep. Edward Wynne, 25 August 1663. Wynne was a co-defendant with Salesbury and others in actions brought by Sir Charles Lloyd in 1662–3: TNA, C6/161/63; C6/170/69; C8/294/45.

50 TNA, C6/158/162.

51 WSTY PA4/6, bundle 7: dep. David Jones, 25 August 1663.

52 WSTY PA4/6, bundle 7: dep. Simon Oliver, 25 August 1663.

53 WSTY PA4/6, bundle 7: dep. Ralph Kynaston, 22 April 1662; PA4/5: breviat for the trial at bar, 16 November 1664.

54 WSTY PA4/5: copy answer of Charles, John and Edward Vaughan, 23 January 1663. Cf. TNA, C9/27/137.

55 WSTY PA4/6, bundle 2: 'Heads of a discourse', 26 June 1662. Charles Salesbury described them as 'the now Vaughans': NEWA (D), DD/WY/6546.

56 TNA, C6/158/164.

57 NEWA (D), DD/WY/6681.

58 WSTY PA4/6, bundle 7: dep. Charles Bowlder, 29 September 1663.

59 WSTY PA4/6, bundle 7: dep. Charles Bowlder, 29 September 1663; WSTY PA4/5, bundle 1: dep. Richard Edwards, *c.*1663.

60 WSTY PA4/6, bundle 7: dep. Charles Kyffin, 22 April 1662.

61 Jan Broadway, *'No Historie so Meete': Gentry Culture and the Development of Local History in Elizabethan and Early Stuart England* (Manchester, 2006), pp. 154, 161–2.

62 Sadie Jarrett, *Gentility in Early Modern Wales: The Salesbury Family, 1450–1720* (Cardiff, 2024); Shaun Evans, '"To Contynue in my Bloud and Name": Reproducing the Mostyn Dynasty, *c.*1540–1692' (unpublished PhD thesis, Aberystwyth University, 2013).

63 WSTY PA4/5, bundle 1: 'A noate of what wilbe deposed', *c.*1663.

64 WSTY PA4/6, bundle 7: dep. Thomas Maurice, 18 September 1663.

65 WSTY PA4/6, bundle 7: dep. John Ellis, 23 April 1662.

66 WSTY PA4/5, bundle 1: 'A noate of what wilbe deposed', *c.*1663.

67 WSTY PA4/6, bundle 7: dep. John Ellis, 23 April 1662.

68 WSTY PA4/6, bundle 7: dep. Thomas Maurice, 18 September 1663.

69 None of Edward Vaughan's three excellent History of Parliament biographies recognise that he was married, for example. Exceptions to this general ignorance of the marriage are the confused references in R. G. Gibson, 'The Vaughan Family of Llwydiarth in the Seventeenth and Early Eighteenth Centuries', *MC*, 95 (2007), 79, and the much more informed discussion in Ruth Bigood, 'Families of Llanddewi Hall, Radnorshire. Part I: The Phillips and the Probert Families', *Transactions of the Radnorshire Society*, 44 (1974), 11–17.

70 K. J. Kesselring and Tim Stretton, *Marriage, Separation, and Divorce in England, 1500–1700* (Oxford, 2022), ch. 5.

71 Shropshire Archives, 894/219.

72 NEWA (D), DD/WY/6674, fo. 34v.

73 WSTY DH/10/15: the prenuptial settlement of James Phillips and Frances Meredith, 1614.

74 For more on the family, and on the marriage, see Bigood, 'Families of Llanddewi Hall'.

75 Lloyd, *Sheriffs*, p. 500.

76 Shropshire Archives, 894/221.

77 TNA, C142/510/58.

78 Shropshire Archives, 894/389–90.

79 Shropshire Archives, 894/220, 221; Clergy of the Church of England Database, *https://theclergydatabase.org.uk/* (accessed 11 June 2023).

80 Shropshire Archives, 894/219.

81 WSTY DH10/15.

82 WSTY DH10/10.

83 WSTY PA5/4, bundle 2: answer of Frances Vaughan, *c.*1670.

84 Shropshire Archives, 894/219.

85 London Metropolitan Archives, P69/Dun2/A/003/Ms010344; T. C. Dale (ed.), *Inhabitants of London in 1638* (London, 1931), pp. 230–5.

86 See above, pp. 50, 69.

87 Shropshire Archives, 849/219.

88 WSTY PA5/4, bundle 2: answer of Frances Vaughan, *c*.1670.

89 Shropshire Archives, 849/221.

90 WSTY PA4/6, bundle 7: dep. Ellis Lloyd, 13 October 1663.

91 WSTY PA4/6, bundle 7: dep. John Price, 13 October 1663.

92 Shropshire Archives, 894/219.

93 TNA, PROB 11/306, fos 420v–21; NEWA (D), DD/WY/6530.

94 WSTY PA6/1: documents concerning Frances Vaughan's dower, 1666–71.

95 Shropshire Archives, P240/A/1/1, unfol.; TNA, C10/159/171.

96 TNA, PROB 11/339, fos 217v–18.

97 WSTY PA4/6, bundle 4: 'The number of sheets in the deposicions', 1663.

98 TNA, C78/1259/4; WSTY PA4/6, bundle 5: narrative of the case, 1664. For interest in the hearing, see NEWA (D), DD/WY/6893.

99 WSTY PA4/6, bundle 6: copy will of Charles Salesbury, 29 March 1666; WSTY PA6/2, bundle 3: breviat of John Anley *versus* Edward Vaughan, May 1676. He was buried at Llanfwrog on 4 April: NEWA (D), PD/59/1/1, p. 72.

100 WSTY PA6/2, bundle 3: breviat of John Anley *versus* Edward Vaughan, May 1676.

101 He was born in November 1649: TNA, C10/159/171.

102 WSTY PA5/4, bundle 1: breviat of Edward Vaughan *versus* William and Gabriel Salesbury, 1667.

103 See his elegy by Edward Morys, NLW, Peniarth MS 115, fos 45–50.

104 NLW, SA1669/159; NEWA (D), DD/WY/6532.

105 TNA, C78/1259/4. Another copy can be found at WSTY PA5/4, bundle 4.

106 NLW, SA1669/159; WSTY PA5/4, bundle 1: Edward Vaughan (via Roger Kynaston *ex parte* Edward Vaughan) *versus* Frances Vaughan and others, 1671; NLW, Clenennau Letters and Papers nos. 790–1.

107 TNA, C78/1261/4; WSTY PA6/2, bundle 1: Magdalen and Katherine Vaughan *versus* Edward Vaughan, *c*.1675.

108 W. J. Smith (ed.), *Calendar of Salusbury Correspondence* (Cardiff, 1954), p. 225.

109 NEWA (D), DD/WY/6519–20; WSTY YA5/4: copy of marriage settlement papers, 1672; Melvin Humphreys, *Plas Newydd and the Manor of Talerddig* (Welshpool, 2022), pp. 130–1.

110 HPO (1660–90): 'Vaughan, Edward III', 'Montgomeryshire'; HPO (1690–1715): 'Vaughan, Edward', 'Montgomeryshire'; HPO (1715–54): 'Vaughan, Edward', 'Montgomeryshire'.

111 Lloyd, *Sheriffs*, p. 226. Curiously, the tablet also records Edward (d.1661) as the son and heir rather than the brother of Sir Robert Vaughan.

112 On the subsequent history of the estate, see E. W. Williams, 'The Vaughans of Llwydiarth and their Tradition of Patronage', *MC*, 107 (2019), 45–56; *idem*, 'The Wynns of Wynnstay and their Llwydiarth Inheritance: Part 1', *MC*, 108 (2020), 99–130; *idem*, 'The Wynns of Wynnstay and their Llwydiarth Inheritance: Part

2', *MC*, 109 (2021), 101–28. For the context of this agglomeration of estates, see Melvin Humphreys, *The Crisis of Community: Montgomeryshire, 1680–1815* (Cardiff, 1996), pp. 96–117; NEWA (D), DD/WY/6225.

113 P. D. G. Thomas, *Politics in Eighteenth-century Wales* (Cardiff, 1998), pp. 150–77.

Conclusion

1   Lloyd, *Sheriffs*, p. 225; J. E. Lloyd, et al. (eds), *Dictionary of Welsh Biography down to 1940* (London, 1959), *s.v.* 'Vaughan family of Llwydiarth'.

2   See above, pp. 7–9.

3   For the archival history of the Wynnstay muniments, see the catalogue entry at *https://archifau.llyfrgell.cymru/index.php/wynnstay-estate-records-2* (accessed 17 December 2023).

4   M. A. E. Green (ed.), *Calendar of the Proceedings of the Committee for Compounding*, 5 vols (London, 1889–92), II, pp. 1626–8. In the late nineteenth century one local antiquarian recognised the importance of this 'mass of [Vaughan] papers' among the committee's archives, and stated his, sadly unrealised, intention to publish them *in extensio*: E. Rowley-Morris, 'Royalist Composition Papers', *MC*, 18 (1885), 80–3.

5   TNA, STAC 5/H35/37.

6   Richard Cust and Peter Lake, *Gentry Culture and the Politics of Religion: Cheshire on the Eve of Civil War* (Manchester, 2020); Jason Peacey and Chris Kyle (eds), *Connecting Centre and Locality: Political Communication in Early Modern England* (Manchester, 2020). In the Welsh context, see also Lloyd Bowen, 'Faction, Connection and Politics in the Civil Wars: Pembrokeshire, 1640–1649', *English Historical Review* (2023), 92–131.

7   Matthew Henry Lee (ed.), *Diaries and Letters of Philip Henry ... 1631–1696* (London, 1882), p. 97. The reference is to Proverbs 10:7.

8   *An Account of the Life and Death of Mr Philip Henry* (Edinburgh, 1797), p. 57.

Manuscript Bibliography

Bodleian Library, Oxford
Add. MS c.177: Welsh pedigrees
Add. MS c.303: William Laud's notes on Star Chamber cases
Tanner MSS: Lenthall papers

British Library, London
Add. MS 46,931A: Fitzgerald correspondence
Add. MS 70,002: Sir Robert Harley papers
Egerton MS 1048: Miscellaneous civil war papers
Harleian MS 255: Sir Simonds D'Ewes papers
Harleian MS 1973: Montgomeryshire pedigrees by Randle Holme

Folger Shakespeare Library, Washington DC
V.a. 278: Index of Star Chamber cases, 1631–41

Hatfield House, Hertfordshire
Cecil MSS

Harvard University, Houghton Library
Law School MS1101: John Lightfoot's Star Chamber reports, 1624–40

Herefordshire Archives and Local Studies, Hereford
DA30/216: Penoyre of The Moor papers

Hertfordshire Archives and Local Studies, Hertford
DE/Lw: Wittewronge and Myddelton papers

Huntington Library, San Marino
Ellesmere MSS: Papers and correspondence of John Egerton, first earl of Bridgewater

Kresen Kernow, Redruth
BU206: Buller papers relating to Welsh estates

London Metropolitan Archives
P69/Dun2/A/003/MS10344: St Dunstan-in-the-West parish register, 1623–45

Longleat House, Wiltshire
Whitelocke manuscripts

The National Archives, Kew
C2/JasI: Chancery pleadings, James I
C2/ChasI: Chancery pleadings, Charles I
C3: Chancery pleadings, series II
C5: Chancery pleadings before 1714, Bridges
C6: Chancery pleadings before 1714, Collins
C8: Chancery pleadings before 1714, Mitford
C9: Chancery pleadings before 1714, Reynardson
C10: Chancery pleadings before 1714, Whittington
C33: Chancery order books
C78: Chancery decrees
C115/107: Chancery master's exhibits, duchess of Norfolk's deeds
C142: inquisitions post-mortem
C219: election indenture returns
C231: Crown office, docket books
E112: Exchequer bills and answers
E113: Exchequer bills and answers against defaulting accountants
E134: Exchequer depositions by commission
SP16: State papers, Charles I
SP18: State papers, interregnum

SP19: Committee for Advance of Money papers
SP20: Sequestration committee books and papers
SP21: Papers of the Committee of Both Kingdoms
SP23: Papers of the Committee for Compounding with Delinquents
SP25: Council of State papers
SP28: Commonwealth Exchequer papers
SP29: State papers, Charles II
SP46: State papers, additional
STAC 5: Star Chamber, Elizabeth I
STAC 7: Star Chamber, additional
STAC 8: Star Chamber, James I
PRO 30/53: Herbert of Cherbury papers
PROB 5: Prerogative Court of Canterbury, inventories and accounts
PROB 11: Prerogative Court of Canterbury, wills
WARD 9: Court of Wards and Liveries, miscellaneous books
WARD 13: Court of Wards and Liveries, pleadings

The National Library of Wales, Aberystwyth
Brogyntyn Estate MSS
Chirk Castle MSS
Clenennau Letters and Papers
Coleman deeds
Great sessions papers
Herbert of Cherbury MSS
Kyrle Fletcher (Second Group)
Lleweni MSS
NLW MSS
NLW Add. MSS
Peniarth Estate MSS
Powis Castle MSS
Sweeney Hall MSS
Vaynor Park MSS
Wynnstay MSS

North East Wales Archives, Hawarden

D/G/3275–6: Trevor correspondence
D/GW/2084: Note of remembrance for Lord Powis
D/HE/875: Note relating to Evan Edwards, 1647

North East Wales Archives, Ruthin
DD/WY: Wynnstay deposit, Vaughan family papers
PD/59/1/1: Llanfwrog parish register

Northamptonshire Archives, Northampton
Finch-Hatton MS 133: Royalist commissions of array, 1642–3

Powys Archives, Llandrindod Wells
M/B/MO/1: Montgomery corporation court book, 1633–50
M/EP/43/R/A/1: Montgomery parish register, 1574–1691

Shropshire Archives, Shrewsbury
212/364: Bridgewater correspondence
894/389–90, 219–21: Hanmer of Pentrepant papers
1037/10/17: More family papers
2922/11/81–2: Dudmaston estate papers
P240/A/1/1: Selattyn parish register, 1557–1724

Index